CONTENDERS
The Tory Quest for Power

PATRICK
MARTIN

ALLAN
GREGG

GEORGE
PERLIN

Prentice-Hall Canada Inc.,
Scarborough, Ontario

Canadian Cataloguing in Publication Data

Martin, Patrick.
   Contenders: the Tory quest for power

ISBN 0-13-171349-3

1. Progressive Conservative Party of Canada.
I. Gregg, Allan   II. Perlin, George   III. Title.

JL197.P76M37 1983   324.27104   C83-099074-7

ISBN 0-13-171349-3

Prentice-Hall, Inc., Englewood Cliffs, New Jersey
Prentice-Hall International, Inc., London
Prentice-Hall of Australia, Pty., Ltd., Sydney
Prentice-Hall of India Pvt., Ltd., New Delhi
Prentice-Hall of Japan, Inc., Tokyo
Prentice-Hall of Southeast Asia (Pte.) Ltd., Singapore
Editora Prentice-Hall do Brasil Ltda., Rio de Janeiro

Design: Joe Chin
Production: Alan Terakawa
Index: Christopher Blackburn
Typesetting: ART-U Graphics Ltd.

Printed and bound in Canada by Imprimerie Gagné Ltée

1 2 3 4 5 IG 87 86 85 84 83

The publisher wishes to thank the Progressive
Conservative Party of Canada for granting permission
to use the party logo on the cover of this book.

"What I don't understand is, why was 67 per cent not enough?"

H.R.H. Charles, Prince of Wales to
Joe Clark, Governor General's Dinner,
Ottawa, June 20, 1983.

Contents

Introduction

The Progressive Conservative leadership convention was undoubtedly the political event of 1983. Not since the mid-sixties has the attention of the Canadian electorate been so clearly focussed on one political gathering.

Many Canadians had been following the drama since that Friday night in Winnipeg when Joe Clark announced he was, at one and the same time, resigning and seeking the leadership of his party. In the four and a half months between that time and June 11th , television viewers and newspaper readers were deluged with reports of "dirty tricks" in choosing delegates, meetings packed by Amway distributors, sharp philosophical swings to the right in the party, and speculation about dark horse candidates and front runners who were sometimes gaining, sometimes losing momentum in the dizzying race for the leadership.   Although the PC leadership campaign was exceedingly well covered by the media, that coverage posed more riddles than it solved.

The riddles begin with the Winnipeg general meeting, where a party enjoying virtually one-half of the electorate's support, as measured by the Gallup poll, contemplates a leadership review because it doubts its current leader's "winability." The leader, the only Tory prime minister in the last twenty years, responds by calling a leadership convention, after fully two-thirds of his partisans claim they don't want one.

At the June convention, the majority of delegates report they are right of centre on the ideological spectrum, but cast a grand total of only four per cent of their votes for strong right-wing candidates. Meanwhile, the incumbent leader initially wins almost 40 per cent of the convention's support, steadfastly holds this vote for nine hours, and is still unable to attract enough delegates to retain power. One of his main rivals, a former Newfoundland Liberal, dubbed by the media as "the man to watch," is eliminated from the race after receiving *more* additional votes since the first ballot than either of his two leading opponents. Curiously, candidates who came into federal politics under Joe Clark's leadership and were appointed by him to Cabinet, throw their support behind others to ensure his leadership *does not* continue. Finally, the PC party, whose litany of failures is in large part due to its lack of support among the Quebec electorate, chooses a Quebecer as its national leader—and this despite the fact he has never run for elective office.

Even on the surface it is a fascinating tale. But a mere recounting of events would ignore the underpinnings of the drama: for there are solid motives for the occurrences we witnessed during the first half of 1983, and these motives continue to play a role in the political life of this country. Moreover, they are important to any understanding of what we, as Canadians, may expect from those people who could very well form the next Government of Canada.

* * *

Since March, 1962, with the defeat of the last Diefenbaker Government, the federal Progressive Conservative party has held office for less than nine months. This record is a matter of fact to the general public. But it constitutes part of the very identity of those who gathered in a sweltering Civic Centre in Ottawa to deny a national leader for the second time in that twenty year period , the opportunity to succeed himself after his power had been wrested from him by his followers.

Many of the delegates who gathered in Ottawa in June, 1983, and conspired against Joe Clark for two years before that, associated him with the division that had disrupted the party over the last twenty years. When Dalton Camp led the first successful attempt to "dump Dief," Joe Clark was there. Since that time, the anti-Diefenbaker wing had been most emphatically "in charge" of the party. Joe Clark was also definitely part of that wing, as were "his" people—those who supported him in his parliamentary caucus, and those who held the key appointments in the party hierarchy.

For many at Ottawa, Joe Clark stood for all that was wrong with the Progressive Conservative party. In him they saw the wishy-washy compromise that blurred the distinction between them and the Liberals, and that had cost them the popularity enjoyed by successful conservative politicians like Margaret Thatcher and Ronald Reagan. Furthermore, his stewardship during the short-lived government of 1979, bespoke an even worse sin...being out-manoeuvered by "the Grits." For many others, the continuing acrimony in the caucus and in the National Executive, between the federal and provincial wings of the Party, and in private meetings wherever Conservatives met, only served as a reminder that the legacy of opposition continued to endure under Clark's leadership.

By June 11, 1983, the issue was not even personal. Joe Clark had become a symbol. And in an attempt to exorcise themselves forever of that symbol, a majority of Tory militants decided that Clark had to go. Having reached that decision, however, the question became "What next?". Not for Joe, but for the party.

Prologue

This is a story of human ambition, of worthy aspirations and, sometimes, less than worthy actions. Its scope is not limited to the efforts of the men who vied for the leadership of the Progressive Conservatives in the spring of 1983, but encompasses the struggle of a political party to come to terms with itself and thereby resolve the question of what it takes to win.

The setting for this story is the entire nation, but the climax fittingly takes place in Ottawa—in the same arena where, seven years previously, the Conservative party assembled to choose a successor to Robert Stanfield...

* * *

The image on the television screens was unfamiliar. "Joe Who?" the headline in the *Toronto Star* would ask next day. No national party leader had ever come to office with so little known about him as Charles Joseph Clark, the fifteenth leader of the Progressive Conservative party of Canada. Joe Clark had been a member of parliament for only four years when he was chosen leader in February, 1976. His entire career before that had been spent in staff roles for others in his party. He had no record, no public persona from which to be judged.

Clark had won the leadership as a compromise. On the first ballot he had placed third with the votes of only 12 per cent of the delegates. The man who had led, Claude Wagner, the first Francophone to contest the Conservative leadership, a former Liberal minister from Quebec who had not become a Conservative until 1972, was unacceptable to many delegates because he had remained aloof from the party during his brief period as a member and held views that many thought were too rigid. The candidate in second place was Brian Mulroney, a bilingual Anglo-Quebecer with an accomplished record as a labour lawyer who was well-connected with the party. Although he had never been elected to office and had had no administrative experience, for a time Mulroney had seemed to be the candidate most likely to attract delegates who opposed Wagner. But he had run an expensive campaign that led many delegates to wonder how much substance lay behind the artifice of his public relations expertise. Thus the anti-Wagner delegates had turned to Clark, a likeable man with moderate views, also well-connected, who had run an effective, low-key campaign.

In one sense Clark's lack of a public profile was an advantage, because it meant that he was free to create his own image from the position of leader, but it also meant his image would be formed on the basis of his performance in uniting the party, a task that had defied and ultimately destroyed many Conservative leaders before him.

Recurring electoral defeats have deprived Conservative leaders of patronage to back their claims to support, attracted to the party some individuals who are by temperament unwilling to submit to internal party discipline, and created an obsessive concern among party members with their role as losers. All of these things have contributed to instability in the Conservative leadership. The party has been fractious and difficult to manage, which has undermined public confidence in its leaders; and as its leaders have failed to deliver electoral victories, the party has forced them out.

Adding to the strains in the Conservative caucus were the residual effects from Clark's own victory and, even more important, those that persisted from the conflict over John Diefenbaker's leadership in the 1960's. Most of the leaders of the group who had fought with Diefenbaker never forgot their bitter defeat in 1967 and many refused to accept the authority of his successor, Robert Stanfield. By 1976, the number of Conservatives who still thought of themselves as belonging to a Diefenbaker faction was relatively small (only 15 per cent of the delegates who attended the 1976 convention), but they remained a vocal and, therefore, potentially disruptive force. For Joe Clark they posed a special problem because he was clearly identified with the old anti-Diefenbaker alliance and his victory at the leadership convention could be seen as a further demonstration of the ascendancy of this faction within the party.

In seeking to master the caucus, Clark was handicapped by the fact that he had no broad base of personal support either within or outside the party. He would be buttressed for a time by the legitimacy of his endorsement from the convention, but legitimacy will not carry a leader for long if he is ineffective. And Clark's effectiveness would be measured by the strength of his popular following. Thus Clark's problem was circular. He needed a broad personal following among the electorate to command the support of potential dissidents within the party, but he needed to demonstrate his ability to master the party if he were to be successful in creating an image that would command a personal following among the electorate.

Using the same technique as Robert Stanfield, Clark tried to build support by distributing his shadow ministerial appointments among every faction within the party. Claude Wagner was made shadow minister for External Affairs and appointed to a new position as chairman of the committee of shadow ministers which was intended to symbolize his status as deputy leader, while Jack Horner, the most vocal of Robert Stanfield's critics from the Diefenbaker faction, was made shadow minister of Transport. Clark also sought to build consensus within the caucus by launching an elaborate process of policy-making in which every member had an opportunity to take part. He hoped through this process not just to provide the party with new policies, but to encourage caucus members to learn to work together and try to find common ground that would bridge their differences.

But these efforts were to no avail. In the summer of 1976, less than four months after his election as leader, he was caught in an embarrassing dispute with a caucus backbencher, Stan Schumacher, who was a member of the Diefenbaker faction. The 1971 census had necessitated the redrawing of federal constituency boundaries and a number of sitting members were forced to seek nominations in new ridings. Schumacher's old riding had partially overlapped Bow Valley, to which Clark had laid claim, but because his hometown was in the new riding Schumacher also wanted to stand there. Both men were adamant and Schumacher challenged Clark to run against him for the nomination. After an extended delay in which the dispute was ostensibly mediated by the Alberta members of caucus, Clark backed down, fearing that it would be even more harmful to have to fight for his constituency nomination. In the eyes of those who had been looking for a sign of the kind of leadership Clark would provide, this was a damaging episode. Clark was the national leader of his party, but he could not even get its nomination in his home constituency.

This was just the beginning. In the fall, Claude Wagner, who had never reconciled himself to his defeat at Clark's hands, resigned his position as chairman of the shadow ministers committee. Then he and Clark became involved in a battle over the election of a new president for the Quebec provincial association, a battle which Clark won, but which further alienated Wagner.

Events in the country also turned to Clark's disadvantage. In the fall of 1976, the Parti Quebecois had been elected in Quebec, which focussed public attention on the Liberal party's strength—its claim to be the only party that could deal with Quebec. By April, 1977, the lead the Conservatives had enjoyed in public opinion polls since Clark's election had passed to the Liberals and in May the Conservatives lost six by-elections, five in Quebec and one in Prince Edward Island in a constituency the Conservatives had held for 20 years.

As the party's electoral prospects began to dim in the spring of 1977, Jack Horner, who had never been able to reconcile himself to Clark's victory, bolted the party to accept a cabinet appointment from the Liberals. Soon after, Jacques Lavoie, who had been elected for the Tories in a Quebec byelection only two years earlier, followed Horner across the floor into the Liberal caucus.

By November, 1977, Clark's position had been so weakened that at the biennial general meeting of the National Association he was forced to allow the national presidency to go by default to Robert Coates, one of the staunchest of John Diefenbaker's remaining supporters, and a man whose views on many issues were out of step with those of Clark. Although the delegates reconfirmed Clark's leadership by a vote of 93 per cent, the election of Coates was a concession to his opponents that could only signal to them and to the country the insecurity of his base within the party.

By early 1978 the image of Joe Clark as a weak leader was firmly established—even his wife, Maureen McTeer, some noted, would not take his name—and the Liberals, although floundering in their efforts to deal with rising unemployment and inflation, looked confidently toward a new general election. The Liberals' expectations for the forthcoming election were shared by many Conservatives. Several members of the Conservative caucus resigned their seats, some of them, including Claude Wagner (who went to the Senate), to accept appointments from the government. But the country's economic problems continued to worsen and, as they did, the fortunes of the Conservative party began to rise. Repeated delays in calling the general election finally forced the government to hold 15 byelections to fill vacant Commons seats in October, 1978, and it was shut out in the 13 contests outside Quebec. The Liberals were on the road to defeat.

But Joe Clark's image continued to hurt the party. In February, 1979, with a general election only a few months away, Clark made a world tour designed to raise his stature as a potential prime minister, but it had quite the opposite effect. Clark was not greeted with the kind of respect that would be accorded a visiting head of government, some of his nervously-made conversational gambits ("What is the totality of your land?") provoked amusement, and there were logistical problems in the organiza-tion of the trip—all of which was reported by journalists.

Moreover, Clark did not handle himself well on television and, because of his inexperience and the limited resources available to him for policy research, he was led into policy mistakes in public statements and inter-views. In the election campaign that began in April, Clark's image remained a liability to the party. The Conservatives won not because of Joe Clark's image, but in spite of it. They won because outside Quebec a majority of voters had had enough of the Trudeau Liberals. Clark became prime minister in a minority government.

The new government was determined to show the country that it was decisive and could provide strong leadership, but it was ill-prepared to govern. For one thing, having been so long in opposition, it took ministers some time to grasp the scope of their departments' activities and to find consensus among the disparate views within the caucus. Lack of adequate research support had produced many policies that were inconsistent or unworkable. This led to conflicting statements from ministers, delays in the declaration of policy, and a backing off from some campaign com-mitments. Far from appearing decisive and competent, the government seemed uncertain of its sense of direction and ineffectual. There was now a complete symbiosis of the images of the party and its leader.

By the end of the summer, as the economic crisis deepened, this merged image had so undermined public support in the government that it was running 20 percentage points behind the Liberals in the Gallup poll. It was in this context that the government was defeated on its budget in parliament and forced into a new general election.

Although there was considerable truth in the Conservative claim that they had not had a fair chance to effect real change, voters were unrespon-sive. They were more concerned with economic problems, the tough measures the government had proposed to deal with the economy, and the image of the party and its leader.

Never was a party leader subject to such cruel personal criticism as in the election campaign of 1980. The devastating effect of Liberal television commercials, which played on Clark's physical mannerisms as well as his public record, was added to by the "Joe Clark" jokes that swept the country. Clark became an object of ridicule. He was not actually disliked, but neither was he seen to have the qualities of a prime minister. And so the Conservative government fell...and Joe Clark began his long, tenacious and doomed struggle to hold onto power.

Part I

WINNIPEG
JANUARY 31, 1983

Do you wish to have a leadership convention?

YES: 795   NO: 1,607

1

"Go, Joe, go…please!"

He had entered as discreetly as a butler; but when Carmen Joynt of the accounting firm Touche Ross and Partners handed Joe Clark a sealed envelope, everyone in the room grew silent. Clark studied the missive for a second before opening it, then briefly scanned the room at the people gathered. They sat in a circle around him: Senator Lowell Murray, Clark's 1979 and 1980 election campaign chairman; Finlay MacDonald, who had advised Robert Stanfield and now Clark; Peter Harder, his young chief or staff; David MacDonald, his former secretary of state now policy advisor; Jake Epp, his most trusted caucus colleague; Marcel Danis, his Quebec organizer; Tony Saunders, a friend of Clark's and principal BC organizer for a number of years, and Terry Yates, Clark's choice as the party's chief fundraiser. Beside him on the couch sat Sandra MacDonald, David's wife and, at the other end of the couch, Clark's wife, Maureen McTeer. They were his political family and the message inside the envelope was addressed to them as well.

For almost an hour the group had chatted superficially in the office of the manager of the Winnipeg Convention Centre while in the main hall hundreds of people revelled. They were Joe Clark's supporters and they sensed that their ordeal was over. They assured themselves that there hadn't been a slip in the three days of the general meeting: the Clark delegates had been overwhelming in their show of support for Joe; the massive audio-visual display, designed to focus the party's wrath on the Liberals and NDP, had been acclaimed; and their leader had given what they all agreed to be a very good speech…"not great but appropriate."

3

As the band struck up "I's the Bye That Builds the Boat" and MP Flora MacDonald, a Clark loyalist, led the crowd in dancing a jig, the news was spreading that the CTV television network had released the results of its survey of delegates leaving the voting booths: 76 per cent were said to have voted against having a leadership convention. It was a great victory for Clark, they had said, and the dancers merrily trampled the discarded signs of their opponents, cleverly worded: GO JOE GO... PLEASE!

The merriment had infected Clark's "operations room" where David Small's staff itched to party too. But Small, who had "tracked" the delegates to this convention, knew that something was wrong with the CTV figures. His own numbers showed that 68 per cent of those *who would express an opinion* would have voted against a leadership convention but more than 16 per cent of the delegates would not tell his people how they were voting. For CTV to be right, almost all of those people would have to be in favour of Joe Clark continuing as leader, and he knew that was highly unlikely. His own best estimate had 72 per cent favouring Clark, but Small kept quiet and prayed: maybe Joe's speech was better than he thought.

The jubilation even spread to the manager's outer office where Jock Osler, Clark's press secretary and many of the Clark staff gathered, drinking from the bottles spread over the secretaries' desks. Jodi White, Clark's former director of communications and one of the two people who had assembled the team that prepared for Winnipeg, decided it was time for a quiet celebration and went back to her hotel to join her husband in watching the good news on television.

To the Clark group at Winnipeg only two scenarios had been thoroughly contemplated: If fewer than 66 per cent of the delegates voted against a leadership convention, then Clark would have no choice but to call for a convention and, of course, run for the leadership himself. If more than 67 per cent voted to retain the present leadership then Clark could feel entitled to stay. What they had not considered was if the vote should fall in between.

Clark loosened the seal of the envelope and took out the paper inside. "Well...," said Clark, his voice barely audible, his eyes still staring at the page. Slowly he raised his head and spoke so everyone could hear: "66.9." Everyone in the room gasped. Clark's gaze met Lowell Murray's. Murray let out his breath, lowered his eyes and shook his head. "It's not enough,"

4

was all he said. Two years before, in Ottawa, Clark had turned to him with a figure almost exactly the same—66.1 per cent had voted against a convention. Then, Murray had told his boss: "You go downstairs and thank them, it's two to one in your favour." But this time it was different.

At the party's 1981 general meeting, Murray was not unaware that his fellow partisans were still suffering a terrible hangover from their 1980 electoral defeat. He knew virtually every detail of clandestine meetings in Quebec involving Jean-Yves Lortie, an old Clark nemesis who was trying to organize support for a leadership convention. He had also heard the innumerable, well-circulated reports of "the cowboys"—a group of the right-of-centre and Western members of Parliament—becoming significantly more vociferous in their criticism of Clark and in their laments of future electoral doom. Murray had heard it all before and had grown immune to any sense of urgency. He simply refused to believe that the party would precipitate another divisive leadership battle.

When Murray formally joined the Clark team in 1977, he had demanded ultimate authority to plan the political strategy necessary to repair what was even then a battle-scarred party and leader. But because of the ongoing in-fighting and bitterness over what had become euphemistically known as "the leadership issue," he found he was unable to obtain what he had demanded. The disunity within the party had necessitated that authority be shared or else the party would have flown apart. As a result, since the 1980 election, Murray had reluctantly acquiesced to those who always believed he had too much power. He gave in to Clark's detractors and accommodated their involvement within the formal party structure. Caucus members who had spoken against Clark during the regular Wednesday morning meetings now held key chairmanships of their regional caucuses. Murray hoped that by making them part of the team, they would exhibit the normal loyalty demanded of team-players.

So when the results of the 1981 vote were brought into the small room in the Ottawa Civic Centre where Clark waited with his supporters, Murray was both surprised and resolute. There was a brief discussion of a preemptive strike by calling a leadership convention immediately. But in the end Murray's view prevailed: a large majority of delegates had voted against a convention and this was a democracy. There would be no tyranny of the minority, no panic, and no convention. Clark would meet the delegates stoically and tell them exactly that... and the next day they would find out what went wrong!

5

Since then, Murray had spent virtually all of his time trying to ensure that there would be no surprise when the next leadership review was held, but he had also seen his authority and ability to develop and execute political strategy whittled away by party members working just as hard to see to it that his goals were not realized. In fact, the first attempt to wrest power away from Murray began the day after the 1981 general meeting.

At the normally ceremonial National Executive Meeting following all general meetings, Allan Lawrence, the veteran MP from Durham-Northumberland and one of the three caucus representatives in the National Executive Committee, made a motion that a sub-committee be struck to supervise and approve the expenditure of all party funds. For many in the room, content simply to be seeing old friends, the significance of this motion was completely missed.

Within the Progressive Conservative party all key appointments—national director, campaign chairman, leader's office chief-of-staff, and policy chairman—were the sole prerogative of the national leader. The budgets for these positions, however, were controlled by the Progressive Conservative Canada Fund, the party's fund-raising organization. Budget approvals, therefore, were a bilateral matter between each appointee and the Fund. The National Executive Committee, the party's elected volunteers, really had no collective say over budget allocations, and in practice, Murray controlled the entire apparatus.

Lawrence's motion was designed to change this and was a direct attempt to undercut Clark's discretion and the discretion of his appointees to spend funds. And in curtailing this discretion, the anti-Clark forces hoped to limit Clark's ability to secure his leadership over the next two years. As it turned out, this was only the first in a series of battles between the National Executive Committee and Murray and the other key figures Clark had placed in the party hierarchy.

Throughout Clark's tenure as national leader, he and his people had never really paid much attention to the National Executive Committee. While they acknowledged committee members had some constituency among the grassroots by virtue of their elected status, staffers and appointees working out of headquarters and the leader's office tended to view them more as an irritant than a resource. For them, the National Executive Committee was made up of "amateurs" who attended committee meetings once every six months and limited their activities to thinking up things for the pros to do. For their part, the group who worked day in and day out for Clark in Ottawa did what they wanted and ignored the activities of the National Executive.

* * *

When 33 per cent of Progressive Conservative delegates voted in favour of leadership review in 1981, the anti-Clark forces recognized his vulnerability; but because they had no say in the national leader's appointments or access to Murray directly, the only place to exploit this vulnerability was from the National Executive. And exploit it they did.

The first item of business of the Lawrence-inspired "audit committee" was to analyze the expenditure of party funds on the leader's tour. As with the original motion itself, although the stated objectives of this investigation were vague, the political objective was well-defined.

One of the political responsibilities of a national leader is to attend various party meetings and functions across the country. On these trips he is supported by staff aides and various "advance men" who travel ahead of the leader to ensure that everything is in the proper order and that everyone is adequately briefed about the events and issues to follow. For an opposition leader, this is virtually the only means, outside of the House of Commons, to attract any press attention to the party's views and positions. Without the excuse of "government business," these travels are also deemed to be solely political and therefore must be paid for out of party funds.

By raising the issue of Clark's touring, the audit committee, made up of caucus chairman Ron Huntington, party treasurer Peter Vuicic and national vice-president for Ontario, John Balkwill, accomplished two things. First, they put into question the legitimacy of past activities. The implied question, of course, was whether Clark was misusing funds to support his leadership by visiting key delegates across the country. Second, they put Clark and his people on notice that even if they had not been misusing funds in the past, the committee would be watching to ensure that he had no advantages in consolidating his support between then and the next general meeting.

The audit committee next set its sights directly on Murray himself. The main allegations were that Murray was drawing an annual stipend of

$60,000 from the party in addition to his Senate salary, and that he had used party funds to furnish his Ottawa condominium with expensive rugs and paintings.

It was further alleged that Decima Research Limited, the PC polling firm hand picked by Murray, was owned by Liberals and therefore should be forced to sever its ties with the party. Some also charged that Murray had misappropriated other funds to support Clark's leadership in Quebec. The charges were of course intended to impugn Joe Clark as well.

Although the allegations were found to be without substance in every instance, the implications of the National Executive Committee activities were clear—the normal prerogatives of the national leader and his senior advisors to run the party were at issue and the elected volunteers were going to take more control.

In no small part, the executive investigations were spurred by a deliberate strategy to undermine Clark by attacking his chief advisors. A number of strong anti-Clark partisans, including Jean-Yves Lortie, John Balkwill and MP's Elmer MacKay, Ron Huntington, and Bob Coates had captured key posts in the National Executive and were using that vantage to assail Clark through his key appointees. Because the spectre of the 1966 revolt against the Diefenbaker leadership continued to hang over all Progressive Conservatives,[1] none of these men wanted to be seen to be making an outright assault on Clark or be accused of disloyalty. However, by undermining Clark's most loyal supporters and attempting to strip *them* of their authority, this group hoped to weaken Clark's power and organizational efforts leading up to Winnipeg. Through what some saw as a sense of equanimity and others viewed as a tacit alliance with the malcontents, PC President Peter Blaikie tolerated these activities.

Although these covert machinations were damaging, Murray recognized an equally grave, though more nebulous, threat to Clark's leadership.

For years, there had been a growing feeling that the grassroots—the elected volunteers of both local and national associations—did not have enough say in the affairs of the party and that too many decisions were being made by paid staff and non-accountable appointees. The disasters of '79 and '80 which saw the Clark government defeated in the House of Commons and then at the polls, highlighted this feeling and added more legitimacy to the claim put forth by those actively trying to remove Clark.

The evidence simply proved the point of the malcontents: If these advisors were so smart, why weren't we still in government? Conversely, if Clark had listened to the grassroots more, then maybe we wouldn't be back in opposition.

By the time delegates arrived in Ottawa to select a new leader in 1983, these feelings had spread throughout the party. Sixty-three per cent (63%) believed that there was an establishment in the Conservative party—that is, an elite group that had a great deal of influence in the way the party was run; however, only 19 per cent of those who accepted this statement considered themselves as being part of or close to that establishment. Even more damaging for Clark, 55 per cent claimed that the leader has been cut off too much from the opinion of ordinary party members and 62 per cent agreed that the party relied too much on technical advisors who were not in touch with ordinary people. By shifting the focus off Clark and taking direct aim at his key advisors and appointees, the anti-Clark group in the National Executive was striking a responsive chord with the grassroots, without their own loyalty becoming the issue. It was a wise, if unintended, move on the part of the dissidents and together with the historic neglect the Clark people had bestowed upon the National Association, it fueled a sentiment for review in Winnipeg that went far beyond any personal animosity to Joe Clark himself. The outs wanted in, and if removing Joe Clark was the only way of gaining more access to influence within the party, then Joe Clark must go.

Taken together, the events of the last two years made it very clear to Murray, as he sat in the manager's office in Winnipeg, that Clark would have to call a leadership convention. Although only 43, Murray had been involved in party politics for over two decades—provincial candidate in his native Nova Scotia at the age of 23; executive assistant to E. Davie Fulton during the Diefenbaker years; chief of staff to Robert Stanfield; and Deputy Minister to New Brunswick Premier Richard Hatfield. For the last five years he had virtually controlled all aspects of the federal party's operations, and everything he had learned during that period told him that Clark and the party could not continue as they had over the past two years. The loyalists had used all the organizational skills amassed over the years to beat back the anti-Clark forces since the general meeting in 1981 and it still wasn't good enough. And for Murray, the reason it wasn't good enough was self-evident…authority in the party had become too

9

diffuse and he and others had lost their ability to control events. They would have to fight for control at the ultimate level available to them...a leadership convention.

* * *

Clark turned away from Murray and looked to Marcel Danis, his trusted Quebec organizer. Danis was perhaps more exhausted and disappointed than anyone in the room, but he too took little time in offering his opinion..."Go for it."

Analysis of the 1981 general meeting results had revealed that Clark's problem was unquestionably in Quebec. By its own admission, the Clark camp calculated that 70 per cent of the Quebec delegation had voted in favour of a leadership convention in 1981. They also found that not just the disaffected, extremist element was working against the leader in Quebec. People who held a formal position on the Clark team in the past were also involved; people such as Keith Morgan, Clark's 1979 Quebec campaign chairman, and Rodrigue Pageau, his Quebec communications director in the same election.

What was especially ironic was the fact that Clark had, as leader, given the highest priority to Quebec in creating the modern party he envisioned. Throughout his tenure he had made a studied and very personal attempt to tap into the province and its political allegiances, by actively recruiting young well-educated Quebec nationalists to the Tory cause. Arthur Tremblay, a former deputy minister in the Bourassa government, was appointed to the Senate by Clark, and also became the chairman of a revived policy committee. Robert René de Cotret, president of the Conference Board of Canada and, at 36, one of the most astute economic thinkers in Canada, was a Clark appointed cabinet minister from the Senate (before suffering electoral defeat in trying to get a Commons seat in 1980). Pierre Laurin, brother of the PQ Education Minister and dean of business administration at McGill, was also "on side."

These were the people Clark needed to make the party credible to Quebec voters and to ensure that Quebec's voice on major issues was heard within the government. Unfortunately, these men knew little about the hard-ball game of organizing at the constituency level in Quebec. That area of expertise belonged to the members of the Clark electoral team who were later to defect from the leader's side after the Conservatives returned to opposition.

The reasons for their defection had less to do with the fall of the Conservative government in 1980, however, than with the manner in which they were treated during the short period of Tory rule. Whether by design or simple omission, Clark and his staff ignored many of the people who had laboured hard during the 1979 campaign. Influence remained concentrated in a small group of advisors around the prime minister, and these individuals were too busy mastering the unfamiliar processes of government to pay much attention to disaffected members of the rank and file.

This neglect was especially hurtful to veterans of an electoral campaign in which the party had once again failed to breach Fortress Quebec. They were looking for some recognition of their efforts in fighting with determination on hostile terrain. On the political level, the failure to have the ear of the leader meant that Quebec workers were not able to secure assurances about forthcoming patronage appointments. They saw the judicious use of patronage as important if the Tories were to improve their standing in Quebec.

One man who did understand the importance of patronage and keeping in touch was Brian Mulroney. The uncrowned heir apparent to the Tory leadership, Mulroney held the additional appeal to the Quebec wing of having come from their native province. Mulroney, for his part, was not averse to welcoming the Quebec dissidents to his side and supporting their efforts at orchestrating a leadership review.

The results of the general meeting of 1981 thus made it very clear to the Clark team that the battle lines were being drawn in Quebec and that for Clark to wage war against a tough and organized opposition, he would have to recruit new troops.

* * *

Marcel Danis was the rather unlikely choice to head up the new Clark forces in Quebec. A boyish-looking 39-year-old lawyer and professor from Montreal, Danis had been a Union Nationale organizer before putting himself forward for federal office under the Progressive Conservative banner in the 1980 election in the St. Hyacinthe riding. He lost to Liberal

MP Marcel Ostiguy by 18,097 votes, but was undeterred in his goal to serve the Clark mission. If the 70 per cent review vote from Quebec could be whittled in half, the impact would be a full 6.7 per cent—enough to give Clark a respectable 72.8 per cent voting against review at the next general meeting in two years time.

Danis was assisted in his assignment by veteran Social Credit organizer Denis Beaudoin, who had moved out of Clark's parliamentary office to head up a revitalized party headquarters in Montreal. Beaudoin immediately went about his task by hiring six full-time organizers where none had existed before. This brought howls of outrage and allegations of misuse of party funds from Lortie, who was now a member of the party's National Executive Committee, having being elected regional vice-president from Quebec at the 1981 general meeting. The National Executive investigated these charges and while they refused to censure the move, it was clear the battle lines had been drawn.

Danis and Beaudoin went about dividing the province up and assigning regional Clark chairmen to oversee the activities that were being organized in all 75 ridings in Quebec. Their aim was to gain control of local riding associations by putting Clark loyalists forward for nomination to their executives. In ridings where they were unable to gain control of the executive, they were to go out and sell party membership cards, in many instances to people who had never even voted Progressive Conservative before, in order to have enough supporters at the upcoming delegate selection meetings to elect Clark slates to the Winnipeg convention. Then they would raise enough money to see to it that all their delegates had their airfare and accommodation attended to in Winnipeg. It was a formidable task, the size of which had never even been contemplated before by the Progressive Conservatives, even in general elections in Quebec. But while the Clark forces organized, so too did the other side.

A parallel organization, with identical objectives, was already in place and operating under Lortie's and Rodrigue Pageau's firm hands. Lortie had worked for Claude Wagner in the 1976 leadership convention and was now firmly behind non-candidate Brian Mulroney. Pageau, who had organized for Mulroney in 1976, worked for Clark from 1977 to 1980 and then returned to Mulroney, together with loyalists Michel Cogger and Jean Bazin. These men believed the key to controlling Quebec was to control the provincial executive. This was the group that would decide who the 38 automatic, delegates-at-large from Quebec specified in the party's constitution, would be. It also had authority to recognize delegate selection meetings and the validity of delegates' credentials. By February of 1982 Lortie and Pageau had the control they wanted. But Danis was undeterred, and the fight for delegates had continued on throughout 1982.

The Clark and Mulroney groups arrived in Winnipeg exhausted from their internecine warfare in Quebec. But in their exhaustion there was also exhilaration because they knew they had done something unique in Progressive Conservative politics. *They* had delivered delegates to the general meeting, and in doing so they had also heralded the beginning of an almost primary-based style of politics in Canada. The combatants might rightfully feel that had earned a respite from their labours. There was little awareness, on either side, that they would have to renew the political struggle beginning the day after the leadership vote. When Danis heard the results of the vote that night, however, there was no question in his mind. He knew he had no choice but to start again…and start immediately.

* * *

It next fell to Jake Epp, the quiet but highly respected member of Parliament from Provencher, Manitoba, to offer his advice. Like Murray and Danis before him, he was no less unequivocal in his opinion… "You've got to call a leadership convention." Epp had risen to national prominence as Clark's lieutenant in the PC's assault on the Liberal government's proposals to patriate the constitution unilaterally. It was considered a great victory for the Tories to have wrought constitutional concessions from the Liberals,[2] although at the time their stand was considered alternatively bold and foolhardy, with as many as 84 per cent of Canadians claiming they wanted to see the constitution brought home to Canada as quickly as possible. But Clark had convinced Epp and others that this was a fight worth fighting. In the end he was proved right, because it was as a direct result of the Tory fight that the government was forced to refer their resolution to the Supreme Court where it was declared in violation of constitutional convention. In the process of leading the opposition to the constitutional resolution, Clark and Epp had formed "a warm, mutual regard."

Notwithstanding this regard and the many victories the PCs had

13

enjoyed in the House of Commons since returning to Opposition in 1980, Epp knew that the Parliamentary caucus still remained deeply divided over Clark's leadership.

After the general meeting of 1981, Clark had been challenged in caucus about his decision not to resign then, and the opposition to him had been so determined that he had been forced to promise caucus to call a convention if his support did not increase in 1983. Epp knew only too well that in view of that promise, caucus would not allow Clark to continue with the vote he had just received.

Divisions within the Conservative caucus—both ideological and personal—have always been legion. Historically, while individuals with a cause to proclaim had a place in the caucus, it was usually the moderates, and those who were closest and most loyal to the leader who held the key positions and control. Because Clark knew his leadership would be under seige following the rather ambivalent mandate he received in Ottawa in 1981, he felt the best way to handle his caucus opposition was to co-opt them. This involved both appointing his critics to key posts and not opposing the appointment of others who sought positions in the caucus and party. While this might have been good strategy in government, it proved disastrous for Clark in opposition.

First Ron Huntington, MP from Capilano, BC, and a strong proponent of the return to the ideological right, defeated Bill McKnight for the position of caucus chairman. McKnight, a respected and well-liked member from Kindersley-Lloydminster, Saskatchewan, was devastated by his caucus defeat—not only because he failed to receive majority support from his caucus colleagues, but also because Clark and his people had failed to use the considerable resources available to the leader of the opposition to help McKnight retain his position.

Next, the caucus demanded the right to elect its own representatives to the National Executive Committee. Except when the leadership of the party was directly at stake, these positions were considered of little strategic value—something to be offered to backbenchers to give them some profile when there was no place for them in the shadow cabinet. After the 1981 general meeting, a seat on the National Executive Committee took on a whole new meaning for the caucus members who wanted Clark out. This concession was also made and the caucus proceeded to elect Elmer MacKay, Allan Lawrence and Peter Elzinga—none of whom had ever been known for their strong support of Clark and, indeed, in the case of

14

MacKay and Lawrence, included two of the most aggressive opponents to Clark in the party.

What was clear by this time was that not only were the anti-Clark forces in caucus prepared to organize and fight the establishment for power and position in the party, but also that the Clark loyalists were *not* prepared to do likewise. In point of fact however, the strong opponents and supporters of Clark in the caucus were probably both a minority of its membership. The majority viewed the issue dispassionately. It was not that they were indifferent; they simply wanted to be certain that the party did nothing to jeopardize its chances in the next election. For the most part, they were ready to go with the flow of events. After a good day in the House of Commons, they were all for Joe. After a bad day, they were ready to listen to almost any alternative to what otherwise might mean ending a parliamentary career in opposition.

With the loss of consensus-building authority came a concomitant inability to establish priorities within the caucus. More and more, discussion in caucus grew increasingly aimless and uncontrolled. Matters which would normally be dealt with as minor items on the agenda were allowed to occupy more attention than they deserved, as Clark learned to accommodate dissent by deferring to every interest. (It was symbolic of this growing drift that in the last meeting of caucus before the summer recess in 1982, with the country experiencing the worst recession in 50 years and the Conservatives 20 points ahead of the Liberals in the Gallup poll, five hours were spent in discussion of the position the party should take on the proposal to change the name of the July first national holiday from Dominion Day to Canada Day.)

Clark, as he always had, would attempt to answer questions and sum up the sentiments aired at each caucus, but he grew increasingly less effective at this task because of the disparate nature of the topics raised. Both situations—the lack of any coherent sense of priority and Clark's inability to articulate a consensus in the face of caucus disarray—frustrated those who had traditionally played a major role in caucus and caused them to question their reasons for supporting Clark. As a consequence, Clark was both giving authority to the views of his detractors and weakening the support of his natural constituency in caucus.

What was happening was that in an attempt to hold onto his leadership, Clark had begun to give parts of it up. Within the constraints of opposition politics, the result was that Clark's would-be supporters felt disillusioned

15

and betrayed, while his opponents were inspired to persist in challenging the party hierarchy.

Outside of caucus, another initiative was being taken against Clark. Because almost all parliamentary members were loathe to be identified publicly with any "dump-Clark" movement, this operation to align opposition against his leadership was of a more clandestine nature. Within the parliamentary group, it began with Elmer MacKay quietly approaching members of Parliament to prepare letters calling for Clark's resignation. In the initial stages he met with almost universal opposition and so he was required to alter his plans. The "fail-safe" MacKay came up with was to guarantee that he would not produce these letters until he had received copies from a majority of the members of caucus. Although these letters were never made public, within six months he had gathered 48 signatures—not enough to allow him to execute his plan, but certainly enough to give the anti-Clark forces a clear indication that, under the proper conditions, a caucus revolt could be organized.

This attempt to force Clark's hand and precipitate a leadership convention was one of many such efforts during the last half of 1981. Typical of such occurrences was the day Mike Wilson was greeted, entering the caucus meeting room, by Epp and Erik Nielsen and informed that the opposing forces had the numbers to bring Clark down. He was instructed to do anything to hold the caucus floor to prevent an intervention from one of the anti-Clark members. As a result he spent almost the entire morning discoursing on the state of the economy and the various options available to the caucus in terms of policy and legislative strategies.

Epp could not get the memory of these events out of his mind as he offered his advice. He had heard colleagues, whom Clark considered loyal supporters, voice their doubts about their leader too often to believe they would have the resolve to stave off the recalcitrants now. There was no choice.

* * *

Terry Yates didn't have to say anything. He just nodded his head in agreement. Yates had spent the last five years working for Clark in one capacity or another, while trying to hold his numerous business interests together. He had been Clark's first choice to head up a revitalized PC Canada Fund in 1977 and had led the party away from the brink of

16

bankruptcy by creating one of the most formidable fund-raising machines in North America. Following the 1980 election defeat, he had also chaired a policy and priority committee, established by Clark to chart party strategy, until ill-health caused him to resign.

By January 1982, when Clark was becoming genuinely alarmed at the events in caucus and the National Executive, Yates was a natural choice to organize the pro-Clark forces for the Winnipeg meeting. In Clark's estimation, Yates had just the right combination of toughness, common sense and the ability to cajole needed to start consolidating his support among the hundreds of partisans who had risen to some level of prominence in the party under his leadership. Together with former communications director Jodi White, Yates was given the mandate to replicate Danis' efforts in Quebec in the rest of the country. Throughout 1982, Yates had had time for little else and he was aware that they had wrung every last vote there was out of the delegates partying on the floor below. He knew this because David Small had been telling him every week for the last 36 exactly where Clark stood among the delegates.

Although only 24 years old, Small was already a political veteran. He was also one of the only backroom operators in the party who had sought elective office in the National Association, having served two years as the president of the Progressive Conservative Youth Federation. Small had sunk his teeth into leadership politics in the 1976 convention while working on the Flora MacDonald campaign. Since that time he had worked in party headquarters and even contested the Ottawa-Centre seat against then NDP Leader Michael Cassidy in the 1981 Ontario provincial election. But his most valuable political experience came under the tutelage of Lowell Murray, who took Small into his office after the 1979 Progressive Conservative victory as an assistant in the planning of political strategy and the distribution of patronage. Murray had a keen eye for young talent. While more of an intellectual and instinctual operator himself, Murray encouraged his young proteges to use the new technology of politics and adopt a professional commitment to what otherwise was seen as the job of "hack." In Small, Murray had, arguably, the most able young mind in the Progressive Conservative party of all he had gathered around him over the years. Yates and White also saw him as their first choice to staff the new committee Clark had asked them to strike. The system Small set up to assist the Yates-White committee was simple, yet

17

ambitious in the scope of information it was to collect. Yates and White were to seek out significant party members to chair or co-chair Clark committees in every province. These chairmen, in turn, were assigned the responsibility of identifying Clark loyalists in each of the 207 non-Quebec ridings. It then fell to Small to determine from these contacts their best guess on the split between pro and anti-review delegates that would come out of their ridings. Based on this initial cut of information, ridings were targeted for directed organizational efforts. In ridings where the pro-review forces were seen to be vulnerable, the riding contact was to organize slates and partial slates of nominees who would stand for election and vote against review in Winnipeg. They were then to go out and get enough party members to come to the local meetings to elect their chosen slate.

Once delegates had actually been selected, Small's task turned to individual-by-individual identification of voting preference for each of the 2,406 delegates who would come to Winnipeg. Information from the local riding contacts was encoded and fed into a computer. Small graded each delegate for ease of comparison. A "1" referred to those with the most solid commitment to Clark, a "7" referred to his enemies. Most fell somewhere in between. At Winnipeg, the discreet anti-Clark delegate wore a tiny blue button with a white "7" printed on it.

Strong Clark supporters were approached directly and asked to become part of the anti-review organization. Strong Clark opponents were ignored. The leaners and uncommitted were targeted for special attention and more information was gathered on them: Who were the other people in the party that influenced the leaners? Would a visit, telephone call or special letter from the leader swing them over? Had they any pet peeves, projects or issues that might forge a greater loyalty to Clark, if promises were made in these areas? This procedure was carried out successively on a day-by-day basis and every week Small would supply his analysis, including a running count of where they stood with the delegates, and recommend what remedial action was required.

Going into Winnipeg, Small had been convinced that they had between 69 and 71 per cent of the delegates committed against a leadership review. As Joe Clark went around the manager's office soliciting opinions, Peter Harder called Small in the operation's room to give him the results. "Shit," was all he said. Small had bought himself a one-way ticket to Europe on a flight scheduled to depart in four days. Now, all plans would be cancelled to take up the fight one more time and, this time, do it right. Back in the manager's office, Terry Yates felt the same way.

* * *

Clark then turned to the oldest and most experienced person in the room, Finlay MacDonald. He had been a candidate for Parliament under Diefenbaker, a co-founder of the CTV television network, chief-of-staff and campaign chairman under Stanfield and had briefly chaired the PC Canada Fund when Yates relinquished it a year and a half earlier. He also had better connections into the outsider camps than anyone in the room, being frequently on the phone to his numerous contacts across the country. The advice he gave Clark at that moment surprised almost everyone in the room. "I don't think we should do anything hasty," he cautioned. Reasoning that one should not yield power lightly, he recommended taking 36 hours to consider the options…talk to the premiers…see where support would come from…assess the opposition. There was nothing to lose by waiting, he argued. "You go out and tell them 'thanks for the support, it wasn't quite what I was looking for and I'll announce my decision to the National Executive on Sunday'." Better to fight from your position of power, he believed.

There was another unspoken option that MacDonald wanted people to have time to consider: calling a convention in which Clark would not be a candidate. MacDonald probably had a better understanding of how formidable Clark's opponents were than anyone else in the room. As a veteran of party politics and one of the most gregarious members of the party, he had often been present when anti-Clark members of caucus and the National Executive freely expressed their views. His belief was that all the organizational wizardry of Murray, Danis and Small would be too little to stem the course of party dynamics as he had come to know them. The enemy would smell blood and fight as never before. How, if Clark didn't have the ability to hang on to power, could he expect to regain it? Perhaps it should be one way or the other. MacDonald believed Clark would never get greater support than he had at this meeting, and his instincts told him that you hang on to power. They were the same instincts that had led him almost a year before to recommend that Clark call a leadership convention before being forced by his opposition to do so. He had written in part:

19

March 1, 1982

The next General Meeting of the P.C. Association will be held in Winnipeg in January 1983, and the total pre-occupation of the delegates and media will be the ballot on leadership review. It is this writer's conviction that—

(a) those who voted in favour of a leadership convention at the last meeting (33%) are still there and a subsequent poll—Maclean's-Carleton University—of those same delegates shows an increase of those who would vote for a convention if they were asked again.

(b) there are aspirants to the leadership who are becoming increasingly militant behind the scenes.

(c) there is a significant increase in response to the mailings of the P.C. Canada Fund in the theme: no more support until you [the Conservatives] get your act together and settle your leadership squabbling.

(d) the caucus cannot be relied upon.

(e) there is no reason to find joy in future Gallup Polls anymore than the recent Gallup Polls enured [sic] to Clark's benefit. There is not widespread acknowledgement of a brilliant parliamentary year on his part.

The moment is on the side of a vote for a convention. *We have no effective means or machinery to reduce the vote to acceptable proportions.* The risk is too great to simply "run out the string."

There is only one alternative to a General Meeting and leadership review. At the appropriate time Clark should request that the *Party Executive call a leadership convention "at the earliest date."*[3]

The memo was signed by MacDonald on behalf of Murray, Peter Harder, Richard Clippingdale and Robert Stanfield. In the past, Clark had sat by impassively when his inner circle discussed his career options. On the occasion when his inner group presented the MacDonald memo, he seemed somewhat more interested in the subject under consideration. Was there provision in the national constitution for voluntarily calling a leadership convention? Would he still perform his parliamentary functions and be considered the leader of Her Majesty's Loyal Opposition if he resigned the party leadership and called a convention? Finally, the question came down to whether or not the National Executive Committee would cooperate with this initiative.

Getting nowhere on this last point, the group dispatched Peter Harder, Clark's newly appointed chief of staff, to feel out National President Peter

Blaikie on his view on the constitutionality of such a move. Blaikie was singularly uninterested in the constitutional aspects of the issue and wanted more detail on the plan itself. Never part of the inner circle, he had travelled the country tirelessly defending Clark publicly, but listening to all the grievances privately and, as often as not, agreeing with the complainant about the leader and his advisors. Now Blaikie felt he would have a chance to get involved in something really important by becoming privy to this new clandestine scheme. Harder would have none of this and in the end he reported back to MacDonald *et. al.* that they probably couldn't expect much cooperation from Blaikie and, in fact, if they didn't give him advance warning of their every move, they might even anticipate some outright opposition. Blaikie's attitude and Clark's indifference to the pre-emptive strike plan thereafter, effectively precluded any initiative being taken regarding a leadership convention.

MacDonald had not pressed the issue further, and the moment had passed. Now he sensed that the opposition to Clark's leadership might simply be too strong for him to retain power. But, as was his custom, he had made his point and did not feel compelled to repeat or elaborate upon it.

* * *

David MacDonald just felt sick. It was times like this when he wondered why he was even a member of this party. A United Church minister, MacDonald had first been elected to the House of Commons in 1965 from the Prince Edward Island riding of Egmont. Since then, he had developed a unique reputation in the PC party as a staunch defender of left-of-centre policies and causes. He had also built bridges for the PC party into the arts and culture community, by actively courting its favour and serving its interest in Clark's cabinet while secretary of state. By virtue of his strong reputation on these fronts, however, he was suspect in the eyes of many caucus colleagues. In fact, his defeat in the 1980 election delighted as many as it shocked; and his detractors created quite a furore when Clark appointed him to his staff as a special advisor in 1982.

Being a Tory had never been easy for David MacDonald and in the last two years it had been even harder. It seemed to him, and to anyone else who considered themselves to be centre or left-of-centre in the political spectrum, that single interests and the right had had a disproportionate influence in the party's affairs during that time. It wasn't that there were

21

more right-wingers. It was just that they seemed to have an added legitimacy within the party that wasn't there in the past. In 1983, being a moderate was beginning to be viewed as extreme.

Nowhere was the legitimacy of the right more prevalent within the formal party structure than in the Ontario youth wing. As Red-Toryism was considered *de rigueur* among Tory youth in the 1960s, the pendulum was once again overswinging, and in the 1980s right-wing rhetoric was the fashion at Progressive Conservative Youth meetings. When these "tiny Tories" spoke of change, they talked about the examples of Margaret Thatcher and Ronald Reagan. Republican memorabilia and photographs of Ronald Reagan were valued commodities and were exchanged freely at social and political meetings. Joe Clark and David MacDonald, as representatives of the 1960s Progressive Conservative youth movement and acknowledged Red Tories, needless to say were not much of an inspiration to this new breed of Conservative youth.

News of this growing swing towards the right in the youth ranks, and their pro-review sentiments, spread throughout the party and found its way into numerous magazine and newspaper articles. The press stories, taken with the sight of such obviously young members of the party working actively against Clark, simply added credence to the notion that the ranks of pro-review supporters were not simply significant in numbers but also extremely varied in composition.

In fact, the swing to the right within the ranks of PC youth was no more pronounced than for the party as a whole. The Young Tories remained, like their elder brethren, a moderately based group. Only 5% reported that they represented an extreme right-wing position relative to their colleagues.

How then does one account for the high profile accorded right-wing youth delegates to the Winnipeg convention? The answer lies in the concentration of right-wing sentiment in the ranks of one provincial youth delegation—Ontario's. In that province, a full 61 per cent of the youth wing considered themselves right-of-centre. Furthermore, as will be seen in a subsequent chapter, the leadership of the Ontario youth wing was strongly behind the candidacy of Brian Mulroney, who made sure that they were well represented at the Winnipeg general meeting.

Given the size of the Ontario youth contingent at the general meeting, it is scarcely surprising that the media should make much of the image of young people lining up against Joe Clark, and this time for another

22

reason—ideology. It was a particularly potent image since youth, after all, is seen as holding within it a hope for the future. Here was a group of young people who saw a future with someone other than Joe Clark as leader.

The defeat of Clark could very well mean the defeat of all the things David MacDonald had stood for. So for him, too, it was a hard but quick decision..."Convention."

* * *

While it was clear there was a near consensus emerging from that room, in the end, the decision would be Clark's. In many ways he had become inured to the assaults of his leadership. In fact, his history with the party and his direct experience at leading it had lead Clark to believe that his troubles were simply part of the job...that any PC leader would have to undergo the same indignities and ordeals, and that he was better equipped than anyone else to withstand the trials his party put its leader through.

Still, the extent of the preoccupation over *his* leadership sometimes puzzled Clark. Why, with all the issues facing the country and all the opportunities available for his party, did the people who he felt close to seem so consumed with his image as the key to electoral success? There were simply too many painful episodes however, where he was reminded of his shortcomings, for Clark to ignore. As he sat listening to his most trusted advisors he could not help but think of others who should have been in that room with him, but weren't because of their doubts about his ability to win. Jean Pigott was one such person.

Pigott had met Clark while she was serving as the accommodation chairman for the 1976 leadership convention. When John Turner vacated his seat, she was Joe Clark's personal choice to seek the Progressive Conservative nomination and run in the Ottawa-Carleton by-election scheduled for October, 1976. Her victory was one of the proudest moments in Clark's early leadership career. He selected her to co-chair the caucus, and sought her counsel regularly on a number of policy and political matters.

After Pigott lost her seat in the 1979 election, she moved into the Prime Minister's Office as Clark's director of human resources in charge of appointments and patronage, where she took considerable personal abuse from party members when Clark failed to fill many vacant positions

23

before the government fell, and declined to make any appointments thereafter. She then attempted, unsuccessfully, to regain a seat in Parliament as the candidate for Ottawa-Centre in the 1980 election. Her rationale for losing in 1979 and 1980 was simple. The party's proposal to cut 60,000 civil service jobs did her in in 1979, and her Government's budget, calling for an eighteen cent excise tax on gasoline, contributed to her defeat in 1980.

By the end of 1981, after returning to her family business and putting some distance between herself and the Clark team, Pigott had convinced herself that the Conservative party was going nowhere under its present leadership. So she phoned the man who had personally recruited her into elective politics and invited Joe Clark for dinner at one of Ottawa's most fashionable private clubs, *Le Cercle Universitaire*. There, she told him point-blank that she felt his image was too deeply and indelibly entrenched in the public mind and could never be changed. His position in caucus was tenuous and any appearance of harmony was simply a facade. Therefore, for his own good and the good of the party, he should resign. MP Frank Oberle had recently proposed that the Tories establish their own think-tank, an organization of party policymakers who would foster programmes for a government-in-waiting. Why not head up such a body? she proposed.

Clark sat listening to all this without rebutting any of the points, but growing increasingly angered that this person, who (he felt) owed her public status to him personally, would have the effrontery to offer this form of advice instead of getting behind him and helping him secure his leadership. But he didn't let his anger show and left *Le Cercle* resolved to start bringing his former stalwarts into line. But it was too late for regaining the support of Pigott, who had been meeting with others to plan John Crosbie's leadership bid for about two months before the dinner with Clark.

Looking at the results before him and listening to the advice being offered, it was obvious to Clark that his efforts had not been enough. He had gotten by without the Jean Pigotts before and he could again in the future. There *would* be a leadership convention, he *would* run and he *would* win it. He had said the same thing to this group before on many occasions. They had always wondered whether Clark really meant it. Now they knew.

* * *

"Go, Joe, go…please!"

Although the decision had been made quickly and authoritatively, there was a significant amount of discomfort in the room as Clark and Murray prepared the draft of the text the leader would read to the waiting delegates. None of them were under any illusion that Clark's hold on the leadership was rock solid. But by the same token, things *should have* gone a lot better than they had. Small's numbers suggested they would, and so had the two days in Winnipeg previous to the vote.

All the disparate groups in the party—the youth, caucus, National Executive, Quebec wing, and Clark team—had converged on Winnipeg on a chilly day three days earlier. The meeting itself had been a *tour de force* of the organizational skills the paid party workers had honed over the last seven years. A 120-foot stage had been constructed and was bracketed by the giant 40-foot screens that would accommodate state-of-the-art audiovisual presentations, designed to dazzle and awe the delegates with the talents of the Clark team. The delegates, however, would focus on one issue and one issue only—what percentage of the meeting would vote against a leadership convention, and what percentage would vote for.

Unlike the 1981 general meeting, however, there was no question that the dominance of this question was taking on a different significance in Winnipeg. The Ottawa meeting, the press and the caucus itself, had established the standard—66 per cent voting against review was the minimum level of support that would allow the leader to continue. Upon arriving in Winnipeg, there was the sense that virtually all the delegates wanted to do the right thing, but it was very clear, very early, that there was no unanimity among the delegates as to what that right thing was. For most, a vote for review meant at least another six months—and probably even a longer period of acrimony, introspection and internal strife which would deflect energies and attention from their mission of defeating the Liberals. For others, a vote against review meant entering another election, probably against the feared John Turner, with a leader whose ability to win was clearly in question. Whatever the outcome of the vote, there would be very serious and enduring consequences for the party.

By the second day, posters began to spring up on the convention walls appealing to the delegates… "It's Too High," (the anti-Clark vote) and imploring them… "To Clear The Air." While these signs were obviously sponsored by the review forces, they struck a responsive chord with the delegates; for they all wanted the air cleared, and sensed that they could

25

not continue indefinitely with the leadership issue hanging over them. One way or another the issue was going to be resolved.

* * *

John Morrison, the self-styled leader of the review forces, was in evidence during the course of the 1983 General Meeting, but he and his followers were viewed as more of a curiosity than a legitimate voice within the party.

Three years earlier, Morrison had emerged as a self-proclaimed media consultant with a mission to dump Clark. His critics claimed his consultancy status was simply Morrison's code word for unemployment and that his prominence was due to nothing more than the fact that others, who *had* a constituency in the party, were too smart to publicly associate themselves with the leadership review.

Morrison, who came from John Gamble's riding in York-North, found a platform in an organization called PC Metro. Nominally an umbrella organization representing 28 federal ridings in the Metropolitan Toronto area, PC Metro had emerged as a vehicle for disgruntled Tories to complain about their ongoing electoral failure in the area. For its part, the party establishment had seen organizations like this before and felt that if they ignored PC Metro, it would fade away. But it didn't fade away immediately, and proceeded to produce a number of resolutions, including a call for an immediate leadership convention. As embarrassing as such resolutions were to the party brass, they produced little in terms of real results; and a frustrated Morrison formed his own review committee in 1980 and then reactivated it in 1982 in his march on Winnipeg.

Working out of his basement, often alone and usually with fewer than six other volunteers, Morrison would prepare long lists of reasons why the Progressive Conservatives could never win under Joe Clark's leadership. This material would then find its way into mimeographed brochures which were mailed to delegates from lists usually leaked by sympathizers with access to the party's headquarters. While he had no organization to speak of, Morrison was highly visible, attending virtually every Progressive Conservative meeting his schedule would allow. There, only the most disgruntled Tories would be seen with him; but he would ask constantly about others attending the meeting and where they stood on the leadership question. If he was given any indication that some delegates might be planning to vote for review, Morrison would note their names and ensure that they got a call the next day to let them know they were not alone in their desire for a leadership convention.

It is questionable whether the efforts of Morrison and his organization had any direct effect on delegates. As a group, they appeared too "extreme" for most of the party regulars. But what Morrison's activities accomplished, along with those of other outside groups such as the National Citizens' Coalition (who were publishing polls showing the public wanting a leadership convention), was to redefine the notion of what was "acceptable behaviour" for delegates to engage in. In the past, it has been political heresy to talk about ousting the leader except under the most confidential of circumstances. By bringing the subject out in the open, Morrison and the other "outsiders" created a new criterion for what was considered heretical. It now became quite acceptable for insiders to actively debate the prospects of leadership review.

But, even with the presence of Morrison and the youth groups carrying signs which read "Go Joe Go…Please," things had gone well for the Clark group at Winnipeg. During his speech to the convention Clark had ignored the cameras and television audiences watching from their living rooms, and spoken directly to the delegates. He told them he had made mistakes in the past but that he had also learned from those mistakes and had moved the party forward since their defeat in 1980. He also used the very words of the review forces, and told the crowd that he too wanted "to clear the air."

The speech had buoyed the Clark forces. As they left the main hall to file into one of the adjacent salons to cast their ballots, many slapped each other on the back, or gave the "thumbs-up" sign accompanied by a knowing wink. While the votes were being counted and the bars opened, this feeling grew. Militants who were publicly associated with opposing factions met on the floor to shake hands and say there were no hard feelings. Otto Jelinek, one of only two MPs who publicly declared his intention to vote in favour for review, went on television to declare that his side had lost and, henceforth, he would be nothing if not supportive of Joe Clark.

The feeling that grew was that "it" was finally over and, with this feeling, came a huge outpouring of visible relief. The party had put the leadership issue behind it once and for all and, whether the delegates liked it or not, they were going to go into the next election behind Joe Clark.

27

But as the band played and youth delegates waved flags from the stage where Clark had spoken earlier, sporadic murmurs could be heard amongst the jubilant crowd. "...It couldn't be taking this long to count the ballots..." Even most of the veterans of these types of meetings dismissed the delay as nothing more than a studied effort on the part of the party to milk a few more minutes of prime time television out of the networks. This notion began to change rapidly, however, when Harry Near, one of Clark's top tour people came on to the floor to tell former national director Paul Curley that he had been dispatched to get Bill Jarvis, Erik Nielsen and Don Mazankowski, Clark's most trusted caucus supporters, for a conference with the leader in the room where Clark and his advisors had received the results of the vote fully 20 minutes ago. Something had gone wrong.

What went wrong, with the benefit of hindsight and information on delegates' voting behaviour in Winnipeg, is now abundantly clear.

* * *

No single group was responsible for the 33.1 per cent vote for leadership review in Winnipeg in 1983. Rather, this vote was the result of a disparate group of Progressive Conservatives coming together, basically out of their concern over Clark's winability—despite the fact that, at the time, they were enjoying the support of 49 per cent of the electorate, as expressed through the Gallup Poll. Having said this, however, a review of the reported behaviour of delegates who attended both the Winnipeg meeting and leadership convention, reveals that this concern was certainly more concentrated in some quarters of the party than in others.

First, while their actual numbers were small, it is very clear that Clark's perennial problems in caucus surfaced in Winnipeg. Fully 50 per cent of Clark's parliamentary colleagues voted for a leadership convention. The extent of the antipathy to Clark in the caucus, in many ways, underscored the thinking behind Clark's decision to call a convention, even though 66.9 per cent voted against one. He simply did not have the support of the one group he had to have, if he were to be able to give credible direction to the party in its role as an alternative government.

Second, the vote against Clark came principally from two provinces. But here also, survey research indicates that much of the conventional wisdom reported at the time simply is not borne out under scrutiny. In the end, Clark's Quebec organization met the goals they set out for themselves in 1981—only 34 per cent of the Quebec delegates voted for review in Winnipeg. In fact, the largest concentration of anti-Clark votes came from Newfoundland, where fully 80 per cent favoured a leadership convention. With the benefit of hindsight, however, it appears that this large bloc of regional votes was not so much a product of a studied attempt to organize pro-review slates, as it was grassroots anticipation of the native-son candidacy of John Crosbie. (The widespread news reports of Clark's vulnerability leading up to Winnipeg, and Crosbie's own public declarations of an interest in the leadership should it become open, unquestionably helped to inspire this grassroots anticipation.)

The next largest percentage of the anti-Clark votes—and the largest single bloc, in terms of numbers—came from Ontario, where 40 per cent reported voting for a convention. Here, there is some evidence that the right-left split in the party and Clark's association with the Red Tory faction emerged as a factor in the voting. In the country as a whole, only 33 per cent of the delegates who identified themselves with the right wing of the party voted in favour of review. In Ontario, however, this number reached 58 per cent.

When asked specifically why they voted for or against a leadership review, however, delegates volunteered that ideology was not the critical factor—not even in Ontario. Among all the anti-Clark delegates from across the country, only four per cent said ideology was a factor in their decision, and in Ontario it was only eight per cent. What this suggests is that, while ideology may have made delegates less sympathetic to Clark— and therefore led to a widespread appearance of dissatisfaction with his leadership—in the final analysis it did not necessarily lead delegates to oppose him.

Judged on the basis of what the delegates themselves said, the most important factor in the decision to vote for a convention was doubt about Clark's leadership competence and about public perceptions of his leadership competence. Twenty-six per cent (26%) of the anti-Clark delegates made negative comments about his judgement, managerial ability, and general aptitude for leadership, while an additional 25 per cent said he had a public image as an incompetent leader. These doubts about Clark's ability and image were translated in the minds of many delegates who voted against him into a concern that, despite the party's wide lead in the monthly Gallup Polls, it still might not win the next election. Twenty-one per cent (21%) of the anti-Clark delegates referred directly to this possibility and another 20 per cent referred to it indirectly.

These findings speak volumes about the peculiarities of politics within the Progressive Conservative party itself. Clark, as the national leader, was more popular among voters than within his own party; and he was more popular in the party than he was in his own caucus. By the normal logic of party politics, exactly the reverse should be the case; but in Winnipeg and for the two years leading up to Winnipeg, it wasn't. By January 1983, the Progressive Conservative party was so consumed with its opposition status that it dominated every thought. The closer the militants in the party were to Clark and the reality of opposition the more consumed they were with the question: Can we ever win with Joe Clark as leader again? For at least 33.1 per cent of the delegation in Winnipeg, the answer was a definite no.

Among the 66.9 per cent who opposed a leadership review, there was a group who qualified as personal followers of the leader—people who respected Clark's abilities, who liked him as a person or felt their interests or views would be better served by his leadership. They did not, however, constitute a substantial majority among the individuals who voted against a convention.

This meant that Clark's personal base—the group who felt their loyalties were to him personally and not just to a symbol standing for an end to division in the party—was relatively narrow. In fact, among the people who supported him at Winnipeg, many shared the doubts of his opponents about his fitness to lead, while others believed that, even if he were acceptable, there were alternative candidates who would make better leaders. What restrained them from voting for a convention was either a conviction that the principle of loyalty to the leader had to be observed, or the fear that to overturn Clark would be to reinforce the party's reputation for disunity and thus jeopardize their chances of winning the next election.

In retrospect, it was not some piece of bad luck or a failure of organiza-tion that produced the unsatisfactory mandate for Joe Clark in Winnipeg. In fact, opinion in the party as a whole appears to have been more strongly weighted against him than his majority would suggest. This is indicated by the fact that among the delegates to the June leadership convention who had *not* attended the meeting in Winnipeg, 45 per cent said that at the time of the Winnipeg meeting they believed a convention should be held. In other words, only 55 per cent of them would have supported Clark had they been in Winnipeg. Thus, it seems that Terry Yates was right—there were just no more votes to be wrung out of the Progressive Conservative party for Joe Clark in January 1983.

* * *

Joe Clark and his supporters gathered themselves up from the manager's office in the Winnipeg Convention Centre to face the delegates with the text they had prepared. As they walked solemnly down the stairs and through the corridors, the din of laughter and gaiety from the convention floor grew louder and clashed with the silence of the sombre group Clark was leading. As the leader's entourage approached the stage, the attention of the delegates was redirected to the podium where Pat Carney and Jean Guilbeault were preparing to read the results of the vote.

…the total votes cast were 2,406. The number of ballots spoiled were four.

The number of votes 'no' were 1,607 which is 66.9 per cent and the number of votes 'yes' were 795 or 33.1 per cent.

It took only seconds for many to realize the significance of what had just happened. The decisive moment of Clark's political career had arrived. Flanked by caucus loyalists—Erik Nielsen, Bill Jarvis, Don Mazankowski and Jake Epp—Clark approached the podium and began to address the meeting.

Ladies and gentlemen, *mes amis*. I've just heard, as you have, the co-presidents indicate the results of the vote on the review. I remind this party that we cannot be seen as a government or as an alternative if we are seen to be divided in the country. This country needs an alternative government and it needs that alternative government urgently

I asked tonight for a clear mandate to carry the party to victory. I received the support of a clear majority of the delegates voting here…but my friends, my friends, that mandate is not clear enough [CHEERING, YELLS]. It is not clear enough to enforce the kind of discipline and to achieve the kind of unity that this party requires…my friends, we know that the greatest enemy this party faces is uncertainty about our unity. Uncertainty about the Progressive Conservative party is damaging to this

31

party. Uncertainty about the future of the Progressive Conservative party is deeply damaging to this country.

Consequently, I will be recommending to the National Executive-
...[SHOUTS OF "NO!", MORE CHEERS]. I understand that feeling. My friends, I have been struggling to hold this party together for the last two years [APPLAUSE]. We have done very well in establishing ourselves as a fighting opposition, but until we have silenced all the serious critics in these ranks, we will not prove our capacity to form a government to the people of this country and, consequently, I will be recommending to the National Executive that they call a convention at the earliest possible time. [NOISE]

I want to take this occasion to announce that if the National Executive calls a leadership convention...I will be a candidate for that leadership.

A handful of delegates in isolated parts of the room whooped and clapped their hands over their head in unsuppressed delight. Most stood silent—stunned, or lost in thought.

By the time Clark and his coterie had descended the stage and left the room, hardly a delegate had moved from the spot where they stood minutes before trying to figure out what to do next. As they slowly filed out of the main hall in the Winnipeg Convention Centre, they didn't even stop to get a drink from the bars that had been set up in anticipation for the merriment to follow.

The leadership race was on.

Part II

OTTAWA
JUNE 11, 1983

Ballot One

CLARK, Joe	1091
MULRONEY, Brian	874
CROSBIE, John	639
WILSON, Michael	144
CROMBIE, David	116
POCKLINGTON, Peter	102
GAMBLE, John	17
FRASER, Neil	5

2

"At least they don't call you 'Joe Who' anymore"

"Clark... one thousand and ninety-one"

On June 11, 1983, Pat Carney and Jean Guilbeault were once again called upon to read the results of another vote to a meeting of PC delegates. This time it was in Ottawa, the occasion was a leadership convention and Joe Clark received 1,091 or roughly 37 per cent of the votes cast on the first ballot. He was running first and, by any political yardstick, it was an impressive showing. What made it all the more remarkable was the fact that, after Winnipeg, many pundits had virtually written Clark off as a contender. "How can someone run to succeed himself, when he is the issue?" they asked. In their view, Joe was slated for a fast fade. Whatever support he had at Winnipeg would slip and those delegates he *was* able to bring to the convention would quickly abandon him to support other candidates, as the mood for change took over.

As it turned out, this scenario in no way foresaw the extent of Clark's support on the first ballot. His strong showing was the result of several factors. First, although Clark had officially resigned as head of the PC party following Winnipeg, he nonetheless retained some of the advantages accorded an incumbent leader. He was, for example, well known in all regions of the country and could draw support from each one. In fact, at Ottawa, he would obtain a more *even* regional distribution of delegates than any other candidate: 46 per cent in the West; 29 per cent in Ontario; 51 in Quebec; and 33 per cent in Atlantic Canada. Moreover, as former leader, he was the choice of many of the party establishment. Forty-five per cent (45%) of the *ex officio* delegates, who were automatically granted a vote as a result of their official status within the party, would opt for

35

Clark on the first ballot. His "incumbency" also permitted Clark to draw upon the instilled loyalty of party members towards a national leader; and this advantage, in turn, allowed him to put together one of the most effective organizations ever assembled for a leadership convention in Canada.

Another factor the critics overlooked at Winnipeg was Clark's appeal as a moderate in a party facing a strong challenge from its own right wing. At the June convention, he would obtain 80 per cent of the votes of delegates who considered themselves centre or left-of-centre within the party.

Ironically, one of the most persistent criticisms of Clark had been that he lacked ideological commitment. He had been depicted as a political careerist whose whole experience was in the backrooms of his party, where he had been preoccupied with the tactics and techniques of winning power and not with the purpose for which power might be used.

The fact is that Clark did have a sense of ideological purpose, but it was confined to the question of *how* problems should be solved, and not *what* the solutions should be. As leader, Clark represented a tradition of pragmatic Toryism that dates back to Sir John A. Macdonald. This tradition embraces two principles. First, while it celebrates the virtues of capitalism, it holds that there are collective social and political values which may transcend the values of the market. Hence, it neither advocates nor flinches from government intervention in the economy. Second, it accepts the inevitability of social diversity and seeks to deal with it not by trying to impose uniformity, but by permitting it to thrive and attempting to accommodate it through compromise and cooperation.[1]

These ideas find resonance in the contemporary party among moderates of every hue, members who strongly identify with the need for a pragmatic rather than a doctrinaire approach to political, social and economic issues. Clark appealed directly to this constituency by repeatedly defending his conception of the Conservative party as a party of moderation, embracing a broad range of interests and points of view.

Coming out of Winnipeg, Clark made this idea a central aspect of his campaign for re-election. He stood as the only candidate who was strong enough to prevent the party from falling into the hands of an immoderate right wing. It was a credible claim in light of the role of the extreme right in the events leading to Winnipeg. And it gained more credibility as the right attracted media attention and other candidates were portrayed as shifting to the right.

This theme also suggested that, without him, the party would undergo a dramatic change in direction from the past; and, in no small measure, past direction was fine with the moderates who had controlled the party apparatus under Clark's leadership.

Among this group were most members of the national campaign organization. In many respects, Clark's biggest advantage in the campaign would lie in the professionalism of this national team and in their dedication to restoring him to the leadership of the PC party. The foundation of Clark's organization had been laid with the reforms to the party that Lowell Murray had made when he became national campaign chairman in 1977. The problem Murray had set out to solve was the most basic of all problems in Canadian electoral politics: that there is no direct means of voting for a party leader in the Canadian system. Elections ultimately are won and lost by individual candidates fighting on the party's behalf in each of the 282 constituencies. Thus, the techniques of advancing the leader's national tour, of using surveys to plan campaign strategy, and of applying research to the choice of target areas and groups for maximum campaign effort, all of which had been put in place during Robert Stanfield's tenure, could only be made fully effective if they were moved down to the local level.

This was the essence of Murray's plan when, in 1977, he set out to change the focus of political organization and the application of the new campaign technology. In doing so, he altered perhaps forever the nature of party politics, and especially leadership conventions, in this country.

Where this change was most significant was in the role played by the provincial campaign chairmen. No longer were these people simply to be sources for regional advice to the national campaign. Each chairman was to develop a parallel structure in his or her province with positions mirroring those on the National Campaign Committee. In every province there would be a tour director, a communications director, a press relations director and a person responsible for every campaign function. Thus, where there was once only one campaign committee, now there were eleven. And each provincial committee had its own team of workers and its own network of contacts reaching throughout the province. Under Murray's system the number of people with a substantial commitment to the national campaign grew exponentially—from less than 50 to literally thousands. And each of them had a role, responsibility and title... in other words, official legitimacy and a place within the party hierarchy.

Animating this expanded campaign organization was a commitment to a revised concept of political professionalism. The "new" style of political campaigning adopted by the Conservative party involved not just the use of modern technologies of communications and research, but the application of principles of scientific management. The people who were recruited into this structure might be volunteers but they were not amateurs. This was a sophisticated form of politics that relied on technical expertise and professional management. Those who participated in it were part of a new system of power and a new organization that demanded professional dedication.

This corps of "professional volunteers," owing their legitimacy and position to Lowell Murray and, therefore, to Joe Clark, formed the backbone of Clark's leadership organization. It was an organization based not so much on personal loyalty but on a commitment to professionalism. Not all of them might have liked Joe Clark personally—many of them didn't—but he had opened the party up to them. Each team member had a job to do, and his or her professionalism demanded that that job be done.

Clark's incumbency, therefore, afforded him a huge advantage over his opponents once the leadership convention was called. His organizers were in place and could function as a team. They also had a vested interest in Clark continuing as leader, not simply because their own positions might be threatened by a change in leadership, but also because the commitment to professionalism, which gave them a role in the party, might be threatened.

Clark's organization had three principal targets. Already many of the party's administrative positions throughout the country were held by Clark's people; they would be used to ensure that as many loyalists as possible were named as *ex officio* delegates to the Ottawa convention. The second target was the hundreds of post-secondary institutions in the country which did not yet have a PC campus club. The party allowed every club to send three delegates to Ottawa, and Clark's strong national team set about organizing dozens of new ones. Finally, and most importantly, the former leader's organization was determined to use its strength to influence the selection of delegates across the country.

"At least they don't call you 'Joe Who' anymore"

In the past, it was relatively easy to predict who would attend PC meetings as riding delegates. In many local associations, small bands of loyal workers would plan social events, membership drives and regular meetings. When the time came for delegate selection, these people were put forward (usually by each other) as the riding's choice to fill their six delegate slots.

Candidates have been able to get committed supporters elected only in the few cases where they have had direct access to local workers or where they could command the support of provincial parties with the resources to mobilize at the local level. Clark was the first candidate for the party leadership to have an extensive enough organization to be able to attempt to elect supporters at constituency meetings on anything approaching a nation-wide scale.

The major battleground for attempts to elect constituency delegates was Quebec, where the process in the past had been most inbred. Because many of the Quebec ridings had no active local associations, delegate selection has usually amounted to little more than a question of who had both enough interest and money to attend the party's meetings. A small and mixed group of Union Nationale members and Montreal West Islanders would draw up a list and assign their friends to various ridings across the province.

Marcel Danis, Denis Beaudoin, Jean-Yves Lortie, Michel Cogger and other members of the opposing Clark and Mulroney factions had changed all that in the prelude to Winnipeg six months earlier. But what these opposing factions accomplished in 1982 paled in comparison to 1983.

* * *

Marcel Danis' office is in the same modern building in old Montreal as that of Brian Mulroney's chief organizer, Michel Cogger, but the two may as well be on different planets. Cogger is a partner in the prestigious law firm of Geoffrion Prud'homme through whose elegant reception room pass representatives of Quebec's most powerful corporations. Danis' practice is criminal law, and his small dark waiting room is crowded with young people who would be thrown out of Geoffrion Prud'homme.

The Quebec constituencies of Clark and Mulroney were just about as far apart as the clienteles of the two lawyers who were running their campaigns.

39

Joe Clark was most popular in the rural communities of the province, among supporters of the old Union Nationale, Créditiste and PQ parties, while Mulroney's support came mostly from disaffected urban Liberals. Marcel Danis, who was himself a Union Nationale worker before joining the Tories, knew both communities well. In 1976 he had worked for Brian Mulroney under Rodrigue Pageau, but joined the Clark team after the convention and stayed. His reasons for switching could be those of most Clark supporters: "One thing belonging to the UN taught us was the importance of loyalty to the leader... it was inbred... of course Clark made it easy to support him. He's a decentralist... wants more for the provinces. That's the most important thing for the real Quebec parties... nationalism." To Danis, Mulroney's view of federalism was little different than Pierre Trudeau's... only the face had changed, and it was exactly that which appealed most to the basically Liberal Mulroney supporter.

So while the white suits and blue jeans of the nationalists packed the rallies for Joe Clark, it was the business suit that seemed to be the costume of the Mulroney advocate.

Whatever the attire, both sides knew how to roll up their sleeves and play tough politics. In 1976 Marcel Danis' job was to get Mulroney delegates elected in the rough east end of Montreal and from there safely to the Ottawa convention. His opposition, the Wagner forces, were led by Jean-Yves Lortie. In 1983 he once again faced Lortie fighting, this time alongside Danis' former boss Pageau, for Brian Mulroney. But Danis had learned well from both of them.

When the National Executive set the June date for a leadership convention and a five-week period for selecting delegates (March 25 to April 30), Danis struck quickly. He ordered all ridings where Clark supporters controlled the executive to hold their selection meetings as early as possible to minimize the amount of time Mulroney forces had to organize. In the first six days about half of the province's 75 ridings chose their delegates. It was the beginning of what the press dubbed the "dirty tricks" campaign.

* * *

It was an hour after the meeting was scheduled to start and 60 people were still lined up to get into the basement hall of the Church of the Immaculate Conception in the riding of Ste. Marie, a poor, French-

40

speaking district in East Montreal. All over the province, church halls like it were transformed into tense, smoke-filled meeting rooms where a crude form of democracy was practised. Each meeting was delayed in starting, as credentials of the party's members were carefully checked. In Ste. Marie, three-quarters of the people had been members for a month or less, and few were known by the officials at the door. A member had to show his membership card, have his name on the riding's list of members, and provide proof he was the person named.

Four men in their forties with bulging middles, cigars and pinstriped suits—looking every bit the caricatures of what they really were, political operators—leaned against a wall near the credentials table. They were from Clark's organization and if any of the members filing in had forgotten their ID, they'd whisk them home and back—that is, if they were on the list of people the Clark organization had sold a membership to. Each of the four men had brought in a group of new members and would receive a commission of $10.00 for each one, but only if the member attended the meeting and with the proper credentials.[2] This was where the battles were really fought... in the streets, as the organizations of each of the two major candidates attempted to outhustle the other for new members who would come to these meetings to vote for "their man." The party only required that a person be a resident in a riding and a member in good standing (that is, pay his three dollars) for five days to be eligible to vote for delegates. In Quebec, with so few permanent members in the party, the choice of delegates could always be determined by new members, the "five-day wonders," and each side worked hard to bring in new people who would vote for their nominees.

The struggle had reached ridiculous heights two nights before when Mulroney organizers in the St. Jacques riding had bussed in a group of "new members" from the "Old Brewery Mission," a home for derelicts. That night, Mulroney's choice of delegates won, but in doing so they left an indelible impression on the campaign.

The party had set no age minimum for its members and it was soon discovered that children of some of Mulroney's and Clark's supporters were also coming out and voting. A nine year-old cast a ballot in Hull, a 10 year-old in Duvernay. In Ste. Marie, the 15 year-old daughter of the riding president (a Clark supporter) signed up 20 of her classmates. The "tricks" didn't stop there. That night in the Church of the Immaculate Conception, both Clark and Mulroney organizers complained that many

41

of their people had received a phone call an hour or two earlier wrongly informing them that the meeting was postponed until the following night. The riding president was telephoned by someone who left the phone off the hook, effectively tying up her line for the evening. But 153 people still came out and, after bumping through the credentials line, were handed cards by representatives of the two candidates.

A dour, heavy-set woman in her thirties wearing a fur coat handed out the names of those delegates Brian Mulroney wanted them to vote for. A tall teenager with glasses and no past experience hesitated to offer people one of her Clark cards. To save time, the party's organizers that evening suggested people needn't mark their ballots with the names of delegates, a simple "Clark" or "Mulroney" would do. Better still, the chairman said a "number one" or "number two" would be sufficient to vote for the whole slate of one candidate or the other. In fact, he added, he would consider one vote good enough for all four delegate positions and all four alternates. It was bending the rules a lot, but no one complained. "We know why we're here," said Casper Bloom, Mulroney's agent at the meeting. Many of the people lined up quickly to vote, then left immediately after. They'd learn the results later—if they cared—that 120 voted for the Clark slate, 33 for Mulroney's. Those who remained let out a faint cheer of…"Joe, Joe, Joe"…as the chairman thanked them for supporting Clark. "That's objectivity," commented a bitter Mulroney supporter.

Such triumphs were the product of organization, of selling memberships and getting out the vote, and in the early days of the selection process the edge went to the Clark people and fueled their morale to work harder. Perhaps their sweetest victory came in Duvernay, in Laval, north of Montreal, where Ronald Bussey, Mulroney's Quebec chairman, headed the slate. The Clark organization sold 1,000 new memberships compared to 800 for Mulroney and then got out twice as many voters as Mulroney to the meeting.

By Easter, Clark had a majority of the delegates that had been selected in Quebec and Mulroney had no chance of getting the 75 per cent of delegates he had earlier boasted he would receive. From then until the end of April, it would get a lot tougher for Danis and in the ridings of west Montreal with their larger English-speaking—often provincially Liberal —constituencies, Clark would get hardly a single delegate. Still, Danis had done it again for Clark.

"At least they don't call you 'Joe Who' anymore"

Of the Quebec delegates attending the leadership convention who were selected from these meetings, 47 per cent would vote for Clark and 50 per cent for Mulroney. 42 per cent claimed they were identified as supporters of one candidate or were opposed by supporters of another, and virtually all reported a Mulroney-Clark battle. The remaining six candidates were not even in the game. And with virtually all delegates sewn up by April 30, 1983, it was already determined that Quebec would be a two-man race.

Through their activities in Quebec, Danis and his organizers laid the foundation for the Clark campaign. They had held the native son Mulroney to a draw in his own province, reducing his base of support and taking away his argument that only he could win in Quebec. It then fell to the rest of Clark's organization to do the same in the balance of the country.

* * *

In the rest of the country the Clark organization had less determined opposition to deal with but its own resources were also more limited because its network, rather than blanketing the country, consisted of concentrated pockets of supporters located for the most part in the major urban centres. Ironically, it was in Toronto, which had been the source of so much anti-Clark activity, that his organization achieved some of its most important victories. Clark's support in Toronto came from two quite different groups: members of the ethnic minority communities to whom he was trying so hard to open the party, and some of the most established of the party establishment.

Clark was proud of his work in Toronto and, while it had caused considerable dissatisfaction in the party, he was especially proud of his activity in the Broadview-Greenwood byelection, held in October 1982. There he had supported the nomination of a local Greek favourite, Bill Fatsis, against that of the outspoken right-wing editor of the *Toronto Sun*, Peter Worthington. Clark's candidate, with the lively support of the Greek community, defeated Worthington for the nomination but placed third in the election when Worthington ran as an independent, splitting the vote.[3] Later Clark said: "We lost a battle but won a war by making it clear that the rights and opportunities of a Canadian whose origin happened to be Greek, are the same as those born in Canada." The Greek community was not the only one that appreciated Clark's efforts. Large groups of South East Asians, Koreans and Chinese under the leadership of Jay Hong, a popular Korean businessman, came out for Clark at delegate selection meetings in Toronto. David Small used their networks to get out large numbers of new supporters in ridings they populated, but not without a price. When a few hundred Asian-Canadians turned out to elect a Clark slate in one of the suburban ridings, newspaper accounts gave front-page treatment to an exercise they somehow likened to the busing of derelicts and the voting of children.

There were, however, some genuine campaign excesses in Toronto. In the inner city riding of Spadina, for example, the riding association passed a resolution requiring people to be members for a minimum of 60 days before being eligible to vote for delegates. A sensible idea on the face of it, but the association failed to inform non-card carrying members about it and the membership secretary was "unavailable" to new applicants. Poor notice of the selection meeting was given and a Clark slate was quickly pushed through with the assistance of a local ethnic ball-hockey team—all 60-day members of the association—who had to be guided through the English spelling of the delegates' names.

Coincidentally, one of the Tory organizers in Spadina was Henry N.R. (Hal) Jackman, president of the Albany Club and one of the many establishment figures supporting Clark. The former leader also received early support in Toronto from such notables as John Bassett, Ted Rogers and Alan Eagleson. It was ironic that Clark, who had once refused to enter the Tory Albany Club in Toronto because of its male exclusivity, was supported by its president and probably a majority of its members. Clark was not one of that crowd, nor on the face of it was he an inspiring leader whom they could admire. What was it that attracted them? Clark himself attributed it to respect for his tenacity: "Their support encourages me. It tends to confirm my view that I'm right for these times." Undoubtedly, for some of them, there was safety in supporting "The Leader" as he was still seen. It is far easier to excuse misplaced loyalty to a leader than support for a disloyal aspirant, should one's candidate lose. And, in a way, because of his personal party organization, Clark had made his own establishment. While this irked the many who were outside of it, it earned the respect of the establishment figures for whom loyalty to the leader—they were themselves leaders—was the expected thing.

The Clark organization contested delegate elections in seven out of the ten provinces.[4] There were no slates in Nova Scotia, but delegates who ran as Clark supporters got effective organizational support. In Ontario, Clark slates ran in all of the Ottawa ridings and in a number of other urban centres. In Manitoba they won an early victory in Portage-Marquette, a riding thought to be a Mulroney stronghold. Clark people had pulled out all the stops, running buses to bring in members from across the riding, and their success encouraged them to run slates in every riding, with considerable success. In Saskatchewan, there were slates in only three urban ridings, but in Alberta and British Columbia almost the entire province had a chance to vote for a Clark slate. As in Quebec, Clark did best in ridings that held early selection meetings, before the opposition could get organized. In Edmonton, Clark slates swept the city, but two weeks later, newly organized anti-Clark slates beat them at their own game in Calgary. From the end of April to the first of June, it fell to the Clark campaigners to make sure he held this support and to woo those in ridings he did not control.[5]

By the end of the delegate selection process Joe Clark had built a substantial lead over his rivals. He seemed to be within striking distance of victory. But his growth had stopped. Of those delegates who decided their first ballot vote before the end of April, Clark won 47 per cent; but, of those who decided after the end of April, only 17 per cent decided to support him.

In part, Clark's momentum slowed because, with the end of the delegate selection process, the campaign entered a new phase in which Clark's organizational advantage was neutralized. In this second phase, the object was to win the votes of undecided delegates and the campaign became much more like a general election. An organizational network reaching across the country was still helpful, but the campaign techniques— candidate tours, media coverage, contact by mail and telephone— assumed a much more central role and all of the candidates could use these techniques.

But that was not all. Clark was making mistakes. The first one to have significant impact was his response to criticism of the tactics used in delegate selection. The packing of meetings and the manipulation of party rules to create new delegateships have always been elements of party conventions in Canada, but they have never received the attention that they did in 1983.

Clark's organization was not alone in seeking to stretch the rules of accreditation for campus clubs or in packing delegate selection meetings. Both Mulroney and Crosbie workers were doing the same thing. But Clark seriously isolated himself when journalists and party members questioned the ethics of these practices. Crombie and Wilson made the ethical question a campaign issue by calling for an investigation by the convention committee. Mulroney quickly moved to join them, telling reporters that he had asked his organizers to conduct themselves in future in "the way I conduct myself in public and private life—with intelligence, probity and honour." In contrast Clark refused to apologize for his workers. He said no rules had been broken and defended what had been done with the comment that "democracy isn't a tea party."

This was a side of Clark that few outside of his immediate circle had ever seen before—a grim determination arising out of his belief that there was a right way and a wrong way for the PC party to go. The campaign simply heightened his resolve in this regard. For Clark, the right way meant a commitment to creating a modern, moderate, and national party that accepted women, young people, new Canadians, and "the reality of Quebec." In his own mind, those who now opposed him were threatening not only his leadership but everything he sought to accomplish.

This attitude allowed Clark to justify and rationalize the tactics practised by his organization. But it also had its drawback since his aggressiveness caused the battle lines to be drawn even more starkly than they had been in the past. Now there was little room for compromise. You were either for him or against him. It wasn't the first time Clark had used such tough language in the campaign. In Halifax, a week before the "tea party" remark, he had paraphrased a Nova Scotia cabinet minister in responding to a question concerned about how he would deal with the party's disunity. It will be "my way or the doorway," he said. It was tough talk and it conjured up memories of Clark's unsuccessful attempt at governing, when he defiantly declared that he would "govern as if he had a majority," despite the obvious fact that he could be brought down at any time by a coalition of the NDP and Liberals. Combined with the emerging Quebec campaign story, it gave many the impression of an unrepentant leader, out for revenge. While undoubtedly some people found this "new"

Joe Clark a refreshing change from the "wimp," it concerned many others, including some of the people closest to him.

But, as the campaign progressed, Joe Clark became increasingly angry. He was angry at having to go through another leadership convention, with its risks to party unity, before he could return to his plan for the nation: a strong, modern and moderate Progressive Conservative party that would be a real national institution. He was especially proud of his efforts in Quebec. "The gains in Quebec are mine," he said privately three months into the campaign, "…to take nothing away from Robert L. [Stanfield]." He referred to the rise of the party's popularity in that province since the time of the constitutional debate when Clark had led his party into a position favouring the right of Quebec, or any other province, to opt out of any federal-provincial cost-sharing scheme. "I had immersed myself in Quebec for four or five years and came to understand and to take that position. That [the popular support won by the position] is personal, it's not transferable."

Clark also saw his work in the province of Quebec as vital for the entire country: "We've done the work in Canada that FDR did in the U.S. five decades ago; we've achieved a new coalition in the country." And he saw himself as indispensable to this work; "I am the only person who can hold together the good forces we brought together and hold back the forces that are bad." By "forces that are bad" he meant the extremists and the narrow-minded, "the guys who fight the metric system and argue for capital punishment so vehemently." Would they be the ones shown the doorway in a Clark-led party? "No, those guys can tolerate me, they've worked out a *modus vivendi* with me. I think they're wrong but I'll keep them in the party, though not in too great numbers."

It was those kind of comments that made his staff bridle. "God," said one senior advisor, "if he does win, he'll be insufferable. He thinks he's done it all himself." Another said Clark reminded him of FDR and Pierre Trudeau, by being so isolated: "None [sic] had the ability to communicate with another human being."

By April, Clark *had* become overconfident: He had entered the race knowing his army of workers was the best organization in the country and, with its early success in getting the Clark slates elected, his attempt to succeed himself had been vindicated. He was tenaciously clinging to power, not for his own sake, but because he genuinely believed he was indispensable to the party's success. His early victories told him that the

47

party would recognize that too. Now, in April, his only regret was that he had been forced to put the party through this procedure, and he was already planning the healing process he would instigate in the summer to reconstruct his party.

Clark's overconfidence got him in serious trouble when his plain speaking escalated to a patronizing treatment of his opponents. On a Vancouver talk show, Clark summarily appraised each of his opponents, laughing at some, criticizing others, at best damning them with faint praise. The next morning his capsule accounts were on the front pages of most newspapers in the country and his lack of judgement, not his opponents' weaknesses, became the issue.

Lowell Murray had mapped out the basic strategy for Clark to follow in the campaign. It was to assume the high ground and allow each of his opponents to be scrutinized under the glare of national media attention, revealing them as the regional or factional candidates they were. The former leader would thus be left as the only truly national candidate. But Clark grew impatient for his competitors' flaws to be uncovered and decided to help the press along. In March and April, Clark's personal campaign showed little evidence of high-minded statesmanship. Concerned, Lowell Murray met with Nancy Jamieson, Clark's former legislative assistant, and Bill Neville, Clark's former chief of staff. Neville agreed to write a high-toned thematic speech Clark could use on the hustings, but when Clark read it, his response was that it was "fine, but not as good as what I've been giving."

What he had been giving had included off-hand remarks about the putative candidacy of Ontario Premier William Davis, whom he had described in one interview (on March 25) as "a regional candidate." In another, he had commented that Davis would not want a recently announced program (providing all French-speaking children in Ontario with the right to a French-language education) "tinged by the accusation of political opportunism." Clark denied that his remarks were anything but spontaneous and well-meaning. At least one observer, however, believed they constituted his own planned attempt to flush Bill Davis out; but "unfortunately, he threw a hand grenade to do it." Whether premeditated or spontaneous, it showed the level of Clark's confidence that he was willing to confront Davis in these terms. Most of Clark's team were aghast. "It was a dumb thing to do," said one, "totally unnecessary."

The response from Davis' side was considerably stronger. Phone lines into Ottawa sizzled the weekend Clark made these remarks as some of those closest to Davis—Eddie Goodman, a past national election chairman and long-time confidant; Hugh Segal, a former aide and close advisor; and Dalton Camp, who still kept up his constant contacts with the Davis team in Ontario—called Clark staff to voice their indignation. These three men had been doves, cautioning Davis against running for the national leadership, and warned the Clark people that they might no longer be able to prevail over the hawks led by Norman Atkins, Camp's brother-in-law and a long-time Davis advisor. In fact, after Clark's remarks, Segal himself became a strong supporter of a Davis candidacy.

Clark had originally sought Davis' support immediately after the vote in Winnipeg. The premier's position, that he "supported the leader" and would continue to do so, was one that still left open his own candidacy. Clark formally resigned the leadership two weeks later, and, in a meeting between the two men in Toronto shortly thereafter, Davis admitted that the situation was "more fluid than the last time we spoke." By that time the Ontario premier had received considerable pressure from Atkins and company and had agreed to keep his options open while they at least determined the viability of his candidacy.

Davis, nonetheless, had stated that his predisposition was to not be a candidate. Before leaving for an Easter vacation in Florida at the end of March, he told one advisor he would announce his decision not to run at a meeting of provincial riding presidents on April 10th. Davis was in Florida when Clark made his remarks and his own reaction was one of patent displeasure. Davis was proud of the stand he had taken during the constitutional debate and also of the steady, if slow, development of French-language rights in his province. It was an injustice to be branded regional or an opportunist for them, he thought, but he did not react immediately. "My wife and some of my colleagues were a lot more upset than I was," he claimed. That was how Finlay MacDonald found Davis—peeved but restrained—three days later when he arrived in Florida.

Clark advisors realized the gravity of the situation when it became clear that, far from discouraging Davis and his advisors by showing them that it would be a tough campaign if they entered, the sleeping Ontario lion might now be wakened. So the eminently presentable MacDonald, with close ties to the premier, was dispatched to Fort Lauderdale carrying a manila envelope. Inside was a transcript of the interview Clark had given in which he referred to Davis as "regional," the newspaper account which had exaggerated the statement (MacDonald did not take any of the material covering Clark's French-language comment, not realizing that Davis found it to be just as irritating), and a letter that Clark had written Davis two days before he had made his first remark. The letter was undelivered because Davis had gone to Florida. This was a handwritten "Dear Bill" note in which Clark politely wrote that if Davis should decide to run he would "bear no ill-will" and, if not, then Clark hoped for his "continued support."

The reaction of Davis and his people was one of bewilderment: Why make an offensive remark after writing such a thoughtful letter? Unless, as some reasoned, it was a heavy-handed attempt to bully Davis into staying out of the race. Its effect was to do almost the opposite. (Upon his return after his meeting with Davis, MacDonald gave Clark the premier's holiday number and advised him to speak directly to Davis. Clark never called.)

When Davis returned from Florida he was greeted by a charged-up company of supporters armed with heavy ammunition. In his absence, they had conducted two opinion polls: one, a survey of the delegates to the Winnipeg meeting showed Davis would have a difficult time winning the party; the other, a poll of the general public, showed Davis as the strongest candidate to run against any Liberal leader including John Turner. If the information from the second poll could become general knowledge, it might influence the delegates to a leadership convention. In view of the Clark remarks and the vigour of his own supporters, Davis could hardly restrain his people. "I knew they were working, working hard, but with no encouragement from me that they would get a positive response," he said later. Nonetheless, Davis indicated he would listen to whatever advice they came up with.

First, the public opinion poll was leaked to the *Toronto Star* and its information did become general knowledge. Once again, a Davis candidacy was a real possibility and the press, hungry for a new slant to the race, began a three-week-long chase of the premier. His response to questions was always the same: "I have no plans to run." He may have had no plans but his organizers did. In the middle two weeks of April, Advance Planning Inc., the consulting arm of Camp Advertising run by Atkins and Segal, was on a campaign footing. They assembled an organization with people ready to work in every province: Malcolm Wickson, the former national director, would run BC, Senator Nathan Nurgitz, a past party president, would handle Manitoba, Marcel Masse, the former Union Nationale cabinet minister then supporting Brian Mulroney, would run the Quebec campaign. At the helm would be Atkins with Paul Curley, the Clark-appointed former national director, and veteran organizer John Thompson. Segal had assembled a policy advisory body staffed by specialists in every field and position papers were already being written. Even a campaign logo had been produced.

Segal and Masse then took to the road and in a whirlwind tour met with the premiers of Prince Edward Island, Nova Scotia, New Brunswick, and Saskatchewan to determine how much support Davis could expect. Premiers Lee and Hatfield said they would endorse his candidacy, and Premier Buchanan agreed that his chief of staff, Dennis Ashworth, would organize for Davis in Nova Scotia. Premier Devine stated that as head of a new government he had to be in a position to work with whoever won; however, he would publicly say he welcomed Premier Davis' candidacy with words to the effect: "If Canada is served as well as Ontario has been, Saskatchewan will be very happy." Even the Social Credit Premier of BC, Bill Bennett, indicated he could be called upon, if Alberta Premier Lougheed came out in opposition to a Davis candidacy, to assert that Davis was not objected to in his province.

It all "made me feel a little humble," Davis said later. "It gave me a good feeling." Still Davis was noncommittal but cooperative. On April 25th, a week before his decision, he delivered an address to Toronto's Canadian Club written and promoted by his people as a national bridging speech. It touched all the bases an aspiring leadership candidate must and ended: "It is time to advance the Canadian dream." Later that week he welcomed a group from Quebec who had been Peter Blaikie's supporters. Blaikie, the immediate past president of the party, had withdrawn his own candidacy for the leadership, and his people argued now that Davis was the man they'd like to support. "I was really moved by their representation," Davis said. People closest to the premier say it was that visit which put him on the edge of entering the race…that is, until the events of the following four days.

Davis and his supporters had always known that the person most opposed to his candidacy was Alberta Premier Peter Lougheed. As Davis went home that weekend for four days of contemplation, the expectation of his candidacy grew and so, too, did the messages from Lougheed.

51

Through "eloquent emissaries" like past party president Michael Meighen, a mutual friend and Mulroney supporter, Darcy McKeough, former Ontario treasurer, and Tom Kierans, president of the investment house McLeod, Young, Weir, Davis heard the same bad news: if he entered the race, Lougheed would do "everything he could to stop him." It seemed to many in the Davis camp bitterly ironic, since in 1976 Davis had called to pledge his support and offered to nominate, should Lougheed decide to run. Since then, it seemed their differing views on energy pricing, the constitution, and the exercise of power in Canada had created a gulf between the two men.

Nevertheless, with the support he had from the other premiers, Davis concluded that weekend he could counter the isolated attack of Lougheed. He would enter the race.

On Tuesday, he arranged a meeting of the Davis campaign team at his house and placed a call to his would-be ally, Grant Devine, in Saskatchewan. What Devine said startled the Ontario premier. It would not be possible, Devine said, to publicly go against Lougheed, since he had encountered some negative reaction in his province. At the subsequent meeting of his advisors, as Davis listened to the report of where his strength came from and how ready the team was, he was still mulling over what the Saskatchewan premier had told him. Later that night, he made his decision.

Davis' advisors agree that it was the Devine decision that kept their man out of the race. "It was *the* factor," says one, bitterly attributing Devine's action "to a distinct failure of courage." Davis himself has told people privately he felt no bitterness but was only "a little disappointed" by the actions of Lougheed and Devine.

Davis' announcement not to run—perhaps the most widely covered event of the campaign—cited his concern not to inadvertently become a controversial force. It was a matter of "what he would have won if he had run," lamented one very close advisor, "a divided party and country. He didn't have the ambition to subject the country to that."

* * *

Clark was spared running against Davis—although some of his people privately mused that they would have liked to have run against and beaten him—but he was not spared the full impact of his remarks. Earlier in the campaign, sources close to Premier Davis had privately told some observers that, unlike 1976, when Davis had kept silent, this time he would announce his support for one of the candidates. Like so many others of the party establishment, Davis was comfortable with the status quo and it was likely that candidate would have been the present leader. Clark's remarks however, and the abortive campaign that followed, ruled out such an endorsement as the sentiment against Clark lingered. Four days before the vote on the leadership, Davis gave a private dinner at Toronto's Albany Club for the 150 people who had organized his campaign. In his remarks, Davis is said to have commented on one Clark remark "...I am not a regional candidate. I believe in Canada, not a community of communities." According to one observer, Davis' eyes filled with tears as he spoke of this commitment and his audience was visibly moved by his words.

At another dinner two days later at *Le Cercle Universitaire* in Ottawa, the "Big Blue Machine" again assembled, this time in the company of its members who had been working for other candidates. In saying grace for the group, and with Bill Davis at the head of the table, Finlay MacDoanld humbly beseeched: "Forgive us for our regional candidate remarks." Everyone laughed.

Not all members of the Clark team were so contrite. While regretting the remark, one leading Clark advisor attributed the subsequent events to gross overreaction on the part of Davis' people, and suggested an ulterior motive for their actions. "They've [the Ontario people] shit on us since day one, doing everything they can do to undermine us." Clark himself remained resolute. "I'm not counting on his endorsement," he had earlier said. "I'm going to win this on my own." Clark believed there was "a certain advantage to getting it without [the Davis] endorsement," almost to the point where he may have wanted it that way.

* * *

Most of the people close to Joe Clark deplored what they saw as his growing arrogance and lamented his occasional lack of skill in dealing with people. Others did not really feel close to Joe Clark at all, but respected his view of the country and shared his dream for the party. For nothing was this respect greater than for his efforts in Quebec. Clark owed much to his wife, Maureen McTeer, for steering him in this direction. Born into an Anglo family in a predominantly French-speaking part of

Ontario, McTeer had buttressed Clark's own sensitivity to the Franco-phone issue. McTeer was seen as a campaign liability in some parts of the country; not so in Quebec where she was used heavily. In fact, in the 1983 campaign, Clark's staff made a conscious decision to keep her separated from her husband as much as possible and used to the best advantage on her own in French Canada.

Clark's work in Quebec organizing the party and on the constitution, and his commitment to developing his language skills had begun to pay off. The party's research confirmed what the Gallup poll showed: that approximately 40 per cent of the province's electorate were prepared to vote for Clark's Tories. But, for the Conservatives, Quebec was not only a target for votes; it was, itself, an issue. While it was natural that a native Quebecer, Mulroney, should have support from the province, the degree of support for Clark made many suspicious. Had he conceded too much to that strange nationalist/separatist province? His enemies focussed on the number of Parti Québecois supporters who were helping his campaign as proof that he had.

There is an expression in French to the effect that the enemy of my enemy is my friend. To a large extent this explains why Joe Clark, the enemy of Pierre Trudeau and his hard line on the constitution, became the "friend" of the PQ.

It is true that a number of PQ organizers did work for Clark's organizer Danis in getting out people to vote for Clark delegates at selection meetings in certain areas of Quebec, and that many more PQ supporters came out to vote for the Clark delegates. It is also true that Clark's organizer in eastern Quebec, Maurice Duplessis, grandson of the former UN Premier, had been active for the "Yes" campaign in the 1980 referendum on sovereignty association. His wife Suzanne, another Clark organizer, had been president of the "Yes" committee in her riding. All these people appear, however, to have supported Clark on an individual basis. There was no "Parti Québecois connection," as some writers reported. They were attracted to Clark because of his constitutional stand, which satisfied part of their short-term strategy for limited independence, and because of Clark's association with many former supporters of the Union Nationale who were now drawn to the PQ over the Liberals. It was their anti-Liberal sentiment which Clark capitalized on when Lévesque called Mulroney a "mini-Trudeau" over his stand against opting out of constitutional agreements. Lévesque had described Clark as "probably the most open-minded English-Canadian politician" on the subject of Quebec, and this remark was evidence enough for many editorialists and cartoonists, in and out of Quebec, to depict him as "soft on Quebec." But the assessment failed to take into account a much more effusive endorsement from the influential Montreal daily, *Le Devoir*, hardly a separatist publication, when, on April 19, it praised Clark for his "courageous and realistic" stand on the constitution. As George MacLaren, publisher of the English *Sherbrooke Record* explained it: "Clark got the intellectuals, not Mulroney."

This was not the impression conveyed across the country—rather, it was of Joe Clark, puppet to René Lévesque. At delegate meetings everywhere Brian Mulroney was quick to exploit the point: "I'm not playing footsie with the PQ," he told his listeners, "another candidate is developing an elegant style in that regard."

By the time Joe Clark appeared on stage in Toronto's Massey Hall on April 30 for the only all-candidates debate of the campaign, the damage had been done. As he stood before the audience, in a city that had never felt fondly toward him, and began speaking in French, many people booed him. Some objected to his use of French, while others wished to show their contempt for "the wimp." Many others, however, were expressing their displeasure towards Joe Clark, patsy for Quebec. The next morning the Quebec press was full of reports of "anti-French" sentiment in Toronto in general, and in the Progressive Conservative party in particular.

Later, Clark said he deeply regretted this interpretation. "I think there is a rather eccentric minority in the Conservative Party who have been around a long time, giving me trouble a long time, who were there, who were giving me trouble again." In typical Clark fashion, he explained that it was all part of his mission: "In a peculiar way, the fact that I persevere in the face of all that helps to make Quebec feel part of a larger family."

* * *

By mid-May, the Clark camp sensed they were in trouble. The delegate selection process had ended more than two weeks earlier, and they had picked up very few "uncommitted" delegates, despite their superior organization. What was becoming clear was that Clark's publicly-acknowledged front runner status, and his attacks on other candidates, had caused increasing polarization within the party, where the main focus was on the Clark campaign and his personality. In short, "Anyone But Clark" was real and the leader's campaign was making it even more real. A change in strategy was required.

Three items gripped the attention of Clark's strategists. The first was that the number of delegates committed to voting for Joe Clark on the first ballot had not changed since the end of the delegate selection process three weeks before. The 1,100 they had at the end of April had not varied despite the number of uncommitted delegates they had attempted to recruit across the country. The second was the belief that the tactics used in getting Clark slates elected, and the arrogant remarks he had made along the way, had reduced the potential for getting additional delegates on a second ballot. If 1,450 votes were needed to win, then Clark had to become the second choice of a lot more people. The third item was that by the middle of May they had come to believe it would be John Crosbie, not Brian Mulroney, whom they would face on the final ballot. Mulroney's growth had stalled; in fact, he was losing delegates in Nova Scotia, Saskatchewan and British Columbia, and his organization was in chaos.

Crosbie had received spectacular press coverage and had all the signs of important momentum. Worse, from the Clark point of view, Crosbie had the greatest second-ballot potential of all the candidates—the anti-Crosbie sentiment in the party was insignificant compared to the anti-Mulroney (or anti-Clark) factions. But facing Crosbie had its advantages. It would enable Clark to focus on the modern, moderate, Quebec-oriented party he favoured compared to the old-fashioned, business-oriented, anti-Quebec party he could argue Crosbie stood for. It would be the old way versus the new, and Clark, for a change, would stand for the new. It was on this basis that Clark hoped to strengthen his candidacy, as he flew westward to begin his final cross-country sweep.

* * *

Clark's tour began in Vancouver and continued across British Columbia. Everywhere Clark sought to generate second-ballot support by emphasizing his commitment to the notion of the Conservatives as a moderate national party. By the time Clark reached Calgary, the tour had learned that the day before in Quebec, John Crosbie had lost his temper under persistent questioning over his inability to speak French. He had reminded reporters that bilingual Canadians were in a minority and not "some kind of aristocracy" with a monopoly on politics. True, he would need an interpreter, he admitted, but so does any prime minister in dealing with China or Germany, and that has never been a barrier to understanding. Brian Mulroney had reacted by calling it "preposterous" that a unilingual be elected leader and was subsequently caught up in a public argument when he denied using the term to describe Crosbie.[6]

Clark saw his opportunity and seized it. At a press conference that morning at his hotel, he refused to endorse Mulroney's sentiments. He said it was a "definite advantage" to be bilingual, but not a prerequisite. "We expect our finance minister to know something about economics ...and we expect our prime minister to know something about Quebec." He added that he had learned about the issues pertaining to the people of that province more easily because he "could speak directly to them in their language." In his heart of hearts, Clark believed Mulroney was right, that the party had come too far to return to a unilingual leader, or at least one who treated French as a foreign language. But Crosbie had already done the damage to himself and Clark's comments, unlike Mulroney's, appeared conciliatory. He went further a few minutes later when he offered his view that it was "unlikely" that he would win the leadership on the first ballot. Until that week it had been Clark's official position that he hoped to. He was now conceding his need for support from the others' delegates—his need for critical "second choice" support. Asked if he were talking to David Crombie's people in particular (they were viewed as the most moderate), he replied that his people were talking to representatives of all the candidates. And then he borrowed a line from Mulroney, giving him credit as he did. "Brian said something very wise the other day ...whoever wins is going to need the help of all other candidates and their advisors, and there'll be a role in my administration for all of them." All in all, Clark sounded like a man who could and would help heal the party. When a local reporter then asked, "If it goes the other way, what will you do—go to the Senate?," Clark momentarily lost his composure. "The Senate?" he repeated, then laughed sarcastically "What do you think. .?" His voice trailed off as he recovered himself and again took the high ground: "I'll be running again in Yellowhead. I think it's in the country's best interest that I do and," he paused only slightly, "I'd be prepared to serve in the cabinet of whoever leads this party." As he left the room, the reporters buzzed about the new "amiableness" of Joe Clark.

That evening in Lethbridge, an agricultural centre of 56,000, 200 kilometres southeast of Calgary, Clark emphasized his record as a conciliator. He met with 20 of the area's delegates in a room closed to reporters. They asked why he had failed to change the civil service during his short term in office and Clark talked about conciliation and pride. The way to have an effective civil service is not by firing everyone, he said, but by getting the most out of them. "The civil service knows me as fair but firm," he said. It's a matter of "professional pride" that makes people cooperate. For Clark, negotiation was the way to get the most out of people. He then proceeded to treat his audience to an extraordinary example: "When we were in government and needed an energy agreement do you know what I did? I went down to New Brunswick and asked Premier Hatfield what he needed out of the deal. He told me and I said 'all right, here's half' and he agreed. I went to Ontario and asked Bill Davis what he needed. He told me 'two things.' First that oil couldn't move to world price—so we agreed on 85 per cent—and second he said 'I need a forum from which to complain.' I said 'all right' and I called a federal-provincial conference...there's no matter that can't be solved this way...energy, the constitution, medicare, the Crow...by good old-fashioned Canadian enterprise."

The next questioner asked if it was "so important to win in Quebec" that Clark would "make a deal with the PQ." Clark assured him it was important to win in the west too, that his support in Quebec was likely to mean eight to 20 seats there and that it had been accomplished without making deals. "I wouldn't make a deal with the PQ for two reasons: The people of Lethbridge would never allow it, and deals don't work."

His answers were indeed interesting, but appeared to fail to satisfy his questioners. It was as if they spoke, and thought, on different wavelengths, neither side wanting to understand the point the other was making—and this only a few miles from Clark's hometown, High River. The trouble was that Clark had transcended his roots. His national outlook no longer jibed with the regional view of his local constituents.

It got worse after dinner, when Clark addressed 200 area residents. They had come out to support the fundraising efforts of the local Young Progressive Conservatives and Clark was obliged to sit as the centrepiece of a head table where no one else was over 21. To his old neighbours it must have reminded them of a high school graduation exercise where everyone smiled awkwardly. Clark was clearly uncomfortable when he rose to speak. His well-worn anecdotes lost almost all their humour as he tied them up in lengthy asides, and his appeal to maintain a modern, moderate, national party got no exceptional response. He chose to emphasize opportunities in Quebec even more than usual, despite the warning that he might have taken from his earlier private meeting with the delegates. And, when no one asked a question about Quebec afterwards, he chose to end the evening by offering an explanation of his position on opting out of the constitution as it relates to Quebec. "I just wanted to say that, because I have learned that you say the same thing in every region of the country, the same thing in both official languages and when there's a misunderstanding you address it directly." It was not a particularly enthusiastic crowd that rose to its feet for a brief ovation as he sat down.

Not content to let Clark get away from his "reunion" without more reminders of the past, Mrs. Edna Campbell, who lives in the Crow's Nest Pass, part of Clark's original Rocky Mountain riding, caught him on the way to the door. "I remember 10 years ago, you coming up our way campaigning," she said, "We called you "Snowy Joe" 'cause you always seemed to bring the snow when you came. "Snowy Joe" looked about ready for the mountains as he smiled and tried to move away. "You've come a long way," she concluded. "At least they don't call you 'Joe Who' anymore."

Later, Clark was to describe the evening as one of the worst stops on the tour. He admitted he felt "distinctly uncomfortable" with the home crowd and had found "no rapport" with them. "In many ways, Peter Pocklington was the quintessential Alberta candidate," he concluded remorsefully. "It's so simple: just blame it all on the Liberals."

* * *

It was with considerable relief that Joe Clark arrived in Quebec to be greeted by two extraordinary news stories and two good friends. The friends were Perth MP Bill Jarvis and former minister of Industry, Trade and Commerce, Robert René de Cotret, both along to warm up the audiences in Clark's three Quebec stops. They joined him at the Montreal airport and together flew by helicopter to Sherbrooke, 150 kilometres south, reading the newspaper accounts as they went.

The first story across the front page of the Saturday *Le Devoir* reported that a survey of Quebec delegates to the Tory convention showed a majority supported Joe Clark over Brian Mulroney, 51 per cent to 44 per cent. Though Clark knew the real Quebec breakdown gave a slight edge to Mulroney,[7] he welcomed the publicity. The second news story was even more flattering, but its source gave Clark pause. Pierre Bourgault, one of the founders of the Parti Québecois, had endorsed Joe Clark as his choice for prime minister in his weekly column in the *Montreal Gazette*. He said he supported Clark because he is "a man of courage and discipline, dedication and respect" and "would be as tough as anyone" in dealing with Quebec separatists. Despite the praise, Clark was concerned about the reaction in English Canada to a separatist's blessing. Bourgault himself addressed the concern in his column: "I don't expect anything from Joe Clark [on the separatist issue] but I want to make sure that as long as I remain a citizen of Canada I can look up to the prime minister with respect and confidence."[8] Clark did the only thing he could, he accepted the endorsement in the spirit in which it was given, and hoped that no one would hear about it.

As Clark arrived at the tavern banquet hall, in the poorer south side of Sherbrooke, he seemed visibly more animated and happy than he'd been all week. In stark contrast to his Alberta meetings, he felt comfortable and among friends, here in Quebec. In fact, as Joe Clark descended the steps into the crowded, windowless room with its low ceiling and tall Clark posters and slipped effortlessly into French, he donned a different persona as well.

The applause was long and rhythmic as Clark took the podium. He seemed amazingly comfortable standing in front of the large illuminated Molson "Export" clock and speaking into the raspy sound system. None of that mattered, it seemed; this was Joe Clark's room. His call for a broad national party seemed all the more poignant among some of the 40 per cent of Quebecers who recently had come to support him. His remarks were liberally laced with humour and that night his stories were genuinely funny. Journalists, who had heard it all before hushed noisy colleagues so they could hear it again, delivered beautifully.

Clark told his audience that he was proud to say "though I speak different languages...I always say the same thing in every part of the country...the same in Alberta as in Quebec." He informed them that the night before in Lethbridge he had spoken of the importance of Quebec to the party and, in a not-so-subtle dig at Mulroney, reminded them that the key to success was to "preserve our reputation as an honest government."

One couldn't help thinking here's a guy from High River, Alberta in the basement of a tavern in Quebec, feeling at one with his audience — speaking well, putting the people at ease — recounting the words he spoke to his Alberta family who the night before had given him not half as much affection.

Sherbrooke was no fluke for Clark, he gave repeat performances of almost as much verve in Trois Rivières and Quebec City before enthusiastic audiences of 125 and 400. At each stop his audience was comprised mostly of former Union Nationale and Créditiste supporters. They were people who dressed and spoke loudly, who knew the important of occasion — with long introductions and expressions of thanks for speakers — and respected the hierarchy in politics, reading telegrams from those who could not attend a meeting, and giving their solemn support to "le chef" — Joe Clark — "l'homme du pays."

Clark was proud of his performance in Quebec and proud of the response he received. Later he said that of all his contemporaries, the politician he admired most was Richard Hatfield who "had achieved the most… in bringing together [his] province." Clark added that "the most important question in Canada" is not about economics but will "always be the unity question." "I've answered that question for our party in Quebec, by my person."

Had Joe Clark become obsessed by Quebec to the detriment of the rest of his national standing? "Not obsessed," he replied, "but I am intrigued by it, yes." He admitted afterwards he did feel more at ease there than anywhere else in the country. "I think," he thought for a moment, "yes, maybe, they like me more [as a person] than Anglos."

* * *

Clark spent most of the final days of his campaign in Ontario, a province where many people did not like him. Yet, there remained in that province, especially in the less built-up southcentre and southwest, a great many uncommitted delegates. So for two days, following his final stop in Quebec, Clark made the rounds, driving to towns like Orillia, Flesherton and Orangeville, the bluest heart of Upper Canada.

This is the country of the National Citizens' Coalition, the unabashedly right-wing lobby, and it has proved fertile ground for the Amway Corporation, the US-based producer of home products that distributes its wares through intense free-enterprise rhetoric and a pyramid-style network. Flesherton is the home of the Canadian Intelligence Service, a private monthly newsletter informing its readers of communist and other subversive plots rampant in the country. In short, the area was not a friendly one for Joe Clark.

Here the loud, exuberant advance men in white suits who had steered Clark through Quebec were replaced by a discreet team of young men from Toronto, each in a blue suit, white shirt, red tie and glasses. They could have been tax lawyers anywhere, and seemed to enhance the negative image of Clark in the area's motels, schools and homes. His now burgeoning press corps further isolated his audience, which was not impressed when as many as six television crews overwhelmed their meetings. These people had a distasteful job to do—pass sentence on their leader—and they wanted to do it in private. At one meeting, Clark asked the people's indulgence to permit the crews to stay: "I think the business we have to do in this party can be done in the eyes of the media," he said.

Once again he boasted of the party he had opened to women and young people, but was promptly criticized for putting senior men in a minority at the leadership convention.[9] He spoke of the inroads the party had made in Northern Ontario by winning the seat in Temiskaming from the Liberals in a recent byelection and held up his cherished example of the Broadview-Greenwood riding where he had "stood for the little guy against the establishment" and opened the party to the ethnic community. But that was not how these people saw it. They liked Peter Worthington and considered him the victim of outside interference.

Behind the closed doors of another meeting they asked Clark what was really on their minds: "Why didn't you get rid of more of the civil service?" and "Why did you lose the government?" For three years they had been bearing their grudge and Clark's few words were unlikely to sway them. One of the things that was different, he confided in one group, was him. "They really used to think I was a wimp, that I'd collapse in a crunch, now they know I won't." The people were surprised to hear him use the term, wimp, which they still liked to believe was only said behind his back. But being confronted with it and hearing him talk did not alter that fact for them. And, when Clark told the story of his daughter

Catherine, whom he called daily to talk to but who sometimes rebuffed him because she had "something important to do," his self-deprecating humour touched them but did not make them laugh. "I guess everyone gets accustomed to that," he added philosophically.

It was a vastly different reception when Clark got off his bus at 19 Rosedale Road in Toronto, the elegant home of his most prominent backer, Hal Jackman. As a number of other wealthy supporters had done, Jackman held a reception for 400 people in his home. Many leading members of Toronto's ethnic communities were included—Jay Hong and Bill Fatsis were there—and a large number of Jewish supporters. One would have been forgiven for thinking it was a Liberal event. Clark had also invited a number of representatives from all camps of the other candidates and, in his brief remarks, he pledged to them that whatever happened on June 11th they would remain "all together in a working family." It was one of the friendliest family gatherings Clark faced. It was how it should be, he might have thought, this marriage between the old establishment and the new Canadians, and he would take the credit for it, confident that the delegates in Ottawa would appreciate its significance.

* * *

The ups and downs of Joe Clark's leadership campaign in early 1983 were indicative of his entire tenure as leader of the Progressive Conservatives. While he clearly believed he stood for something—moderation and a broader base for the party—and believed that a vision contrary to his would be disastrous for the Tories, he was really a man without a strong constituency within his party for the seven years that he led it. Here was a born and raised Westerner who became increasingly uneasy with Albertans. Here was a Conservative who could not relate to his party's heartland support in rural Ontario. He would adjust and attempt to accommodate, but as often as not, that adjustment and accommodation were simply regarded as weakness and vacillation by his opponents.

Another problem Clark faced was his inability to generate among his followers any feeling of intense personal loyalty to him. For many, however, this situation changed appreciably during the challenge to his leadership. For the first time they realized that more than just Clark's career was at stake, and that by demanding his ouster, perhaps Clark's opponents meant to do more than just replace the leader. They were also setting out to change the whole orientation of the party. Consequently, Clark's supporters became the most loyal and committed of any of the delegates attending the leadership convention.[10]

But for others—and as it turned out, a majority—exactly the opposite was the case. The campaign simply confirmed their doubts about the leader and made them more committed to "Anybody But Clark." If they had no particular affinity for Clark during his seven-year term, the campaign simply made it clearer that he was incapable of any change in direction or in his "image." Moreover, if he *did* win again, it would amount to an endorsement of both his record and his plans for the party. Such an outcome was unpalatable to this group, who were adamant in their belief that Clark was a liability in any effort to return the Tories to power.

* * *

At Thursday's convention opening ceremonies, some of the crowd booed when Joe Clark was introduced. They were a minority of the 3,000 delegates gathered in the Ottawa Civic Centre and their volume was nearly drowned out by the cheers of the Clark supporters, but the nagging undercurrent served to remind everyone why they had come.

Seven years and three months before, Clark had stood on the same stage and heard only the cheers. His "little-engine-that-could" campaign had taken him to the top; and now the best political organization in the country was trying to keep him there.

It is about three kilometres from the Civic Centre to the Chateau Laurier Hotel, whether one goes along the park-lined Rideau Canal, dodging cyclists and joggers, or straight north on heavily trafficked Bank Street to the downtown hotel district. About halfway between, at number 175 MacLaren, stands a fine old three-storey red brick house that served as Joe Clark's national campaign headquarters. William McAleer, the campaign manager on loan from the Big Blue Machine, had an office there, but he spent most of his time working out of Clark's MP office in Parliament Hill's East Block. Jock Osler, the press secretary, was there when he was in town, and John McDermid, the convention organizer, holed up there for the final few weeks of the campaign. For the most part, however, the place was overrun by young people, 30 or more at any one time, none of whom looked older than 25.

"At least they don't call you 'Joe Who' anymore"

This was the nucleus of David Small's convention network. Having 1,100 Clark-elected delegates at the end of April, Small had "baby-sat" them until June, keeping them informed of campaign activities with reams of literature and campaign newspapers. He knew the best, most reliable delegate was the one who was actively involved in the campaign, and so he put as many of them as possible to work. Five hundred of them were designated as "buddies" each with a "key" delegate in his charge. A "key" was someone whom Small had identified as uncommitted or wavering in his support of a candidate (that candidate could be Clark). The "buddies" stayed close to their "keys" throughout the hectic convention and made a report on any shifts in commitment at the end of each day to their respective provincial desk at the Delta Hotel. At 11 o'clock each night the reports were entered into Small's computer and by two a.m. he had a reading on any trend or shifts in support. At the seven a.m. senior staff meeting each day, he would then present an analysis and make recommendations about what line all Clark workers should push that day. If, at any time, a "buddy" thought a "key" was wavering, there was a telephone number he could call to learn where Clark could be found at that moment in order to spirit his man over to the candidate. Alternatively, he could arrange to have a VIP (a supporting MP or Senator, preferably with some connection to the key) come to meet them. He could even arrange for an instant personal note from "Joe" to be delivered to the delegate's hotel room.

The system was well designed and worked beautifully, but it had very little business. At each breakfast meeting Small reported that nothing much had changed.

Clark had very little choice but to stage as big a show as possible at the convention to attempt to persuade those not in his camp that his election was inevitable. In 1976, Clark had been unobtrusive; this time he was almost oppressive. There was a greeting by hundreds of loud supporters at the airport when Clark arrived in Ottawa on Monday, a crowded party for workers on Tuesday, a packed reception for delegates on Wednesday, and a rally to end all rallies—with a 40-foot backlit Canadian flag and a Patton-esque Clark standing in front of it—on Thursday night. His organization's presence overwhelmed that of every other candidate—only Crosbie came close and Mulroney deliberately didn't try to compete. It was an ostentatious show of strength and it didn't change a thing.

Clark spent most of the week lounging at Stornoway, the residence of the official leader of the Opposition (Clark had relinquished his right to live there when he had resigned four months before, but interim leader Erik Neilsen had invited him to remain). He had caught a cold and despite the June heat, remained wrapped in his favourite yellow cardigan as he pored over versions of his speeches.

As all the candidates did on Thursday afternoon and Friday morning, Clark addressed the three policy sessions—on economics, social issues, and foreign policy—which the party had arranged to show the public that the process of choosing a leader involved more than mere hoopla. But in none of the sessions did any of the major candidates put forward an idea that distinguished him from the rest. Each stood for free enterprise and the elimination of waste by government, considerate but not profligate social assistance programs, and a strong, defence-oriented foreign policy The only way to tell the candidates apart was by the nature of the questions asked and the size of the crowd they attracted: Clark's and Crosbie's sessions were always packed, Crombie's and Wilson's never were.

Nothing in this research of policy discussions had prepared Clark for the first question he received in the very first of the social policy sessions. "Are you naive or just opportunistic," asked Scott Newark, a Crosbie supporter who had been elected a delegate on a free enterprise (read Amway-endorsed) slate, "when you make a deal in Quebec with the PQ?" It did not matter that Clark gave an excellent, angry answer that brought his supporters to their feet cheering. The people with similar questions for him weren't listening.

* * *

Joe Clark's finest moment, and the one that best expressed the nature of the fight within the Progressive Conservative party, came on Friday night just prior to his speech to the convention.

The Civic Centre was stifling in the June heat, with the television lights and thousands of excited Tory supporters moving the thermometer even higher. As paper Mulroney and Clark fans fluttered throughout the hall—even in the sections of other candidates, delegates desperate for relief took the fans and disguised them with their candidate's stickers—the eight men running for leader trooped to the stage to address the party and the nation. They paraded with varying degrees of fanfare, but none could match the demonstration for Clark. On stage to salute him were over 50

66

members of the House and Senate, nearly half of the Tories' parliamentary caucus. Every former member of the Clark cabinet still sitting in Parliament was there, except John Crosbie, David Crombie, Michael Wilson, Allan Lawrence, Ron Huntington, Sinclair Stevens and Elmer MacKay. The latter two stood with Brian Mulroney, directly facing their former colleagues. Mulroney and Crosbie had each been endorsed by about 20 MPs but, unlike the people on stage with Clark, few had enjoyed influence or power under his leadership. Otto Jelinek, Michael Forrestall, Bob Coates and George Hees could testify, as they sat with Brian Mulroney, how they had been ignored by Clark, and MPs Bob Wenman, Pat Nowlan and Lorne Greenaway could tell Crosbie the same thing.

Two Conservative parties stood facing each other that night, and between them was Joe Clark. To those behind him he was a symbol of the kind of party they wanted to have and their rightful place in it. To those opposite he was an obstacle.

3

"Ya dance with the lady what brung ya"

"Mulroney...eight hundred and seventy-four"

One of Brian Mulroney's favourite expressions is "ya dance with the lady what brung ya" by which he conveys the principle that is most important to him: one is loyal to one's friends. Eight hundred and seventy-four "friends" had brought Brian Mulroney to Ottawa as the number one contender for Joe Clark's title. To some of them he was the long-time acquaintance they were happy to toil for; to others he held out the prospect of future benefits a grateful friend would provide, and, to all of them, he offered a better chance of reward, a better way to win the next general election.

It was something of a paradox that loyalty was Brian Mulroney's first tenet because it was not something he really applied to his own leader, Joe Clark. In fact, with the possible exception of Clark himself, Brian Mulroney was most responsible for his leader's eclipse and the calling of a convention.

He was not alone in the subtle encouragement of antagonism to Clark. When the Tory delegates assembled in Winnipeg many had the impression that both Alberta Premier Peter Lougheed and Ontario's William Davis were less than elated with Clark's leadership, but neither had planned or organized for his downfall as Mulroney had. John Crosbie had assembled a team ready to make a run at the leadership, but had covered his tracks so that fewer people looked to him as a reason for ousting Clark.

The explanation for Mulroney's actions is simple: Brian's "rule" didn't apply. He did not look upon Clark as a friend; rather he saw in him the cause of his own defeat in the 1976 leadership contest. He was convinced, moreover, that the party had made a dreadful mistake in choosing Clark

"Ya dance with the lady what brung ya"

and was not slow to offer his personal opinion to that effect, although publicly he maintained that "Joe won fair and square."

* * *

Brian Mulroney had waited a long time. He had had seven years to reflect on his defeat—second to Claude Wagner on the first ballot, third when he was eliminated—and to weigh the prospects for another chance at the leadership. On March 9th, 1983 his wait came to an end; but, standing backstage of the Grand Salon in Montreal's Queen Elizabeth Hotel, about to appear to 2,500 well-wishers and announce that he was "considering" running again, the final few moments must have seemed interminable.

It was the unofficial launch to his campaign—the official declaration would come 12 days later, the day after his 44th birthday, before the national press corps in Ottawa—and was designed to give an impression that the people were demanding his candidacy. An organization called "The Friends of Brian Mulroney" had staged the affair and brought out a parade of notables from business, politics, sports, and the arts to tell the crowd—bussed in from as far away as Quebec City—why Brian Mulroney was the best candidate for the leadership of the Conservative Party. Paul DesRochers, a prominent Liberal—the *éminence grise* in Robert Bourassa's days—was the chairman of "The Friends." The organizing had been left to Fernand Roberge, manager of The Ritz Hotel, and Bernard Roy, Mulroney's former law partner. Brian, they said, had merely agreed to attend. So he stood backstage among the folded chairs and discarded backdrops with DesRochers, Leo Taylor, the former head of the Seafarers' International Union, Bobby Orr, the Pulse (a local news program) weathergirl and a bevy of others, waiting for his turn to come.

In the hall, the crowd and press had gathered. Not as many people as expected had shown up[1] and some of Mulroney's people were a little concerned. The organizers had set up large closed-circuit TV screens in the corridors for the expected overflow. But the crowd had not filled the main room where 3,000 could stand and the other rooms were ordered closed off.

Nonetheless, the crowd of roughly 2,500 was impressive enough and Michel Cogger was pleased. Although "The Friends" were credited with having organized the whole event, Mulroney stalwarts Michel Cogger and Jean Bazin had a hand in everywhere. They had not come this far to let someone else jeopardize their man's candidacy.

Cogger had been Brian Mulroney's campaign manager in 1976; he acted in 1983 as his chief strategist and spokesman. Like so many others in Mulroney's inner circle—Bazin, Michael Meighen, Peter White—he had first met Mulroney in law school at Laval in the early 1960s. Then, it was Jean Bazin who had been the star on the political scene. In the 1963-64 year "ti-Baz" became president of the university student council in a tough fight. Brian Mulroney, secretary to the council the year before, had worked for him. The campaign of his chief opponent, who had lost by a mere 50 votes, was organized by Cogger. Bazin was subsequently elected president of the Student Federation of Canada and spent the next year at its headquarters in Ottawa. In partisan terms, Bazin was already a Tory. In 1961-62 he had been vice-president of the national PC Student Federation, having lost the presidency on the toss of a coin to a young Alberta Tory named Joe Clark, but left the party over the Diefenbaker leadership issue. In Ottawa in 1966 he had a chance to get involved again as the Chief was forced from office.

Cogger had never been a Conservative, but he too encountered Clark early on. In 1960 each served as editor for his respective university newspaper, and the two met at a conference hosted by Cogger. By 1967, Cogger was persuaded by Brian Mulroney to get involved with the Tories and went to work for Davie Fulton on his leadership bid. He was not alone. Lowell Murray and Brian Mulroney were the principal organizers of that campaign, while Jean Bazin was Fulton's Quebec coordinator and Joe Clark wrote his speeches.

Following Fulton's defeat, Cogger became the party's associate national director under Malcolm Wickson, Murray and Clark joined Stanfield's staff and Mulroney returned to Montreal to practise law and act as party organizer in the city. Bazin also went back to Montreal, but ended up in party headquarters in Ottawa in 1972 and 1974. It was Mulroney and Cogger who came up with the name Claude Wagner as the kind of star candidate the Tories needed in Quebec in 1972. Four years later they fought their "discovery" in the battle for the leadership, only to have their old friend Joe Clark take it away from both of them.

Since then Cogger had worked to keep alive the prospect of a Mulroney candidacy. A short, cherubic-looking man—he bears a striking resemblance to Pierre Trudeau's former principal secretary Jim Coutts—Cogger had been a popular press secretary to Robert Stanfield in 1972, charming, if often evasive. In recent years, his law practice had dwindled to only a couple of clients—the Government of New Brunswick and a helicopter manufacturing company—as he increased his business activity, entering into partnership with Walter Wolf, the Swiss race car owner, to market a line of men's toiletries.

Michel Cogger once likened Brian Mulroney's run at the leadership to the attempt by Ted Kennedy to displace American President Jimmy Carter: Each a handsome Irish Catholic, part of the establishment but still in touch with the masses, launching an inner party attack on the sitting party leader, whom they considered to be inferior. In both cases, the candidate faced the same obstacle: distrust by the electorate. Cogger had read about Kennedy strategies and style from 1960 to 1980 and had learned from them and from their mistakes.

The first requirement was to ensure that the candidate was not blamed for the challenge to the leader; the second, to win people's trust by personal appeal and keeping his head down; and, the third, to organize and organize again. It was to help ensure the first, that the candidate not be blamed, that the reception in Montreal was held. Mulroney would be seen as answering a call to arms, not instigating it.

Backstage, Mulroney fidgeted. He held a package of du Mauriers and a "Cricket" lighter in his right hand and was forever switching them to his left to shake someone's hand, parking the perennial cigarette in his mouth as he did so, wincing as the smoke bit his eyes. His wife Mila said he hadn't been able to sleep the night before because of the tension. But even the evident nervousness could not conceal the fact that Mulroney was better looking than ever.

Lean and fit, he flattered the day's styles with their natural soft and unobtrusive lines, and only his continued indulgence in hand-sewn loafers revealed his self-consciousness. His hair, now gray, had softened the effect of his prominent jaw. It appeared to be a very different Brian Mulroney from 1976.

But, when he opened his mouth to speak to a familiar face backstage, one realized little had changed. It may be because he's been around politics and the law so long, or because of his reputation at school as a debater, but every time Brian Mulroney speaks, it's a performance. He likes to speak slowly, so that his audience can savour the deep timbre of his voice. Though charming in front of small groups, he often converses in

71

clichés, using well-rehearsed lines that often lack a natural flow. His topics hardly ever vary: politics, the party, himself. "We had no choice in 1976," he explains when someone asks about the style of his upcoming campaign, "as outsiders, we had to make our presence felt. But, this time it'll be different." In 1976 Mulroney had been chided for being too slick, his campaign too lavish. Now he promised "a frugal, delegate-oriented campaign." As a walkie-talkie crackled an "all systems go" message to a Mulroney aide, one wondered just how different his campaign would be. Outside in the hall, dozens of men with two-way radios were scurrying to check last minute details: "have the band move to the front," "tell the people to face their signs to the cameras, not to Brian." The stage was adorned with provincial flags and an enormous pale blue square suspended by wires. Across the square was handwritten a large white signature: "Brian," the campaign logo.

In the corridor 40 to 50 pretty young women, each wearing a high-necked white blouse adorned with a blue carnation, handed out cards to the guests, encouraging them to volunteer for the campaign. Behind one table, two professional artists hand-lettered the "homemade" signs which people were brandishing in the hall. They would write out just about anything one asked for. "We love Brian" and "Mulroney = Le Quebec" were popular choices.

As the speaker over the walkie-talkie had said, the signs were for the benefit of the people watching from home and many would see them. All the television networks and most of the national news organs had reporters out for the event. Even the "almost" candidacy of Brian Mulroney was a lead story, for they knew that the man who had lost before, and who had still never run for office, was, nonetheless, the one to beat.

On stage Rodrigue Pageau introduced his performers, "some great personalities of Quebec and Canada who *insisted* that they be here tonight," and in the fashion made famous by television award shows, two beautiful women escorted each guest to the rostrum.

DesRochers, the old Liberal, told the crowd he was "sick and tired of the way the country's running" and that "lots of Liberals in the province will vote for Brian Mulroney." One speaker called Mulroney a "straight-shooter" when he dealt with labour unions, another a "stabilizer…and we've got to have less destabilizers and more stabilizers" like him. Still another praised his "down to earth and original way." The main act then began as Brian and Mila walked onto the stage.

"Ya dance with the lady what brung ya"

Brian Mulroney seldom waves. The wave, it seems, is used by many politicians to appeal to unfamiliar faces or to express acknowledgment of an anonymous crowd's applause. Brian Mulroney accepts the applause by pointing. Standing slightly to one side he looks down his long arm and straight into the face of his supporters. It is an act of personal recognition performed as much for the cameras as it is for his delighted pointee. That night Mulroney and his wife did a lot of pointing.

"They look so gorgeous," one envious female voice could be heard saying. In fact, they did, and they knew it. Their smiles flirted with the audience and, as the crowd pulsed faster and faster with its chants of "Brian," the candidate cried "Stop it! I love it."

He had little to say to them that night, only to thank them for coming out "in historic and record numbers" and to assure them that he considered it "a great and humbling experience to seek the leadership of a national political party" and would give them his answer "very soon." He then left as quickly as he had come, leaving his audience hungry for more.

* * *

How had Brian Mulroney managed to establish himself as the number one contender for Joe Clark's job? He had never run for public office and had for six years been keeping a low profile as president of the Iron Ore Company of Canada, a corporation few Canadians had ever heard of. He was, moreover, a resident of Quebec, where being a Conservative has all the popular appeal of hockey in July. How then could he universally be seen as the logical replacement to the leader? The simplest answer is that since first trying for the leadership in 1976, Brian Mulroney had not stopped running.

Mulroney had made a big splash in his 1976 effort. He had the money, the looks, the organization, the establishment, and the press with him and had lost, some would argue, because of all of that. He had been distrusted by delegates who thought the brash 36 year-old had not yet earned his stripes. But he had cut a wide swath and many would remember the handsome Quebecer for years to come, especially if the candidate helped to keep the memory alive.

He did not take his defeat well. During the next two years, he was known to have drunk heavily on several occasions and was blunt in his assessment of the party's choice of leader. Ottawa reporters were frequent recipients of phone calls from Mulroney, reminding them that he would have been a better selection. In addition, Mulroney's behaviour at the 1976 Parliamentary Press Gallery dinner and the 1977 PC party general meeting in Quebec City, where he repeatedly criticized Clark to anyone who would listen, created a very unfavourable impression.[2]

Gradually the bitterness dissolved and Mulroney put more energy into his work, but he never stopped massaging his network, keeping it in shape. Every day he called some of its members, the gang from Saint F.X. (St. Francis Xavier University in Nova Scotia), the group from Laval, his workers from '76, and the ones he continued to court.

Jean-Yves Lortie, a Montreal bailiff and one of Wagner's chief organizers in 1976, had come over to Mulroney not long after the '76 convention. In a fight for the presidency of the Quebec wing of the party in 1976, Lortie had lost to the Clark-backed candidate Roch La Salle. Wagner, meanwhile, had grown obstreperous in Clark's caucus[3] and Lortie had seen no future allied with him. Thus, he turned to Mulroney.

Another of Wagner's workers who came over to Mulroney was Peter White, an old friend of his from Laval. White had actually joined Mulroney during the '76 campaign and was the source of information on the controversial $300,000 trust fund established on Wagner's behalf when he joined the Tory party in 1972. White, Wagner's former assistant, had privately told journalists, just prior to the convention, that Wagner had lied when he claimed the fund had been established only after his election. The information was intended to harm Wagner and enhance Mulroney's position, but when White's involvement became evident it had the opposite effect.

After 1976, White served as a considerably more important intermediary. In 1969 he and a partner went into the newspaper business in the Eastern Townships of Quebec. That partner was Conrad Black, the newspaper business grew to become the Sterling chain, and in the late 1970s White became a partner with Black, Black's brother Montegu, and David Radler in a company called Western Dominion Investments. (WDI controls the Ravelston Corporation which owns 97 per cent of the voting shares in a company called Argus.)

It was White who had first introduced Mulroney to Black, and throughout the late 1970s Mulroney moved closer to the powerful businessman, eventually sitting on the boards of four Black companies (Hollinger North Shore Explorations Limited, Labrador Mining and

Exploration Company Limited, Standard Broadcasting, and the Iron Ore Company of Canada itself). He also sat with Black on the board of the Canadian Imperial Bank of Commerce (of which Black is a member of the executive committee). This connection, in turn, enlarged the Mulroney network into new areas of the Canadian establishment and diversified his holdings away from the Desmarais group at Power Corporation, with whom Mulroney had been associated up to 1976.

Mulroney was of considerable service to Black. In 1981, Black asked Mulroney to undertake the delicate task of assuring his bosses at Hanna Mining in the United States (which then controlled the IOC) that he, Black, although poised to attempt a takeover of Hanna, was not unfriendly. In the struggle for control which ensued, Mulroney acted as peacemaker between Black and Robert Anderson, the chairman of Hanna, as a result of which Black was able to gain a substantial share of Hanna and sit on the executive committee of an American blue-chip company's board of directors.[4]

Mulroney effectively sat out the 1979 election. He neither sought a nomination to run, citing his commitments to the Iron Ore Company, nor did he do much to aid the Clark campaign. When the short-lived Clark government fell and then was defeated in 1980, Mulroney recognized Clark's vulnerability and began to work on his own campaign to replace him.

He first assembled a team of disgruntled Quebecers. Two of his people — Rodrigue Pageau, who had worked for him in '76, and his old friend Jean Bazin — had gone to work for Clark. Pageau had been Clark's Quebec director of communications and Bazin first his Quebec organizer from 1977 to 1979, then a member of the transition team in Ottawa preparing for a Tory takeover, and finally a member of the Clark PMO. Embittered by Clark's perceived mishandling of power, both returned to Mulroney's side. Keith Morgan, a director of marketing for Bell Canada, was another convert. He had worked for Wagner in the 1970s, then replaced Bazin as Clark's chief Quebec organizer in 1979. By 1980, he too was resentful and very receptive to the overtures made by Mulroney who, as Morgan recalls "dined [him] right after the campaign."

Together with Jean-Yves Lortie and Michel Cogger, they began to work for Clark's removal: their target, the 1981 general meeting and the question of leadership review. First Mulroney began to make a series of public and private speeches citing the failure of the party in Quebec — the

Conservatives only had two seats in the province in 1979 and one in 1980—as the reason for Clark's defeat. His message was clear: Mulroney could do better. Then Lortie with Pageau and Morgan began the first in a series of organizational campaigns that would culminate three years later. Using Lortie's campaign to become the party's regional vice-president, they organized throughout the province and delivered to Ottawa 70 per cent of the Quebec delegation voting for a leadership convention. That amounted to 13 of the total 34 per cent opposed to Clark continuing.

Yet, while all this was going on, Brian Mulroney denied any desire to see Clark removed. He said in an interview, broadcast December 7th, 1980, on CBC Radio's *Sunday Morning*: "Joe Clark won one and lost one [election]...this is an old baseball town and we don't put .500 hitters on waivers...I'm going to vote for Mr. Clark."

Despite the Mulroney group's efforts at the 1981 meeting, Clark decided to carry on as leader and further resolved to take steps to defend himself against any future insurgency. Unfortunately, for Clark, Mulroney would be a much tougher foe in their next encounter.

The occasion was the February 1982 meeting of the Quebec wing of the party. The provincial party executive was controlled by Joe Clark's people under Quebec president Marcel Danis. This body had a legitimate means of organizing and, at any national convention, had the authority to appoint 38 voting delegates-at-large. In 1981 these positions had gone to Clark people and Mulroney's group resolved that would not happen again. They decided to fight for control of the provincial executive.

Marcel Danis knew a bitter fight was building and proposed a compromise. He made a deal with Rodrigue Pageau, for whom he had worked in 1976, that a neutral, Danis' law partner Robert Brunet, would run unopposed as Danis' successor to the presidency. They also agreed that two of Clark's choices and two of Mulroney's would seek positions without opposition. The only races, therefore, would be for treasurer and the posts of vice-president (English) and vice-president (French).

The campaign was hotly contested and, for a time it appeared that Clark's choices were headed for a narrow victory.

Then, only moments before the deadline for nominations, Clark's candidate for treasurer, Marc Legris, withdrew unexpectedly and Mulroney candidate Dugre won unopposed. Danis believed "someone persuaded him to do so" and National Party President Peter Blaikie, scarcely an avid Clark supporter, exploded and accused the Mulroney forces of "playing politics."

The rout of the Clark team was completed on voting day, when Mulroney took the unusual step of going down on the floor and campaigning for his choices for the two vice-presidencies. His timely personal intervention undoubtedly affected the vote and his candidates squeaked through. The provincial executive was his, and he would put it to good use in both Winnipeg and Ottawa.

Early in 1982, two groups began a series of secret meetings. Their aims were, respectively, to remove Joe Clark as leader and replace him with Brian Mulroney. One man played a key role in both cabals: former Newfoundland Premier Frank Moores.

In Ottawa, Moores chaired a number of secret meetings of a small group of anti-Clark MPs which included Bob Wenman, a BC member and later a prominent organizer of John Crosbie's campaign, Chris Speyer from Cambridge Ontario and an organizer for David Crombie, and Nova Scotia MP Elmer MacKay, a strong supporter of Brian Mulroney. Together, they coordinated a campaign to create disruption in caucus, to challenge the leader's authority, and to encourage other MPs to make clear their opposition to Clark.

Like many Conservatives, Moores had given up on Clark's ability to win and, for him, winning and the redistribution of power were all that counted. He later explained to Claude Arpin of the *Montreal Gazette* (February 3rd, 1983): "…it had to be done for the country's sake."[5]

To many observers it was unclear whom Moores would support in a leadership convention. As a loyal Newfoundlander, many assumed John Crosbie could claim his endorsement, but others recalled his personal friendship of many years with Brian Mulroney.[6]

If observers had known of Moores' participation in another group's meetings, there would have been no doubt about whom he was supporting.

In Montreal, sometimes meeting at the exclusive Mount Royal Club, the inner council of Mulroney's network was getting down to business. Almost always present at meetings throughout 1982 were Mulroney, Peter White, Michel Cogger, Jean Bazin, Nova Scotian Fred Doucet from Saint Francis Xavier, a Toronto lawyer and close friend of Elmer MacKay, Fred von Veh, Ken Waschuk, an advisor to Saskatchewan premier Grant Devine, and Frank Moores. Sometimes joining the group were former

77

Toronto MP Sam Wakim (who had been at Saint F.X. with Mulroney) and former party president Michael Meighen (who had been with him at Laval).

This was the team that would plan Mulroney's campaign in the event of a leadership race. But at one meeting, early in 1982, the talk turned to how to ensure a convention was called. Some of those present objected to the topic, and at length it was agreed that Mulroney, for his own good, should not be directly involved in managing Clark's ouster, that it should be left to others to do.

Thus, the actual work of getting out delegates to vote against Joe Clark in Winnipeg would again fall to Rodrigue Pageau, Jean-Yves Lortie, Keith Morgan and the province-wide organization they assembled. But through Michel Cogger, who met regularly with Pageau, Brian Mulroney would be kept informed of their activities.

While these groups met, Mulroney took to the road again for another series of speeches. This time he told Tory audiences in Montreal, Ottawa, Toronto and Vancouver about his industrial prescription for Canada based on his success at the Iron Ore Company but, as Alexander Ross reported in *Canadian Business* "for the Tory faithful, the unspoken message was clear: here is a man with a program for uniting the country and getting it back to work; here is the man with the charisma that Joe Clark lacks; here is the man who could beat the Liberals."[7]

Then, in November, Mulroney made an extraordinary move. He was in Toronto for Grey Cup week and, while visiting a friend, wrote out the list of people in Quebec whom he knew to be opposed to Joe and list of those in his favour. He could see that Clark's organizer Danis was doing a fine job of countering Pageau's organization in Quebec with one of his own. He then took out another piece of paper and hand wrote a statement which said he would support Joe Clark in Winnipeg. But it was a carefully crafted statement that left open the possibility of his own future candidacy and emphasized that the party was entitled to make a change if it chose to do so. He was pleased with this formulation and telephoned Finlay MacDonald, Clark's advisor in Ottawa, to say he had an offer to make. MacDonald went to Toronto on the Friday and, at a lunch at Winston's, Mulroney produced his notes. He would read this, he said, if Clark would meet him in Montreal for a press conference.

MacDonald jumped at it. Although a Clark loyalist and advisor, he was also a close friend of Mulroney's, and had spent a week with him in

Brian Mulroney declares his support for the leader—Montreal, Dec. 6, 1982.

"[the] mandate is not clear enough"—Winnipeg, Jan. 31, 1983.

Canapress Photo Service

Brian Mulroney assails Joe Clark's position on Quebec—Contenders' debate, Massey Hall, Toronto, Apr. 30, 1983.

Progressive Conservative Party of Canada

Neil Fraser (left) and John Gamble (right)— 'no place to go'.

William C. Stratas

Canapress Photo Service

Clark organizer Marcel Danis (left) and Mulroney strategist Michel Cogger (right) fought long and hard for control of Quebec.

Courtesy: Mr. Small

Progressive Conservative Party of Canada

Dave Small, delegate tracker for the Clark camp.

Elmer MacKay, one of Mulroney's early caucus supporters.

Bill Davis' tantalizing "candidacy" frustrated Joe Clark.

The Toronto Star Syndicate (Larter)

Two issues proved harmful to the contenders in Quebec—Both Mulroney and Clark suffered accusations of 'dirty tricks' and Clark was tagged as being soft on the separatists.

The Toronto Star Syndicate (Macpherson)

Allan King

the summer at his fishing camp in Labrador. As the man who had persuaded Robert Stanfield to run for the leadership in 1967 and had served him so well in Ottawa, MacDonald had proven his devotion to the party. All he wanted was peace in the family, and this statement might be the armistice it needed. He went back to Ottawa and told Clark it was a legitimate offer he should accept. Clark agreed.

Michel Cogger supported Mulroney's "withdrawal"—it satisfied the first of his strategic requirements, that the candidate not be blamed for the leader's ouster—he only argued that it "be done right and appear to be done right." They must be seen pulling their supporters out of the field. Mulroney agreed. Cogger, Bazin and Wakim were present when he called Pageau, Lortie, Morgan, and their team to his house the week before the press conference with Clark. Mulroney told them what he was doing and read them the statement. "I don't want anyone organizing in my name," he said. The Pageau group was upset by the news and replied that many workers would continue to organize against Joe anyway. Mulroney pointed to the careful wording of his statement and told them they must "make [their] own decision."

On Monday December 6, 1982, Brian Mulroney and Joe Clark posed together for photographs in Montreal and reporters recorded the surprise endorsement.

Why Mulroney undertook this initiative is not entirely clear. Had he given up hope of unseating Clark when Danis' organization proved so effective in Quebec? But surely, he was aware of the extent of dissent to Clark in Ontario and Newfoundland as well, that there was still a chance of getting a convention called. Had he taken this action, then, in an effort to disassociate himself from what he hoped would happen, and so avoid being blamed for Clark's removal? Or, had he genuinely changed his course and decided that it was in the party's best interest to stay with Clark? In view of the continued work by Lortie and Pageau, even if not "in his name," the ongoing activities of the Moores group of anti-Clark MPs, and the deliberately careful wording of the statement, the last possibility is unlikely. Certainly the effect of the endorsement was more beneficial to Mulroney than Clark. By going to Mulroney, in Montreal, Clark gave him a clean white shirt to wear in the campaign that followed. Then too, there are the words of one senior Mulroney organizer, "I was laughing my ass off. Why did Joe do it?"

* * *

79

Shortly before his "Friends" extravaganza in March, Brian Mulroney was confidently predicting he'd get a near sweep—80 to 85 per cent—of the Quebec delegation. He told one reporter "by the time we get finished, Clark won't have enough support in Quebec to get a bridge game."

Mulroney had expected that, once the campaign was above board, he would be able to do better than Pageau and Lortie had done "unofficially" for the Winnipeg meeting. At that time, they had been able to deliver only about 34 per cent of the Quebec delegates against Clark. In fact, for the Ottawa convention, the numbers did substantially improve, but not nearly as much as expected. Like Mulroney's, Clark's organization merely continued the work it had begun. There was only one significant defector. Clark's Quebec City organizer Bernard Côté joined Mulroney's camp, and in that area Mulroney increased his support. The only other substantial increase he enjoyed was in the Montreal area, where five more ridings were captured for Mulroney slates. Only three of the area's 21 ridings went to Clark.

Mulroney had been caught slightly off-guard when Danis called half of the selection meetings for the first week of the campaign. His organization had little difficulty selling new memberships—they offered a $10 incentive in many ridings—but experienced problems in getting their new recruits out to vote. The situation improved after they followed the Clark method of paying their recruiters only for new members delivered to the meetings.

Like Danis, the Mulroney organizers played hardball—derelicts, kids, and motorcycle gangs played a role in some ridings—but, by and large, it was a contest of organization. Mulroney, however, had to contend with a problem that Clark did not face. Having been hurt by his attempt to discredit Wagner in 1976, and the more recent battle to control the Quebec organization, Mulroney needed as clean an image as possible in the month's ahead. So Jean-Yves Lortie and Rodrigue Pageau, who had done so much to help him get this far, were given a lower profile. Lortie established an office separate from the Mulroney headquarters and looked after the organization of ridings in East Montreal. Pageau remained evident in the Montreal office, but as deputy to a new man Mulroney brought in, Ronald Bussey, the handsome young chairman of the Executive Council of the City of Laval. He was, in Mulroney's words, "a new man...the kind I'd like to show I can attract to the party...with new ideas." Most of all he was clean: "Till three weeks ago, I was a Liberal," he stated in one interview. But, unfortunately, he was not the best organizer.

"Ya dance with the lady what brung ya"

In his own riding, Duvernay, where he headed the Mulroney slate, Bussey had sold 800 new memberships, but Marcel Danis, smelling blood, had persuaded Bussey's rival on city council to join Clark and together they sold more, eventually defeating Mulroney's slate 483 to 258. Bussey handled defeat graciously, but it was a serious setback and his position as chief organizer evaporated.

While it was true that Mulroney had to maintain a trustworthy image if he was to win delegates in English Canada, it was no less true that he had to win big in Quebec if he was to have a chance at the leadership. He needed the base for its numbers alone but mostly to validate the principal argument for his leadership bid that, of all the candidates, he could best deliver Quebec.

Controlling the provincial executive helped and his people unabashedly filled all 38 at-large delegate positions with Mulroney people, including the candidate and his wife. But Mulroney was forced to restore Pageau and Lortie to positions of more control, and the latter could once again be seen more frequently in Mulroney headquarters. The candidate also called in his 1976 public relations expert, Roger Nantel, to work on keeping his hard-won cleaner image intact. Using Pageau and Lortie was a calculated risk, but it seemed to pay off. When the smoke had cleared from the last delegate selection meeting, Mulroney and Clark were about even.

The result was, nonetheless, a far cry from what the candidate had predicted. Even in the highly manipulative area of PC campus clubs, with dozens of new organizations springing up in secretarial schools and CEGEP's across the province, Mulroney's organizer, Jean Dugre, was able to manage only a draw with Danis. And, to be safe from embarrassment, the candidate had felt obliged to change his plans about running as a delegate in his home riding of St. Henri-Westmount: the outcome was just too uncertain to predict.

Mulroney had expected more than 600 delegates from Quebec but had to settle for around 400, and the oft-proclaimed Mulroney promise of massive support from Quebec began to take a beating in the province's press. As Ted Kennedy found with Jimmy Carter, a party leader can be more resilient than expected. If Mulroney was going to defeat Joe Clark he would have to come up with a lot more non-Quebec delegates than he had planned.

* * *

Caraquet is a charming, French-speaking community of 4300 on the Bay of Chaleur in the northeastern corner of New Brunswick. The spruce forest has been peeled back from the coast just enough to let two rows of neat clapboard houses line the north shore highway. It's a prosperous town—the lobster catch has been plentiful the last few years—and the people are friendly.

On May 6, a week after the last Tory delegates had been selected, Brian Mulroney came looking for support. The people here send Conservative members to Fredericton and Liberals to Ottawa. Their local provincial member, Jean Gauvin, is Premier Hatfield's fisheries minister and rumour had it he would like to run for the Tories federally if Mulroney won.

The candidate was two hours late and his anxious hosts, Mr. and Mrs. Fernand Lanteigne, peered through their front window onto the now darkened street at the sound of every passing car. In their recreation room, 30 friends and neighbours, including the six local PC delegates, waited, emptying Lanteigne's wine cellar and putting a big dent in Mrs. Lanteigne's popular crab dip. As a luxury camper van pulled up to the front of the house and Lanteigne announced the arrival of their famous guest, the room tingled with excitement. Gauvin and two delegates from the adjacent riding descended from the van with Mulroney and his wife.

The candidate had started the day in Fredericton with an 8 o'clock breakfast meeting for the provincial Conservative caucus and area delegates. He'd next met privately with Premier Richard Hatfield, and had then covered 400 miles with three stops at private homes for meetings with delegates before reaching Caraquet. All in all, the candidate would spend only 43 hours on this trip to New Brunswick, but would manage to meet with the Premier, the provincial caucus, and visit all 10 federal ridings. He would also log two nights sleep. This was the style of Mulroney's campaign. Long days, long miles and personal, private sessions with the delegates. This was the frugal, delegate-oriented campaign designed to counter the impression Mulroney had left since 1976. His advisors had correctly identified that, of all the candidates, Mulroney was distrusted by more delegates than any other. In part, this was a result of the style of his '76 campaign: the young aide Stephen always ready with a cigarette, the private jet, the expensive entertainers at the convention. And it was amplified when he refused to divulge the sources of the considerable funds he had used although party rules required it and he had promised to do so.

"Ya dance with the lady what brung ya"

Since then he had been tagged with the accusations of plotting against his leader and becoming too close to Conrad Black. Still others pointed to the members of Parliament who had become identified with Mulroney — Coates, Jelinek, MacKay — dissenters who had made Clark's life in caucus difficult.

John Thompson, Mulroney's convention organizer, summarized in writing the problems the candidate had faced in the campaign and would face at Ottawa. In a memo dated May 22nd, he outlined the main concerns of the Mulroney candidacy: "People are scared of your candidacy because a) they are scared off by your organization b) they don't trust you."

Thompson explained the lack of trust as arising from three factors:

> 1) image is fuzzy...not certain who you are and what you stand for...2) it is perceived that you are not your own man — that someone else is pulling the strings — Conrad Black or some big business organization — that someone who is always perfect (changing shirts, Christian Dior shirts, Ken Doll image) should be suspicious(sic); that you are opportunistic — here today gone tomorrow...3) people around you are not acceptable: certain party workers from Headquarters fired for being double agents, Lortie's tough...image and your own stabbing Joe in the back, your convention tactics at Winnipeg, etc., all contribute. Your campaign is a threat.[8]

Of course, the Mulroney team had been aware of some of these criticisms well before the Thompson memo, and had taken measures to counter their impact.

To allay public distrust of the candidate, the Mulroney staff had first sought to moderate his big spender image. They did this, in part, by issuing a rigid set of rules all workers were to follow. For example, under no circumstances was the candidate to travel by private aircraft. On one trip in southern Ontario, tour organizers were obliged to book Mulroney on a commercial American flight from Buffalo to Detroit, in order to make an event near Windsor, rather than charter a small craft. (In fact Mulroney later resolved that he would use charter craft, but only after the other candidates did so. By May they had become an acceptable, if still generally secret travel option.) The rules also stipulated that Mulroney's entourage be kept to a minimum, that the press be excluded from meetings, and that no, repeat no, alcoholic beverages be served at Mulroney sponsored events.

But frugality in the campaign would not, in itself, be sufficient to construct a trustworthy image for Mulroney. The candidate also needed to counteract the negative impressions he had left before.

To do this required establishing a personal rapport with the delegates, so as to convince them that Mulroney was not, after all, such a bad guy. In practical terms this meant personal visits to the delegates' own homes, where the candidate and his wife could exert their charm. Caraquet was just one in a long series of such encounters.

* * *

The team of Brian and Mila Mulroney works a room well. They enter, usually holding hands, and immediately divide as an amoeba, each half now a whole, moving around the room, one in a clockwise direction, the other counter. Brian works faster at greeting the guests, exchanging nothing more than pleasantries, and usually crosses Mila's path before she has reached the halfway point. Sometimes they jokingly greet each other before moving on.

Mila (Pivnicki) Mulroney is a tremendous campaign asset. Only 29 years old, she conveys a happy youthful image that her guests find refreshing after the seven sober years with the sometimes outspoken Maureen McTeer. Seldom more than an engaging smile leaves Mila Mulroney's lips.

She sits, usually with some of the room's older women or young children, as her husband moves to make his remarks. At each meeting the two of them engage in a little routine: Mulroney greets the people by telling them "we've been at this now for... how many days, Mila?" And Mila would fill in the blank. That day in Caraquet was their 46th day of campaigning.

Mulroney is marvellously adept at using both languages, and weaving them together. His French is more provincial than the patrician speech of Pierre Trudeau or the acquired elegance of John Turner, and his northern New Brunswick audience was made comfortable by his use of the patois.

Mulroney began with two claims to the leadership of the party. First, he was a Quebecer. "There are 102 ridings in the country with a Franco-phone population over 10 per cent. In the last election the Liberals won 100 of them, we won two. You give Pierre Trudeau a head start of a 100 seats and he's going to beat you 10 times out of 10." His audience took its cue and grimly nodded. Things would be different under his leadership, he assured them. Fortress Quebec would be breached. "For every seat I win in French Canada, and I'm going to win a chunk, Pierre Trudeau's going to have to win two in the West." Mulroney never explained this mathematical conundrum, but everyone laughed at the thought of Trudeau scrounging for votes in the Prairie wasteland.

Mulroney's second claim was that he had, as president of a large corporation, experienced "the real world." It was a dig at the Liberals who had been in office too long to know about the real world, and at the hated Ottawa bureaucrats who his audiences liked to believe didn't care about this world. It was also a dig at Joe Clark who, as everyone knew, had only worked in political backrooms before going to Ottawa.

But it was the "friends" approach that was the key to Mulroney's pitch. In every room he first established that he was one of them. "You're looking at the only native New Brunswicker in the race. I've got roots here…went to school just down the road…" Then he employed the names of his bigger friends to convey an impression that all of official Torydom would be supporting him. "I look at Richard…uh…the Premier…we're old friends… and see what he's done…"[9] After that he quickly assured the people that his administration would bring them all personal rewards. "I look around this room and see half a dozen senators, maybe one or two judges."

Mulroney's audiences were almost always charmed by his performance. For many of them, it was the first time they felt at ease with the man. He too tried his best to appear relaxed, but found it hard. At every stop he looked for a prop to stand behind; sometimes a chair, at others a bar stool, became his rostrum. After his remarks he liked to sit to take questions but always on the edge of his seat, never back and never unbuttoning his jacket. A cigarette quickly appeared in his mouth. But although his words seemed genuinely easy, they were well rehearsed. Asked in Caraquet how he'd respond to the Kirby Report on Atlantic fisheries he said only that "Michael Kirby wouldn't know a trout if he fell over it" and lashed out at the "typical" Liberal appointment. His approach, he promised, would be different: "When Jean Gauvin [the provincial fisheries minister in the audience] talks, Brian Mulroney listens."

That's the way he'd govern he said. "Oh, there'll be jobs for Liberals and NDPers too, but only after I've been prime minister for 15 years and I can't find a single living, breathing Tory to appoint." It was all said in jest of course, but it struck a responsive chord with his audience. It reminded them that the fruits of power had not been their's to taste for a long time, not under Liberal rule nor under the brief reign of Joe Clark, and that Brian Mulroney would not forget them. "I'm going to dance with the ones who brung me. That means Tories... That's what this is all about." Then thanking the Lanteignes for their hospitality, he departed to begin a two-hour drive to his next stop on the campaign: a breakfast meeting in Newcastle.

Before boarding his van the candidate paused to reflect with a lone reporter on the day he'd had. He was very satisfied and sucked deeply on his cigarette. "What a great day...did you see our schedule? You see, when those other fellows are on TV, ol' Mulroney's out in the 'boonies,' talking to the people...there were nine votes in there."

But Mulroney liked to have it both ways. At breakfast the next day, the national media was encouraged to attend and television dutifully recorded his "reunion" with the people with whom he had lived while going to St. Thomas High School 30 years before. The day after, in Antigonish, Nova Scotia, he played hide and seek with the cameras.

The occasion was the graduation exercise at Mulroney's alma mater, St. Francis Xavier University. Mulroney was on the university's board of governors, and was a prominent fundraiser. In the previous three years he had collected $11.5 million dollars for the institution, more than $4 million above its target. Mulroney particularly wanted to attend the ceremony that day since his "old friend," Peter Lougheed Premier of Alberta, was receiving an honourary degree. Lougheed's was by far the most coveted of Tory endorsements, and it crossed the minds of more than one observer that perhaps it was no mere coincidence he received his honour from Mulroney's grateful university in a convention year. That was what reporters asked him as he stood outside the President's dining room waiting for the honoured guest to arrive. He denied it vehemently, but must have realized the delicate situation that his ambitions had placed him in. He very much wanted Lougheed's blessing; or, if that was not possible, at least a perception of closeness to the premier that would allow others to infer that a blessing was forthcoming. But he could not appear heavy-handed in pursuing the task; his image simply could not stand it.

Mulroney's staff were caught in the bind too. The day before, Fred Doucet, Mulroney's Nova Scotia organizer and a friend from Saint F.X. days who still worked as an administrator at the university, called Father Gerald Power at the school. Father Power, who had written the speech the university president would give honouring Premier Lougheed, listened as Doucet complained that the proposed text did not mention Mulroney's name. He added that had Mulroney known that he would not be acknowledged, he probably would not have come down for the commencement.

Towards midnight Doucet placed another call to Father Power. This time he informed the bemused priest that Mulroney was worried that his presence at the university was making the convocation *too* political. He now wondered if he should not appear at the ceremony after all, and wanted to meet with the president to discuss it.

The next morning Mulroney did meet with the president and, as he stood nervously awaiting the arrival of the premier, it appeared all would proceed after all. But, after posing for photographs with Lougheed and Nova Scotia Premier John Buchanan, the candidate unexpectedly left. It surprised the two premiers who heard the news only as the convocation procession began to file in to the hall. And it caught the network television teams totally off guard as they found themselves filming Colin Chisolm, mayor of Antigonish, who at the last moment was asked to sit in the seat intended for Brian Mulroney.

That evening in Halifax, Del Archer of CTV News cornered Mulroney at a dinner gathering of Young Conservatives. Why had Mulroney run out? he wanted to know. He had not run out, the candidate assured Archer. "I was in Saint F.X. to meet with delegates. I met with delegates from three adjoining ridings. I had lunch with Premiers Lougheed and Buchanan then I drove here…I was invited to participate [in the commencement] but unfortunately had to decline." He explained that he had to "drive down here" to speak to the YPC dinner and was, therefore, unable to stay for the commencement exercises. "But didn't you fly down?" Archer asked, referring to a private plane he had heard Mulroney had chartered. "No," Mulroney responded. "Keep your eye on the ball." The truth was that Mulroney *had* flown into Halifax that day. His aide Michael McSweeney had admitted as much, privately, only a few minutes before.

This was not the only time Mulroney attempted to avoid mildly irritating issues with the press (for example see also the question of the Edmonton free bar (Chapter 3, footnote 10) and the use of "preposterous" to describe Crosbie's unilingualism remarks, p. 99). Why he elected to duck such easily verifiable facts is a mystery, but its impact has been to foster considerable suspicion among a number of national reporters as to how far this tendency will extend.

* * *

To the 1,026 young Progressive Conservatives who would attend the Ottawa convention, Brian Mulroney was a fresh commodity. Most had not been around in 1976 when distrust of Mulroney first surfaced. A large portion of these delegates came either from Quebec (a Mulroney power base) or Ontario where Joe Clark's moderate image clashed with their own new right tendencies. Better still for the candidate from Baie Comeau, John Crosbie had enjoyed limited success in organizing any youth contingent, outside of Newfoundland. Thus, Mulroney had the opportunity to capitalize on his chief rivals' weakness among a key constituency. In order to make the most of this advantage, his director of operations, Peter White, took personal charge of the youth campaign.

Of the 874 votes Brian Mulroney received on the first ballot in Ottawa, about 45 per cent were cast by delegates from Quebec. Of those, 156 or approximately 46 per cent were delegates under 30, drawn either from the ridings' youth associations or from the province's 57 campus clubs. Credit for cultivating this group belongs to two young men: the fiery Jean Dugre, who had won the position of provincial treasurer in 1982, but had been forced to resign when he had replaced photos of Joe Clark at provincial headquarters with ones of Brian Mulroney; and Marc Dorion, a young law student who had been Mulroney's choice for the uncontested position of provincial youth vice-president. The two served as critical components in the campaign's Quebec organization, first surfacing in Winnipeg in January when Dorion contested the presidency of the national youth association against Clark favourite, Randy Dawson. (Dorion lost narrowly when he and a number of Quebec delegates were banned from voting at the election, having arrived a few moments late.)

Of the approximately 450 votes Mulroney received outside Quebec, about 47 per cent were cast by youth delegates—almost half! Since the youth accounted for only a third of all delegates to the leadership convention, Mulroney enjoyed considerably more success with them than he did with the seniors.

While it was expected that a disproportionate share of Mulroney's support on the first ballot would come from Quebec, as it did, his very large share of the youth vote was not widely foreseen. Yet it was the product of the same factor that delivered him Quebec votes: organization. Only in this case it was not his own.

Ontario, which provided Mulroney with the bulk of his English-speaking youth support, has had a deeply entrenched youth organization for years. It came about as part of the battle for the ideological soul of the party that had been waged in Ontario for a dozen years, and it offered the right suitor a majority of the more than 270 delegates it would send to Ottawa. Like healthy young men and women everywhere, the youth of the Progressive Conservative party in Ontario have been consumed with an idealistic approach to politics: that principle must come before convenience. The vast majority agree with this, but disagree among themselves as to which set of principles they uphold. Since 1966 and the struggle over the removal of Tory leader John Diefenbaker, the battle has raged between left and right wings of the party, and each side has experienced its successes and setbacks.

Thirteen years ago, reacting to the presence of "Red Tory" Robert Stanfield as national leader and the selection of moderate William Davis as premier, a group of right-wing youth sprang up under the direction of a young, brilliant, well-spoken, and tireless Hamiltonian named Sean O'Sullivan. O'Sullivan went on to be an MP and later a priest, but before he did, he assembled an organization that took control of the provincial youth association and made him its president. So fervent was the zeal of the right wing that some of its members even formed a secret society called "The Shysters," which was dedicated to the pursuit of their ideology. (The society's rituals included an oath burning ceremony and the kissing of a sacred ring.) Lacking any suitable Canadian political heroes, they admired the work of Richard Nixon and the ideas of Barry Goldwater.

By the mid-1970s the right wing leadership had been replaced by a considerably more moderate group which called itself the "Killer Bees." Many of its members learned about organization in the Flora MacDonald campaign of 1976 and were quite content with the election of another Red Tory, Joe Clark, as leader. Until 1980 they controlled the province's youth association. Then another force intervened. A young "Killer Bee" named John Polack, was elected president of the Ontario Progressive Conservative Youth Association (OPCYA). Polack was seen by most as an agent for one of the province's cabinet ministers, the moderate Larry Grossman, who aspired to be William Davis' successor when the premier stepped down. This development worried the right wing of the party and another aspiring cabinet minister, the very conservative Gordon Walker, from London, Ontario. The right wing found a new home in another youth body, the Ontario Progressive Conservative Campus Association (OPCCA) and in 1981 a new champion in a young London law student named Tom Long. Backed by Walker, Long zealously worked to expand the influence of the right wing in the province. They turned their sights on the general youth association (Ontario PCYC) and heavily backed Ken Zeise, a rising young man in the association hierarchy. Zeise had been elected to the lowest position on the youth executive the same year as Polack, but the ambitious 16 year-old quickly distinguished himself as an indefatigable organizer. Armed with the party's WATS line and, a provincial publication called "Outlook Ontario" (which he turned into a personal vehicle), Zeise developed riding youth organizations all over the province loyal to a right-wing viewpoint and to him, and in 1982 was elected president for a two-year term. Thus, by the time the national party met in Winnipeg, the youth delegates of Ontario were firmly in the hands of the right wing and Gordon Walker's young men.[10]

A large majority of Ontario's youth delegates voted in Winnipeg to have a leadership convention. As previously mentioned, Clark's moderate image offended their new right sensibilities[11] and they resented his continued efforts to influence their organization through paid party organizers. Thus, when the convention was finally called, the leadership of the Ontario youth stood ready to continue their fight.

A number of factors contributed to the delivery of this leadership and its concomitant organization to Brian Mulroney. The first was that these young people were staunchly ABC (Anybody but Clark). At the March meeting which chose a new president of the Campus Association,[12] the leadership met and resolved to unite against Clark regardless of whom they supported. The second factor was that John Crosbie, while personally attractive to many of this group, had not gotten off the ground fast enough to recruit them. Brian Mulroney had, and that was because of Peter White.

In the fall of 1982, White, a Londoner who knew Walker, had correctly identified the ringleaders of the Ontario youth organization, and began actively courting them. Both Long and Bocock, the new OPPCA president, were among the first to announce their support of Mulroney following the Winnipeg meeting, but White knew that Zeise was the key. Peter Pocklington had recognized the young man's talents as well and had flown him across the country in the fall of 1982 to promote a leadership review among various youth groups. White decided to attempt courting the young man too. Making no secret that his efforts were on behalf of Brian Mulroney, White told Zeise he would like to help young Conservatives get to Winnipeg to vote for a leadership convention. He said he had money which could be used to defray some of their expenses and asked Zeise if he would distribute it. In January, Zeise received $3,000 from the Halton riding association of pro-Mulroney MP Otto Jelinek which he proudly divided up among some of the Ontario youth delegates who were attending a reception in Toronto for Marc Dorion, the Mulroney-backed candidate for youth president. At the same weekend youth gathering in Toronto, Zeise received a further $3000 from Bill Campbell, Peter Pocklington's organizer, which he distributed as well.

The shrewd 19 year-old continued to keep open his choice for leader, but after a concerted campaign by White,[13] through his friends Long and Bocock, and a lengthy personal visit with Brian and Mila in Toronto, Zeise climbed aboard at the end of March.[14]

In Nova Scotia, Mulroney had split the youth vote with Clark, taking control of the right-wing provincial youth association which organized in the ridings, while the former leader won over the more left-leaning campus association. It was the former group Mulroney addressed that day in Halifax, where he gave an excellent speech. He spoke concretely about an industrial strategy for the country and of ways of increasing productivity. He promised them a chance to participate in helping him and to rebuild the grand coalition of the East, West and Quebec envisioned by Sir John A. MacDonald. Together he concluded, they would "walk the road to victory." It was a forceful speech and he was sweaty by the time he finished. His audience of mostly young men in good suits and silk ties with pretty, attentive girlfriends gave him their rapt attention and a heartfelt standing ovation. Only one question still disturbed his listeners, "Why didn't he give more of such speeches?"

* * *

Mulroney seemed determined not to narrow his delegate constituency by being specific on any issue, unless that issue was one on which everyone agreed, such as increasing productivity. Therefore, he spent very little time talking about issues other than winning a general election and rewarding his friends. Asked his view of the National Energy Program, he usually replied that it "resembled a 3:00 a.m. holdup of a gas station" because it introduced confiscation and retroactivity. "That's an odious provision…against the British common-law tradition," he declared, but never quite explained how he would change it. And what about moving to the world price for Canadian oil? "That's under negotiation," was all that he would say.

When the federal government introduced legislation providing a civilian security service, Mulroney's response was equally noncommittal: "I'm suggesting we have to be extremely prudent in agreeing to any concoction the Liberals throw at us in regard to our civil liberties."

While Mulroney did expand on his views concerning productivity in a handsome paperback book, *Where I Stand*,[15] published during the campaign, most of Mulroney's policy statements more closely resembled the one given to the inquisitive New Brunswicker asking for his reaction to the Kirby Report on fishing: replacing a Liberal with a Tory was about the extent of it.

Mulroney never apologized for his policy omissions; he was fond of saying: "all of the candidates have good policies but all of these policies aren't worth the powder to blow them across the street if we don't get elected." The issue he reduced it all to was winning. Don't worry about what I stand for, he seemed to say, just worry whether or not I can win.

The single response which Mulroney could be depended on to provide at any meeting was his devotion to conciliation. Avoiding confrontation, he would have his audiences believe, was his hallmark. Perhaps his career as a labour lawyer, addressing the disputes between labour and management, or his enviable labour relations record at IOC, caused Mulroney to overrate the benefits which his brand of conciliation would bring. Wherever he had been, he said, he had "reaped peace." He elevated this approach to a panacea for every area he would touch as leader: within the party, of course, it was the only way; for the Canadian economy, it was the secret to increased productivity, and for the country, it was the answer to federalism.

That latter inclusion astonished Quebec reporters. Mulroney, they said, had become known in Quebec for privately saying that as prime minister he would "kick ass" in the province. His emphasis on conciliation was not enhanced by the constitutional position he hastily provided to hostile French-speaking reporters when they demanded more precision in his statements. Although it consisted mostly of generalities, Mulroney also reiterated his view that Quebec should not be financially compensated if it chose to opt out of any federal-provincial agreement. As he explained to his audiences: "I wouldn't give a plugged nickel of the taxpayer's money to René Lévesque until he told me what he would do for *Canada*."

"Why, this could have been written by Pierre Trudeau," a Chicoutimi journalist complained, when he was handed the statement.

"Watch it there," replied an offended Mulroney. "There are no similarities between the type of conciliation I've practised all my life and Mr. Trudeau's emphasis on confrontation." As one reporter later wrote: "It had to rank as one of the candidate's more amusing lines..."[16]

Quebec's influential editorialists, however, were far from amused. Professing to be conciliatory while taking a position of confrontation was not a sufficient solution they said. Jean-Louis Roy of *Le Devoir* noted that Mulroney continually portrayed Clark as soft on Quebec for his constitutional position, yet offered no alternative policy. "We remain entirely ignorant of the principles of candidate Mulroney," he wrote. His style, Roy concluded was a limited one, "rich in form, but empty of content."

The lack of an explicit position on Quebec and other matters did not detract from Mulroney's right-wing support. This was exceptional, since the right normally demands of a candidate a specific set of acceptable principles in order to gain its support.

In this case, right-wing members of the party seemed to have overlooked some fuzziness on the issues and accepted Mulroney as one of their's. This despite the fact that in his 1976 campaign he readily accepted the label given him of "progressive," usually anathema to "conservatives" and that even in 1983 he would sometimes describe himself as "a Stanfield Conservative." In announcing his candidacy Mulroney had also pointedly emphasized that "we Conservatives must show the Canadian people that we have about us...a dimension of tenderness." In the run up to Ottawa, however, the tenderness played a less prominent role. Instead, the candidate expressed the kind of judgements that the right wing had come to expect: that he would arrest "the Swedenization of Canada," throw out the dreaded bureaucrats "with a pink slip and a pair of running shoes" and introduce government to "the real world" by cutting back its expenses. He was a credible messenger to them because he had tasted the real world as president of IOC, had "met a payroll... balanced a budget." The right, in their haste to remove Joe Clark, seemed to rely most on that and gave the former "progressive" the benefit of the doubt. Rather than tempt his fate, Mulroney continued to offer little more in the way of policy and concentrated almost entirely on the politics of winning.

* * *

As Brian Mulroney jetted into Western Canada in the middle of May his campaign looked far from being a winner. Feuding was rampant in his camp and he appeared to lack the organization, or the money, needed to win enough votes to stay ahead of the rapidly rising John Crosbie.

Mulroney and his closest advisors had been shaken by their failure to win an overwhelming majority of the Quebec delegates. It had meant they would have to win more in English Canada where the going was considerably tougher. And that meant they would have to have a campaign manager able to operate effectively outside Quebec. Mulroney had begun his campaign without an overall manager. Quebec was well administered with Bussey, Pageau, Bazin, Lortie, and company, but he had decided not to put Michel Cogger, his former national manager, in the same role, preferring to use him as a strategist. For a time he had coasted this way until the less than ideal vote in Quebec had created the English imperative.

Among his trusted coterie he had no one appropriate to name. Michael Mieghen, his friend for 20 years, was one of Mulroney's greatest assets but not a manager. The grandson of Prime Minister Arthur Meighen, this former Montrealer had twice run unsuccessfully for Parliament against Bud Drury in the riding of St. Henri-Westmount and had been elected party president in 1974. He offered Mulroney what he most needed, someone the people could trust but, by his own admission, he could not organize his way out of a paper bag. Sam Wakim and Peter White lacked the necessary skills as well.

Mulroney had shopped among Ontario's Big Blue Machine (BBM) for someone, but found the best people "waiting for Bill"—delaying any decision until they found out if their preferred candidate William Davis would run. By the middle of April, Mulroney could delay no longer and he appointed as campaign manager Ontario veteran Paul Weed. In fact

94

Mulroney had been using Weed unofficially for some weeks before his appointment. Weed was another figure whose presence would not enhance Mulroney's image and the candidate had hoped to keep him in a less visible role. He had worked with the Big Blue Machine in backing Allan Lawrence for the Ontario leadership in 1971, had been unpopular with the press during the Ontario election later that year, and had fallen out with the leaders of the BBM during the 1974 national election. In 1976, Weed had managed Claude Wagner's hardhitting campaign and his reputation as a tough operator had been reinforced. Yet, Mulroney had no choice but to take a chance on him.

Weed's arrival, however, soon provided the culmination to a period of internecine squabbling within the Mulroney camp. For weeks Rodrigue Pageau had been upset with his upstart superior Ronald Bussey as Quebec organizer and had not been appeased until Bussey was shunted aside. In Ontario, the outspoken Wakim had had frequent clashes with the highly secretive "operations director" Peter White. Even Michel Cogger and Jean Bazin, friends for more than 20 years, were said to be fighting. But the worst, most demoralizing clash occurred between Paul Weed and Michael Meighen. Meighen was the titular Ontario chairman, a position from which he could manage his extensive network of political contacts and promote the good name of his candidate. He was also one of the two designated spokesmen for the candidate, Cogger being the other, and it was to this role that Weed took exception. The attractive, well-spoken Meighen was always a favourite contact for the media and Weed criticized him for "stealing the show." On May 5, not content with verbal abuse, Weed physically threatened Meighen in the parking lot of a Toronto "gentlemen's" club. For the final weeks of the campaign Michael Meighen did not set foot inside a Mulroney campaign office nor was he presented, until the convention, on any Mulroney platform. However, he continued to work for his candidate by making countless phone calls, writing letters soliciting support, and by never letting on about the indignity he had suffered.[17]

Weed's organizational abilities apparently matched his diplomatic skills: By the middle of May the convention campaign had collapsed into chaos. Only 17 days before the convention was to open in Ottawa John Thompson, whom Paul Curley had persuaded in the middle of May to join the campaign as a new convention organizer, sent Mulroney a memo.

It included the following observations:

1) Convention campaign is out of control;
2) No direction or focus;
3) Will cost a lot more than it should;
4) Currently insolvent — many overdue bills in Ottawa — Bell Telephone have frozen the phones and called National Headquarters;
5) Most opportunities for an Ottawa based organization have been missed. I don't perceive that we have one competitive point of view;
6) Few delegates in organization;
7) Too many people are being paid;
8) Space is fragmented in Ottawa causing lack of communication; and
9) Our competitors and National Headquarters think we are poorly organized.

Not even the obligatory campaign song had been written and this only days from the convention and Mulroney's ultimate test. With all of this ringing in his ears, Mulroney flew to Saskatchewan to be greeted by an even greater blow.

* * *

Every morning, regardless of where he is in the country, Brian Mulroney receives a package delivered by courier containing clippings of the previous day's newspapers. At every opportunity during the day, on planes, in cars, before bed, he reads them voraciously. Quick to contact journalists with whose work he agrees and equally quick to call those who disappoint, Mulroney cajoled and bullied, leaked and stonewalled his way into the professional lives of many journalists, until he became able to do a little "trafficking" of his own.

Ottawa columnist Douglas Fisher has written: "He raised the leaking of information to preferred sources into an art. Over the past three years he sponsored a clever operation on Parliament Hill that fed a regular stream of anti-Clark tales to reporters through two men on the staffs of pro-Mulroney MPs."[18]

But the news Mulroney read on his arrival in Regina was not of his making. Southam News had published the findings of a delegate survey conducted by Carleton University which showed Joe Clark firmly in the lead in the race for delegates with John Crosbie the most popular second preference.[19] Brian Mulroney, the survey implied, was the big loser.

Mulroney's own delegate tracking had confirmed such findings. Their committed vote total was not high enough to keep ahead of the momentum John Crosbie would have as "everyone's second choice" in the balloting. So Mulroney, for the last time, flew into Western Canada with a different game plan.

Whereas in the past he had excluded the press from most of his delegate meetings now he was again actively soliciting their company. Seats on charter planes became available to a select few and he told some reporters: "Every night I want to be on the 11 o'clock news. It's fine to shake delegates' hands but you can't win them in five minutes. You've got to reinforce it." Reinforcing it would prove a challenge.

* * *

Perhaps it was because of his new approach, or perhaps because western Canadians expected more, but Mulroney began providing more lavish meals at his meetings—scrambled eggs and sausages replaced doughnuts and coffee for breakfast—and for at least one large lunch meeting in Edmonton he broke his own campaign rules and provided free liquor.[20] But nothing seemed likely to shake the commitment most of these people had given to Joe Clark, Peter Pocklington and to a lesser extent John Crosbie, and Mulroney appeared very nervous at some of his sessions. At his major Edmonton lunch he grew very disturbed at the incessant chatter during his speech and awkwardly chided the culprits: "Gentlemen by the bar…gentlemen by the bar…there's a rule in this campaign that anyone talking except the candidate picks up the bar bill."

Mulroney's big hope in Alberta was to win many of the *ex officio* delegates. Federal MP Gordon Tower was his provincial chairman and he looked to the provincial Conservative caucus as a good prospective source of support. But he did his effort no good at all by remarks he made at a breakfast he held for the Alberta MLAs. Mulroney appeared in Edmonton two days after Michael Wilson had announced he would not come before the Lougheed panel which had been struck to interview all leadership candidates and report to the full caucus on the "acceptability" of each to Alberta. Wilson's decision had been both praised and criticized depending upon what one thought of the Lougheed panel. The night before Mulroney's breakfast, the caucus appeared to indicate where it stood as not one MLA showed up for a Wilson reception to which they had been invited. Yet, however disapproving they were of Wilson, they were not prepared for Mulroney's greeting to them: "Welcome to the Michael Wilson memorial breakfast." An uneasy room of 15 MLAs could barely force a smile, and days later some would still talk about the "tasteless remark."

Mulroney was in fact hoping for deliverance by the hand of one man, Peter Lougheed, whose endorsement he counted on. The candidate defended his appearance before the Lougheed panel on the grounds "when I go to New Brunswick and meet with my friend Richard Hatfield, he wants to know what I'll do for New Brunswick. It's the same thing here with my friend Peter."

Mulroney had nothing concrete to report when he emerged from his meeting at Edmonton's Government House, but assured journalists that he was number two in Alberta and growing as he sped off to his next meeting. Later, he quietly told one national reporter: "You can have this...I don't know if it's useful but...Premier Lougheed is chartering a jet to take all his delegates to Ottawa." With another he shared a not-for-publication secret. He had, he said, a "40-minute *private* meeting" with Peter Lougheed following the session with the whole panel. The Premier, he said, had told him: "Just keep doing what you're doing Brian, every-thing will be fine." Lougheed eventually decided to endorse no one publicly.

* * *

As Mulroney flew back east, to rest over the May 24th weekend, the jury was still out over whether or not he would be able to turn his flagging campaign around. On holiday Monday, May 23rd, the verdict appeared to be in the negative. The night before, Mike Duffy on the CBC National News had reported on a meeting involving a number of leadership candidates, including John Crosbie and Brian Mulroney, the result of which, he suggested, was a pact which provided that whichever of the anti-Clark candidates was ahead at the convention would receive the support of the other candidates. Brian Mulroney was livid. He announced to the press on Monday that he would take legal action against Duffy and the CBC for making such libellous remarks. His astonishing outburst received much more attention than the original story, which was highly conjectural, and told observers two things: a man firmly in second place in the race would not have seriously objected to a story which predicted his ultimate victory; and a confident man, regardless of his standing would have merely brushed off the suggestions instead of drawing attention to them. Mulroney, it appeared, was neither firmly in second place nor confident of getting there. And that was the state of affairs with less than three weeks until the vote on the leadership. Then two things happened: one deliberate, the other a blessing of fate.

* * *

The arrival of John Thompson in the Mulroney camp the week of May 23rd was a stroke of genius. Experienced in Ontario campaigns and at national party headquarters, Thompson had all the qualifications of an organizer, rolled up in an attractive, personable and unambitious package. President of his own industrial equipment manufacturing company, he had been slated to run William Davis' leadership campaign with Norman Atkins and Paul Curley, but the decision of the Ontario premier freed him to listen to the persuasive arguments of Curley, who had quietly switched to Mulroney's camp. Thompson quickly assessed the problems Mulroney's campaign faced and immediately took charge of the chaotic convention preparation. The Mulroney team had just breathed a tentative sigh of relief at his addition when fortune again smiled on them.

John Crosbie, who enjoyed a surge of delegate support in the month of May, had stumbled badly. Two weeks before the convention opened he had lost his temper while touring in Quebec, upset at the incessant attack by reporters over his inability to speak French. Mulroney had reacted instinctively when the outburst came and called it "preposterous" that a unilingual be elected prime minister in a bilingual country. He then almost blew his advantage. Apparently mindful that his second and third ballot support would have to be drawn from the delegates backing other candidates, he sought to soften his criticism of Crosbie and for a while denied he had used the word "preposterous." When the transcript of a radio reporter's tape recording confirmed the use of the adjective Mulroney had no choice but return to the attack. Yes indeed, "it *was* preposterous," he said. "How many seats do you think the Conservative Party is going to win in the province of Alberta if the leader can't speak English?", he demanded of an audience in St. Catherine's, Ontario. "Not a damn one," he answered himself. The argument proved very effective and as Crosbie's support began to wane, Mulroney's again picked up.[21]

* * *

Brian Mulroney tried not to smile. It was Friday night of the leadership convention and as he sat in his box, John Crosbie, his chief opponent for the right to contest Joe Clark on the final ballot, was fighting his way through the pronunciation of his first French lines. It was a bold gambit and, as Crosbie progressed, tackling his greatest handicap head on, he won full marks, but Mulroney was convinced it was too little too late. In the two weeks prior to the convention Mulroney's delegate trackers showed the Quebecer picking up enough support to put him 400 to 500 votes ahead of Crosbie, whom they expected to have fewer than 500 delegates.[22] Crosbie's weakness was Mulroney's greatest strength and the man who had been worried only three weeks before was now comfortably confident. Mulroney didn't know that two days before his campaign had run out of money and a number of his senior organizers had been forced to sign personal promissory notes totalling $50,000 in order to get needed convention materials. Mulroney had placed himself in John Thompson's hands and Thompson had done a fine job.[23] He had tackled Mulroney's greatest weakness, lack of trust, with a clever convention strategy designed to co-opt the delegates more than persuade them.

In a memo to Mulroney, Thompson had identified the two biggest hurdles:

1) Your organization poses a threat because of the people and because it is unknown;
2) They don't trust you because of the slickness, smoothness...feeling there is no substance, plastic image and the feeling that you are someone's candidate—big business or Conrad Black; and
3) Our campaign [convention] strategy must focus on both of these weaknesses.[24]

He correctly predicted that both Clark and Crosbie would conduct "presidential style campaigns" at the convention, with ever larger crowds attempting to persuade other candidates' delegates that their's was the bandwagon on which to jump. Mulroney, Thompson had argued, must attempt the opposite. To go the route of large crowds would only show Mulroney as a threat and perpetuate the distrust.

The very first thing Mulroney must realize, Thompson wrote, is "that the campaign in Quebec is over and that the battle is for English delegates. To win their confidence, he added, the candidate must recognize that "the average English delegate wants to know that you have French support, but he really doesn't want to get too buddy-buddy with the French." For this reason it was essential that convention organizers disperse the French contingent so as to make them appear less threatening. The same logic would apply in the case of the right-wing youth, spreading them out to avoid any disturbing concentrations.

The second concern was to bring directly into the organization as many of the delegates they were wooing as possible because "involvement breeds involvement." So the Mulroney campaign set up a volunteer headquarters on the Sparks Street Mall and simply asked people to work...they needed their help. The unspoken message was clear: "come inside...see, we're not a threat." To subtly boost the team spirit of this growing organization, 1,000 shamrock pins were made up and each member of the organization proudly wore one. To symbolize the idea that the candidate needed the delegates, rather than the idea "hey, you better come with us" which the others were pursuing, Mulroney went out to the airport to greet incoming party members, reversing the usual roles. Never mind that the only flight he ended up greeting was one filled with Clark supporters from Edmonton, the TV cameras were there to record the act, and word of mouth accomplished the rest of the desired effect. To reduce further any chance of being seen as a threat, the decision was made to have only two relatively modest "events" during the convention. In 1976 Mulroney had been severely criticized for his lavish soirées and hiring the expensive Ginette Reno to sing for the crowds. Not this time. A modest early evening reception on Wednesday and a barbecue of hotdogs and hamburgers late Thursday afternoon were Mulroney's only social offerings. They stood in stark contrast to the efforts of the other two major candidates, who attempted to outdo each other.

In keeping with the bare-bones approach, the distribution of signs and campaign newsletters was held back considerably until the final day and the candidate tried to dress more genuinely casually than usual, to get out of the "plastic clothes" as Thompson had recommended.

101

Finally, following Thompson's advice, Mulroney had to somehow demonstrate that he was "his own man." The vehicle for this was his speech, not so much what he said but the way he delivered it. Introduced without fanfare by Saskatchewan MP Len Gustafson and New Brunswick cabinet minister Brenda Robertson—two people whom 90 per cent of the delegates had never heard of before—Mulroney spoke without a prepared text in front of him. In 1976, he had plodded through a wooden speech unable to lift it from the page. This time, with only cue cards, Mulroney spoke "off the cuff," he understood what he said, he was his own man. The result was an adequate speech in which the candidate once again reminded the delegates that they were winners at leadership conventions, but losers in general elections. He, Mulroney assured them, could change all that by winning in Quebec and "rekindling the spirit of an entire nation." "If you honour me with your trust," he pointedly concluded, "it will never by sullied."

* * *

Of the 874 delegates who voted for Brian Mulroney on the first ballot, roughly half were from Quebec and about a quarter were Anglo youth delegates. Approximately 13 per cent were an assortment of *ex officio* delegates—MPs, provincial members, past presidents, etc. Only about 13 per cent, somewhere between 100 and 125, were actually senior English riding delegates. These people formed the vast majority of the PC Party, yet only a handful had elected to make Mulroney their first choice.

Could they trust him?

That was not the question most considered when they weighed their choices on the first ballot. Mulroney had succeeded in not making himself an issue in the campaign. The only question that mattered was "Can we win with Joe Clark or Brian Mulroney—Do we want four more years of the same or is it time for a change?" For those who supported Mulroney on the first ballot, that was enough. But were there 650 more people in the arena who felt the same? After all, there was another contender for Joe Clark's job whom the delegates trusted and respected more—John Crosbie, the former finance minister, whose exceptional campaign had made him the party's most popular second choice. The Newfoundlander had gained considerably more votes than Mulroney had expected and once again the tense Quebecer might have wondered: If he's come this far, am I safe from him yet?

4

"Je suis canadien"

"Crosbie... six hundred and thirty-nine"

The May 23rd issue of *Maclean's* magazine featured a cover story which its editors entitled: "The Tory to Watch." The subject of their flattering gaze was John Crosbie, the enigmatic former finance minister who, then in third place in the hunt for delegates, looked like a winner to *Maclean's*.

Were they wrong to focus their attention on a candidate who remained in third place on each of the three ballots in which he ran, and who obtained only three quarters as many votes as the number one contender, Brian Mulroney?

Not at all. Because, for a few weeks in the spring of 1983, the leadership of the Progressive Conservative party was within John Crosbie's grasp. That it slipped from his hands was something that might have been foreseen, but never really expected. After all, this paradoxical character from Newfoundland had waged the most remarkable campaign of all the contenders. He had made a Newfie jokester prime ministerial; a former Liberal one of the most respected Conservatives and a shy introvert the most popular candidate of the race. Yet the very qualities which took him to the top were also the ones that pushed him over. To use the language of that other sport which gripped Canadians in 1983: he was a long-ball hitter who couldn't check his swing. Nonetheless, until he fanned on a wild pitch thrown near the end of his campaign, it looked like John Crosbie was going to hit a homerun.

* * *

"All right, now we've got to get you out of here." The words were directed at John Crosbie, two hours after Joe Clark announced his decision to call a leadership convention and run to succeed himself. The scene was Crosbie's suite in the Winnipeg Holiday Inn where a crowd of Newfoundland well-wishers had flocked to celebrate following Clark's announcement. The speaker was Ross Reid, Crosbie's astute young assistant who, after the merry-makers had left, grew concerned about the combination of his unpredictable boss with the hundreds of reporters covering the convention. The plans, so carefully laid in the previous two years, could be undone by one intemperate remark. So first thing the next morning, John Crosbie was hustled out of the danger zone and onto a noon flight to Toronto.

Fellow Newfoundlander Reid had done well to spirit Crosbie away. In serving "John" (said with an East-coast drawl) he had learned his boss' weaknesses: a frankness that left little room for subtlety and a temper which could colour his most decorous remarks. An ever-smiling Reid had kept Crosbie from trouble scores of time before, acting as his executive assistant from 1976 to 1980. While part of the Clark administration, he had won almost universal praise, from Liberal as well as Conservative, for being "the best E.A. in Ottawa." His mere 30 years, exaggerated by his round boyish features, belied his wisdom. When the Clark government had fallen, Reid had returned to St. John's to open a branch of the successful P.A.I. (Public Affairs International) consulting firm. Following Winnipeg he would leave the company to once again serve Crosbie, an edge which no other candidate enjoyed.

Reid had not been part of the organization whose plans for Crosbie's leadership bid he sought to safeguard. This group had assembled in St. John's, Ottawa and Toronto a total of nine times in the two years since the party's general meeting in Ottawa in January 1981. Under the chairmanship of John Laschinger, a former national director of the party, the participants had produced a blueprint for a successful Crosbie campaign long before the leader decided in Winnipeg that there would be one.

John Laschinger had first met Crosbie in the fall of 1976. National director from 1973 to 1978,[1] he had helped to organize the Tory byelection campaigns in Ottawa Centre and St. John's West that brought Jean Pigott and John Crosbie to Parliament Hill. Subsequently he had gone to work for Crosbie's former colleague, then Newfoundland Mines and Energy Minister Brian Peckford, managing his successful campaign to succeed Frank Moores as Newfoundland PC leader and premier. He also helped Peckford in winning both the 1979 and 1982 provincial elections.

Until 1983 he served effectively as a senior civil servant in the Ontario government (Assistant Deputy Minister of Tourism and Recreation was his final post) and kept well hidden his impressive efforts to prepare John Crosbie for a run at the national leadership.

It had started on St. Patrick's Day, 1981, only a few weeks after Joe Clark had received a disconcertingly low vote of confidence at the Ottawa general meeting. Three men, Basil Dobbin, a successful Newfoundland businessman, Frank Ryan, Dobbin's partner in some offshore ventures and the campaign manager of the 1976 St. John's West byelection, and John Laschinger met with John Crosbie in the latter's St. John's home. Together they took on the task of developing a leadership strategy. Laschinger was charged with drafting an overall scenario and the New-foundlanders the task of raising the monumental sum of money that would be needed. Adopting some of the island vernacular, partly in good fun and partly for purposes of secrecy, Laschinger became known as the "Toronto Codfather" ("T.C.") and Dobbin and Ryan were the "fisher-men" whose financial "catch" would be spoken of as "tons (thousands) of fish (dollars)." It was a good-natured group with a serious purpose: to make John Crosbie Prime Minister of Canada.

Two weeks after the first meeting the nucleus of a national organization was in place. There were eleven people, including the candidate and his wife, who met every few weeks for the next two years and drafted an impressive program for victory. To the original group had been added Chester Burtt, a bright, affable young man whose most recent assignment had been as secretary to the Sykes committee which proposed administra-tive reform for the Office of the Leader of the Opposition. Rob Parker and Jean Pigott, two former MPs, were also part of the team. Parker had worked for Crosbie in his 1969 campaign for the leadership of the New-foundland Liberal party and became Crosbie's press secretary following his defeat in the 1979 election. Pigott was a successful Ottawa business-woman, a part-time advisor to the Ontario government, and, most significantly, a key recruit from the Clark camp. In addition, Chester Burtt had signed on Howard Dean, the former head of computer opera-tions at party headquarters, and Crosbie had asked a young reporter for

the St. John's *Evening Telegram*, Jim Good, working on a Ph.D in philosophy, to become his policy coordinator. Bob Wenman rounded out
the group. The MP from Fraser Valley West, British Columbia, was an
overt right-winger who would later join the secretive Moores committee
of disgruntled MPs determined to make life tough for Joe Clark.

The group had two sets of strategies: the first for the period until a
leadership convention was called; the second, for the actual leadership
campaign. They worked fast. By the summer of 1981 they had set up an
elaborate speaking schedule designed to get Crosbie into the regions of the
country from where most of their potential delegates would come.[2] The
Toronto Codfather, Laschinger, kept the candidate supplied with a steady
stream of new speech material, and to spare the candidate excessive wear
and tear, limited his load to one speech per week. Meanwhile they built.
Reasoning that favourable contact with the future delegates to a yet
unannounced leadership convention was the key to their success, they
assembled lists. Lists of delegates to past party meetings, of party workers,
of anyone who had ever corresponded with John Crosbie. By the summer
of 1981, 12,200 names were stored in their computer, broken into categories
of issue interests and known attitude to John Crosbie. As the candidate
travelled and the organization quietly built its national network, new
names were added and categorized. A sophisticated correspondence
system was established that mailed appropriate speech material or personal
greetings from "John" to the key target groups. In his confidential
memorandum outlining the system Chester Burtt wrote: "With the right
list of data we can pinpoint any message, to any person or group, and
target that message right at them. We can do it formally or personally. We
can talk to our campaign team, to regions of the country, to urban groups
or to everyone."

By the end of 1981, after carefully analyzing the 1976 convention, the
group had produced a complete strategic plan for a leadership campaign
with special emphasis on what to do in the first hours, days and weeks
following a convention call. They had taken 1976 figures and projected a
budget of approximately half-a-million 1981 dollars and were well under
way producing major position papers. Their list of "personal hard-core
supporters" had grown to more than 600.

As the Winnipeg meeting approached, they refined their plans. They
drafted a non-committal statement Crosbie would read in the event a
convention was called and summarized their platform in a twelve-point

106

program emphasizing encouragement to the private sector, changes to the National Energy Program, attractions to foreign investors, a mortgage interest and property tax credit and a "sober review of...our relationship with the U.S." They wrote notes for Crosbie to use in response to questions he might receive on his regional origins, his "buffoon" image and his lack of French.

All of this was achieved with remarkable efficiency and yet it also maintained the primary objective of the campaign agreed to on April 1, 1981, that the candidate "keep a low profile." They would "allow others to speculate about a possible candidacy" but would "do nothing overt to cause controversy or appear to be pushing Clark."[3] Twenty-one months later, John Laschinger and his team were beaming with pride. When Joe Clark announced his decision to call a leadership convention, none of his wide-eyed, weary party, except for eleven people, knew what was about to hit them.

* * *

Why did John Crosbie want it? What was it about the job of leader that so attracted him that he was willing to undergo the regimen of a two-and-a-half year campaign? When asked that shortly after Winnipeg he replied, with a shrug, "because it's there." He likened it to any other ambition: "If you're in business you want to become president of the company, if you're in politics you want to become leader." He did say that for the good of the party Joe Clark had to go "because he lacks the stature...I doubt that Joe could ever win a majority." But his responses were mostly personal, "I can do the job," he said, "I've been a bridesmaid long enough."

In fact, since the late 1960s John Crosbie appeared to have caught three bridal bouquets, the only trouble being no one had thrown them. As Minister of Finance in the Liberal government of Newfoundland Premier Joey Smallwood he looked to be next in line. But a dispute over financing the oil refinery at Come-by-Chance had led to his resignation from cabinet.[4] In 1969, Smallwood called a leadership convention; but, when Crosbie declared his candidacy, Smallwood abruptly reversed his earlier decision to retire and successfully ran to succeed himself. Crosbie then joined the provincial Progressive Conservatives and served in the cabinet of Premier Frank Moores. He had eyed the top job there again, but Moores looked well entrenched so he moved to the bigger pond in Ottawa to wait for a turn in national government or a run in another leadership race, whichever came first.

Crosbie had no doubt about his ability to do any of these jobs. A brilliant man—he won medals at Queen's University and Dalhousie Law School—he had been able to perform any task he attempted. The only thing that had eluded him was the leadership of a political party. Coming from a family and province where politics was all pervasive, it was a recognition he missed. Crosbie had to overcome considerable adversity to get as far as he did in Newfoundland politics. Being a diffident speaker is a considerable disadvantage in a province that prizes oratory, so Crosbie had enrolled in a Dale Carnegie public speaking course. It was in the bearpit of the Newfoundland legislative, however, in daily and painful battle with Smallwood, that he learned the speaking skills for which he is nationally known today. Vestiges of his shyness can still be seen when he sometimes closes his eyes, mustering his inner strength, to reply to difficult or awkward questions.

From 1981 to 1983, under John Laschinger's direction, he continued to open his eyes further. He shed the physical trappings that had marked him as an outsider, the loud sports jackets, wide-rimmed glasses, the long sideburns and unruly hair. He focussed his humorous remarks so that there were fewer gratuitous, caustic jokes thrown at the Liberals and more messages with mirth. But for all his work, his planning, and his history of overcoming handicaps, there was one thing John Crosbie omitted. He could not speak French and, after one frustrating attempt at French immersion, chose not to try again.[5]

Nowhere in the stacks of documents from the two years of organizational meetings is the problem confronted, until the last meeting of the group, one month before the Winnipeg general meeting. If asked in a campaign about his linguistic deficiency, Crosbie was advised to say simply:

1. I don't speak French, that's true (some also say I don't speak a form of English that they recognize).
2. However, I believe I understand the Quebecer and Franco-Canadians ...values and aspirations.
3. French Canadians and all other Canadians have the same desire for fiscal and economic leadership to solve the pressing issues of today— jobs and inflation—mortgage and interest rates.[6]

While Crosbie genuinely believed all that he said regarding his lack of French and believed he was capable of convincing the delegates of his worth despite this handicap, he had unwittingly planted a land mine beneath the surface of his campaign. The only question was whether or not he would step on it before reaching the convention.

* * *

John Crosbie liked to tell delegates at every meeting across the country that he had a lot of support in Newfoundland. "Yup," he would say, "about 99 per cent of the Newfoundland delegates will be supporting me...and if we can find the other fellow, he'll never make it across the gulf." He wasn't far wrong. The "other fellow" was the only other Progressive Conservative member of Parliament on the island, Jim McGrath, a staunch Clark loyalist. A few delegates followed McGrath but, in the end, 94 per cent of the island's delegates voted for Crosbie. That the percentage was so high was mostly a mark of provincial pride in their "favourite son"; but that the actual number of delegates was so high, was a mark of imaginative organization.

Across the country most of the positions for delegates to a leadership convention are fixed. Each of the 282 ridings can send four senior and two youth delegates and every sitting Conservative MP or candidate has a place as well. Tory members of provincial legislatures and an assortment of executive posts and at-large appointments (the number of which are set) make up most of the rest. However, in one category, there is flexibility: that of delegate positions from campus clubs. Each club is eligible to send three delegates—that much is fixed—but it is the number of clubs that remains undetermined. Given the number of major post-secondary institutions, there is a rough ratio of campus delegates to riding delegates (because of the normal ratio of institutions to the population of the province). As it turns out, in almost every province, the number of campus delegates is usually equal to the number of ridings. In Nova Scotia, with a disproportionately high number of universities, the number is higher. In Quebec, because of the extensive efforts by Mulroney and Clark organizations to establish clubs at the CEGEP (or community-college) level, the ratio was approximately two campus delegates to every one riding. But in Newfoundland the ration was 9 to 1! With seven ridings, 28 senior and 14 youth were entitled to attend the convention from the constituency associations, but 63 delegates from 21 "campuses" were also eligible to come and vote.

When the campaign following Winnipeg began in earnest, the Crosbie team had established clubs on the "campus" of every institute of higher learning. No driving academy, flying school or beauty college escaped their notice and, aided by the province's minister of education and her premier, most of these were able to meet the only criterion the party had established: that they be recognized (by the province) as degree or diploma-granting post-secondary institutions.

John Crosbie and his team had learned well the Newfoundland style of campaigning. Candidate slates and packed meetings were not a new occurrence there. What is surprising is that Crosbie did not export this talent to his campaign in other parts of the country. While Clark ran slates with organizations designed to elect them in half of the country, and Mulroney and Pocklington did the same in various regions, Crosbie did next to nothing. His organization had made a conscious decision not to do so. Only by maintaining a low profile in their hidden campaign, by not being seen as contributing to any push Clark might get at Winnipeg, could they run the high-road, bandwagon campaign they envisioned. As a result of their caution, Crosbie's team lacked the organizational network needed to pack delegate selection meetings. Except in the province of Newfoundland where their activities would go unnoticed, organizing slates and campus clubs were inconsistent with their low profile priority.[7] It was a calculated risk they took, based both on their confidence in their candidate—no one, they believed, could campaign better than him—and on their polling which showed distrust was the biggest hurdle facing their chief rival Brian Mulroney. They had successfully avoided that obstacle themselves and so John Crosbie steered his campaign machine onto the highroad leading to Ottawa.

* * *

As the seemingly ageless Gray Coach bus barrelled down the highway from London to Chatham in southwest Ontario, John Crosbie tapped his foot to the time of the music streaming from the driver's stereo speakers.

Country singer Kenny Rogers wailed "The Gambler," the adopted campaign song, and the journalists on board sang along. Even Crosbie picked it up, substituting his own words: "You never count your *delegates* when you're sittin' at the table. There'll be time enough for countin' ...when the dealin's done." "Give 'em a blast Doug," Crosbie called out to Doug Ferrier, the retired Gray Coach driver who had offered his bus and services to the campaign. Cars overtaking them on the highway noticed the John Crosbie logo painted on the side and honked their horns in greeting. Doug replied.

It was a convivial atmosphere on the bus that day, but it might have been just about any day on the Crosbie tour, easily the most enjoyable of the campaigns.

Well controlled through a strict chain of command in Ottawa, the candidate's tour ran efficiently, almost always on time, had its candidate eating at least one good meal a day, and in bed by eleven. Without the chaos or hurried schedules that plagued some campaigns, the staff actually enjoyed themselves and the mood was infectious. No one who came on the Crosbie roadshow could fail to be touched by it. The crowds who turned out were large, the candidate usually performed well, and one could sense the momentum building.

The delegates liked John Crosbie. For all his imposing character and his newlook suits, he was still one of them. The rural delegates thought him folksy; the urban liked his reserve. Not at all slick, he was a diamond in the rough. And not the most snobbish among them could resist the way he talked. "You see this here," he would direct his audience's attention to a piece of paper he took from his pocket and unfolded. "This little piece of paper cost you $200 million. Yup, that's the price you had to pay when Marc Lalonde became the first Canadian politician ever caught in the act of leaking." (He was referring to Lalonde's inadvertent exposure of budget documents to a television crew during a ritual "photo session" which subsequently required that an increase in public expenditure — in this case $200 million — be made in order to perpetuate the notion of budget secrecy). "Sure, he called over the cameras, said 'here boys', and leaked right on national television." It wasn't subtle but it was very effective. The barrier between leader and led is most easily scaled by laughter, and by the end of most meetings Crosbie had the delegates swinging with him from the rafters.

But what a strange fish this Newfoundlander was. It was disconcerting to see a politician *avoid* having attention drawn to him, yet that's what Crosbie did. At almost every meeting he preferred to slip into the room unobtrusively — he was standing among the delegates before they knew he had entered. Invariably his first stop was the bar — a cash bar was set up at almost all Crosbie meetings — to pick up a scotch and water. Between

111

awkward exchanges of pleasantries, he took large gulps from his glass. Crosbie does not chit-chat comfortably. In fact, a stranger to the scene would say that the large and rather ill-at-ease man jingling the change in his pocket was the last one he would expect to turn and address the room.

* * *

One hundred and twenty pairs of eyes grew fixed on the man taking his place behind the podium, as friend nudged friend and husbands drew wives away from the cheese table to watch. "Here he comes, here he comes" they excitedly said, their faces beaming with expectation. The delegates of London, Ontario were happy "the show" was about to begin. Some had heard Crosbie speak before, all had come expecting a treat. They were not disappointed.

The recipe of a John Crosbie speech is one part Winston Churchill, one part vaudeville comedian, and one part country hick. It's a potent concoction that seldom failed to please. He'd tell them, though 52 years old, he'd been a Canadian only 34 years, since Newfoundland joined Confederation, "the only time an entire ethnic community entered at once." He would speak quickly, listing his many bits of experience, pausing only for effect when he came to that innately funny job he once held: "Minister of Finance in Newfoundland…now there's a job for ya," and as the laughter subsided he would stoke it again: "…Course it wasn't much better as Finance Minister of Canada." As they laughed and he listed, the point was well made: he had done just about everything. "Yes sir, I've been up and I've been down; I've been in and I've been out, I have even been buried 10 feet deep. That's where Joey Smallwood said he had put me, but, like another famous J.C., I rose again." At this point he sounded like a medicine-show barker hawking his universal remedy.

His panacea was to restore the health to the free enterprise system. "Economic growth has to be the number one priority and to achieve that we have to set the environment in which the private sector can freely operate, by rewarding the investor, the risk-taker, the doer, the *intrapranure* (a Crosbyism). Pierre Trudeau has said 'the economy is performing well.' But there are 2,000,000 people out of work." He shouted in exasperation, almost screaming. "The economy is not performing well: it is performing dismally, it is performing abysmally, it is performing abominably." Everyone in the room followed this man on his oratorical roller coaster.

London is known as a small "c" conservative city. Shown a list of the delegates on the plane ride in, Crosbie learned who were supporting which candidate. It was a crowd he knew he could work well: almost nothing for Joe Clark and a large number of undecided. Mulroney had a few delegates; the Quebecer's national operations director, Peter White, lived in London and he had organized well among the youth. He had also made a deal with a group of Pocklington supporters in London East to run two Mulroney candidates on a delegate slate with two of Pocklington's. This was Pocklington's home town and also the site of the Canadian headquarters of the Amway corporation, so the Alberta-based entrepreneur had a sizeable following. The four person slate won comfortably. Crombie and Wilson had next to no support in the area and in mid-April Crosbie didn't have much either, but he eyed with a smile that large group of undecided.

This crowd welcomed Crosbie's right-wing economic message. He extended his arm and held his hand straight out in front of him, slicing the air with a downward motion, "The way I see it, the middle is here. Now, if you're to the left of it," he said waving his hand off to that side, "you're a Liberal or part of the NDP. If you're to the right of it you're a Conservative." Again, with exasperation, he demanded: "What would be the point of having a Conservative party if it is not to the right? We might as well be liberals or socialists." "I am to the right," he solemnly assured his now cheering audience.

Having reduced the range of Canadian political philosophy to an invisible spectrum before their very eyes, Crosbie proceeded to stick humourous swords into a boxful of Canadian issues. Not even the most complex matter could escape his simplistic skewering…crown corporations…"Canadair…it should be called How Can They Dare!"…the metric system… "they brought in metric so no one can understand what's going on…the Liberal theme song is 'Nothing could be sweeter than to fool you with the litre'." Allan MacEachen's "reform" budget of November 1981 was so bad, Crosbie told them, that he was forced to "throw off this reform and then that one" (Crosbie pretended to cast off his garments) "until he was left as naked as a newt. He became the Gypsy Rose Lee of Canadian politics!" As the crowd doubled over with laughter,

113

a suddenly very serious Crosbie composed himself: "I'm supposed to be going through this campaign not being funny, so please expunge that last remark." He was referring to the problem of his "buffoon" image which clashed with his prime ministerial aspirations. He had tackled it head on in his announcement speech in Toronto, even then getting a laugh when he promised to campaign "as though I'd been weaned on a pickle." But at every meeting since, his humour had been omnipresent and the delegates loved it. And if there was any question that Crosbie was just simple-minded there were the degrees and academic honours to remind them otherwise. "No," the crowd in London concluded, "Crosbie just fires from the shoulder, that's all and it's about time someone did."

Their own questions to him confirmed that his right-wing pitch was on target. They wanted to know where he stood on junking FIRA, the Foreign Investment Review Agency, on selling Air Canada, on dismantling Petro-Canada, on cutting back foreign aid and on balancing the federal budget. But what they heard did not please most of the audience. "Balancing the budget... that's the theory, but its very difficult to achieve. I favour *reducing* the deficit to make it more manageable." Yes, Crosbie assured them "I'd sure want to change FIRA... but, no," he equivocated, "I'd still leave it in place... to learn what's going on." Selling Air Canada was "a possibility" but Petro-Canada would have to stay. "I think most Canadians *want* to have a presence in the oil industry." "But," he tried to assuage them, "we'll redefine its role." His answers were not as simple, nor as funny, as his earlier pitch and the crowd grew restless. "I don't think we should reduce our foreign aid," he said, "for humanitarian reasons and to develop international trade." He tried to give his humanitarian response an economic coating which the delegates might find palatable but they found it hard to swallow. Crosbie, it seemed, was not as consistently right wing as he led people initially to believe. Later he explained to an interviewer: "The Canadian people are moving to the right... and I'm to the right in my business and finance positions. I try to emphasize that but, no, I wouldn't cut a dollar from any social program."

Crosbie's social conscience stemmed, in part, from a genuine concern for people's well-being, an attitude born of the *noblesse oblige* philosophy his wealthy family practised in impoverished Newfoundland and, in part, from his pragmatism. Sometimes this pragmatism seemed at odds with his conscience, as it was on the matter of capital punishment. Asked where he stood on the issue, Crosbie would always go into a song and dance that he "thought" himself an abolitionist, but had promised the police force in St. John's that he'd support having a free vote on the issue. As the campaign wore on, Crosbie admitted having second thoughts about supporting abolition. But, in London, the people were a little disappointed in their "straight from the shoulder" right winger. As the Crosbie bus left London and moved on the next day to Sarnia, the candidate realized this. Two prominent local papers each carried the same two stories on their front page, from the United States the story, "Killer Executed in Alabama" and from Canada, "Prison Guard Killed at Archambault." Their message was clear. Crosbie's was not.

*　*　*

Throughout the campaign, Crosbie felt defensive about two issues: his proposal to consider free trade with the United States and his inability to speak French. Wherever he went, the questions were always asked. Although he had never announced free trade or a "common-market arrangement with the United States" as a firm commitment, Crosbie found himself constantly back-pedalling from what he had said. "These were interesting ideas," he said, "worth considering," But a few weeks before he had called them, or something like them, imperative. "We need a new *partnership* (emphasis added) with the United States..." he told the Canadian Club in Toronto. "I am not afraid to have this issue discussed, to put it before the Canadian people and I believe that any further steps taken along the road of so-called Canadian economic nationalism will doom the people of this country to a dubious and diminishing economic future." "This is not a pro-American approach," he told inquiring delegates and reporters alike, "it is pro-*Canadian*."

Still Crosbie's opponents hounded him. "Didn't you know his family in Newfoundland supported union with the United States not Canada?" some reminded delegates. "He's really a continentalist," others lectured, "He was a Liberal once you know." Crosbie believed, correctly as it turned out, that most Conservatives *were* in favour of free trade with the United States, so he struggled all through the campaign to find the formula that would solicit enthusiasm from the delegates and silence his critics.[8]

In dealing with his other problem issue, Crosbie did not back away. He *was* unilingual, he couldn't get around it and so, making a virtue of

115

necessity, he became defiantly unilingual. "There are 18 to 19 million unilingual Canadians," he told every audience, "and I don't think they should be disenfranchised." He would joke that "it is better to be honest and sincere in one language than a twister, a trickster and a twit in two."[9] The impact words like these had on many English-speaking audiences did not escape Crosbie's notice. At one large gathering in Ottawa, which most of the region's riding delegates attended, Crosbie had a pretty tough time pleasing his audience. He was tired from a week of travel and none of his usual lines were igniting the crowd. Four or five times he tried to end his remarks, but lacking the climax with which he always liked to finish, he continued talking. His Grit-bashing fell flat, even his "pro-Canadian" American partnership couldn't deliver. Finally he addressed the issue of his lack of French and told them his attitude was that unilinguals have rights too. The crowd cheered enthusiastically the more he drove home the point. Having obtained the desired response, Crosbie finished his remarks. In the cloakroom, afterward, people discussed his comments. "I liked what he said about the French," said one man, and a group of others nodded their agreement. Crosbie hadn't said anything about "the French," but these people and many others across the country took what he said, in his own defence, as being a euphemism for an anti-French sentiment.

"I can't help the interpretation people put on it," Crosbie said later. "I have to say something... if I had another answer I'd give it." But he did agree it was sometimes inflammatory. "I'm not going to deny that there are bigots in our party, and some of them are supporting me. But I'm not going to be anti-French." Would he clarify that to these people? "I'm not turning away any votes," he replied.

If his outspoken treatment of this issue had paid an unexpected dividend in the form of votes from bigoted delegates, so be it, he seemed to say. It might make up for the "brainless" delegates he lost because of his unilingualism.

* * *

Being outspoken usually worked well for John Crosbie. Stopping in Sarnia at the end of his major sweep through southern Ontario, he avoided the equivocation that hindered his answers in London and successfully explained that many of the issues were too complicated to

116

solve simply. When he took the time to elaborate without waffling, he lost none of the edge his cut and thrust approach gave him. The delegates in their Canadian Legion jackets and service club pins gave him an enthusiastic send off.

There were also times when Crosbie's outspoken nature got him into trouble. Asked at a press conference before leaving Sarnia whether he favoured the legalization of marijuana, Crosbie was momentarily speechless. It was not a question he had ever thought would be raised. Looking to the side of the room where his now apprehensive aide Ross Reid sat, Crosbie quickly recovered and replied to the reporter. "No, I don't favour reform. I don't want to encourage its use." A relieved Reid could finally take another breath, but Crosbie wasn't finished. "Actually," he added, "I'm against all smoking in general...marijuana and every other kind of smoking." A shocked Ross Reid buried his face in his hands as another reporter, smiling, asked Crosbie if he knew how far away the region's nearest tobacco fields were.

That day it was only an offhand remark about smoking that haunted Crosbie and, when he got far enough away, it would soon be forgiven. But not all of his outspoken comments could be so quickly forgotten.

* * *

On May 15th, the Crosbie campaign headed West for the final time. Crosbie's message was aimed at playing on the sense of community among the provinces outside Central Canada. Addressing Victoria's Chamber of Commerce, he wryly observed that in his quest for delegates he was doing very well in Newfoundland and in British Columbia. But as you all know, he reminded his audience, "it's the part in between that gives us the trouble."

He entertained his audience with the explanation of why his particular origins gave him an advantage:

> Of course, all of Western Canada knows it can trust me. I am not from the east—I am from the *far east*. You can't go any further east in Canada than my riding of St. John's West. If you go any further easter you'll be up to your keester in the North Atlantic. And, as all you bright people know, the earth is round. If you keep going to the east, eventually you'll come to the west.

"I am the third western candidate," he concluded triumphantly.

Crosbie didn't stop there. He reassured them that even as an outsider he knew what's what. "The people of central Canada have nothing to fear from me. I know that if their industrial heart misses a beat the fibrillations would be felt throughout Canada." At this, Crosbie extended his arms at his side and shook them in mock trauma. "I am not some wild-eyed, rubber-booted Attila the Hun riding in from Newfoundland to plunder Central Canada, and they know that."

Crosbie was really rolling that day and the audience got its money's worth. Crosbie got his too. The Conservatives of British Columbia were mostly right wing and they embraced his message. There were a substantial number committed to him already, mostly in the interior and the suburban Fraser Valley. Pocklington had picked up a few in the same areas and Crosbie looked there for second-ballot support. More importantly, some of the declared Clark supporters, especially on Vancouver Island were known to have misgivings about their commitment. Don Munro, the MP from Esquimault-Saanich who had recently come out for Crosbie, told him that although most of his riding's delegates were bound by a constituency-wide survey to vote for Clark on the first ballot, they really preferred Crosbie. But perhaps most important to Crosbie on this trip was that he sensed he had the number one contender, Brian Mulroney, on the ropes. In the West, in particular, Mulroney's support appeared to have peaked and Crosbie believed he had a chance to knock him out.

With unilingualism less of an issue in Western Canada, Crosbie felt he could criticize Mulroney more freely. "Unless you've been in the trenches, unless you've been 'over the top' as a corporal, or a sergeant or a captain ...you should not expect to become the commanding general." Crosbie then reminded his listeners that he *had* the experience. "I have a seat in Parliament. If I'm elected leader, I only have to move over two places."

It was going very well and Crosbie knew it. That morning the Southam poll had been released which showed him to be the clear second choice of the party and, as he left Victoria, Ross Reid told him that the Ottawa office had informed him that a very favourable cover story had just appeared in *Maclean's* magazine. As Crosbie and his wife Jane walked to the sea plane that would take them back to the mainland and the last lengthy leg of their campaign, he slipped his arm casually, protectively, around his wife's shoulders.[10]

Crosbie continued to perform very well throughout most of that week. An arduous tour through the interior of British Columbia led him to

Calgary and a triumphal speech before 850 people at a luncheon sponsored by the local women's caucus. Afterward he signed his autograph to the cover of dozens of copies of *Maclean's* which the delighted Calgarians brought to him. Although much of the Alberta delegation was committed to Joe Clark and a smaller number to Peter Pocklington, Crosbie's delegates appeared to outnumber Mulroney's in the province. Further-more, Crosbie believed he was the most likely second choice of those Pocklington delegates once their man had been eliminated. Perhaps most importantly, Crosbie even had a real chance to pick up a lot of the provincial Tory caucus. Don Getty, the province's popular former energy minister and a possible successor to Peter Lougheed, had just come out for Crosbie, and was quietly telling anybody who asked whom he was supporting. "I believe there is good support for Crosbie at the Alberta government level of delegates (MLAs and at-large appointments)," Getty opined. "In the ridings, he lacked the organization to pick up a lot of delegates, but he's a popular second choice, especially with Pocklington's people."

"You see," he explained, "a lot of rural people support Pocklington and I think they see something rural about John...they can relate to him ...people are impressed by what they perceive to be his straight talking ...they also like that he is less than 100 per cent serious about himself all of the time."

While Crosbie welcomed the support of a man as influential as Getty, it was the endorsement of Getty's former boss that most concerned the Newfoundlander. Peter Lougheed and his committee had interviewed all the willing major candidates except Crosbie. The candidate knew he was something of a longshot to get the Premier's nod — as if they needed any reminder, Albertans were recently being reminded by someone that Crosbie as finance minister had referred critically to Lougheed as "the Ayatollah" during energy pricing negotiations — and as he flew north to Edmonton for his meeting all the candidate could hope for was a promise that Lougheed would not publicly support anyone. Crosbie had heard often enough that the premier and Mulroney were "friends," and merely denying the Quebecer the endorsement he seemed to expect would be a victory of sorts.

As his chartered flight drew close to the Albertan capital, Crosbie must have had some doubts about his chances. During the flight, the plane had hit some severe turbulence and Crosbie's glass of white wine had spilled down the front of his vest. With no time to change before his important appointment, Crosbie was obliged to enter Government House in his marinated pinstriped suit. Crosbie's meeting, nonetheless, went very well—the premier even allowed a flattering photograph of him and Crosbie to be taken on the mansion's balcony—and a relieved, though weary John Crosbie completed his Alberta tour looking forward to a long weekend of rest and beyond that, to the end of the campaign.

* * *

The elevator doors parted and John Crosbie stepped into the lobby of the Longueuil Holiday Inn and into the open arms of a crush of eager reporters. He had arrived on his bus at this Montreal suburb only moments before from Quebec City. His press secretary, Diana Crosbie (no relation) reported that a number of journalists from Montreal had come out to see him and were complaining that there was no press conference scheduled during his visit. Crosbie agreed to hold an informal scrum for them and Diana Crosbie went ahead downstairs bearing the announcement. As Crosbie stepped out to confront them, he walked about four feet forward and stopped. The reporters jammed around him and began firing. With his hands in his pockets, Crosbie looked almost relaxed for the first few minutes. Then the reporters, as they had the day before, began to zero on Crosbie's lack of French. This time there was none of the self-deprecating humour that Crosbie had used earlier to deflect their questions. He was angry and it quickly showed.

"I am not some kind of criminal," he pleaded. "I'm just an ordinary Canadian who has been in politics for a long time and has a lot to offer. Just because I'm not fluent in the French language doesn't mean a disaster is going to occur." Had he stopped there Crosbie probably would have won his point effectively but as the reporters, mostly from Montreal, sensed they had wounded him and the level of their attack rose, so too did Crosbie's blood pressure.

Red-faced, he reminded them that "there are 20 million of us who are unilingual English or French...I don't think that the 3.7 million who are bilingual should suddenly think themselves some kind of aristocracy and only leaders can come from their small group." He insisted that he understood many of Quebec's problems and could talk to the people of that province. When a reporter then asked how he could do that only in

English, Crosbie snapped: "I cannot talk to the Chinese people in their own language either...I can't talk to the German people in their own language. Does that mean there should be no relationships between China and Canada or Canada and Germany, or whatever?...there are many different languages," Crosbie lectured. The reporters had heard enough. As they scribbled their notes and raced for the phones the French headlines had already been framed. *Le Journal de Montreal* was typical: "For Crosbie, French is Not More Important Than Chinese or German."[11]

Grattan O'Leary records in his memoirs that the late George Drew, former Premier of Ontario and leader of the federal Progressive Conservatives from 1948 to 1956, had once reminded French Canadians they were a conquered people. Despite years of efforts by O'Leary and other friendly advisors Drew was never persuaded to go into Quebec and attempt to undo that remark. (For their part, the people of Quebec were never persuaded to go into the polling booths and help make Drew prime minister.)

John Crosbie did not wait so long to apologize. Within a week he had attempted to explain away his Chinese-German comparisons but, like fly paper, the more he pulled, the worse he became entangled.[12] His opponents enjoyed watching him squirm. Mulroney made great mileage out of his "preposterous" remarks asking Albertans to consider if they would vote for a unilingual francophone and Clark, though publicly generous, began privately to draw the George Drew comparison.

Tory delegates from Cape Breton to Queen Charlotte were asking themselves: "Can we take a chance on Crosbie?" A party so long in the wilderness could not afford to take another detour on its way back.

Opinion leaders across the country were split over the basic argument. Don Braid of the *Edmonton Journal* called Crosbie's reference to a bilingual aristocracy "a burst of insight." For this "self-satisfied ruling elite... mostly Liberals..." he wrote in an opinion piece for the *Toronto Star*, "bilingualism has become a ritual chant...they demand it of national leaders, thus guaranteeing their continued membership in the club. They dismiss dissenters as red-neck bigots and intellectual lightweights, while exercising a powerful bigotry of their own."[13] But the more pervasive opinion was recorded by Southam columnist Allan Fotheringham: "The incredible insensitivity [Crosbie showed] quite stunned Quebec and made everyone reassess Crosbie's credentials as a future prime minister."[14]

Those credentials were not enhanced by a spate of endorsements he received from avowedly right-wing opinion leaders in the last few days of the campaign. The *Toronto Sun* and its two most outspoken columnists, Peter Worthington and Lubor Zink, called for his selection and a survey of the National Citizens' Coalition membership, released by its executive, proudly showed John Crosbie as the favourite of its members, with almost double the support expressed for their second choice, Brian Mulroney. For a man who had already painted himself into a corner the last thing he needed was another can of paint.

* * *

"I shall overcome," John Crosbie cried as he raised his clenched fists in the air, resembling a weightlifter triumphantly thrusting a record load skyward. Crosbie addressed the assembled delegates to the Ottawa convention and the millions assembled in their homes with the kind of passion seldom seen in Canadian political speeches. If any doubted at the start of the campaign his ability to deliver an unfunny but inspiring address, those doubts were laid to rest by the Crosbie "barn burner," perhaps the best political speech of his entire career. Crosbie knew that it had to be. The speech remained the only means left to throw off the effects of his Longueuil remarks and restore the momentum he had enjoyed before that dreadful day.

Crosbie knew he was a more popular second choice of the delegates than Brian Mulroney but, if the most dominant objective of the assembled delegates was to replace Joe Clark, then he'd have to be close to Mulroney on the first ballot—within 150 votes reasoned Laschinger—in order to carry the ABC banner.

"If you select me as your leader, I will listen as I lead," Crosbie promised, touching the nerve which Joe Clark left exposed by not returning calls, never listening to rank and file's views.

In the same breath he added that the party's challenge was "to *continue* (emphasis added) to recognize that in our party, as in this nation, unity is only possible where *diversity* is *permitted*...we must not simply welcome diversity but provide the forum to reconcile and accommodate differences." It was a direct appeal to the people sitting in Joe Clark's section in words the former leader himself might have used.

This double-barrelled approach worked and as Crosbie progressed through his text, enthusiasm for his words grew. Unlike any other speaker

122

that evening, he was applauded from every section of the arena. Still, their support was guarded. It begged the one question everyone had about John Crosbie. He tackled it head on.

"Je suis canadien et je suis fier," he began defiantly. Struggling with the French text, but determined, like a man breaking from his chains, Crosbie haltingly continued: "Je m'engage ce soir à continuer d'apprendre le français, à faire des efforts particuliers pour comprendre et discuter en français. Je le promets."

"By the next election, in 1985, I will speak to Canadians in both English and French," he told the cheering crowd. "It will be un plaisir ('un plaisyu' he pronounced it) to overcome this challenge."

Crosbie had attempted to reduce his handicap to the simple matter of his unilingualism, but he had more than that to live down. It was the years of frustration, the lifetime of opposition and the perception that because of his outburst, he was more a part of the problem than of the solution.

Crosbie knew this and against the judgement of many of his advisors chose to risk making one more point to deflect the delegates' attention and get the Quebec issue off his back. He played off the fact that the other two major candidates had made Quebec an issue. Signs abounded proclaiming "CLARK + QUEBEC = CANADA" and "MULRONEY = LE QUEBEC" and the Newfoundlander used them to his advantage "I say to you that Crosbie plus Newfoundland, Nova Scotia, Prince Edward Island, New Brunswick, Quebec, Ontario, Manitoba, Saskatchewan, Alberta, British Columbia, the Yukon and the Northwest Territories *equals Canada*." There was more to consider than Quebec, he told them in effect. It had bordered on Crosbie's earlier defiant approach, but the delegates understood and as the "best candidate" stepped back a pace from the podium, many were applauding and many besides the Crosbie section were standing. Said one devout Crombie supporter among the large number who had leaped to their feet, "I couldn't help myself. It was just...so powerful."

If any speech could have turned it around for John Crosbie, that was the one. Long after the other delegates had left the arena on Friday night, Crosbie's contingent lingered, chanting for their candidate, swinging their signs, not wanting to break the exciting spell their man had cast. But for the people who left, other memories persisted. They saw John Crosbie twirling an interpreter's earpiece as he addressed the convention's policy sessions waiting for the inevitable questions in French. They recalled the

123

shameful scene in Toronto's Massey Hall six weeks before when a Conservative gathering had booed Joe Clark's reply (in French) to John Gamble's comments on French Canada. And they remembered Brian Mulroney's haunting statistics: Of 102 ridings with substantial Francophone populations, only two with Conservative MPs.

5

"...but I don't think he can win"

Within all three of Canada's major political parties, there are a number of sayings that are regularly expressed by the various people who plan and execute campaigns. Of these maxims, none would have more Conservative heads nodding in agreement than the favourite of Norman Atkins, god-father of Ontario's Big Blue Machine: "Party politics is only about three things; friendship, loyalty and principles...in that order." Atkins' second favourite saying is "Remember who your friends are, Daddy." Both these mottoes make the same point: that no single factor better explains the functioning of the Conservative party than collegiality. The camaraderie generated by political campaigns forms a lasting bond among party workers that extends beyond politics into business and their social lives. To many outsiders, the intensity of that bond is difficult to understand; but, for an insider, it is what politics is all about.

That bond, in turn, creates a complex networking system among those who have fought in the political wars of the past. John Laschinger, John Crosbie's campaign manager, for example, has a card file with one hundred names and telephone numbers in it. When he was national director of the party from 1974 to 1979, he made sure that every one of these people received a call regularly from the party's chief operating officer. It kept them "on side," provided Laschinger with a valuable information base, and gave him a constituency in the party which ensured his position was secure. When he left the party to take a senior civil service position in the Ontario government, he maintained his card file...and kept making his calls even though he was no longer part of the formal party apparatus.

And the calls continued during every day of the '83 leadership campaign. Never asking for favours. Never twisting arms. Just finding out how things were going; what his contacts thought; and relating small tidbits of information about the campaign that let them know that they were still part of "Lasch's" network, no matter what side they were on in this particular war.

This became John Crosbie's quiet campaign. In effect, it let the network (and, through them, the delegates) know how far reaching and impressive the Crosbie organization was.

While John Laschinger may approach his network in a more systematic and dedicated manner than others, all political adherents have networks or else they are without influence...and influence within the party, especially when you are in opposition, is what partisanship is all about.

The enduring nature of partisan collegiality also goes far beyond mere card files and telephone calls. It shapes the lives and relationships of the key people who make up political parties. Joe Clark's chief strategist, Lowell Murray, shared an apartment with Clark and Michel Cogger of the Mulroney campaign during the early Stanfield years. In addition to being godfather to Clark's daughter Catherine, he was also an usher at Brian Mulroney's wedding and shared a room with him and another Mulroney confidant, Pat MacAdam, at St. Francis Xavier University in Nova Scotia. Hugh Segal, a chief operative of Bill Davis, went out with Maureen McTeer before she married Clark. He now works with Norman Atkins who, besides chairing the 1981 PC campaign in Ontario, is Dalton Camp's brother-in-law. Joe Clark himself worked at Camp Advertising one summer and lived at Norman Atkins' house. He also managed Michael Meighen's successful bid for the party presidency in 1973. Meighen, in turn, was introduced to his wife Kelly by Hugh Segal, went to law school at Laval with Brian Mulroney, and ended up as Mulroney's Ontario campaign chairman during the leadership campaign.

The delegates that attended Ottawa were also very much committed partisans. Fifty-one per cent (51%) had attended the general meeting in Winnipeg earlier in the year. Twenty-nine per cent (29%) had also attended the 1976 leadership convention. Eighty-three per cent (83%) also mentioned that they had worked in election campaigns in the past and 96 per cent reported that they planned to work in upcoming ones. In fact, the average delegate reported 15 years involvement in the party—far in excess of any of the five candidates who trailed on the first ballot.

The five men who together obtained only 384 votes, or less than 13 per cent of the delegate support on the first ballot, were not part of this or really any other partisan circle. Of the five, only David Crombie had attended the 1976 leadership convention, and none had ever played any formal role in the party structure or had any real connections in the informal structure before 1977. In 1976, Mike Wilson was working on Bay Street, David Crombie was mayor of Toronto, Peter Pocklington was an enterprising businessman in Edmonton, John Gamble was practising law in North Toronto and Neil Fraser was employed in the civil service.

In leadership conventions, the ultimate exercise of party politics, the lack of a network, constituency, and history in the party can be devastating (Trudeau, in 1968, being a notable exception). Unlike general elections, where popular appeal, partisan identification, name recognition, and "image" are the key to success, leadership conventions require gaining the support of people who have their own mission, network, and history within the party.

In the past, it was always good enough to wait until the delegates were selected and then go and see them or convince them to support you through your oratorical skills or campaign literature. 1983 was different. Owing to the unprecedented organizational efforts of the Clark and Mulroney camps, some 40 per cent of the delegates who came to Ottawa were part of an elected slate of delegates or were otherwise pledged to a particular candidate. For outsiders like Wilson, Crombie, Pocklington and Gamble, the task of changing the commitment of these delegates would be extraordinarily difficult.

In many ways, John Crosbie could have been victim of the same outsiders syndrome. Like the others, he was without a real constituency or network within the federal Progressive Conservative party. Thanks to his years of experience in Newfoundland, however, he clearly understood party politics and could take advantage of the resentment towards the other two major candidates. Besides, John Laschinger had his card file, and that, as much as anything else, was the difference between 639 and 144 votes on the first ballot.

"Wilson ... one hundred and forty-four"

Michael Wilson shivered in the rain. His large athletic form made an even greater target for the cold early March wind as he stood in the parking lot behind his Etobicoke riding office, waiting for his driver Sandy Miller to arrive. She was ten minutes late to take him to a meeting of his Etobicoke Centre riding executive, where Michael Wilson would inform them he was "running to be prime minister." Moments before he had closed up his constituency office for the night, having little difficulty with a tricky lock, for he had locked up by himself many times before. Since 1979, when he had beaten Liberal cabinet minister Alastair Gillespie for the seat, the two-room imitation wood panelled office in a nondescript three-story suburban "professional building" had been his political home. It was a long way from the oak-lined boardrooms of Bay Street.

Almost two years before his election, Wilson had called on Bob Jones, counsel and director of Eaton's, completely unannounced. Jones was then Ontario campaign chairman for the party and Wilson opened the meeting by declaring he wanted to run for Parliament and needed his advice. Jones was surprised, but not at all unhappy with the prospect. As a senior vice-president of a leading stock brokerage (Dominion Securities), Wilson was a strong candidate. "Three things struck me about him then," Jones said: "his intelligence, a magnificent smile and the fact he had never had any involvement with the party." Jones reported the good news to Lowell Murray and Rich Willis at headquarters and the party contacted organizers in Etobicoke Centre to work for Wilson in his bid for the nomination. A local, Bob Wells, had already entered the field, however, and Wilson would not win without a struggle. The nomination meeting was postponed once, giving Wilson more time to organize and, in the end, more than two thousand new memberships were sold, giving the decisive edge to "the fresh face" from Bay Street.

With the accession of the Clark government, freshman MP Wilson made the cabinet in a portfolio created for him: International Trade. This served to emphasize the Clark commitment to economic expansion and to showcase one of the "new people" Clark had brought into the party. After the government fell Wilson was made energy critic; then, when John Crosbie's intentions to seek the leadership became too evident and he was shunted aside to shadow external affairs, Wilson was moved to the role of finance spokesman. He made his reputation as a thoughtful, well prepared

128

critic and, in the internal struggle over Clark's leadership, as a loyalist to his leader.

At the 1981 party meeting in Ottawa, Clark asked Wilson to introduce him to the convention. Although Wilson's pedestrian style of speaking failed to win much support for the leader on that occasion, he persisted in his endorsement of Clark's leadership out of loyalty to the man to whom he owned his rapid political climb. Yet even before that 1981 meeting — only 18 months after he had first achieved public office — Mike Wilson had decided to run for the leadership of the party. He explained privately that many of his friends had been pushing him into it "even if not to win, just to raise my political stature."

Wilson's friends hailed mostly from the circles of the Toronto financial community and the governing Ontario PC party. Neither group had been adequately represented in Clark's Conservative party and the new member from Etobicoke Centre was attractive to both of them.[1] He was bright, well connected, handsome, and educable, even if a little dull (that too is considered a virtue by both the Ontario Tories and the financial community). Wilson began to see himself as the flag-bearer for these sectors. He was comfortable with the role because it fit well his moderately right-of-centre economic orientation and his growing ambitions.

By the spring of 1983, standing in the cold rain, he was able to justify his dark-horse candidacy, having realized "not everyone has the capability to do the job [of leader] but, if you've got it then you should run."

Michael Wilson's head had been turned by his early political success and his popularity in certain circles, but he was smart enough to realize that his success in the federal party was primarily because of the sponsorship Joe Clark gave him. For that reason he remained publicly loyal to his leader until the events of January, 1983, when Clark's decision to call a convention freed him of that commitment.

"I was surprised he called it," Wilson said as Miller's small Japanese car finally pulled up. "I wasn't surprised at the numbers [Wilson had won $20. betting that Clark would get less than 69 per cent] but I thought he could have hard-nosed it through." For just a moment he allowed a touch of regret to creep into his voice: "I think my entry [in the race] will hurt him because...I was seen as so loyal to him, not like the others." As quickly as it had come, the regret was gone: "Joe knows his leadership is not now strong enough and it's hurting the party... Frankly, I got tired of having to defend him."

129

With that, "the future Prime Minister of Canada" struggled into the front seat of the little car, tucked his big knees up under his chin and with two briefcases pressed against his chest, sped off into the dark.

Michael Wilson was right that his entry into the race would be a blow to Clark but what he had not counted on was that it would also rebound on him. The party had become quickly divided between those favouring Clark and those opposing him. The latter group viewed Wilson as a loyalist to the leader and tended to support other more obviously anti-Clark candidates. Clark supporters were not drawn to him because they had the real thing to vote for.

Wilson banked on the third-man scenario, that he would appear to a divided party as a god-sent compromise; and, in later ballots at the convention, when Clark's forces realized their cause was futile, they would turn to the former loyalist. To this end, Wilson's theme was "unity" and he did everything he could to place himself in the middle of his party, to be all things to all people. The problem with the strategy was that it required enough votes on the first ballot to position him properly for the later ones. That was where his friends in Ontario came in. They would be his priority and constitute his base.

A more experienced politician would have realized that Ontario is a many-sided lady who is very difficult to lay claim to; furthermore anyone who too obviously woos her must contend with her jealous sisters: Quebec and the West. It was a political obstacle course that Michael Wilson had chosen to run and, without much experience in the party, he hardly knew where to begin.

Wilson's first hurdle was, in some ways, the highest: to staff an organization. Prior to the Winnipeg meeting Wilson had asked Pat Kinsella, principal secretary to BC's Premier William Bennett, to manage his campaign. Kinsella was formerly the executive director of Ontario's PC party and the two had met when the new Minister of International Trade was cultivating his domestic political contacts. Kinsella was noncommittal because of a pending election in British Columbia and, following Winnipeg, he recommended his former assistant, Michael Perik, then in the office of Ontario Treasurer Frank Miller, as a *pro tem* "coordinator." Wilson believed he had little choice but to agree to the young man's appointment. As Mulroney had found, many of the talented Ontario organizers were "waiting for Bill."

Perik brought another Miller staffer with him, Ted Matthews, to handle advance work, and Sandy Miller, the former director of communications for the national party in Ontario. Bob Jones became his Ontario organizer and through him Jean Pearce and Hugh Hanson, veterans of Flora MacDonald's 1976 campaign, joined the team. Hanson was seen as especially valuable, having been MacDonald's principal speech writer and advisor during her time in cabinet. Carl Beigie, former Head of the CD Howe Institute, was named head of the policy advisory group. In theory, it was an organization with strengths in Ontario, policy and speech writing; but, in practice, it dissolved without proper direction into fratricidal sniping.

Perik was abrasive with people other than his friends and earned the enmity of many workers. "He had no people skills," said one, "he wouldn't even say hello to the volunteers." As a result, the organization suffered. Missing a proper campaign manager, Wilson contacted Murray Coolican, who had been on Stanfield's staff in the early 1970s and had been one of the principal organizers of Flora MacDonald's leadership bid, to ask him to take the job. Coolican was well connected—he was married to Stanfield's daughter, Mimi—and lived in a region where Wilson was weak: Nova Scotia. But, while Coolican considered his decision, Perik announced he would resign if Coolican were appointed and would take Matthews and Miller with him. Believing he could not afford to lose his Ontario connection, Wilson withdrew his request to Coolican.

Without an organization, Wilson had no chance to cultivate the delegate selection process and thereby secure important first ballot votes. He had to rely on convincing the uncommitted delegates of Ontario to vote for him first and those in the rest of the country to make him their second preference. He thought he had a chance to achieve the latter in Quebec, where his claim to be a conciliator might carry considerable weight.

* * *

Wilson stood in the middle of the room with his hands in his pockets and tried to make his impressive size as unobtrusive as possible. Twenty-two people were crowded around him in a Montreal hotel suite meant for six. The delegation was what was left of Peter Blaikie's organization in Quebec. Two weeks before, Blaikie, the past party president, had announced his withdrawal from the month-old campaign, citing his lack of experience with the issues. He had left his workers and a handful of committed delegates flabbergasted and, while some made their personal peace with Clark or Mulroney, most of Blaikie's Quebec workers decided to act as a bloc. They had first visited Ontario Premier Davis to encourage him to run and, having failed there, moved on to Wilson. They had never met him before but, if he gave the right answers, they were prepared to support him.

As they took seats on the arms of the sofa and the coffee table, crunching raw vegetables and potato chips, Wilson began: "I'd like to give you some of my French...so you can have some fun with me." In fact, Wilson was proud of his second language capacity: He had worked hard to speak and answer questions solely in French. Nonetheless, he was far from fluent. Some listeners fidgeted as he struggled with the construction of a sentence or tried to find the right word; but, generally, his audience appreciated his efforts with a second language.

In his remarks, Wilson called himself a man who balances the negative and positive approach to politics, who can lead and unify the party. The caucus, he said, had assured him that they would happily serve him as leader. Wilson reiterated the policies he had become known for: a balanced federal budget in five years, and the sale of any crown corporation if it no longer performed a needed public service.

But this group was more interested in talking politics than policy. One man who described himself as "to the right of Attila the Hun" agreed with the sale of crown corporations "especially Air Canada" but was distressed that the public was reluctant to accept it. "It's a matter of marketing to the general public," he said. "they don't have the tools to understand the difference between denationalizing and dismantling."

The balance of the meeting turned to the topic foremost in the guests' minds: party organization in Quebec.

"Would you establish a provincial Progressive Conservative party in Quebec? asked one.

"If we tried to organize one before the next federal election, it could hurt our national cause," replied Wilson. "I think it's better to wait until after an election and allow the grassroots to build it, not the national party." "That's what they all say," one shot back, "it's never the right time."

"Look," said another, "Joe Clark has carried on a relationship between the federal Progressive Conservatives and the Parti Québecois for years. This really upsets *les bleus* of Quebec. Will you clean up this act?"

"Yes," said Wilson firmly, "and it's better that an outsider do it, so we can go beyond this infighting."

As Wilson left to make his way through a busy day of performances, some of the Blaikie people stayed behind to talk with Ted Matthews who had arranged the meeting. They told him they liked what they had seen and were prepared to go to work for Wilson, for a price. They wanted to become the Wilson organization in Quebec with complete autonomy to run the campaign there and a budget of $75,000, to do with as they saw fit. (A few days later, the group announced they were supporting Michael Wilson—they received autonomy and a $50,000 budget.)

* * *

Michael Wilson squirmed in his seat. He was sitting at the boardroom table of Lise Bissonnette, editor of the influential Montreal daily *Le Devoir*, with Bissonnette and two of her reporters. For almost an hour they had peppered him with questions and Bissonnette was clearly dissatisfied with the responses. Wilson wanted to keep the discussion on the economy, "the important issue today"; Bissonnette was equally determined to test him on matters affecting Quebec's place in Canada. For Conservatives to overcome their historic handicap in the province, she knew they would have to impress Quebecers with their genuine understanding.

"Joe Clark," she said, "favours a full compensation clause for Quebec, do you?" (In any future amendment to the constitution giving provincial powers to the federal government, Clark favoured allowing any province the right to opt out of the allocation, handle the matter itself and receive proportionate funding for its administration.)

"No," Wilson said, "I think we must keep an open mind about this…it depends on the issues."

"Should Quebec have the right to veto?"

"Actually, it almost does if it gets support from some other provinces…"

"That's not a veto," Bissonnette snapped.

"I understand the concern but, to be frank, there are greater priorities today. It's far more important to spend time on the economy than get involved in two more years of constitutional wrangles."

"Joe Clark has told the press that you favoured opting out in April, 1981—why have you changed your mind?"

"I haven't said I'd oppose opting out," replied an exasperated Wilson, "I just want to be flexible."

Bissonnette was astounded that the candidate wouldn't face the issue.

Wilson slammed his fist on the table, "What are you getting at, what do you want to know? I've answered your question on opting out!"

The editor replied without looking up, "It's more than just *speaking* French."

Wilson had not understood her point; he had not understood that Quebec would not be content with symbolic gestures. If Crosbie had offended Quebec by claiming that he did not need to know French to understand Quebec problems, Wilson had blundered just as badly by believing that it was enough to speak the language.

It had been a tiring and frustrating two days in Quebec. The *Le Devoir* encounter was followed by more press interviews, in French and English, and each time Wilson was buffeted with the opting out issue and his incomprehensible position on it. He held two more receptions in Montreal, one for the west-end, largely Mulroney, ridings, another for the mostly Clark east island. Each brought out about 20 curious and polite delegates all committed to one or the other of the major candidates.

Leaving Montreal, Wilson had driven to Sherbrooke, Quebec, stopping on the way to meet a single delegate, the mayor of the hamlet of St. Alphonse de Granby, in his home, and arrived at a reception for five area ridings to find only three people in attendance. Twice before, in Western Canada, Wilson had been faced with no-shows and those times had been able to blame it on the "dirty tricks" of opponents' supporters who had called his guests and reported a change in venue. This time there was no excuse and no one felt like eating the raw vegetables and chips or drinking the wine intended for 20. Then, crowding into one car, he and his party drove to Quebec City for a final evening reception. Burned once that day, he approached it with trepidation.

But Wilson was pleasantly surprised: Twenty-seven delegates, including the area organizers for both Clark and Mulroney and the president of the Quebec Youth Association, came out. It was almost an even split between the two main camps and the delegates formed a horseshoe around Wilson, the Clark people on one side, Mulroney's on the other. Wilson rose to the occasion. He spoke for 15 minutes, and took questions for an hour. He never uttered a single word of English.

"...but I don't think he can win"

Wilson was calm and forceful; his speech, delivered without much hesitation, had his audience surprised and attentive.

He told them he thought he had a good chance of winning and volunteered "I have a very good opportunity to get big support in Alberta. Premier Lougheed and four of his caucus are interviewing each of the candidates and I think I have a good chance to get their support," he said. "They respected my work in the energy area as our party critic."

Looking down both sides of the room, he said that only he, of the "bilingual candidates," could bring the major factions of the party together.

Wilson's addresses were never stirring. At best he surprised his audience with a competent performance and won marks for his thoughtful and earnest positions on the economy. Seldom lighthearted in his remarks he appeared to the delegates as bright but sober. He would joke that Canada had endured 15 years of dazzling charisma with Pierre Trudeau and "look at the mess it got us into," but left most people wondering if there wasn't something in between a Trudeau and a Wilson. Of all the candidates, Mike Wilson changed a room the least by walking into it. The persistent joke about him was that he was like Clark Kent, only when he emerged from changing in a phone booth, he was still Clark Kent. Occasionally he allowed displays of touching innocence to show through.

One such incident occurred just prior to his Quebec City meeting. Weary and irritated from his frustrating campaign into Quebec, he had not looked forward to the evening's event. But when reminded that afterward he'd be able to view the first game of the NHL playoffs on television, he became a changed man. An eager smile lit up his face. He announced to his staff that regardless of what happened, the reception that night must end promptly at nine and ordered steaks in his room afterward for all of them. Even the delegates approved and cheered him when promptly at nine he announced the start of the game and made his exit. It was a relieved man who put his feet up in front of the TV to enjoy himself. His team lost.

* * *

The news came as a surprise to almost everyone: "Michael Wilson announced today he would not appear before a select committee of the

135

Alberta legislature chaired by Premier Peter Lougheed..." The committee had been struck to interview each of the leadership candidates and advise the MLAs which candidate or candidates met Alberta's needs. In private, almost all of the candidates spoke with derision about "the demeaning process" but each agreed to appear before the "inquisition," as one dubbed it. A storm of "who the hell do they think they are?" columns rocked the eastern press with Dalton Camp, former party president, promising to vote for the first candidate who refused to appear before the committee. Descendants of Camp's in the Big Blue Machine of Ontario were still stinging from the rebuke Lougheed had given their Premier Davis when he had considered running, and the formation of the Lougheed committee added insult to their injury. None of this went unnoticed by Michael Wilson and when, following the Davis decision not to enter the race, a number of Ontario organizers joined Wilson's already Ontario-dominated advisory group, they told him it would be clearly to his advantage to shun the committee. So the day before his scheduled appearance, Wilson announced his decision saying a national leader "cannot afford to look like a headwaiter to the premiers."

In the narrowest of terms, Wilson had little to lose by this action, since it was highly unlikely he would have received the committee's endorsement. In fact no more than a handful of delegates west of the Lakehead were inclined to support Wilson on the first ballot and his vote total was unaffected by the outrage his decision triggered in the West. But there was a greater issue at stake. This self-proclaimed "unity candidate," whom a divided party was supposed to find to be an acceptable compromise, had shown he knew very little about the most persistent and serious causes of strain in the party and the country. By offering this gratuitous insult to Peter Lougheed in an attempt to score some political advantage in Ontario he demonstrated that he did not understand that much of the cause of regional conflict in the country is the perception outside central Canada that national policy has been dictated by the interests of Ontario and Quebec.

Michael Wilson succeeded in his effort not to appear as a "headwaiter" to Premier Lougheed but in so doing came out looking like something much worse for Premier Davis.

And what of the prospect for an electoral coup in Ontario? The province's Big Blue Machine and the men closest to Bill Davis had

136

scattered in many directions, backing a variety of candidates when their premier had decided not to enter the race, and those who believed Wilson was owed a vote of gratitude were left with very few votes at their disposal.

Nonetheless, Ontario did not forget Michael Wilson's actions. His name was mentioned very warmly at a private Albany Club dinner William Davis had for the 150 or so people who had organized his putative campaign, and Hugh Segal, a former Davis aide, spent much of the week prior to the convention on the telephone telling national reporters of a "movement to Mike" for "having the courage to say what a lot of people thought." The one Ontarian most taken in by this talk was Michael Wilson himself who, by the time his "unity train" arrived in Ottawa, had become convinced he would receive about 300 votes on the first ballot. It was a rude shock to learn that the train had only been pulling a caboose.

"Crombie... one hundred and sixteen"

David Crombie stood at the corner of King and Church streets in the middle of the oldest part of Toronto. It was February 25th; two days later he would be a candidate for the Conservative leadership.

"I love this city," he said. And it loves him. As he walked the eight city blocks to his Rosedale constituency office, no fewer than three policemen, two street cleaners and 15 "civilians" stopped him to say hello. Some shook his hand and a number of drivers honked their horns at the familiar diminutive form. These people knew Crombie, not as their MP, but as their mayor of six years. Some say the best ever. He was a one-term junior alderman when he sought and obtained the mayor's chain in 1972, running on a reform ticket. His policies were moderate and "neighbourhood oriented" — he smoothed the edges of a radical city council. In two subsequent elections, Crombie faced no serious opposition and enjoyed boasting of the 93 per cent of the vote he received in his last race.

Many were surprised to learn he was a Progressive Conservative. His visible supporters had always seemed more "trendy" NDP-types. In 1976, he stood before the delegates to the Tory leadership convention to place the name of Flora MacDonald in nomination. Still, some doubted his conservatism. But in 1978 he made it official by running as the Progressive

Conservative candidate in Rosedale against a Liberal star, former University of Toronto President John Evans, in the "safe" Liberal seat vacated by Donald MacDonald. Once again "little David" was a giant killer.

Two general elections, two victories, and a brief turn as Minister of Health and Welfare had followed, during which Crombie maintained his image as independent and a champion for the little guy.

Crombie had made few friends in the Conservative party, either federally or provincially, and liked it that way. "David Crombie's nobody's man" his constituents could say. When he first ran in Rosedale he even discarded the party colours; one had to look hard in his literature to find that he was the Progressive Conservative candidate. Once elected, his people took over the riding executive, displacing Hal Jackman and Warren Armstrong, two prominent, influential party members. He paid for his independent line, however. As a minister in the Clark government, Crombie had expected to be the senior political minister in Toronto, but Premier William Davis objected. His message to Clark was "anyone but Crombie" and Ron Atkey was designated instead. "He's not a team player," said Atkey. In February, 1983, however, it was David Crombie and not Ron Atkey who was looking to captain the team. As he walked north on Church Street that chilly afternoon, the driver of a car stopped at an intersection and rolled down his window to shout "give 'em hell, David." Crombie shook his fist in the air in a gesture of defiance.

* * *

Four weeks into the race, David Crombie was in trouble. His organization was dispirited and rumours abounded that its collapse was imminent. Crombie had gone to his small group of friends to staff his office: Bill Marshall, a Toronto film producer who had been his strategist and speech writer in past campaigns, returned to that role; Chris Speyer, MP for Cambridge, and a friend from Ottawa, served as chairman; Tom Watson, who had run Speyer's last local campaign, directing as well his unsuccessful bid for the party presidency, became national manager, and David Dyer, who knew both Speyer and Watson from his days as a party organizer in southwest Ontario, kept track of delegates. John McFadyen from Crombie's constituency office became his chief aide and McFadyen's wife Nancy ran the tour. Only Speyer and Dyer had anything resembling national political experience. Bill Saunderson, who had chaired Crombie's mayoralty races, had been the party's Ontario campaign chairman in 1979, but this time he was Crombie's finance chairman and was asked to do little more. The team did not perform well. Watson had spent half of the first month in Austria on business and Speyer divided his time between Ottawa and Toronto. Dyer had been refused much authority and Marshall was never in the office. "There was no team spirit because we were never together," one of them said.

The situation was not helped when, annoyed by the national press treatment of their campaign as a long shot, the Crombie team took out a full-page ad in the national edition of the *Globe and Mail* asking for money and workers. It was designed to enhance their presence in the campaign, but it served more to fuel the rumours of a candidacy in trouble. This then made it harder to sell Crombie to the delegates and, more importantly, consolidate a "base" vote in greater Toronto. Tom Watson was disappointed, "I had translated his mayoral success to delegates." But as more and more delegates were selected, Crombie was seldom mentioned as a first choice for leader.

Crombie had decided four years before to run for the leadership but had done little to prepare for the event. "I was totally surprised when Joe decided to call a convention," he explained. Surprised or not, in politics David Crombie usually flies by the seat of his pants, relying on good ears, good judgment, and a good voice. They've served him well. He listens to people's concerns and echoes them as his cause.

On his first visit to Prince Edward Island, for example, Crombie's briefing notes were a scant two paragraphs and yet, he was at his best. He asked his driver for advice and used it in his remarks to the provincial caucus. He made mental notes of the caucus' questions to him and repeated them later to a television interviewer as his concerns for their province. What he learned from the interview he applied at the next and, in this manner, leapfrogged his way across the province (and the country).

This was the Crombie strength and he decided to make it the basis of his campaign strategy. "I decided this was just another aldermanic race," he said. "There are 3,000 constituents—that's fewer than the smallest ward in Toronto—and I'll get out and meet all of them." David Dyer was not happy, but had little choice: "If you have to play without a hardball organization, then Crombie's the best one to pitch to the delegates." So the workers at Crombie headquarters dug in and covered the walls with clippings of the '76 leadership race. They especially liked those which told

139

of underdog Joe Clark begging reporters for attention only weeks before his victory.

* * *

On May 4, Crombie's candidacy appeared to receive a boost when Bill Davis decided not to enter the race. Crombie had done a jig when a radio reporter informed him of the news during a campaign stop in Charlottetown. After very nearly kissing a stunned security guard in the halls of Canada's oldest legislature, the candidate composed himself sufficiently to tell the reporter he was "sorry to hear that, he'd have been a good candidate." This was the biggest weight Crombie had carried throughout the nine weeks of the campaign. At every stop he'd been asked: "What will happen if Davis enters the race?" And he'd always given the same lame response: "It'll scramble everyone's numbers a lot but I think it'll hurt Joe and Brian more than me." Now the load was lifted.

Reading the *Globe and Mail* the next morning on the plane from Charlottetown to Sydney, Crombie was noticeably less ebullient. He read aloud the analysis that Davis's decision would benefit Clark, Crosbie, and Wilson more than him. "They're doing what they've always done: writing down our campaign. They're wrong," he said firmly. What could he expect to get from the decision? Support from Davis? "No, I've always figured he'd stay neutral publicly."

And privately...?

"I think he'll probably support me. I expect Frank Drea and [Roy] McMurtry will come out for me now. That's what I've got to do this weekend, start talking to them."

His immediate concern, upon his arrival in Sydney, was the ritual "conference" with the local press. For the past three days in the Maritimes, Crombie had performed well with the delegates and poorly with the press. That day was no exception. His energetic manner and smiling face made no impression on the six reporters in the room as they plodded through their questions. Two days before, Crosbie and Wilson had been though town doling out praise for the crown corporations of Atlantic Canada.

"What's your position on crown corporations?" they asked. Crombie didn't help his own cause when he refused to attack his opponents. He thought the Crosbie-Wilson position was hypocritical, coming from the two who promised to sell off many of the same corporations, but didn't say so!

"I think each corporation should be viewed independently," was the sum of his answer. "Of course I'm in favour of the crown corporations in Cape Breton," he offered.

He asssured the skeptical reporters that his campaign was building and that he'd "win in Ontario." The reporters appeared to be merely going through the motions. When the CBC radio reporter's tape ran out during the session, she didn't bother to reset it and only one of the reporters stayed for the delegate reception that followed. During this event, Crombie stood squarely in the middle of the room, his feet spread, his chest swelled and his jaw clenched as he told them in ten minutes why he was the one to lead their party. He stressed his winning seven out of seven elections, his balancing municipal budgets, and his unifying an unruly city council. He said people wanted the Conservatives to have a "mainstream" political party "not some ideological association or private club." His audience was attentive and appreciative. He then raised "the three objections people have to me becoming leader. First they say: 'What about French, Crombie? Isn't it time the leader of the party be able to speak *both* official languages?' And the answer to that my friends is most emphatically, yes!" At this point, as always, he broke into a few lines of broken French and repeated in English that he had been studying the language for two years and would continue to do so. His audience smiled with him and applauded. "The second objection," he said, "is that I'm from Toronto and everyone hates Toronto. Well I love that city. I love its streets, I love its people. And wherever I've been in this country I've never had it held against me. I'm proud of that city." It was what the audience wanted to hear and they cheered and clapped a man who boasted of his home.

"Now the third concern is a little more difficult to deal with. That's the one you read in the *Globe and Mail* that says: 'That Crombie, what a nice guy. He's honest, sensitive, intelligent and capable—too bad he can't win.'" At that, as audiences did everywhere he mentioned it, the people laughed, then shook their heads sadly. He finished his remarks by asking for their support to help show that those "old-fashioned values could win." He was visibly moved when everyone leapt to their feet and gave him the best round of applause he'd had in the campaign. In questions afterward, the issue that headed the list of the delegate's concerns, even in far-away

141

Cape Breton, was: "Can you win in Quebec?" Crombie gave his stock answer: "Sure I can win in Quebec. I can pick up a few seats there, but no one's going to win there overnight. The next election's going to be won or lost in Ontario and I can win that BIG. Then, next time we'll win in Quebec. Once they see that we're going to be in Ottawa for 20 years, they'll come along."

In his parting words, Crombie confided "a secret" that he left in every meeting—it was his encoded attack on the three main contenders: "The people of this country want a change, they don't want the same old leadership. That may be hard for some of you to accept but it's true" (his attack on Clark). "The people won't trust an untried, inexperienced leader" (Mulroney). "And, finally, they don't want to give up to those who would sectionalize the country or give up on the Canadian dream." Few guessed that the last point amounted to his attack on John Crosbie. He finished in the same way at every meeting: "So when you're in that ballot box and the balloons and banners have all been put away and no one's looking over your shoulder, mark your ballot for the party, for the country and for me." Again they rose and cheered him.

The delegates were tight-lipped about whom they'd support: "Oh we don't have to say down here," one replied when questioned. When pushed, he offered, "I'm leaning to Crosbie or maybe Mulroney."

"What about Crombie?"

"Oh, I like him, he's a fine speaker, but I don't think he can win."

"That's just what he said people say about him—do you think that's fair?"

"Oh yeah, but he's from Toronto."

"Didn't he answer that too?"

"Well, I'll tell you who I won't support...Joe Clark."

Bill Manson, a delegate from Cape Breton-East Richmond, liked Crombie a lot, "like he says, he's a nice guy—he's a good grassroots Tory. But I'm for Clark...on the first ballot." He explained "most of us were with Flora in 1976 and then we went to Joe when Flora did. Most of us are still there." Manson was taken aback when reminded that Crombie had nominated Flora MacDonald in 1976, "I'd forgotten that," he said, scratching his head.

Afterward, in his room, Crombie was asked why he hadn't mentioned his link to Flora in this her home ground. "I never thought of it," he groaned. He walked over to the window and spent a long time watching the boats in the harbour.

* * *

Politicians lie awake nights imagining the circumstances of the perfect speech — when the speaker, his message, and the time for delivering it are in such accord that the spines of his audience tingle. For Joe Clark it may have been that evening in Sherbrooke, for John Crosbie, his speech to the convention but, like Edward Kennedy at the 1980 US Democratic convention, the moment for David Crombie came only after he had accepted that he could not win the leadership of his party. It happened one morning in Victoria, British Columbia two weeks before the convention in front of 22 people.

Two days before, in Toronto, Crombie had come out of the closet and declared himself a Red Tory. From the start of the race he had avoided the label but, when it became apparent he did not have the numbers to win, he confronted the issue. "If my work with the people of my city and setting my priorities on looking after them as individuals and caring for the community makes me a Red Tory, well then I'm proud to wear the label," he told Toronto delegates. Dropping his veiled attacks on his opponents, he charged that the right-wing policies advocated by Wilson, Mulroney and Crosbie would lead the party "down the path where the Canadian people will not follow." He cited the "currently fashionable tough talk about social policy cutbacks" and called it "dead wrong." "Canadians don't want a mean or petty government. They want good government and frugal government." In Victoria, Crombie repeated this along with his usual pitch to delegates, and delivered it beautifully. His audience let their scrambled eggs and sausages get cold as he spoke from the head of the table. He added what being a Tory meant to him: "glorifying the individual whose rights and liberties are sacred" and from which flows our system of free enterprise; and "cherishing the community" which provides "security for all individuals." This, he likened to "God's work," and said that "the day the Conservative party thinks it's only concerned with economic growth and not social justice is the day Canadians will forget about the party." When he was finished, his audience stood and cheered. Pat Croften, a Clark supporter from Esquimault-Saanich, spoke for

143

everyone, "David, we've heard a lot of political speeches in the last few years but I've never heard a better one than you just gave," and they stood and applauded again.

Flying in a small seaplane from Victoria to Vancouver, a relaxed David Crombie spoke easily about his shift in emphasis: "This is my turf—I'm comfortable on it." Did he think he could win? "I know it's a long shot—I've got to work for victory and be happy in defeat." He thought back to the day in caucus a year before when almost all his colleagues had revolted against the appointment of former Clark Secretary of State David MacDonald as the leader's policy advisor. MacDonald was known as a Red Tory and Otto Jelinek, a strong supporter of Brian Mulroney, denounced him as a friend of communists. "I stood up," said Crombie, "and defended him as the kind of guy who should be in this party."

David Crombie seemed pleased that he had stood up again.

* * *

Just a few minutes before the results of the first ballot were announced, Crombie turned to David Dyer, sitting behind him in the candidate's box, and asked how many votes he should expect. "I didn't have the heart to tell him," Dyer later said, "and so I *doubled* what I really thought and told him '140'. I was the most pleasantly surprised person in the box when we got 116."

Two things had contributed to Dyer's accidental accuracy: a fine and touching speech to the convention and a small stampede of "white knights" riding in from Ontario.

Once again Crombie had taken the high road in his remarks on Friday night. He walked proudly, and confidently from his box directly to the stage, escorted by supporters who twirled bright yellow umbrellas which amplified their strength. He had drawn the poorest speaking position of the lot, following John Gamble with only Neil Fraser to come. Moments before, runners from the Mulroney, Clark and Crosbie camps had gone through the crowd imploring their people to stay through Crombie's speech. They were not disappointed they stayed. In remarks addressed more to the television audience than to the delegates he sold his party as one in which "we are our brothers and our sisters keepers" in upholding social justice and in a "hunger for a sense of community." He told them what it meant to be a Tory and appealed to everyone to consider joining

144

the party, even Canada's native people—he was the only candidate to refer to them. "If you believe that we are only as old as our doubts and despair, but we are as young as our faith and our dreams, you are not alone. There are three thousand hearts beating with your's here tonight." Crombie directly attacked John Crosbie when he defiantly said "we are not second-class Americans... not Little Orphan Annie" and obliquely criticized Brian Mulroney for painting a "scenario of desperation" and chided him for offering women chivalry instead of justice. "It may be sweet, but it's not equality."

At the end, a lot more than Crombie's supporters stood and clapped. The loudest cheering came from Joe Clark's section where everyone stood. They applauded a voice of moderation and a potential ally. Clark went over to the railing that separated his section from Crombie's and enthusiastically pumped his hand. Flora MacDonald kissed him. "That's the speech I'd have liked to give," she said proudly.

Crombie's supporters were delirious: their candidate had done them proud. When Ontario's Deputy Premier Robert Welch then joined them in Crombie's box, raising David's hand high, a few even entertained a thought of the impossible. Was Welch's visit a signal from Premier Davis or the Ontario organization? In a way it was. For days it had been assumed that a number of delegates controlled by Davis would be supporting Michael Wilson. Crombie had been disappointed, but not surprised at this prospect. Having shunned them in the past it was hard to ask their support. He tried calling a number of Ontario cabinet ministers at different points in the campaign—"I gritted my teeth, prayed to my God and dialled the numbers"—but met with little success. But on Friday afternoon, Premier Davis told some of those closest to him that neither of the candidates from Ontario should be embarrassed. And so Welch joined Crombie with the premier's blessing and Ontario Attorney General Roy McMurtry worked the crowd that evening asking everyone he could find for "one vote for David."

* * *

Among the losers, Michael Wilson and David Crombie stood apart as national political figures. Both had been prominent ministers in the Clark government, both had reputations for accomplishments. But Crombie and Wilson were never in the game of convention politics as it was played

145

in 1983. Both of them waged creditable public campaigns but neither had an adequate organizational network. As a result, neither or them was able to contest delegate elections and, outside their own province their efforts to win support were almost totally unproductive. Seventy-five per cent (75%) of Wilson's vote and 60 per cent of Crombie's came from Ontario. In all of the other nine provinces Wilson received only 36 votes and Crombie 46.

It was not just that they lacked contacts outside Ontario. They were not in touch with the attitudes and concerns of people in the other provinces. Wilson had demonstrated a fundamental misunderstanding of the nature of regionalist feeling in the Western and Atlantic provinces and, despite his commendable efforts to learn French, had shown that he did not really understand the complexities of relations between Quebec and the rest of the country. Crombie seemed to have a better understanding of the elements of regionalism, but he could not escape the symbolism of the fact that he had been mayor of Toronto.

Crombie had another problem with symbols that was more of his own making. By insisting on calling himself a "Red Tory"[2] he placed himself on the fringe of the party. The term is not one that party members feel comfortable with because of its left-wing and extremist connotations. This was all the worse for him because in 1983 the symbols that were important in the party were those that proclaimed pride in a right-wing identity.

On the positive side, by the end of the campaign both Crombie and Wilson had preserved their dignity and enhanced their reputations. Wilson's standing was more improved by campaigning than any other candidate's. Forty-three per cent (43%) reported that the campaign had raised their opinion of him. Crombie's Red Tory identification had made him less attractive, but the qualities that had helped him win the affection of his constituents in Toronto had the same impact on the delegates.

The personal qualities of these two men and the campaigns they ran confirmed that they belonged in the major leagues of public life. 1983, however, was simply not their year to win the pennant.

"Pocklington... one hundred and two..."
"Gamble... seventeen"

In its cover story of April 11, *Maclean's* magazine told its readers, "the voice of the new right will be heard clearly at the June 10-11 Tory leadership convention in Ottawa. More important, its votes could decisively shape the party for years in the future."[3] For most journalists and many Conservatives this was the big story of the 1983 convention campaign. The party was heading toward a showdown over its ideological direction. Its commitment to the pragmatic interventionist style of government that characterizes welfare-state capitalism would be challenged by neo-conservatives supporting a return to a purer free market system.

The new right is a movement which advocates the unravelling of the web of state regulation of the economy, the elimination of virtually all of the redistributive activities of government, and massive reduction in the public sector share of national expenditures. Its prescriptions are based on the belief that collective well-being can only be maximized if each individual is encouraged to pursue self-enrichment.

While the new right finds its identifying focus in economic theory, it has attracted people with a wide diversity of concerns. The anti-government thrust of its liberal ideas permits the new right to absorb almost any group which has a grievance that can be redressed by curtailing or rolling back government's involvement in society. In addition, it has found allies among moral conservatives who deplore the secular values of contemporary society, and social conservatives who believe the fabric of society is being threatened by welfare and by a justice system that is too lenient with criminals.

In the United States, which has provided both the intellectual inspiration and the organizational model for the Canadian new right, the leaders of the movement have come not from the corporate business world, but from entrepreneurial sectors such as real estate and the service industries. They tend to be people who have become wealthy through their own enterprise and salesmanship, successful wheelers and dealers who operate in rapid growth areas of the economy that have been relatively free of government control; people like Peter Pocklington.

* * *

Peter Pocklington looked out of place, waiting in the lobby of the Toronto Tory establishment's staid Albany Club. Some of the men who filed past him to the cloak room below and the myriad of private dining rooms beyond recognized him. His longish golden hair, full beard and ice-blue eyes combine to give him an evangelical, almost Christ-like appearance that one doesn't forget. Few noticed the expensively tailored suit, but everyone stared at the dark Gucci purse he clasped in his hand. Pocklington felt a little out of place too. Two of the things Peter Pocklington is most proud of are his uncanny ability to know what people want, which explains his financial success, and the fact that he has reached the top on his own terms, with no major benefactors and no government assistance. The Albany Club, by contrast, is symbolic of a world in which knowing or caring what people want and making it on your own are less urgent priorities than making the right connections, socially and politically.

Pocklington hated government of any political party and studiously avoided politicians. But he had gone to the Albany Club that spring day in 1982 to ask the advice of one of the few political types he knew, Ralph Lean, who had most recently raised money for Art Eggleton's mayoralty race in Toronto, (Although Eggleton is a Liberal many Conservatives supported his candidacy in order to oust the left leaning mayor, John Sewell.) Lean is a Toronto lawyer who met Pocklington in the mid-1970s, when both men joined the board of directors of the Holiday Rent-A-Car Company. He had always admired the Edmontonian's business acumen, but what he heard that day at the Conservative stronghold made him doubt his sanity. Pocklington wanted to be prime minister, and to accomplish that had decided he should run for the leadership of the Progressive Conservative party. Never mind that there was no leadership vacancy at the moment—"We'll see about that," Pocklington had answered—where would support in the party, to which he was a stranger, come from, Lean wondered? But he knew enough about Pocklington not to question his resolve and so Lean nodded his agreement to help, and suggested first that they hire a pollster to determine exactly where "the candidate" stood in the public's eye. Michael Adams, president of the small Toronto-based Environics firm, was engaged and by May his work showed that Pocklington had fairly high name recognition throughout the country; although many people confused him with another Western entrepreneur and (then) hockey team owner, Nelson Skalbania.[4]

* * *

Pocklington decided to run for the leadership because he believed the government was ruining the country. More specifically, the Liberal's National Energy Programme was ruining his financial empire. Pocklington's principal corporate vehicle is the Pocklington Financial Corporation, which controls the financial institution, Fidelity Trust. Fidelity's cash enabled Pocklington to expand his holdings in the 1970s by buying heavily into the booming Alberta real estate market. But, when the NEP was passed in 1980, business in Alberta suffered and the floor fell out of the real estate market. The value of the declared assets of Fidelity Trust plummeted, and the all-important, government-regulated ratio between assets and consumer and corporate deposits was violated.

The federal government closely monitored Fidelity Trust, and when it determined that its borrowing limits had been exceeded, ordered Pocklington to inject new capital into the company ($16 million, according to Pocklington) or sell. The company's yearly permit was reduced to running on a series of two-week operating licences.

Pocklington was depressed and began to talk privately to people that "someone" was out to get him. He looked to the Conservatives but saw that they had squandered power, and his knowledge of "the people" told him that Clark would never be popular enough to win a majority government and reverse the disastrous Liberal policies. The solution to the conundrum, he said later, was to "stop Clark at any cost." So Pocklington began a speaking tour in the fall of 1982 designed to raise his profile and promote the cause of getting rid of Joe Clark as a first step to ousting the Liberals. His message was his own story of how he had gone from rags to riches and would be damned if he was going to rags again. He had never been a public speaker before, but his tale was told convincingly and hundreds came out at each stop to listen to the quixotic entrepreneur from Edmonton.

It was all "designed to cause discontent," Pocklington explained. He wanted Conservatives to consider that there was an alternative to Joe Clark. "[I was] a new guy trying to crash the gates of the party, but I was the only one saying what the people were thinking."

Whether to cause discontent or to raise Pocklington's profile, his tour was highly successful. It had been organized by a young staff assistant, Bill Campbell, who had political ambitions of his own. Campbell, an admirer of the success of the new right movement in the United States, had sought the PC nomination for the riding of Edmonton East in 1982. Although he brought out a large number of like-minded people to support his

149

nomination, superior Clark forces backing candidate Bill Lesick simply out-organized his team. Campbell, nonetheless, learned a valuable lesson about managing a political candidacy and discovered a new organizational resource: the many Amway distributors who were also sympathetic to the new right ideology. In 1982, Campbell would draw on the Amway network across Canada to help get out the crowds for Pocklington as he toured.

The Amway network comprised the extended chain of dealerships and sub-dealerships that makes up the company's sales force. Amway is itself more like a movement than a business. Its simple product line has been transformed into the basis for large profits through the use of highly-sophisticated motivational techniques. These techniques reinforce the message that anyone can become rich relying only on resources of personality and the drive to succeed. Amway dealers are animated by a religious-like commitment to the spirit of free enterprise and this commitment has got them deeply involved in the new right in the United States. Amway's leaders had provided platforms for Pocklington at dealers' meetings in 1982. He was also invited to speak at the company's convention in Vancouver in the fall of that year.

As the Winnipeg general meeting approached, Campbell focussed his efforts more closely on the delegates going to the meeting. Knowing his own style as a salesman was most successful with young people, Campbell attended a number of meetings of YPC's and PC campus associations in December and January to promote the idea of voting in Winnipeg for a leadership convention. In Toronto, at the large gathering of the Ontario PC Youth Association in January, Campbell took a suite in the luxurious King Edward Hotel and invited up a steady stream of young men and women to encourage their dissent. He handed out $100 cheques to those favouring a leadership review and claiming to be financially strapped. "Perhaps a dozen," he admits.

On January 19th, Campbell's cause was helped by the appearance of a public opinion survey, released by the Gallup organization, which stated that most Canadians believed that the Conservatives under Joe Clark could not beat the Liberals under John Turner. The poll showed, however, that Alberta Premier Peter Lougheed and Ontario's William Davis could defeat Turner. The impact of this nationally reported story was enormous. The Turner candidacy was the question in the back of most Tories' minds and this answer confirmed their worst fears. It was never established who had commissioned the poll or distributed its results. The material arrived on the desks of a number of national news organizations in unmarked brown envelopes and, when contacted, Gallup would only admit that the material received was, in fact, a copy of a Gallup document. They would not identify its sponsor nor whether they had actually conducted the poll or merely verified the analysis of some other company's research.

A few weeks before, Bill Campbell, on behalf of Peter Pocklington, had asked Michael Adams of the Environics research firm to conduct a poll on the Turner candidacy and other questions, the responses to which, according to Campbell, were "uncannily similar" to the Gallup material. Both he and Pocklington denied that they paid Gallup to run or verify their survey, although the latter agreed that it was "virtually identical" to the one he received from Adams.[5] Whatever the poll's origin, the Gallup imprimatur gave the survey credibility and left the door open for Pocklington and others to challenge Clark. It was, as Bill Campbell described it, "the trigger" of the gun aimed at the leader's head.

Politically, Pocklington's candidacy had three practical advantages. He had the personal wealth to mount a national campaign, his prominence attracted media attention, and he had connections to a network (Amway's) outside the party which gave him a means to fight in the constituencies.

Ideologically, Pocklington remained, both in self-identification and the perception of others, a candidate of the new right. His orthodoxy was perhaps most clearly expressed in his proposal for a flat rate tax system, eliminating all of the subsidies and incentives of the existing system. In addition, he proposed deep and broad-scale cuts in government spending, deregulation, and the "privatization" of all crown corporations performing functions that "can better be provided through the private sector" (including Petro-Canada, Air Canada, and Canada Post.)

Not all of his political ideas, however, squared with those conventionally identified with the "new right." For one thing, Pocklington believed that in Canada the tradition of a mixed economy "contributed significantly to our development," and that collectively members of society had a responsibility to one another that required government to maintain "a safety net below which no one should be allowed to fall." In addition, he extended the libertarian orientation implicit in the theory of limited government to justify legalized abortion and the legalization of the use of marijuana—two positions which run counter to those of moral conservatives.

While Pocklington may have seemed an idealist in his campaign for freedom from too much government, he quickly showed himself a pragmatist in organizing his campaign to win the leadership. His initial (pre-campaign) planning team consisted of Bill Campbell, Ralph Lean, and Michael Adams. They recommended that Pocklington not attend the Winnipeg meeting so as to avoid being tagged by the press as one of the persons behind the review initiative. Once the results and Clark's decisions were announced, however, Pocklington was on the phone immediately, "ecstatic" about the results and urging that the campaign begin. Lean shopped for a campaign manager and, when Paul Weed, who had managed Claude Wagner in 1976, turned them down, he settled on Erick (Skip) Willis, a consultant who had some experience with PC politics in Manitoba. Willis in turn recommended academic and pollster Peter Regenstreif for the role of campaign strategist. Both Willis and Regenstreif were hired by the Pocklington Financial Corporation for handsome amounts plus, in the best sporting style, incentive bonuses. (Regrettably, neither one qualified for the additional payment as the unstated number of votes was not attained.)

It was Pocklington himself, however, who pulled off the biggest coup when he successfully recruited the eminent Edmonton accountant Eric Geddes, senior partner of Price Waterhouse, to co-chair the campaign with Lean. As a former national vice-president of the party, a major fundraiser for Peter Lougheed and a prominent, mainstream Conservative, Geddes' support gave the Pocklington campaign considerable credibility. "He was a good friend who came to me for help," Geddes explained. "He's been very good for this city [Edmonton].... and while his causes are simply stated, they're deeply felt." Geddes recognized Pocklington's naiveté in party matters but, with an experienced team now at the helm, and an almost unlimited Pocklington budget, he was confident the brash candidate would make his mark.

On other fronts, Bill Campbell, adopting a tactic from the American new right, had set up a separate organization to mobilize the Amway network. Officially no longer part of the campaign, Campbell, nonetheless, directed his efforts towards winning delegates for Pocklington. Campbell's Canada Project 2000 Limited held seminars across the country to explain to groups largely recruited by Amway dealers, how to pack delegate selection meetings to elect "free enterprise" slates. This effort resulted in the running of slates by Pocklington in almost as many ridings as Crosbie and more ridings than Crombie and Wilson combined.

While Bill Campbell's recruits worked the ridings and Pocklington jetted across the country enjoying and using the media attention attracted by his celebrity status, the other candidate of the new right, John Gamble, was waging his own grim battle to achieve recognition as a serious contender.

* * *

John Gamble was first elected as an MP when he defeated the Liberal Defence Minister Barnett Danson, in the Toronto area York-North riding. From the outset, Gamble was ill-at-ease with Clark as leader. When the short-lived PC government fell, it only confirmed his reservations about "Red Tory" leadership. In his own riding of York-North, an organization promoting Clark's ouster sprang up. Chaired by riding association president, Tom Viersen, the PC Review Committee advocated a leadership convention as the only means to "clear the air" following the Tories' defeat, and promoted the candidacy of "men like John Gamble" for the job of leader. At the 1981 general meeting in Ottawa, the Review Committee was the only outwardly visible, organized dissent to Joe Clark and when 33.9 per cent of the delegates voted in favour of a convention, the committee and John Gamble took much of the credit.

In the two years between the meeting and Winnipeg, Gamble had also discovered the Amway Corporation. On two occasions he journeyed to the United States to speak to the organization's conventions and confirmed to them his steadfast commitment to rid Canada of statist Liberals. Like Pocklington, he believed the only way to do that was by removing Joe Clark and replacing him with a staunch small "c" conservative. At that point, Gamble was the only candidate who fit the bill.

Unfortunately, by January 1983, the question of who would replace Clark had become rather more problematical. Better known and more influential members of the party seemed more likely to benefit from Clark's discomfiture. The MP from York-North persisted, nonetheless, in his goal of attaining the leadership. His frustration with the direction of both the party and the country would find an outlet in his candidacy and an articulation in the central theme of his campaign.

"This is a democracy! The public will *will* be done!" Thus spoke John Gamble to 150 cheering supporters in Victoria Square, a tiny hamlet north east of Toronto. The occasion was the formal announcement of his candidacy for the leadership of the Conservative party; the subject under discussion was capital punishment. "We will have the reintroduction of capital punishment in this country because the majority of Canadians want it." With those words Gamble climaxed a thirty-minute tirade against the nation's "elites": the Liberals who were "an elected monarchy"; the NDP who were "tied to union bosses"; the bureaucrats who were stealing our money, and the national media who distorted the truth. These were the groups that thwarted the public will, who refused to give the country back to the people. From crown corporations to social assistance programmes to foreign aid, all would fall under this Jacobin's blade. "We must stop the handouts," he exhorted his audience.

The crowd cheered John Gamble that day in March, but three months later when he arrived in Ottawa for the convention there was no one to greet him at the airport. In between he had criss-crossed the country telling the people he knew what they wanted. There were always audiences to address, but no swarm of volunteers rallied to the Gamble banner; no big-name party leaders pitched in with his campaign. Even the Amway contingent, who provided a platform for both new-right candidates, preferred the more polished and better organized Pocklington candidacy. It had become clear that what the people wanted was not to be found in the new-right proselytizing of either Peter Pocklington and John Gamble.

* * *

The truth was, that for many Tories, Gamble and Pocklington were outsiders who made them feel uncomfortable. The measure of this feeling became clear when delegates were asked if there were any candidates for whom they would never vote under any circumstances: 47 per cent of the delegates named Gamble, and 37 per cent named Pocklington.

It is true that on some issues their views were close to those of the delegates. Eighty per cent (80%) of the delegates said they wanted to restore capital punishment, 60 per cent (60%) thought Canada should support President Reagan's tough line in dealing with the Soviet Union, 55 per cent said they would cut spending on foreign aid, and over 60 per cent wanted a significant reduction in the degree of public ownership in the economy. Yet when the delegates were asked which candidates held sound views on policy, only 14.5 per cent mentioned Pocklington and only 5.7 per cent named Gamble.

What the delegates saw was that the new right involved more than a set of issue positions. It embraced a general outlook, an ideological view that sought to reduce all problems to simple elements.

The delegates rejected this reductionism because, as one put it, the world "isn't all *that* simple." That this is a common view was illustrated by the delegates' reaction to Pocklington's flat-rate tax proposal: over 71 per cent of them opposed it on the ground that "because their problems are often distinctive, different groups and different sectors of the economy need different kinds of tax treatment."

Perhaps even more important in the party's response to Pocklington and Gamble was the fact that the ideological position they struck was not consistent with the party's tradition. Robert Stanfield had made this point repeatedly in urging the party to avoid the prescriptions of the new right. In the Conservative party's tradition, he pointed out, "economic policy was and is subservient"[6] to the party's larger goals. The party has always accepted that state intervention may be necessary to achieve national objectives or fulfil social responsibilities that transcend the values of the market. This is not just an element of the party's heritage, it is what the party believes today.[7]

Thus while deregulation, reductions in government spending, and a curtailment of public ownership are all part of the agenda of most Tories, a majority of delegates approach these issues pragmatically.

Stanfield has also made the point that the Conservative Party has always been a party of consensus, trying to bring together different groups and different interests. The delegates also affirmed their commitment to this principle when, by a 2-to-1 margin, they said "the party should not take extreme stands but should try to appeal to as broad a group of opinions as possible."

It is this point, that the party values diversity and not exclusiveness, that in the final analysis explains why Peter Pocklington and John Gamble could spend over a million dollars in their efforts to win the party leadership and between them only attract four per cent of its support.

"Fraser...five"

On the Friday before balloting, the delegates and the Canadian viewing public were treated to the speeches of the leadership candidates. In the interest of fairness and the normal traditions of conventions, each candidate was alloted an equal amount of speaking time and the order of their presentation was determined by the luck of the draw. Neil Fraser, the anti-metric crusader, was to speak last.

Outside of the public accounts of his civil service firing for criticism of the federal government's metric conversion policy, little was known of Neil Fraser within the Progressive Conservative party. He had no real history in party politics or the Progressive Conservative party and he knew virtually none of the partisans who met in Ottawa to select their new leader. During the convention, he wandered the corridors and elevators, alone, without the normal coterie of followers, aides, and cameramen attending the other candidates. He sported a tartan ribbon on his jacket as his campaign symbol, but only he could be found wearing one. His isolation within the party was probably best typified by his choice of the man who was to introduce him that Friday night, Mike McCutcheon. McCutcheon, another champion of single-issue causes, had been unable to get either delegate or press credentials to the convention. He had met Fraser only one time before and agreed to introduce him just 24 hours before the speeches were to take place, since it was the only way he (McCutcheon) could get onto the floor of the Civic Centre.

Yet, despite his outsider status, Fraser had put up his $5,000 deposit and managed to gather the necessary signatures for his nomination. Now he was to have his 25 minutes of prime-time television, in a time slot normally reserved for top-rated shows such as *Dallas* and *The Dukes of Hazzard*. CTV had decided well in advance they would cut Fraser off after five minutes and resume with their normal programming; and while the CBC agonized over a similar decision, in the end they covered his speech in its entirety.

So under the auspices of the Progressive Conservative Party of Canada and before a national television audience, Neil Fraser gave his vision of the country which included more than the abolition of the metric system. In part he said:

> ...The Conservative party along with the Liberal party has followed a policy of appeasement towards Quebec and I tell you it never works. You see we have one seat in Quebec. Diefenbaker was reasonably fair; he had a minimum of eight and a maximum of fifty. Think about it.
>
> You see what has happened in Quebec under the Liberal regime is like [sic] every part of Canada is giving a blood transfusion to Quebec. We've

got New Brunswick air base in Chatham … gone to Bagotville.[sic] Halifax-the naval reserve goes to Quebec. We've got a rip-off by Quebec Hydro for Newfoundland power. We've got a federal government that brags about the end of the Crow Rate for the benefit of Quebec farmers. Now I tell you, why would you say that with all that transfusion, Quebec is not the strongest province in Canada? I'll tell you why…

…at the same time that they are getting that transfusion, they are cutting their wrists. Our blood, their blood is rolling out on the floor, because without English signs they're killing their tourist trade. They're sending their entrepreneurs out of Quebec. Those who speak English — whether they be Scottish, Jewish or what have you — they've sent over a hundred and fifty thousand out in the last ten years. Well it's up to Quebecers for you to change that. You see my father taught me that the majority of people in Quebec are fair and reasonable people, and I believe that.

Above the dwindling crowds, in a lounge set aside for CBC commentators, Lise Bissonnette, editor of *Le Devoir*, watched the speech on television in disbelief. Turning to the other observers who joined her she said, "If Radio Canada is broadcasting a translation of this, it will set the Conservative Party back 10 years. Everything he's saying fits the Quebecer's stereotype of a typical Tory."

In the end there were no more than 100 people left in the Civic Centre when Neil Fraser was almost forcibly removed from the stage by convention co-chairmen Peter Elzinga and Claude Dupras. The next day he would receive five votes on the first ballot…the second lowest total ever accorded a PC leadership candidate.[8]

* * *

In many ways, Neil Fraser's candidacy tells much about the Progressive Conservative party. Whether one can agree with him or not, and whether one believes such views have or do not have a legitimate place being aired on national television, there is no denying that Fraser believes passionately in what he is saying. His message is one of protest against a system that will not accommodate his form of individualistic expression. And there are thousands of people in Canada who share his opinions.

The Progressive Conservative party attracts people like Neil Fraser because it provides the only legitimate channel through which they can express their political views. The Conservative party performs this function both because it is a right-of-centre party and because it is a party that is usually in opposition.

Some of the people the Conservative party attracts are simply those who, like Neil Fraser, have developed, for idiosyncratic reasons, a passionate concern with one issue. Others have more general anti-elite feelings arising from the fact that they belong to middle-class groups who feel themselves under social pressure. The Conservative party appeals to this group because it is not part of the liberal-bureaucratic establishment. The problem for the party is that, although the angry views these outsiders express are as much outside the mainstream of the party as they are outside the mainstream of the country, the fact that they are expressed from within the Conservative party means that the party becomes identified with them.

In many ways, the NDP in Canada suffers from the same dilemma. Any public perception of extremism will attract extremists, and any suggestion of extremism is met with public opposition and, ultimately, electoral failure. Leadership change within the Progressive Conservative party has not and will not alter this fundamental truth of Canadian politics. For the very reason Neil Fraser had no place else to go in 1983, the Progressive Conservatives will continue to attract people like him.

Part III

OTTAWA
JUNE 11, 1983

Ballot Two

CLARK, Joe	1,085
MULRONEY, Brian	1,021
CROSBIE, John	781
CROMBIE, David	67

6

"If the numbers are right..."

The vultures had gathered at the foot of Michael Wilson's section of the Ottawa Civic Centre. Smaller groups of Clark, Mulroney and Crosbie workers had clustered in front of David Crombie's and Peter Pocklington's boxes too, but it was Wilson's carcass that was thought most worth picking. For one thing, they reasoned, he would be the fattest, with more delegates than the others; for another, no one was quite sure what Michael Wilson would do faced with a vote too low to realistically continue in the race; and, for a third, many doubted that Wilson's grip on his delegates was very strong. Crombie and Pocklington, it was assumed, had a much firmer hold over their people—delegates who were drawn to a person or an ideology, a commitment which they would find it hard to abandon. By contrast, Wilson supporters had been attracted by his Ontario origins or his middle ground policies; further many viewed his merely as a stop-gap candidacy, a place to deposit a vote until it was clear how the convention was going. So the vultures waited and, when the results of the first ballot were announced, moved in to feast.

Wilson and his supporters were stunned. One hundred and forty-four votes was less than half of what they had expected. The vaunted Ontario backing had failed to materialize and the fanciful dream of a Wilson compromise victory, which some had entertained for a few hours, had been dashed. A few supporters left quickly, their minds already made about whom they would turn to next. The half dozen apron-clad Clark workers who were waiting to pin campaign buttons on the defectors managed to grab off a couple of the Wilson contingent. Ron Atkey, a

161

Clark loyalist, led away one woman he had been courting all week, her hand clutching the bright yellow Clark scarf he had given her. The majority, however, remained. Would Wilson stay in for a second ballot, his delegates wondered, and would they continue to support him even if he did? It was a time of shock and most sat forward in their seats letting their faded emerald green Wilson signs fall limply at their sides, as they waited for Wilson to announce his decision.

But Michael Wilson wasn't sure what to do. As dozens of reporters craned from the floor to see him, hollering for news of where he was going, Wilson's chief aides and advisors shielded him from scrutiny. Wilson was the most devastated of all the people in the arena that day. He'd come so far, worked so hard, been promised so much…for a lousy 144 votes. He was visibly shaken by the results and, for a moment, seemed oblivious to the voices of his advisors imploring him to make a decision. The telephone ringing in his box broke the trance. It was Pocklington informing him that he was dropping out, would be announcing his support for Mulroney, and asking Wilson to do the same. Wilson pleaded for time.

His press secretary, Sandy Miller, called down to a group of reporters demanding to know how much time was left before the option of withdrawal was removed. If Wilson had not submitted his official notice of withdrawal within 15 minutes his name would appear on the second ballot. "Get me Crombie," he told his convention coordinator, Gord Moore, sitting by the telephone. In the conversation that followed David Crombie informed Wilson he was staying on for another ballot and urged him to do likewise. "We got nothing to lose Mike," he advised. Again Wilson asked for time, and again Miller called down to the reporters to find out how much time was left.

The advice of those around him was unanimous: "Get off the ballot." They did not want to risk further embarrassment. Wilson finally agreed and scribbled his name on the sheet proffered him. Bob Jones, his official agent, who five and a half years before had welcomed Wilson into the party, rushed it through the jammed arena to the officials' table, cancelling his candidacy. That much had been decided; but it was still not clear if Michael Wilson would attempt to deliver his delegates to another candidate.

Only a few moments before he had entertained the idea that Peter Pocklington and David Crombie might come to him as the leader among the second tier candidates. Pocklington had even made public his decision to do so, "if the numbers [were] right," and all three had agreed to consult with each other before making a move. Together, they had reasoned, their numbers might represent a potent force, a community of candidates able to compete with the front-runners for influence. That notion had vanished with the results of the first ballot.

Wilson had been courted by all three of the major contenders. Early in his campaign, rumours abounded that he was merely a stalking horse for Joe Clark and that, when the final decision had to be made, the loyal Clark supporter who owed his high standing in the party to the rapid promotions given him by Clark would return to the fold. A chastened Clark would then welcome back a now more politically potent Mike Wilson. Believing this hearsay to have been started by Clark's organization, an angry Wilson had cut off all communication between his group and the former leader's. For his part, Clark continued to praise Wilson (as he did Crombie) at every available opportunity, content in believing that, in the end, he would return.

Lines to the camps of the other two contenders were left considerably more open. Wilson's closest political advisors all seemed predisposed to Brian Mulroney as their second choice. Throughout the latter part of the campaign, Michael Perik and Pat Kinsella met frequently with Mulroney representatives Frank Moores, Peter White and Michel Cogger, and Sandy Miller arranged for Wilson to meet quietly with Moores while on a visit to Montreal. Wilson's closest personal advisor, his brother-in-law Doug Lawson, regularly consulted former national director Paul Curley, who was also quietly helping Mulroney. Lawson and Wilson often went to the protean Curley for advice. Wilson had countered this pull towards Mulroney with his own meetings with John Crosbie. On two occasions he had personally sat down with Crosbie "to discuss scenarios." At one meeting late in May, Wilson had gone to Crosbie's Holiday Inn suite in Toronto for breakfast, but had insisted that the talks be kept a secret even from Wilson's own staff.

It is a delicate business when two competing men, or representatives of each, meet to prepare the way for a possible alliance. If it is to be fruitful, the stronger contender must be ever mindful of the lesser's pride. Both Crosbie and Mulroney were careful never to let Wilson hear that they anticipated his defeat. Whenever either of the major contenders met with Wilson, there was always praise for the way he had conducted his campaign, a sharing of information, and the subtle establishment of the grounds of mutual interest. Crosbie and Mulroney each believed he had a shot at getting Wilson, until events at the convention almost scuppered the chances of one of them.

As the convention opened, rumours once again were flying. The most persistent had Michael Wilson, David Crombie, and Peter Pocklington in a deal with Brian Mulroney. Depending on what Joe Clark's vote was on the first ballot Saturday, the story went, the trio would either go to Mulroney right away or stay on a second ballot to determine the flow of events. (If Clark had between 1,000 and 1,150 votes they'd go to Mulroney, otherwise they'd stand pat.) When Michael Wilson was confronted with this rumour on Thursday morning, he was furious. His people *had* met with Mulroney's and the number of delegates Clark received *was* the subject of some of the scenarios they drew. But Wilson, still confident at that time of receiving a rush of support from Ontario, had made no deals and Mulroney's people tactfully had proposed none. "If that's the word they're putting out," Wilson vociferated, "there will be no deal." That was how Clark had played the game earlier and Wilson would not stand for such presumptions from anyone.

Mulroney's people had quickly assured Wilson's that they were not the source of these rumours and Wilson appeared calmed by this, but for the final two days of the convention there were no further official talks between the two sides.

Wilson had not been the only candidate to suffer from the inadvertent exuberance of Mulroney's organizers. On Thursday night, a large horde of supporters had accompanied Mulroney on a visit to David Crombie's tent in the park adjacent to the National Arts Centre—an ingenious drop-in centre where delegates could sip draft beer and listen to the music of the Tommy Ambrose orchestra. Mulroney perhaps expected to cement good relations with Crombie; instead, he only succeeded in upsetting tentative plans made between the two sides.

The impromptu visit had been arranged earlier in the day between Chris Speyer, Crombie's point man in talks with other candidates, and Mulroney's Michel Cogger, who had seconded Speyer's nomination in his unsuccessful 1981 bid for the party presidency. Cogger and Frank Moores had called on Speyer and Crombie campaign manager, Tom Watson, with the idea. After consulting with Crombie by telephone, the Mulroney people were assured their candidate was "welcome to come over for a beer." What followed was a lot more than a casual drink. Senior Mulroney organizers claim that in their talks they had come "close to an understanding with Speyer" that if the numbers [were] right (Crombie out of the running and Mulroney leading next to Clark), Crombie would go to them. The visit, they said, was intended to show this, pointing, as proof to the fact that Speyer had asked for the sheet music to Mulroney's campaign song so that the band could properly herald his arrival. So all evening, a number of Mulroney's people began leaking word of the upcoming visit to key national reporters. By 10:00 o'clock, the appointed hour, a mob had filled the Crombie tent waiting to witness an endorsement.

The Quebecer arrived on cue to the strains of his "Together" theme and as the fervour of the crowd chanting "Brian…David…Brian …David" rose, so too did David Crombie's anger. When Mulroney left, the normally easy-going Crombie was shouting, complaining about their visitors' assumption of a deal. He ordered his communications advisor, Bill Marshall, to change the headlines on the "Daily Runner," Crombie's morning tabloid circulated to all the delegates, to read "Crombie to the others: LET'S NOT DO A DEAL" in order to offset the inference of Mulroney's visit.

The following day, Mulroney attempted to make up for his embarrassment. He sent an apologetic, handwritten note to Crombie and his wife Shirley, who had been accidentally shoved by the jostling crowd, and his organizers ordered large numbers of their people to attend Crombie's presentations during the day's policy sessions and his plenary speech that evening. As they had in the case of the Wilson rumours, Mulroney organizers were once again forced into a hasty retreat and could only hope their ill-advised initiative would not be fatal to their overall plans.

However upset Crombie was, the incident at his tent was not a major factor in his decision to remain on the second ballot. Two other things were. First, as Crombie had told John Crosbie on Thursday morning, when the Newfoundlander had paid a secret call to his Chateau Laurier hotel suite, Crombie was in the race to the bitter end, "till they throw me out," he said. Second and more important, Crombie wanted to stop Joe Clark! Crombie and his organizers, perhaps optimistically, reasoned that Clark's vote was soft and that many of his delegates would likely desert the former leader on the second ballot. Crombie, as the only other moderate in the race, would be a logical place for some of them to go. Conversely, if Crombie dropped out of the race, his endorsement of another candidate would probably not prevent a number of his delegates from going to Clark anyway. So for both reasons—to enhance his position and to hurt Joe Clark, Crombie stayed on the ballot.[1] Besides, he told Wilson on the telephone, with Fraser and Gamble in the race, the first ballot was like a dry run. The votes of the two low men would merely up the ante for the real game which would start on the second ballot, now that everyone was aware of the level of support for Clark. Wilson wasn't sure. Pocklington had seen it differently, he said.

Peter Pocklington shared with David Crombie the same overriding concern in making his decision: how best to eliminate Joe Clark; but he had interpreted the results of the first ballot in another way. Clark was, as he saw it, only 400 votes from victory and that was too close for comfort. To Pocklington, all that mattered were the numbers and that meant Mulroney. The Quebecer was the only safe choice to stop Clark—and the most effective way of ensuring that he did was to support him now.

Pocklington had been wooed actively by both Mulroney and Crosbie. He had surprised them with his organization and what most people believed to be his large number of supporters (estimates ranged from 150 to 180). Further, because of the ideological nature of his campaign and the zeal with which his delegates supported him, it was assumed that he would deliver most of his votes to whomever he chose after his own withdrawal.

His advisors were divided over who should be their second choice. Erik Geddes, his Edmonton-based co-chairman, and Skip Willis, his campaign manager, favoured Crosbie; while Ralph Lean, his Toronto co-chairman, Peter Regenstreif, his strategist, and Bill Campbell, his former employee and organizer, all leaned toward Mulroney. But this was a decision Pocklington would make on his own.

He had conferred privately with each man[2] and had formed his own opinion. In Edmonton, at a secret meeting arranged by Geddes, the Albertan and Newfoundlander had met at the latter's Westin Hotel suite. Crosbie had just returned from his meeting with the Lougheed committee and Pocklington found him to be "uncomfortable."[3] The meeting was strained, with each side only querying the other's progress. Neither man was skillful at small talk and, while Pocklington believed he and Crosbie had much in common on the issues, the outspoken entrepreneur left the meeting less than impressed by his eastern brother.

The two had a considerably more satisfying meeting in Ottawa. At midnight on the Friday night (June 10), only a dozen hours before voting began, Crosbie, along with his manager John Laschinger and his aide Ross Reid, called on Pocklington at the Albertan's hide-out in the Delta Hotel.[4] The Albertan was waiting with his manager Willis and advisors Lean and Regenstreif. Pocklington wasted no time getting to the point. Numbers would be the principal determinant of where he would pledge his second-ballot support, as long as anyone he considered met his minimum terms: a role in a future administration. Specifically, he said, he wanted to head a Royal Commission on taxation, with a mandate to rewrite Canada's income tax laws and to consider his favourite proposal of a flat 20 per cent tax rate for everyone. Crosbie gently suggested that perhaps a House of Commons committee would be a speedier means of reform and that he hoped Pocklington would run for Parliament and play a direct role in the committee. Pocklington agreed that perhaps he should run and suggested that, if he were successful, the finance portfolio might put his talents to best use. Crosbie would not agree to anything specific but assured the businessman that he would have a prominent cabinet role in a Crosbie government. Pocklington seemed pleased with that pledge and said it would all depend on the numbers.

Only moments after the door closed behind the Crosbie party, another group arrived to talk with Pocklington. Brian Mulroney brought with him manager Paul Weed, who had met previously with Ralph Lean, and a surprise guest: the council chairman of Metropolitan Toronto, Paul Godfrey. Mulroney correctly identified Lean as the most influential of Pocklington's advisors and the presence of Godfrey, whom Lean had supported in municipal politics, made the desired positive impression. Pocklington and Mulroney had had one previous secret meeting in late May over breakfast at the Westin Hotel in Toronto. Then, little more had been said than that the two sides would "keep in touch." Not this time. As he had been a few moments before, Pocklington was frank in his demands. Mulroney, like Crosbie, was assuring but not much more specific—the Royal Commission was a possibility, an unspecified cabinet seat a certainty. Pocklington was again pleased and told Mulroney it would all depend on the numbers.

He asked Mulroney what he figured those numbers would be. Paul Weed replied: Clark 1,050; Mulroney 875 to 900; Crosbie 500.

If that was the case, Pocklington said, he would be with him on the second ballot. A few minutes before he had asked Crosbie the same question and Laschinger had predicted: Clark 1,050; Mulroney 800; Crosbie 700.

If *that* turned out to be true, Pocklington had assured them, he would support Crosbie even though he trailed Mulroney. Pocklington's surveys, as well as those shown him by Laschinger and the ones already made public by Southam News, had clearly indicated that Crosbie had greater potential than Mulroney for growth on later ballots. Pocklington had come to find both men acceptable as leaders—they were not Joe Clark and the economic perspective of each seemed similar to his own, although they both were more moderate. His choice would be based on simple arithmetic. Because of Crosbie's greater growth potential, Pocklington was prepared to spot him a number of votes. After Mulroney left, at close to 2:00 a.m., Pocklington and his advisors agreed that 200 would be the cut-off point. If Mulroney's vote exceeded Crosbie's by more than 200, then they would consider the Newfoundlander out of contention.

Pocklington relished his role as potential kingmaker. He had worked long and hard to remove Clark and desperately wanted influence in the system that had hitherto stymied his aspirations. It was he who had forged the potential coalition with the other also-rans. He had spoken frequently to Wilson on the road, and had met privately with Crombie when the two were in Vancouver the last week of May.[5]

The Albertan entrepreneur already believed he had made the difference in keeping Clark's support base low. As his strategist Regenstreif told a gathering of Pocklington supporters less than six hours before the vote, "we've stopped Joe Clark. If it weren't for us there would not have been another western candidate. If we hadn't entered, that stinking little wimp might have gotten in." Now, Pocklington figured, as he left for the arena on voting day, his team would finish Clark off.

When the results of the first ballot were announced, it seemed obvious to Pocklington what had to be done. The also-rans all had disappointingly low totals, and Crosbie had fallen short of the threshold Pocklington had set for him. Mulroney, he concluded, was the only one in a position to stop Clark. There was nothing to be gained by fooling around. "Let's do it now," he had urged Crombie, but Crombie had repeated his decision to stay in. Pocklington could not understand it, any more than he could understand Michael Wilson's dithering.

Wilson faced a dilemma. Like Pocklington, Wilson had data which

168

showed Crosbie as the more popular second choice of the party, but none of his advisors advocated supporting the Newfoundlander. Said one prominent Wilson organizer, "John made it difficult to go to him." He was too much "a one-man show," "stubborn," and with a "temper." He added that some of the Wilson people "saw another Diefenbaker" in Crosbie. All that, plus Crosbie's resistance to learning French, made it next to impossible to recommend endorsing him. Wilson agreed. At a meeting he held that morning with his advisors, Wilson had ruled out Crosbie, unless he were the only alternative to Clark. At the same meeting, some of his people suggested doing nothing was an option to consider. If Crosbie, or Clark (God forbid) did win, it might be in Wilson's best interest to not be tarred by Mulroney's brush. Furthermore, campaign research showed that Mulroney was not popular among Ontario's delegates, the very group Wilson was seen as representing. It was possible, they reasoned, that a large number of Wilson's supporters would not follow him to Mulroney. Endorsing the Quebecer might both disappoint his people and further embarrass him.

Hugh Hanson had been one of the strongest supporters of making no endorsement, but when the results of the first ballot were announced and Wilson again turned to his advisors for input, Hanson was nowhere to be found. The campaign's coordinator Michael Perik, a strong supporter of Mulroney as second choice, had made it clear he was not welcome in the candidate's box. Hanson, from his isolated position at the side of the arena, only learned later that Wilson had twice called out for his advice.

All this was going through Wilson's mind when the telephone again rang. This time he told Pocklington he would join him in walking to Mulroney. The Albertan entrepreneur wasted no time. Wilson had barely stood up and straightened his tie when he heard his name being called. At the foot of his section, beside the gaggle of reporters, stood Pocklington without a jacket, his sleeves rolled back to the elbow, his tie unknotted. He was asking, no demanding, that Wilson "come down here." Wilson's section of the arena was adjacent to Mulroney's—only an aisle and ten feet separated the two men. Obviously unsure of himself, Wilson descended the steps to stand with Pocklington on the floor and together the two men began walking through the crowd, past Mulroney's section in the direction of John Crosbie. Straining reporters, still ignorant of the decision the two had made, began screaming into their microphones, "they're going to Crosbie!"

169

From where he sat, Brian Mulroney must have thought this too. In 1976 he had sat in almost the same spot in the Ottawa Civic Centre and watched others cross the floor in front of him—some heading to Joe Clark, others to Claude Wagner. Mulroney had been in second place on that first ballot too, but no one came to him. It appeared as if there was about to be a replay of 1976; but then Pocklington and Wilson suddenly reversed direction and quickly mounted the stairs where a relieved Mulroney waited to greet them.

Wilson smiled a little sheepishly as Mulroney supporters passed among his former delegates handing out "Brian" stickers, pins and signs. He and Pocklington, along with their wives, took their seats beside Brian and Mila. Michael and Kelly Meighen were also present in the Mulroney box, completing this display of the new Tory "first family." From the floor, David Angus, Mulroney's finance chairman in 1976 and since then a neutral director of the PC Canada Fund, called up to Wilson and signalled his approval of the choice as he mouthed the words "thank you." Wilson nodded his reply.

Not everyone, however, was as happy with the course of events. Some of the people in Wilson's section were refusing to don the Mulroney paraphernalia, while others were visibly upset by the decision. And a number of Crosbie signs also began to spring up. Dissatisfaction was not nearly so evident in what had been the Pocklington section but some supporters were undoubtedly displeased. As the call to vote on the second ballot was issued less than half of the delegates who filed out of the two sections would second Pocklington's and Wilson's choice of Mulroney.

The pessimists among Michael Wilson's advisors had been right and the general view about Pocklington's support had been wrong. On the second ballot, neither man was able to effectively control for whom his delegates would vote. When all the ballots were again counted, John Crosbie, endorsed by only John Gamble and Neil Fraser among the candidates, had enjoyed a vote increase about equal to that of Brian Mulroney. Most of the new arrivals had come from the ranks of the two men who had so authoritatively thrown their support to Mulroney.

Only 49 per cent of his delegates followed Michael Wilson's example and voted for Brian Mulroney. A handful did not vote at all and a few went to David Crombie. 12.5 per cent returned to supporting their former leader, Joe Clark and a full 35 per cent voted for the man Wilson and his organizers had thought unworthy, John Crosbie.

170

Among Peter Pocklington's supporters the results were even more revealing. Although it was widely assumed that Pocklington "could deliver," only half of his delegates accompanied him to Mulroney, the same number voted for John Crosbie anyway.[6] Tory delegates have minds of their own.[7]

Mulroney had held a remarkable 98.8 per cent of his own vote on the second ballot. The handful he lost appears to have gone to Crosbie, but this was more than offset by a group three times as large that he picked up from the Newfoundlander. That was Crosbie's only significant loss—a very small number had gone to Clark and about the same to Crombie on the second ballot.

David Crombie had not fared so well. Only 54 per cent of his delegates remained to fight another ballot. About twelve per cent (12%) joined the ranks of Clark supporters and the same number were drawn to the "clear alternative" Mulroney. More significantly, 23 per cent anticipated their candidate's decision in going to Crosbie.

In one sense Joe Clark had fared best of all. Against almost all predictions he had held 97 per cent of his vote, but the few delegates he had gained from the ranks of Wilson and Crombie delegates could not even make up for those he had lost.

The delegates to the Tory convention in Ottawa were quietly going about their own business. Deals and expectations had little to do with their movement. That didn't stop some people, however, from trying to effect the biggest power brokerage of them all.

* * *

John Laschinger, Crosbie's campaign manager, had hoped to meet with Pocklington's manager Skip Willis right after the first ballot to try to persuade the Albertan to support his man. They had previously arranged to meet after the first ballot at the corner of the stage, but Laschinger had been delayed and Willis was forced to return to his section, so that he could be with Pocklington when he made his move to Mulroney. Thus when Laschinger finally arrived, Willis was not in sight; but, next to the CBC tower, he did encounter three surprisingly friendly western MPs. Bill McKnight, Don Mazankowski and Jake Epp, three Clark supporters, were depressed by their candidate's showing on the first ballot. There was no way, they suspected, that Clark could defeat Mulroney now. He was not close enough to majority; yet, someone had to stop Mulroney. This was a position held by many of the MPs supporting Clark. They had fought tenaciously against their fellow caucus members who were now supporting Mulroney. The ascendancy of these dissidents would do Clark's insiders no good at all. What these three proposed to Laschinger came as a delightful surprise. If Joe's vote did not increase significantly on the second ballot, "to well over 1,100", and Crosbie's did, then they would be prepared to come as a unit to Crosbie on the third ballot and bring as many people as possible with them. A buoyant Laschinger returned to Room 65, the Crosbie dressing room cum command centre to be greeted with more good news.

Crosbie's executive assistant Ross Reid had been standing in his candidate's box shortly after the first ballot vote had been announced. He had just returned from what seemed to be a fruitless mission into Wilson's section and was still wiping the sweat of disappointment from his brow with one of Wilson's green scarves when Doug Black, a Clark emissary carrying a walkie-talkie, informed him that David Small, Clark's delegate tracker, wanted urgently to talk to him on the phone. The two young men were good friends and Reid called immediately. They agreed to meet in 10 minutes beside the barbeque in the parking lot.

At the meeting, he and Small discussed the likely outcome of their candidates' vote on the upcoming ballot. Both were pessimistic about their respective candidate's chances against Mulroney without help from the other and so they quickly came to an understanding. Small proposed that if one of the two candidate's vote fell off and the other's rose "significantly" then there could be the makings of a deal between the two sides. Reid agreed "on that basis" and the two returned to their camps to have the tentative arrangement approved. Laschinger and Crosbie readily agreed to the plan. Combined with what he had heard from the three Clark MPs, Laschinger allowed himself to be a little less pessimistic than he had been when the first ballot results had been announced. Now they waited to hear from Small.

David Small had gone straight to Clark with the proposal. The former leader's initial reaction had been to doubt if he could deliver his vote, especially his Quebec delegates, to the unilingual Crosbie. Small assured him that it was highly unlikely that he would have to try. He knew the delegation intimately from months of tracking and could "almost guarantee" that they would hold fast. But Clark had already been surprised by the size of Crosbie's first ballot showing and thought that anything could be possible over the next two ballots. "I wouldn't entice him with something I couldn't deliver," Clark said later and so refused to make any firm deal. But he did approve sending Lowell Murray and David Small back to meet with Crosbie's people on an exploratory basis after the next ballot. Small went to a pay phone and called Room 65. The meeting was set.

* * *

When John Crosbie heard the results of the second ballot announced, he rose and held his clenched fists in the air. His vote *had* risen "significantly" and Clark had obviously peaked. While the gap between Crosbie and Mulroney remained at 244, he now believed there were a lot of his supporters among those voting for Clark. Now they would realize that the former leader could not win, he reasoned, and that they should come to him. There was still a chance.

Clark too stood when the results were read out, but wasn't sure whether to cheer or not. He was still in first place — his vote had held — and there was no question of him going to Crosbie now. But would the Newfoundlander come to him? Although his vote had gone up, Clark reckoned, Crosbie could not catch either him or Mulroney on the next ballot. He *should* come to me, Clark thought, but then so should the others and no one had come.

* * *

The literature on Canadian politics abounds with theories on the importance of regionalism, ideology, and personal loyalty as principal motivators which determine partisan behaviour. Yet the results of the second ballot — and Joe Clark's lack of growth on that ballot — seem to defy all these theories. While Peter Pocklington had a definite regional basis in his delegate support, neither he nor his supporters would move to Clark despite the fact that he was the only other Western candidate. Mike Wilson's career in politics arguably had risen faster than any other federal politician in the country since 1979, and it had risen, in no small measure, because Joe Clark personally had promoted Wilson into prestigious positions within his caucus and Cabinet. In fact, Mike Wilson liked Joe Clark as a man, and had been one of his staunchest defenders throughout the political storms of 1981 and 1983. Yet, despite personal friendship and political indebtedness, Mike Wilson also could not cross the floor to support Joe Clark. And then there was David Crombie, who, by refusing to declare any intentions and waiting out the second ballot, deliberately hurt Clark's chances of winning—the *only* significant bloc of delegates with any likelihood of supporting Clark as their second choice were Crombie's—as surely as if he had declared outright support for another candidate at that time. Similarly, Crombie himself made much to do about the importance of moderation and compassion for the Progressive Conservative party, and Clark clearly was the only other candidate with any kind of the "Red Tory" credentials Crombie was advocating by the end of the campaign. Yet he too would consider both of the front runners before he would ever even contemplate supporting Clark.

In theory all of these three men—Peter Pocklington, Mike Wilson, and David Crombie—had good reasons to support Clark, as did their supporters. After all, Clark had been national leader for seven years, they knew where he stood, and there should have been a certain comfort sticking with a known commodity during the height of their political fortunes. But *in practice* each of the three men had decided well in advance that they would never support Clark in the event they were forced out of the race.

And they had made their decision precisely *because* Clark had been leader for the last seven years and they knew where he stood. For them, there was no comfort sticking with a known commodity despite a 50 per cent showing in the Gallup Polls, because they had seen their political fortunes slip away all too many times before under Joe Clark's leadership. In short, it was not Pocklington, Wilson and Crombie that sealed Joe Clark's fate on the second ballot. It was seven years as leader and the politics of opposition.

* * *

Clark's leadership had been born under a dark cloud. "Joe Who?" became "the wimp"; Stanfield's detractors became his. Clark could never escape his image. As long as he was winning—the leadership, by-elections, the '79 election—he was tolerated. He was still "the wimp," but "the wimp" had clout. But whenever Clark lost—personal confrontations,

Bill Davis arrives in Ottawa firmly uncommitted.

Optimism as the week begins in Ottawa.

The Policy Sessions

A pensive Clark.

Canapress Photo Service

An assertive Mulroney.

Canapress Photo Serv

Ross Reid prepares John Crosbie for his Friday night speech to the convention.

In 1976, Sinclair Stevens went to Joe Clark—in 1983, he stayed with Brian Mulroney.

Silent to the end, Alberta Premier Peter Lougheed casts his ballot.

Eva and Peter Pocklington in their convention box. In the foreground, Ralph Lean, Pocklington's campaign co-chairman.

Lowell Murray and William McAleer confer in Clark's box. Behind them, John McDermid, Clark's convention organizer.

Jim Merrithew, Ottawa

John Laschinger, John and Jane Crosbie, and Newfoundland Premier Brian Peckford welcome the results of the second ballot.

William C. Stratas

An anxious moment in Clark's box—in the foreground, Jock Osler, Clark's press secretary, Bill Parsons, his executive assistant, and Scott McCord, his youth organizer (telephone), await further results. To McCord's right Finlay MacDonald, Clark's long time advisor.

ⓒ Jim Merrithew, Ottawa   Progressive Conservative Party of Canada

(left) Tension mounts in the Crosbie box as Crosbie urges his supporters on. Beside him is Basil Dobbin, behind him, Frank Ryan, his two principal Newfoundland organizers. In the centre, in glasses, is Frank Moores, former premier of Newfoundland and a pivotal Mulroney organizer.

(right) Confidence builds in the Mulroney contingent that now includes Peter Pocklington and Michael Wilson. Applauding behind Mulroney is his long time associate, Jean Bazin.

Pocklington and Wilson move to an excited Brian and Mila Mulroney after the first ballot.

If the Numbers ...

An emotional Brian Peckford delivers the message—you can lose to us or lose to Mulroney.

David Crombie walks over to John Crosbie after the second ballot.

… are Right

Rebuffed, Peckford and Crosbie await the outcome of the third ballot.

byelections, the '80 election—it was back to square one. Victory gave Clark a respite but made his falls that much greater.

With hindsight, Clark's victory in 1979 and his brief tenure in power probably caused him more personal problems than all the earlier ups and downs combined. It wasn't that party members felt Clark and his team were doing a bad job in government. In fact, except for a few caucus members who felt slighted as a result of being passed over for cabinet positions, euphoria tended to dominate PC meetings between June and December 1979. Even when the election was called in December 1979, the troops rallied faithfully and went out to sell their government's record. But when they started knocking on doors that winter, there could be no question that they were in big trouble.

After their defeat, it wasn't the record of the government that Tory workers blamed for their humiliation. It was the fact that the election had even been called that focussed the anger of the militants. Again, the charge was bad judgement and the evidence: power lost. Once more, Joe Clark was the one accused and this time, the crime was the most heinous of all…returning the party back to the wilderness of opposition.

* * *

Because Clark's personal fortunes had been so inextricably tied to the party's political fortunes, he and his advisors believed that the task of addressing the concerns of party workers was as important as that of dealing with the concerns of the electorate. This, and the constant problems of internal party disunity, caused them to focus much of their attention on finding new and innovative ways of portraying Clark as "a leader." And as often as not, this portrayal was for the benefit of his own supporters as much as for the electorate at large.

When Lowell Murray came to Ottawa as Clark's principal strategist in 1977, the first "event" he organized for Clark was something called the Kingston Conference. By bringing the (then) four Progressive Conservative premiers to Kingston to discuss national unity with Clark and then issuing a PC declaration on the subject, they would put Clark in the same league as these proven leaders. The choice of Quebec City as the site of the party's 1977 general meeting, four months after the election of a PQ government, was designed to show Clark as a battler, capable of taking on the feisty

175

Lévesque in his own backyard. The disastrous world tour of January 1979 was meant to portray Clark as a statesman, dealing with world leaders on a one-on-one basis.

But as often as not, these "events" did not work, and if anything produced results that were exactly opposite of those intended when the plans were designed. The schizophrenia caused between constantly trying to position Clark as a leader, and so often failing in the setting chosen, produced a contrary tendency to try to hide Clark and downplay the importance of leadership. In the 1979 election, for example, the PC campaign team produced over 20 television commercials. The ones that even mentioned Clark were never aired until his advisors were convinced that, in the minds of the electorate, the election was over and no damage could be done.

In hindsight, the combination of the two strategies did little to help Clark. On one hand, constantly attempting to display Clark in such obvious leadership situations simply caused pundits to comment on the obvious... if he were a natural leader or were already seen to be a leader, then there would be no need for such a strategy. On the other hand, by "low bridging" and trying to ignore the leadership issue, Clark's advisors simply signalled the fact that he was a liability and that they knew he was a liability. Taken together, these, and the vacillating fortunes of the PC party under Clark's leadership, provided all the evidence needed for those who chose simplistically to believe that the PC political troubles began and ended with Joe Clark. But in politics, as with magic, perception is reality. And Joe Clark's tenure as leader of the Progressive Conservative party had come to symbolize the politics of opposition. Always losing ...even when it looks as if you will win; and always the victim, never the master, of events controlled by your opponents.

In many ways, this symbolic depiction of Clark was extremely unfair. He was fond of explaining publicly to Tories that their 1980 election defeat came about because... "the pool in which we fish is too small" — the base from which the PC party drew its support, its natural constituency, was too narrow and unless they broadened that base, they would be a perpetual minority party whose fortunes rose and fell exclusively on the basis of how frustrated the public was with "the natural governing party," the Liberals.

Rarely, if ever, had a national political leader gone out so assiduously and worked so deliberately to broaden that base…among young people, women and Quebec. In doing this, Clark was breaking one of the oldest political maxims—"go to your strength"—but as he continued his work, he became more convinced that his personal political problems were inextricably tied up with those of his party's. As long as the Progressive Conservative party represented narrow interests, he would be captive to those narrow interests, and his long experience finally made it clear to him that he would never find a personal constituency among those groups. Similarly, as long as the party failed to establish a more lasting coalition of broad-based support, they would be contenders and contenders only. Without more and different kinds of Canadians considering themselves to be Progressive Conservatives, the party's fortunes would be forever unstable. And if instability marked the party's fortunes, so too would it mark those of the leader.

But even while he and his advisors were consumed with placating the party regulars, Clark continued to attempt to redefine the Progressive Conservative party more in his own image. Time, however, was at a premium, as the general meeting in Winnipeg loomed ahead. Consequently, Clark himself, and his team attempted to accomplish the goals at once. At McMaster University in Hamilton, after spending a full-day session where party members were deliberately invited to vent their collective spleen about his and his advisors stupidity in losing the 1980 election, Clark laid out the type of party he chose to lead:

> "I think it is time that we ask ourselves whether we are as well accepted by Canadians, whether we are as well recognized by Canadians as being a party committed to positive and compassionate action to help those Canadians who need help. We, ladies and gentlemen, can concede to other parties the reputation of financial irresponsibility, but we must never concede to anyone the reputation of caring for the people of Canada. In fact, that reputation is deep in our history as a party in this nation; we're the only Canadian party that accepts the dual mandate of financial responsibility and compassionate action. We of the people; the Flora MacDonald's; the David Crombie's; the Jim McGrath's; the Ray Hnatyshyn's; the Joe Clark's; we have the tradition of a party that has pioneered responsible social programs, from health insurance to the indexing of income tax. It is time we took a hard look to ensure that we are being true and that we are seen to being[sic] true to the mandate, to those

people, and to that Progressive Conservative tradition of compassion and social justice."

Many cheered. Others simply shook their heads and lamented, "There goes Clark missing the point again."

Part IV

OTTAWA
JUNE 11, 1983

Ballot Three

CLARK, Joe	1,058
MULRONEY, Brian	1,036
CROSBIE, John	858

7

"You can lose to us or lose to Mulroney"

When David Crombie, following his elimination on the second ballot, walked to join John Crosbie in his box, no one was more stunned than Joe Clark. "I had no idea the desire for change was so great," the former leader said later.

Of all those attending the Tory convention none more closely resembled the Clark delegates than David Crombie and his supporters. Their desire for a moderate, progressive, mainstream party was virtually identical; and most observers saw Crombie, however reluctantly, voting for Clark when his own candidacy failed. That was not how Crombie saw it.

True, Clark *said* many of the same things he did; but, in practice, Crombie believed that he had run a closed, mean-spirited party. "It wasn't an *open* party," Crombie explained later. From his regional organizer in Toronto "to Lowell Murray at the top...all were amateurs who did nothing but politics. It was always Joe's closed shop". And no one else could come in, complained Crombie still bitter about not being asked into Clark's inner cabinet in 1979 after leaving his mayoralty chair to run. "His 'my way or the doorway' was just the latest manifestation of this attitude."

So when Crombie and his band of organizers first retired to his arena dressing room after being knocked from the race, it was clear to them that they would not be endorsing Joe Clark. And, when the telephone rang and an aide handed it to Crombie with the words: "It's Joe," there was little to say.

Clark pleaded that for "the integrity of the party," Crombie must

181

support him. Crombie, shouting to be heard, had to repeat his reply: "I can't support you...I'm sorry, I'll explain why some other time."

Crombie hung up the phone and turned back to his grim-faced friends. Every one of them had agreed with that decision. But now they differed over what to do next. They were evenly divided between those who favoured Mulroney, the obvious winner, and those who would refuse to support him. For all of them, the memory of Mulroney's heavy-handed visit to the Crombie tent lingered and one of Crombie's closest advisors asked him to consider whose style of politics he most admired. As Crombie took his wife Shirley into a corner of the room for a final quiet word, she reminded him of that comment.

Others had argued that to go to Crosbie when the convention was moving to Mulroney might be interpreted as a negative judgement against the new leader. But the independent-minded Crombie didn't see it that way. He made each individual decision based on its own merits, on what he liked, and let the subsequent interpretation be damned. He turned and announced: "It's Crosbie."

* * *

Over 200 other delegates had reached the same conclusion as David Crombie over the course of the second and third ballots, and had decided to vote for John Crosbie. Before being eliminated, Crosbie's vote had risen by more than that of the number one contender, Brian Mulroney—on the second ballot they had risen almost equally; on the third, Crosbie had gone up by 77 votes to Mulroney's 11—despite the fact that with each ballot Mulroney's victory appeared more and more certain. There was no better testimony to John Crosbie's popularity among the delegates, a popularity reflected by the fact that he entered the convention with more second preference support than any other candidate.

At the beginning of the campaign many journalists and some party insiders questioned whether Crosbie's candidacy would be taken seriously. His reputation as a "jokester" was seen as a liability that would deprive him of credibility as a potential prime minister. Yet, by the time of the convention, Crosbie's most important asset was his image of competence. In a survey of delegates during May he was ranked among the top three candidates on six out of eight dimensions of leadership, and the dimensions that he did best on were "overall ability and competence," "the ability to make tough decisions," "sound policy views" and "the ability to earn the respect of international leaders."

Crosbie's campaign literature had been carefully designed to develop his reputation for competence by emphasizing his academic achievements and administrative experience. In part, this was to dispel the negative effects of his rhetorical style, but it was also meant to appeal to what was seen to be a major concern of the delegates. The Clark government had been defeated because of its mistakes. Clark's personal image problem involved public doubts about his competence to govern. By attempting to convince delegates of Crosbie's strength on this dimension, his strategists were also trying to appeal to the party's desire to find a leader who could both win power and hold onto it.

These perceived strengths of Crosbie's in part stemmed from the simple respect the delegates had for the qualities of the man, but respect alone would have made little impact had it not been for the effectiveness of the Crosbie campaign. As he toured the country, Crosbie continually impressed those with whom he came into contact, including the press. This was his campaign's major tactical achievement: to have convinced journalists that he had a real chance to win.

The role of journalists in politics is often exaggerated. They tend to facilitate the formation of opinion rather than create it. Journalists did not create the idea of Crosbie as the alternative to Clark and Mulroney, but as the campaign developed, they began to realize that Crosbie *might be* the alternative and to take a harder look at him. When this happened many of them came away with a fresh and positive opinion, and their coverage began to treat him with greater seriousness. This, in turn, had an impact on the delegates, more than half of whom relied entirely, or in a substantial way, on the mass media for information about the candidates during the campaign.

By the logic of the normal process of movement within conventions, John Crosbie might have been expected to move rapidly ahead after the first ballot because of his strong second choice support. This was what happened in 1976 when Joe Clark, the most widely-acceptable second choice, rapidly overtook Brian Mulroney. Crosbie was, however, unable to capitalize on his widespread secondary support.

The reason lay in two problems forged in the dynamics of this convention. The first was that, for many delegates, the most important question was not which of the alternatives to Joe Clark would make the more attractive leader, but how best to ensure that Joe Clark was not returned as leader. For these delegates the only safe course of action was to vote for Mulroney, because he was better placed to win. This attitude hurt Crosbie not just by impairing his ability to win votes from the supporters of the candidates who ran behind him, but also by making it difficult for him to hold his own existing votes. On the second ballot Crosbie lost seven per cent (approximately 44) of his first ballot votes, and on the third ballot he lost six per cent (approximately 47) of those who had supported him on the second. Had he retained these supporters, Crosbie would still probably not have overtaken Mulroney on the third ballot; but their loss did deprive him of the momentum he needed to demonstrate that he could still move into second place.

The other problem for Crosbie was that most of his secondary support was among delegates who had voted for Clark and Mulroney on the first ballot. Between them Clark and Mulroney held the votes of nearly two-thirds of the delegates, and if Crosbie was going to be able to mobilize his second preferences, he would have to attract Clark or Mulroney delegates. Since Mulroney was in second place and had advanced to within 65 votes of Clark on the second ballot, there was little hope of finding votes there. Everything depended on winning votes from Clark.

* * *

Two hundred and fifty Crosbie workers had been positioned all day among the Clark supporters at the east end of the arena. They stood ready to escort any and all Clark delegates to the far end of the hall, should a decision be made to support their candidate. While they waited for word, a group of nine men met beneath the stands in Room 65 to determine if they could agree to a means of preventing the apparently inevitable election of Brian Mulroney.

On one side of the room stood Crosbie campaign manager, John Laschinger, Crosbie aide, Ross Reid, and MP Lorne Greenaway, a prominent supporter who was respected by Clark's group. On the other, Lowell Murray, Clark's strategist, stood between manager Bill McAleer and advisor David Small, while Finlay MacDonald hovered in the background. It looked like a showdown with no apparent winner, except for the presence of two other men who appeared to tilt the balance toward

184

one side. MPs Don Mazankowski and Bill McKnight, still wearing their "Another MP for Clark" buttons, were sitting on *Crosbie's* side of the room.

As agreed, when Laschinger had heard the results of the second ballot announced, he hurried to the CBC tower on the floor of the arena where he had previously met with Mazankowski, McKnight and Manitoba MP Jake Epp. The results of the second ballot had given Crosbie a "significant" advance, whereas Clark had obviously stalled, and Laschinger hurried to collect the MPs who had earlier offered support in just such a situation. At the tower Laschinger found only a despondent Jake Epp, who told him he was going to hang in with Clark after all. Disappointed, but not surprised, Laschinger returned to Room 65 to find the other two MPs waiting for him.

Lowell Murray was surprised to see them when he and his company arrived a few moments later. He knew there was talk among Clark's MPs and some other advisors that the only way to stop Mulroney was for Clark to throw his support to Crosbie — just outside the room, Murray had encountered MP Bill Jarvis and London businessman Don McDougall, two Clark loyalists who told Murray they thought Clark should do exactly that — but the meeting David Small and Ross Reid had arranged had not called for anyone's presence except representatives of the two candidates. "What was so important about stopping Brian Mulroney?" Murray would say later.

For a moment there was an awkward silence. Murray was the first to speak. Before he had entered the room he had told Small that as far as he was concerned Joe Clark would be on the third ballot — about that, "the issue was closed." He proceeded to repeat his message in front of the group and hoped that Crosbie and his staff would support the former leader on the third or fourth ballot.

Laschinger quickly countered: "But you've stalled...besides," he said, "our people prefer Mulroney two to one over Clark...we couldn't deliver them."

"Face it," he concluded, "you can lose to us or lose to Mulroney."

"You people have to choose," chimed in Mazankowski, looking straight at Lowell Murray.

For Murray there was nothing to decide. The former prime minister of Canada was atop the ballots in an all-out campaign to retain his leadership; he wasn't going to advise a move as humiliating as withdrawing in favour of a third-place candidate, 300 votes behind. What would the country think?

Not only would it appear humiliating, it would be seen to most as a gang up against French Canada. Then too, could Clark deliver even if he wanted to support Crosbie? Murray knew that their Quebec organizer Marcel Danis had already met with Mulroney confidante Jean Bazin and he doubted if Clark's sizeable French Canadian delegation would follow him to the unilingual Crosbie.[1] Besides, thought Murray, what the hell was so superior about John Crosbie? It was a stalemate and, as the Clark delegation filed stoically out of the room, leaving Crosbie's people shaking their heads in dismay, no one doubted what they had just done. "It's beyond our control now," David Small had concluded. "Brian Mulroney is going to win."

One last desperate effort was made to try to convince Joe Clark himself to withdraw in favour of Crosbie. Be realistic, Premier Brian Peckford of Newfoundland had pleaded with Joe Clark, former prime minister of Canada, while millions of Canadians eavesdropped on the conversation on national television. "You can't win," he said. "But we're still going up...come with us." The entire nation watched as Joe Clark bit his lower lip, shook his head and turned away.

* * *

In retrospect it was totally unrealistic for Crosbie to expect Clark, while still leading, to withdraw. For one thing Clark was a man whose life was bound up in the party and his career within it. It was improbable that, having come so far in defence of his leadership, he would give it up while there was even the remotest chance he might still win. And, if he did attempt to block Mulroney's election and the Quebecer won, it would deprive him of any influence in party affairs under Mulroney's leadership. In addition there was a question of pride and dignity. As Lowell Murray pointed out, it would have been demeaning for a former prime minister to end his leadership by trying to use his remaining influence in what would be viewed as an act of attempted vengeance.

Beyond these motives of a purely private nature, there were also Clark's concerns about the party and what he had tried to accomplish for it. Any attempt to gang up on Mulroney to prevent him from winning, no matter what the outcome, would leave a legacy of bitterness that would make it more difficult for the party to re-establish unity after the convention. And what would become of Clark's proudest accomplishment as leader, his opening to Quebec? Could he really endorse Crosbie, a unilingual Anglophone whose attitudes toward Quebec, in Clark's opinion, reflected a fundamental misunderstanding of that province? Clark was certain that if Crosbie were chosen leader, the party's opportunity in Quebec would be lost.

In the final analysis it was not Joe Clark's rejection of Crosbie's overtures that cost Crosbie the chance to win. Crosbie was a victim both of his vulnerability on the Quebec issue and of the convention process.

Crosbie's inability to speak French was only one part of his problem with the Quebec issue. In consciously choosing not to make the effort to learn French he appeared, in the eyes of Francophones and those concerned with finding an accommodation in French-English relations, to show that he did not care about the issue, or at the very least that he did not understand it. Crosbie was not a bigot, but he had never been forced to confront this issue. As a Newfoundlander, he knew little or nothing from his own experience of the traumatic impact of problems in French-English relations on the history of the country and the history of the party. It was this ignorance that allowed him to discount the importance of attempting to learn French and that led him to the intemperate flare-up in Quebec in which he had seemed to say that he would deal with French Canada as with any other foreign culture. He did not seem to understand that his words challenged the fundamental concept of Canada as a political community.

Crosbie's handicap was compounded by his outburst in Longueuil, Quebec. Word spread quickly: Crosbie had stumbled and stumbled badly. To the delegates this was his greatest weakness. Above all else in 1983, the Progressive Conservative party was determined to find a leader who could win and hold on to power. It did not want to risk choosing another error-prone loser.

Had Crosbie been able to stay on the ballot through further votes, under a system like that in the United States, where the low man is not eliminated, there might have been a chance to manoeuvre — to make the Clark delegates realize the futility of their efforts, to spring from among them the closet second-choice Crosbie supporters — a chance to bring into play the delegates' high estimation of his abilities as a potential leader.

Clark knew, however, that by staying on the third ballot he was

187

probably handing the convention to Mulroney and ensuring Crosbie's elimination. The more Clark thought about it, the more he imagined he saw the ghost of George Drew welling up in John Crosbie and, in his supporters, a nostalgia for days gone by, days which Joe Clark believed the party must never return to. If the delegates *really* wanted John Crosbie, they would have to go over Clark's head to get him. Clark was resolute — he would remain on the ballot — and the delegates would have to choose.

John Crosbie entered the third ballot hoping that Clark's delegates would feel differently. He needed about 130 of them (combined with his gains from Crombie's delegates) to leave Clark and vote for him. He knew there were that many and a good deal more within the Clark delegation who would prefer him to Mulroney as a new leader.

Clark, his advisors, and his supporters were not blind to this fact. By the end of the second ballot most believed it was over — the gambit that began 135 days before in Winnipeg had failed.

After Winnipeg, some of his advisors had said that Clark's defeat there resulted from the fact he had to run not against real candidates with flaws of their own, but against an abstract standard of an ideal candidate with an unblemished record. They had said he would fare better when he was compared to flesh and blood rivals. But when the delegates to Ottawa made that comparison, it didn't work out as Clark's supporters had expected.

Clark's standing in the estimation of the delegates reflected little of the strength he might have been expected to have. Beyond his own core bloc of delegates he was viewed, at best, with ambivalence. The only dimension on which he had more first, second, or third place mentions than any other candidate was regional appeal. On every dimension related to competence he ran behind Crosbie and this was what was most damaging. The delegates themselves seriously doubted Clark's qualifications for leadership. Only 58 per cent of the delegates ranked him among the top *three* candidates for overall ability and competence, only 55 per cent for the ability to make tough decisions, and only 54 per cent for the ability to earn respect from international leaders.

Even Clark's own delegates recognized the liability of his image. In evaluating the candidates' appeal on television, just 11 per cent of the delegates ranked Clark first. The seriousness of his image problem is demonstrated by the fact that on this dimension half of the delegates did not rank him among the top four candidates.

Standing at the other end of the arena, John Crosbie eyed the Clark delegates hopefully. He was sure they could see the futility of their continued support. Would they not leave Clark now?

They wouldn't. Despite the misgivings and despite the fact he was stalled, most of the delegates who voted for Joe Clark on the first ballot were fiercely loyal to him. For some that loyalty was based on ideological commitment. Both Mulroney and Crosbie, however pragmatic they might be in reality, had embraced the right symbolically. They had shown themselves to be willing to deal with elements of the party whose ideas and approach to politics were anathema to many Clark followers. For some, as well, there were considerations of party career. They had committed themselves so completely to Clark, been so closely involved with his cause, and fought with such intensity on his behalf, that they were certain to have very limited roles in a party headed by a new leader.

But probably the most important factor in the loyalty of the Clark delegates was emotional commitment. While politicians are usually portrayed as people whose every action is dictated either by public policy concerns or by personal ambition, they, as often as other people, also act on their emotions. Friendships, feelings of empathy with or antipathy toward particular groups, anger, resentment, or a sense of moral obligation, all can have an effect on a politician's decisions. When relationships of support or opposition are formed on the basis of feelings of this kind, they tend to be particularly hard to change. Emotion is a powerful force in politics which tends to set its own course. Those whose actions are governed by it tend to take uncompromising positions and to be unmoved by other considerations.

Most of the delegates who voted for Joe Clark on the first ballot stressed the importance in their decision of reasons involving emotional commitments. In part, these commitments reflected attitudes toward Clark himself and in part they reflected a more general feeling of group identification. There was a sense of group solidarity among the Clark delegates that had developed from the years of conflict over his leadership.

As the people in the stands around Joe Clark and Maureen McTeer began to sing, one could see the exultant determination in their eyes: "Oh we ain't got a barrel of money, maybe we're ragged and funny, but we're travellin' along, singin' a song, side by side."

Internal party conflict always tends to produce emotional effects contributing to this kind of group bond. On the one hand, it generates feelings of comradeship among those allied in a common cause; on the other, it generates negative feelings toward those who fight on the opposing side. The longer any conflict goes on, the more intense these types of feelings are likely to become. Thus, the protracted struggle over Joe Clark's leadership had created a hard core of Clark loyalists whose views of party affairs were shaped primarily by their experience in battling on his behalf. For as long as Joe Clark was there to support, they would support him.

* * *

When the results of the third ballot were announced, the 250 Crosbie workers who had been sitting in Clark's section rose as one and filed down the steps to the arena floor. Tight-lipped, the despondent lot marched past the horde of reporters who demanded to know what they would do next. They paraded through the crowds to the far end of the arena to dwell in the melancholy silence that surrounded the member from St. John's West. They believed their champion had been thwarted by the bull-headedness of Clark's delegates. Now they, 858 of them, would determine who would be the party's next leader. Only 22 votes separated the two remaining contenders—a bare majority of Crosbie's delegates could determine the outcome. Most had already made up their minds, but many would follow the direction of their hero, should he decide to give one. "What would John do?" They waited for the answer.

In Room 65 one final meeting took place. John Crosbie too had already made up his mind what he would do in this situation. Seventeen hours earlier before retiring for the night, he had told his closest advisors that he would prefer to sit it out, to give his endorsement to no one. He knew full well that, left to their own, his delegates would choose Mulroney over Clark, probably by a margin of two to one. That was as it should be, Crosbie had concluded. The party could not win a majority with Clark and that was what mattered most, but he saw no need for a final public reproach. Clark had brought him into the cabinet, had given him the biggest job, and made viable his own candidacy. He owed him something for that.

Now Crosbie listened to determine if there was any reason he should alter his opinion. David Crombie, who with his wife had joined Crosbie's advisors in the room, said very little. Supporting Clark was out of the

190

question for him and he had already made it clear he preferred Crosbie to Mulroney. A half-hearted endorsement of Mulroney would have only appeared opportunistic. No one in the room disagreed—that was how they all felt. There was nothing to make Crosbie change his mind.

As David and Shirley Crombie left to take their seats among their original supporters, Finlay MacDonald in his loudly-checkered, Palm Beach sports jacket, pushed his way through the crush of reporters outside Room 65 and to the sanctum inside. The group there held the fate of the party in its hands and MacDonald had come to make one last plea on behalf of his boss Joe Clark. "For the sake of the party…" he had started to say, when Jean Pigott burst out: "After what that man's put me through you can't expect me to support him." No one else said a thing. That had about summed it up for all of them.

MacDonald said no more. He pursed his lips and gave a little nod of resignation, then moved aside as the proud party streamed from the room. John Laschinger remained behind for a moment with MacDonald. They and all the others who had left knew that Brian Mulroney would be elected on the fourth ballot.

* * *

Over two ballots, Joe Clark lost a grand total of 33 of his first ballot votes.[2] That he had been able to hold this support was testimony to the fact that he had come to symbolize the type of party these partisans wanted. The fact he was not able to add to his total was just as strong a demonstration, that for many other partisans, Clark had also come to symbolize something quite different…a loser.

Clark's inability to enhance his front-runner status showed that the desire to win was stronger, for more PC delegates, than was the desire to follow the course laid out by Clark. In effect, what was evident was a profound split among delegates as to what was the best way in which to win…more of the same or time for a change? A majority could simply no longer suffer more of the same.

Part V

OTTAWA
JUNE 11, 1983

Ballot Four

| MULRONEY, Brian | 1,584 |
| CLARK, Joe | 1,325 |

8

"Right on the numbers"

If it had not been clear earlier, by the beginning of the fourth ballot it was a foregone conclusion—Brian Mulroney was going to be the next national leader of the Progressive Conservative party, and odds-on favourite to become the next prime minister of Canada. Of John Crosbie's supporters, 40 per cent stated before the convention that their second choice was Mulroney and only 17 per cent Clark. They had seen nothing in Ottawa to make them change their minds. Moreover, even if Crosbie had personally gone over to Clark in an effort to stop Mulroney, it is doubtful that it would have had any effect on the outcome, as 78 per cent of his supporters also claimed they would vote their own second choice rather than follow their candidate to someone else.

Clark's inability to capture the convention after leading on the first ballot was one story—a story of failed expectations, seven years of acrimony, and the politics of opposition. Mulroney's victory, however, was quite another. After all, other candidates, including Clark, were seen as more likeable, more competent, and tougher than Mulroney, and were considered to have a sounder grasp of policy. More delegates even considered that John Crosbie would be better able to unite the party, and had a more appealing television image. Further, there were just as many delegates reporting they would never vote for Mulroney (21%) as were reporting they would never vote for Clark (20%). In other words, the Anyone But Mulroney sentiment was as real and large as the Anyone But Clark feelings. The major difference was that the Anyone But Mulroney

195

camp was housed almost exclusively in the Clark delegation, while the ABC movement was spread throughout the convention.

So it would be easy to conclude that Mulroney was the choice of the majority of delegates, in the end, because he was the *only* candidate in a position to stop Clark, given his placement on the first ballot. He was that, but this kind of analysis woefully underestimates the skill, experience, and appeal of Brian Mulroney. It also seems potentially misleading inasmuch as delegates reported after the convention that in a hypothetical last ballot, with Crosbie facing Mulroney, the so-called "best candidate" Crosbie would have lost to Mulroney by 58 per cent to 42 per cent. They wanted to stop Clark and the majority wanted Mulroney.[1]

The principal reason Brian Mulroney won, despite the fact he was not seen as the "best candidate," has to do with the overriding concern of Conservatives: their quest for power. When asked how influential various factors were in their choice of a candidate, three-quarters of the delegates said finding a candidate who would best help the party win power was "very influential." No other reason figured as greatly. In 1983, the Conservatives were looking for a winner. And Brian Mulroney looked like a winner.[2]

Why did the delegates think Brian Mulroney was the best candidate to help the party win? Part of the explanation is a negative assessment of the other candidates. Joe Clark, a decent and able man, was bedevilled to the end by his image; and John Crosbie had lost credibility as a winner when he stumbled on the language issue. But to say that Mulroney did not appear to have such flaws is not enough to explain his success in relation to *all* of the candidates. How could he, a man who had no national prominence outside his party, indeed a man who even within his party was known mainly for his work in the backrooms, emerge a winner over former ministers and active members of Parliament who were portrayed almost daily in the news media as leading political figures?

The answer to this riddle lies in Mulroney's knowledge of the PC party and its membership.

Mulroney was fond of telling delegates that he had been involved with the Progressive Conservatives for 29 years. While many saw this statement as nothing more than an attempt to deflect attention away from his parliamentary inexperience, the fact is that Mulroney's 29 years of experience made him as professional a politician as anyone in Canada. Mulroney understood the enduring nature of party politics—and it showed in his networks and the lasting loyalty he was able to extract from the men and women he had met during that time. He also understood the changing nature of politics and that showed in his ability to adapt political tactics to meet these changing realities; for, across the country and especially in Quebec, only he, along with Clark, was equipped and prepared to play the game under the new rules. But, most importantly, Mulroney had a shrewder appreciation of the Progressive Conservative party than the other candidates, including Joe Clark. And that understanding showed in virtually everything he did, said, and stood for throughout the campaign.

One thing that Brian Mulroney understood was that during Joe Clark's leadership there had been a great number of Progressive Conservatives who thought of themselves as "outsiders" in the party: people who felt they had little or no influence in the direction of party affairs, or were cut off from a leader who relied too much on technical advisers. More than half of the delegates interviewed mentioned these items, saying that they believed there was an establishment in the party and that they were not part of it. And on the last ballot nearly two-thirds of those delegates voted for Brian Mulroney.

There are different reasons why many Conservatives considered themselves to be outsiders in their own party. Some party members had nursed personal grievances, because they felt their talents had not been properly recognized; others were frustrated because they had been on the losing side in most of the conflicts in the party since the battle over John Diefenbaker's leadership in 1966-1967.

At a deeper level, many party members felt themselves to be outsiders because of their social situation. Although comfortable financially, they felt insecure because they perceived themselves to be socially remote from the centre of power in Canada, which they saw as dominated by a technocratic elite operating through the bureaucratic structures of big government and big business. These individuals were proprietors of small businesses, farmers, fishermen or members of the lower middle class; they were residents of the smaller communities across the country, and/or inhabitants of one of the hinterland provinces of the Atlantic region or the West. These "social outsiders" were attracted to the Conservative party because it is both the party of opposition and a party that is conservative. The problem for many of them was that they saw the same style of technocratic power entrenching itself within the Conservative party.

They looked with suspicion on the growth of the party's bureaucracy, with its commitment to the uses of the new techniques of political organization, and on the leader's dependence on this bureaucracy and these techniques.

To many outsiders in the party, John Diefenbaker was the symbol of what they stood for ... or, rather, what they stood against. Diefenbaker's populism had been directed toward them. Thus, when Brian Mulroney constantly reminded delegates of his affection for, and connections to "The Chief," and when he won the endorsements of such prominent Diefenbaker loyalists as Alvin Hamilton and Robert Coates, he identified himself with those outsiders.

Mulroney had made the mistake in 1976 of looking too much the prisoner of technocracy. His campaign had offended people because of its slickness and sophistication. He did not make the same mistake in 1983. Mulroney was still a showman, but his campaign played in the rec rooms of the nation. He let the delegates reach him personally in homey surroundings.

And even though Brian Mulroney was the president of one large corporation, held directorships on the boards of several others, and often lunched with Conrad Black of Argus and Paul Desmarais of Power Corp., he knew enough not to flaunt such connections in the presence of delegates. Instead, he reminded them that he was "one who has worked as a labourer and truck driver and whose father was a unionized electrician." His humble beginnings included not simply a childhood in the North Shore town of Baie Comeau, but "a father who, during his entire life held down two jobs to provide for the needs of his family with neither complaint nor regret."

Mulroney's description of himself was, of course, unashamedly sentimental. Yet it appealed not just to the "social outsiders" in the party, it also identified him with the "average" Conservative delegate. Most of the Conservative delegates are people with family incomes putting them in the top 10 per cent of the population. They are high achievers in their careers, yet most of them report they came from families which were "just able to get along" or were "badly off." By portraying himself in this way Brian Mulroney was displaying his understanding of the party and its politics. And when delegates made the inevitable comparison of his roots to his current status, they saw a man who had arrived—a winner, like the one they were looking for.

There was another thing that Brian Mulroney understood about the

Conservative party that was very important in his victory, and that was a change in the ideological disposition within the party.

Mulroney is as much a Tory pragmatist as Joe Clark, but he was able to capitalize on the mood of conservatism among Tories. There had been considerable shift in ideological identification within the PC party since 1976. At the convention that year only 43 per cent described themselves as being on the right of the party. By 1983, 57 per cent placed themselves on the right. As Mulroney's support grew from ballot to ballot he drew his major strength from these delegates. On the fourth ballot 75 per cent of right-wing delegates voted for Brian Mulroney.

This does not mean that his base lay exclusively among this group. Thirty per cent (30%) of the delegates who placed themselves on the left and 38 per cent of the "centre" also voted for him. Nor does it mean that Mulroney would be forced to shift the party to the right to satisfy his major constituency.

While delegates may identify themselves as being at the right end of the ideological spectrum, the positions they take on specific issues may not. For instance, while a majority said they would sell all or part of several crown corporations, 60% said they believed in government ownership. And while a majority called for cuts in government spending, they didn't want them across the board: a majority called for *increased* spending on defence and high technology development as well as for education, manpower training and assistance to the disabled.

There is nothing inconsistent in this. The Conservative Party in Canada has always embraced two different traditions: the first, of social respon-sibility—a sense of duty towards others in society;[3] the second, of individual enterprise or self-reliance. Historically, within the party, the balance between these two traditions has fluctuated in adapting to social and economic conditions.

Responding to hard economic times in the 1980s and the resulting burden on individual taxpayers, Conservatives have placed their emphasis on individualism and self-reliance, although their attitudes on most policy issues have not changed dramatically from 1976.

Brian Mulroney understood this attitude and responded by stressing the virtues of individual enterprise while never abandoning a commitment to social responsibility or "tenderness" as he called it. His rhetoric soothed the right wing without troubling its conscience.

Although strong positions on specific issues did not form an integral

199

part of the Mulroney campaign, he and his organization did take special steps to ensure that the candidate would not be tagged as "insubstantive" or "plastic." The book he released during the campaign, *Where I Stand*,[4] was designed precisely with this aim in mind. 3,000 delegates received a free copy of book; and those who took the trouble to read it doubtless found a view of the nations's problems and a prescription for their cure remarkably like their own.

The remedies were never very complicated: Federalism isn't hard to master because "...(t)here is nothing that Canadians cannot do in a reasonable and thoughtful way once they set their minds to it. We must begin by purging the negativism and the vitriol from our public life and our private manner."

In equally succinct terms, Mulroney states that the nation's economic sickness has one "principal cause...the productivity factor." To revive the economy, he proposes an industrial strategy based upon cooperation, capital and human resources, as well as increased research and development. To finance R and D will require "dramatic and innovative fiscal reform" and the candidate reiterates established Conservative policy to control government spending through fiscal and parliamentary accountability.

In another area, however, Mulroney adopts an approach that is diametrically opposed to the policies of his predecessors, Clark and Stanfield. The issue is that of constitutional accommodation. Says Mulroney: "In any discussion of constitutional reform, I start from the premise of an indivisible Canada...I do not believe in a theory of two nations, five nations, or ten nations...Nor do I believe in any concept that would give any one province an advantage over any other." These words seem to be an invitation to the Conservative party to return to the days of Diefenbaker's unhyphenated Canadianism. Updating the issue to the 1980s, Mulroney declares that "no one can make a separate deal with the province of Quebec without involving Ontario, Alberta and all of the other provinces." In other words, no special rules and, above all, no special status.

Once again Mulroney expressed well the view of most Conservatives. Sixty-five per cent (65%) of the delegates said they were opposed to the idea that Quebec should have special recognition within Confederation and 69 per cent said no province should be allowed to have powers that the others don't. Special status implies an entrenched privilege and any granting of privilege is incompatible with the individualist's concern for equal opportunity.

The heart of the book is found in "A View from Baie Comeau." In this chapter, his personal view of the world and how it can be used for utmost political advantage, Mulroney offers not a reminiscence of his childhood, but his defense of the new Progressive Conservative touchstone... individualism. According to Mulroney, Baie Comeau was a place where investors, managers and workers took "great risks... in the development of the North Shore." But the risks were worth it: "We have all been, *as it should be*, rewarded for our efforts." The author concludes with a paean to liberty and free enterprise:

> Was it a demeaning life experience — as some fancy pants leftists would lead us to believe, those who would discourage new capital from entering Canada and penalize the existing pool — for you, for me, for many others who found here a sense of belonging; important degree of tolerance and pride; moral strength; a legitimate ambition to do, to build, to acquire and to share, the capacity to suffer defeat; and, to start again toward new challenges
>
> These are qualities that are instilled into us, perhaps unknowingly, by an independent and audacious life on the North Shore. Such are the values and liberties we have acquired here, and which are slowly being taken away from us, quietly, gradually, surreptitiously, by our leaders behind a smokescreen called "democratic collectivism." For me, it is just like an insidious illness which will, inescapably, diminish our strength and our duties as independent citizens.

Without reading too much into the actual wording, the reader cannot help but get the sense that each and every member of Mulroney's intended audience grew up with him in Baie Comeau. And in a way, they did. For while Mulroney's analysis of the country's problems and the necessary prescriptions to solve those problems would surely make a professional economist or public policy analyst blanch, they would almost bring a tear to the eye of a pollster or professional politician. For in those words, Mulroney and his team, have captured the very essence of what makes "the average" PC delegate live and breathe. In the pollsters' parlance, they were "... right on the numbers."

For the PC delegates, and for Brian Mulroney, as he campaigned across the country, the government which they so desperately sought to capture was neither inherently good nor evil. But it most definitely had the potential to abet or impede individual initiative. The difference, for them, was not a question of dogma, but a question of practice: whether our leaders "would quietly, gradually and surreptitiously erode our values and liberties" or whether they would allow us the "legitimate ambition to do; to build, to acquire…" and in so doing permit us to exercise…"our strength and our duties as *independent* citizens."

This view is expressed as much by the role of opposition — by acquiring the ability "to suffer defeat, sometimes with difficulty, and to start again towards new challenges" — as by the role of conservative. Few politicians in Canada are astute enough to recognize this. Caught up in the media coverage of "shifts to the right" and supply-side this and single interest that, candidates for the Progressive Conservative leadership in 1983 alternated between republican totems, socialist bogey-men and Red Tory shibboleths. Through a combination of keen political instinct and weekly polling on delegates' attitudes towards issues, the Mulroney camp was able to avoid these pitfalls.

From what started on the first ballot to be an impressive, but narrow, support base made up of Quebec delegates, Ontario youths and a smattering of senior delegates from across the country, Mulroney was able to build an impressive coalition on each successive ballot. By the last ballot, that coalition consisted of 50 per cent of all *ex officio* delegates; 82 per cent of all delegates supporting candidates other than him or Clark on the first ballot.

Brian Mulroney *was* the symbol to kick the ins out. But he also positioned himself, very deliberately over seven years, to become that symbol. Even though he may not have been seen as "the best" candidate by the majority of the delegates, he had the organization and foresight to neutralize that handicap on the first ballot.

Mulroney also was the only candidate who set out to exhibit more of those qualities a power starved party *required* of a leader, regardless of what non-partisan observers might deem to be the "best" qualities.

There is nothing paradoxical about all this. There is no conflict between the image of the hard-ball playing politician and the man with the vision from Baie Comeau. Brian Mulroney knew that the first rule for any politician is to know your constituency and secure it. That may require an adaptability that seems cynical in the eyes of those who want politicians not just to be true to principles, but always to be seen to be true to them. Brian Mulroney *did* talk about the things he believed in during the campaign; but what he was most concerned with was winning and Mulroney won because he followed the first rule of politics and shrewdly applied it to the realities of the Progressive Conservative party in 1983.

Asked what factors most motivated delegates to make the leadership choices they made, they replied: first and foremost, who was the most electable; second came the candidate's stand on issues; third, the fact the other candidates were less attractive; fourth, the personal attraction to the candidate; and fifth, personal friendship.

Probably no criteria better reflect the kind of campaign Brian Mulroney waged, and the kind of candidate he set out to portray to the PC delegates. Winning was his constant theme. Even the emphasis he constantly placed on his Quebec origins had little to do with accommodation, national unity or federal-provincial relations. It was a way of reminding conservative delegates of their successive electoral defeats and it associated his candidacy directly with these people's first concern—the quest for power. On the issues, he avoided detail, but what he did put forward fully satisfied the right-wing faction of the party, without hampering the party's electability. Through his public utterances and campaign publications, Mulroney was able to speak directly, not simply to the delegates' issue concerns, but more importantly to the unique mindset that produced those concerns.

Without ever having been elected to public office, Mulroney was also able not only to be the obvious alternative to Clark but the only alternative, given the choices offered. His business background, his fluency in both official languages, his "image" and even the altered style of campaigning he adopted, were all cultivated *in contrast* to the other candidate's attributes and not simply as desirable characteristics, unto themselves. He was the "complete candidate"... who developed his image as a counterpoint to all the deficiencies Conservatives traditionally associated with their leaders.

Finally, there is the question of personal friendship. Rarely, has a Canadian politician understood the importance or used the influence of personal friendship in party politics more than Brian Mulroney. The team he assembled, his constant references to patronage and the cultivated charm that has become a Mulroney trademark is testimony to this fact.

In short, and in the simplest of terms, Brian Mulroney prevailed in the fourth ballot because he was the most studied and professional politician of the bunch. Like so many, his strengths are his weakness. What is seen as smoothness by some will be condemned by others as vacuousness. What is viewed as consummate organization skills from one perspective, will be seen as manipulation and guile from another. But in the final analysis, all of it is part of politics. And the politics of the Progressive Conservative party—the politics of opposition—is a unique game for which few are equipped to play. Brian Mulroney, the unelected professional politician, played that game with a vengeance.

Epilogue

The Party and the Leader

In his victory on the fourth ballot Brian Mulroney put together a more broadly-based coalition than either of his predecessors, Robert Stanfield or Joe Clark. He won in every province except Prince Edward Island, Nova Scotia, Quebec and Manitoba and even in these provinces he was supported by substantial minorities. His majority cut across cleavages on virtually every dimension of social identification and interest. But Mulroney's greatest strength lies in the fact that he has provided a focus for uniting groups that have been fundamentally divided for a generation — and even longer.

One uniquely important opportunity lies in the bridge he has built across the cleavage between the French and English within the party, a cleavage that has caused more disruptive conflict in party history than any other. While on the fourth ballot he did not have a majority of the Quebec French, he had very close to a majority and in the post-convention survey these delegates gave him a strong endorsement. At the same time he had a majority of the delegates who have opposed bilingualism and concessions to Quebec. He is uniquely positioned, therefore, to bring these groups together, particularly if he can provide the party with some success in Quebec. A stronger Francophone presence in the party caucus would alleviate much of the cause of the difficulties of the past because it would leaven the effect of the small minority of anti-French members and make others who have been cut off from discourse with Francophones more sensitive to French-Canadian concerns. In the interim he can count on the support of the Anglophones because most of them believe that he is going to help the party win seats in Quebec.

A second important opportunity is presented by the fact that he has the support of most of those Conservatives who have felt themselves to be outsiders in the party. Many of these people have been losers in internal party battles for nearly 20 years — since the beginning of the struggle over John Diefenbaker's leadership. It was from the ranks of these outsiders that most of the dissent came during the leadership of Stanfield and Clark.

205

Now they are winners, positions of power and influence are open to them not as symbolic gestures to conciliate them from leaders whom they did not want, but from a leader who is leader by their choice. And, although a small majority of the *ex officio* delegates at the Convention voted against him on the fourth ballot, Mulroney will also have the loyalty of the party's established elite. While most of the Clark appointees in the key roles around the leader will be replaced by Brian Mulroney's men and women, the elite as a whole will support him because they will continue to hold their power and because they, above all, are committed to the principle of loyalty to the leader.

Mulroney, thirdly, has the opportunity to unite the party ideologically. He understands the vitally important distinction between using right-wing symbols and advocating right-wing policies. Because, in the use of symbols he captured the "conservative" mood of the party, he carried with him the vast majority of the delegates who *think* of themselves as being on the right, but because he articulated a political view that was pragmatic and emphasized the basic Progressive Conservative sense of social responsibility he appealed to their basic issue positions. Three-quarters of the delegates expect Mulroney to lead the party in a direction which is more to the right than the direction in which Joe Clark tried to lead it. But, given his positions during the campaign and his insight into what the party wants, that probably does not mean much in the way of change on basic issues of social and economic policy. However, the party under Mulroney will be more right-wing on symbolic issues and on issues that are remote from the daily concerns of Canadians such as foreign and defense policy—an area in which the party is substantially united in seeing the world in "we/they" terms.[1]

As important for Mulroney as the breadth of his base in the party is the fact that the party has the will to unite behind him. More than anything else it wants power and its members are deeply conscious of the harm internal division could do to their chances of winning power. In addition, most party members believe that despite their divisions there is a basis for consensus and accommodation within the party. Even most of those who say that there are big ideological differences in the party do not believe these differences are so big that they cannot be reconciled. A large majority of Conservatives also believe the outcome of the convention was a good thing for the party—good for its chances of uniting and good for its chances of winning. Seventy-one per cent (71%) of the delegates believe

206

Mulroney will have greater success than Clark in uniting the caucus, while 68 per cent believe he will have greater success in uniting the party as a whole. Most importantly, 73 per cent say Mulroney's election has improved the party's chances of winning the next election.

For all of these favourable circumstances, Brian Mulroney will still have to be adept in the exercise of his leadership. The real test for him will be in the caucus. His majority is not monolithic; it is a coalition of diverse groups and individuals. Moreover, while public dissent is officially disapproved of by most party members, it has become part of the culture of the party, something that is accepted because of the Tories' individualism and because little can be done to prevent it in a party that is out of power. What makes Mulroney's task more difficult is that the party's rivals and journalists will be looking for the slightest sign of discontent because of the party's reputation for divisiveness. Internal conflict is what is expected of Conservatives. The big political question for party watchers then, is whether this time that expectation will truly be unfulfilled.

In approaching this problem Mulroney can choose from three alternative models of leadership. The first is the model of Stanfield and Clark. That is the model of conciliation through the widespread distribution of appointments and consensus-building through an attempt to engage caucus members directly in policy-making. That model didn't work—for three reasons. First, there were members so hostile to Stanfield and Clark that they were not prepared to work with the leader. Second, neither man articulated a clear vision or found a concept to articulate a clear vision around which the party could unite. In pursuing the politics of consensus they allowed the course of the process to determine the direction rather than providing a concept to give coherence to the process. Third, neither man possessed at the beginning, nor was able to develop, a strong independent popular base to sanction his authority in caucus.

The second model is the model of strong one-man leadership provided by John Diefenbaker. Diefenbaker's style worked for a time because he did have a vision and he did have a base in the country, but it ultimately failed because government is too complex for one-man leadership to work and because he included no one in his inner circle who was not completely a Diefenbaker loyalist and, therefore, had no independent channel of advice.

The third model combines elements of both of these and, judged by what the delegates say, it is a model that seems to fit what the party wants.

The delegates want to share in party decisions, but they are prepared to follow a strong leader who will provide them with a sense of direction.

Brian Mulroney's life experience as a man from working-class background who is a high achiever and his attempt to express that experience in a coherent vision for Conservatives provide a basis for purposeful leadership to which most Tories can commit themselves. That gives him the opportunity to take strong stands. If he tempers strong leadership with the understanding for conciliation, the patience to seek accommodation and compromise that Stanfield and Clark brought to the leadership, he will have fulfilled two of the three requirements for achieving success. The third is to develop a base in the country and even there his prospects seem promising.

The Party and The Country

For more than six decades the Conservatives have been contenders for but seldom the holders of power in Canada. Some party members and commentators have blamed the party's minority status on its alienation of Quebec. From an historical perspective that is certainly part of the problem: the party's loss of French Canada helped precipitate the situation in which it finds itself today. Yet, for some time, the Conservative party has been a minority not just in Quebec, but in all of Canada — English as well as French.

The party's minority status is best represented by the fact that over the past 25 years the number of Canadians who have been committed Conservatives — those who have felt some sense of identification with the party — has always been less than the number who have been committed Liberals. Even at the beginning of the 1979 campaign, when the parties had about equal shares of the intended votes of the electorate, there were 10 per cent fewer people who declared an attachment to the Conservatives than to the Liberals.

Consequently in the 1980 election, when Liberal government performance was no longer an issue, and the state of the economy had been associated with the present Conservative incumbency, it was quite natural for those Canadians who considered themselves to be Liberals but voted PC in 1979, to return to their traditional partisan moorings. From this perspective, the 1979 PC victory can be seen as an aberration, only to be

208

repeated when a sufficiently large number of "Liberals" become disenchanted enough with "their" party to vote Conservative.

The party under Joe Clark spent a considerable amount of its time grappling with the "minority party" problem. Research uncovered the fact that the Progressive Conservatives were viewed by the electorate as old-fashioned, out-of-step with the 1980's and narrow-minded; representative mainly of farmers and businessmen, while providing little room for women, "ethnic" groups and the poor. The research showed further that the perception that the party had a narrow political base preventing it from widening that base.

Canadians gravitate toward broad-based, representative organizations and avoid narrow-based, unrepresentative ones. They value compromise and seek consensus. Political parties which are seen to serve exclusively the interests of one group over another, are viewed by the electorate as politically unacceptable.

Still another problem for the Conservative party has been the popular belief that it was not as competent as the Liberal party. It was seen as a party that has been less able to manage its own internal affairs, and lacks the level of skills the Liberals possessed to provide effective government.

The Conservatives who gathered in Ottawa may not have known but might have sensed intuitively that the image of their party, in relation to that of the Liberal party, had changed profoundly since their last electoral defeat in 1980.

* * *

As long ago as 1975 there was evidence in party polls that the Canadian people had begun to sense that something was wrong—that the world as they were seeing and experiencing it was becoming increasingly different from the world they wanted it to be. This feeling deepened and became more widespread as the economic crisis in the country increased in intensity. Nonetheless, people retained the basic sense of confidence in the strength of the country and in themselves. What they began to re-evaluate, was the performance of the people who were running the country. If there was nothing fundamentally wrong with Canada, then there must be something wrong with the way in which it was being managed. Thus, the difficulties in the country soon became associated with the government and, in turn, with the natural governing party, the Liberals.

Given the lasting nature of partisanship and political identification, the Liberals did not immediately fall victim to this reassessment. At first, "the blame" became highly personalized—"it was Trudeau's fault." Over time, however, as more Canadians began to associate the problems they were experiencing with the very prescriptions that were being applied by government to solve them, "the blame" began to shift away from personalities—Trudeau—and towards institutions—the Liberal party.

The PC victory in 1979 arrested this trend. While the Conservatives entered that election with 10 per cent fewer partisans than the Liberals, they were on a sounder political footing at that point than at any other time in recent history. But, by the end of the 1980 election, there were 22 per cent fewer self-confessed Conservatives in Canada than there were Liberals! By forming the government, the Progressive Conservative party—elected as an agency of change—had shifted the association of problems with the Liberal party to the association of problems with all political parties. Nothing had changed, the problems still existed, and therefore there was nothing to choose between the Liberals and the PCs. In the 1980 election the issues for the average votes once again came down to the question of "which political party is most like me?" and "which one is most for me?" —in other words, "which one do I identify with?" Given the Progressive Conservative party's chronic image problem, it was no contest.

But with the Liberals' return to power, the trend once again began to emerge and by May 1982, *for the first time ever* , the Progressive Conservative's national polling showed that there were more Canadians who considered themselves to be Progressive Conservatives in federal politics than there were Liberals. This erosion of Liberal partisanship had been incremental, but steady and continuous with each successive poll. The implications for Progressive Conservative party fortunes, although difficult to assess, were undeniably positive. Back in 1978, after losing 13 out of 15 by-elections and trailing the Tories by 10 points in the Gallup poll, the Liberals were still seen as the most competent, practical and moderate of Canada's three major political parties. In the PCs' May 1982 poll, however, the Liberals were virtually tied with the NDP as the most incompetent, impractical and extremist. In other words, the Liberal party had lost the association with those very qualities which had made it synonymous with "government" in Canada.

Epilogue

Someone looking at the nation-wide Gallup poll for the 18 months preceding the Progressive Conservative leadership convention might quite naturally conclude that the decline in Liberal party fortunes, would be paralleled by a rise in Progressive Conservative party fortunes. But while there can be no question that the Progressive Conservative party's image and electoral position has improved considerably since 1980, the party has yet to inherit the Liberal mantle as Canada's natural governing party. Doubts still exist, as they exist about all the political parties in Canada.[2]

Surprisingly, the Winnipeg general meeting in early 1983 did not seem to raise more doubts about the party. Instead of seeing the calling of a leadership convention as a foolish act, considering the Tories' high standing in the polls, most Canadians took the view that the party was "doing something" to clean up its' own problems, and, they hoped, those of the country as well.

In many ways Brian Mulroney is inheriting a party that has never been in a better position to cast off its minority status. For the first time in modern history more Canadians identify with the Progressive Conservatives than the Liberals. For the time being the party has put aside its leadership problems and has the opportunity to demonstrate its competence to govern by uniting behind a new leader. That does not mean that Brian Mulroney will encounter no difficulties in his quest to lead the Tories to victory.

Between 1956 and 1983 the Progressive Conservative party of Canada had three national leaders. Two—John Diefenbaker and Joe Clark—went on to become prime minister of Canada. Both were forced to contest their leadership by their own party and both failed. The other—Robert Stanfield—resigned shortly after losing his third bid for federal office in six years, undermined by his failure to impose unity on a fractious party.

When Joe Clark announced on January 31, 1983, that he was calling a leadership convention, there must have been a keen sense among some delegates that they were "doing it to themselves again."

On the following day a resounding majority voted to amend the leadership review clause in the party constitution to ensure that in future, a review vote would only occur at the first general meeting following elections when the PC party failed to form the government. To many, this amendment might have appeared to be a public declaration that the Tories had overcome their fixation on leadership. But, in fact, a mere five months later, in Ottawa, 67 per cent of these same delegates were reporting that they thought the leadership convention they were attending was a "good thing" for the party.

* * *

All of this behaviour and reported opinion is perfectly consistent...if you are a federal Progressive Conservative in Canada.

The fact of the matter is that for all of its recent history, the Progressive Conservative party *has* been obsessed by the so-called leadership issue. But this obsession is rooted in neither malice nor mischief.

An historian of the party wrote nearly 30 years ago that "the Conservatives have been searching for another Sir John A. Macdonald and when a new leader turned out to be an ordinary mortal he was subjected to constant criticism until he was forced to resign."[3] The standard used to measure Macdonald's successors is the standard that gives him his hero's status in the party. He was a winner. For his successors the party's failures have become the leader's failures.

This dilemma has not been eased by the Tory electoral record. Repeated defeats have manifest themselves in conflict, bitterness and acrimony which the leadership of the party has been unable to manage due to the kinds of members that the Progressive Conservative—a right-of-centre, opposition party—attracts and attempts to accommodate, and to the limited resources available for managing conflict in a party that is in perpetual opposition. This conflict, in turn, creates severe doubts among the public about the Progressive Conservative party's ability and competence to govern. When the leader of the party cannot exhibit that ability and competence by imposing his authority on the party, then the doubts expressed by the public tend to focus on the leader as well. And finally the leader becomes "the reason" for these doubts. The problem is structural but the solution is personal: change the leader.

Brian Mulroney made a point of reminding delegates that they, like him, were winners. What had made them losers were the people in charge—of the party and the country. For them, all that was required to be winners was to "recapture that spirit, that belief in ourselves."

For Progressive Conservatives it is an appealing posture. It is also one which Mulroney deliberately adopted in fashioning his leadership victory.

Now, after the convention, Brian Mulroney has what may be an unprecedented opportunity to transform the Progressive Conservative Party of Canada and, in doing so, change the entire complexion of Canadian politics. Fifty-three per cent (53%) of the voters who were interviewed for the Decima Quarterly Report in mid-June said they would be more likely to vote for the Conservative party with Mulroney as its leader. What is most important for the party is that Mulroney was most popular in central Canada where the Conservatives must develop a base if they are to become effective competitors for power.

Because Brian Mulroney was elected as "a winner" and because he understands the nature of party politics and his party so well, there is every reason to believe that he may be the very personality to alter the Progressive Conservative party's structural problems. But to do so, he must continue to win. And this is his dilemma. For to win — to convince the Canadian population that the Progressive Conservative party deserves the right to govern — Brian Mulroney and the Progressive Conservative party must overcome (or at least appear to overcome) its internal problem and appear as a governing party. To be winners they have to stop appearing as contenders; and to stop appearing as contenders the Tories must be winners. So, even though, in the final analysis Progressive Conservative leadership problems have centred on their electability, to ensure their electability, Brian Mulroney, like all Progressive Conservative leaders since MacDonald, must first contend himself with his party. Or, as Mulroney himself recognizes… "a condition precedent to electoral success must be tangible proof to the Canadian people that the Progressive Conservative party is genuinely united."[4]

Acknowledgements

Many of the people who have provided us with information have requested anonymity in exchange for their candour. For this we are frankly grateful, for to list all the individuals whose information has been invaluable to the writing of this book would be a herculean task, so we list none.

May we simply express our gratitude to the six front running candidates who gave generously of their time and assured us access to their staffs and in many cases their private meetings. None ever asked us how we would treat the things we learned. And may we thank those in the six organizations who patiently answered our queries and in so many instances went out of their way to direct us to the truth.

We would like to thank the Progressive Conservative Party of Canada and its president, Peter Elzinga, its former national director Pierre Fortier, and the many members of the staff who enabled us to conduct our delegate surveys.

The people at Decima Research were gracious in withstanding our intrusion on their time and facilities and we thank them all for their understanding. A few must be named here: Joanna Davis, who day after day typed and retyped without complaint; Russ Wilton who managed data processing for the project; Greg Vickers and Elizabeth Copeland who administered the project in shop and took part directly in the fieldwork in Ottawa; Ian McKinnon for his continuing advice (he and Cory Herrera also participated in the fieldwork); and Carol Schnell who kept us organized.

We are also deeply grateful to the 55 interviewers, most of them students at Queen's University, who conducted the interviews for the Ottawa survey; and to Dan Shea who assisted in the administration of the project in Kingston.

Some years ago the Canada Council provided Patrick Martin with a generous grant to conduct research into the PC party, work which formed the basis for much of this book. Their encouragement and patience is gratefully acknowledged. We would also like to thank the Social Sciences and Humanities Research Council for financial support to George Perlin's earlier work on party conventions, some of the data from which have been used in the analysis for this book.

To the CBC we owe a particular debt of gratitude. Only because Arnold Amber of CBC-TV News Specials and Nicole Belanger of CBC-Radio *Morningside* showed such interest in our project and airing some of our findings were we able to successfully carry out our work.

Nancy Colbert and Denise Schon, our agents, acted quickly and effectively to ensure publication; and our acquisitions editor, Janice Whitford, and the staff of Prentice-Hall were wonderfully attentive and patient.

Two journalist friends, Geoffrey Stevens of the *Globe and Mail* and Richard Gwyn of the *Toronto Star*, whose work in the coverage of Canadian politics we greatly admire, were kind enough to read our manuscript and offer us comments.

Three wives and four children tolerated an enormous burden this year, witnessing the poorer side of their husbands'/fathers' behaviour with none of the better. Next year...

Finally, two individuals must be singled out for particular thanks. John Mykytyshyn of Decima Research and Chuck Macli, our editor at Prentice-Hall, served us far better than any authors have a right to expect. For their patient devotion to the detailed accuracy and comprehensible presentation of this book and for their friendship, we will always be grateful.

For this book's inadequacies, the authors take full responsibility; for its value we share the credit with the people above.

Patrick Martin   *October, 1983*
Allan Gregg
George Perlin

Appendix A

Memo from Finlay MacDonald to Joe Clark

CONFIDENTIAL   March 1, 1982

The next General Meeting of the P.C. Association will be held in Winnipeg in January 1983, and the total pre-occupation of the delegates and media will be the ballot on leadership review. It is this writer's conviction that—

(a) those who voted in favour of a leadership convention at the last meeting (33%) are still there and a subsequent poll—Macleans-Carleton University —of those same delegates shows an increase of those who would vote for a convention if they were asked again.

(b) there are aspirants to the leadership who are becoming increasingly militant behind the scenes.

(c) there is a significant increase in response to the mailings of the P.C. Canada Fund in the theme: no more support until you get your act together and settle your leadership squabbling.

(d) the caucus cannot be relied upon.

(e) there is no reason to find joy in future Gallup Polls anymore than the recent Gallup Polls enured [sic] to Clark's benefit. There is not widespread acknowledgement of a brilliant parliamentary year on his part.

Conclusion

The moment [sic: read "movement"] is on the side of a vote for a convention. *We have no effective means or machinery to reduce the vote to acceptable proportions.* The risk is too great to simply "run out the string." There is only one alternative to a General Meeting and leadership review. At the appropriate time Clark should request that the *Party Executive call a leadership convention "at the earliest date."*

Rationale

At the closing speech of the Policy Conference in May (but not later than the close of the session) he would indicate that 1983 must be a year of renewal for the Conservative Party. The Canadian people look to the Party as their only hope and alternative to the most incompetent government in our history. The Party must accept their responsibility to the nation. That responsibility comes first. We must put our house in order. We must resolve our internal differences.

217

Advantages

(a) He both challenges the Party and places himself in their hands. He silences all who say he is afraid, clinging to his office-hoping for a miracle. He becomes the master of his own destiny not the victim of a time clock ticking to a trial. He places the emphasis on those qualities which even his detractors credit him for—courage, honesty, energy, vigour. He sets the agenda for the convention—the engagement of the Party and their responsibility to the nation.

(b) With the co-operation of the National President there is less likelihood of insistence that his resignation should be contemporaneous with the announcement of his intention.

(c) By requesting a leadership convention at the "earliest possible date" he can be quite confident that it would be in January '83 at the time and the site planned for the general meeting. Public pressure would be against those who would have a right to set a later time (and it would be logistically almost impossible to have it earlier).

(d) The Premiers of Ontario and Alberta will be otherwise engaged.

(e) There is little risk in a call before summer. A call in September might be seen as not giving other candidates a fair chance. It would be unlikely that a *candidate* would insist upon Clark's resignation as a pre-condition of the call. It would be counterproductive. Any alleged campaign advantage to him because of incumbency would be offset by the public necessity of carrying on his Opposition Leader responsibilities (but Clark might hold out an option).

(f) The decision would have public and media support. It is not a pre-emptive strike.

Disadvantages

1. Why would a leader "quit" when the party is so high in the polls?

2. The national executive would probably interpret the constitution as requiring his immediate resignation and therefore he might be seen as abdicating his parliamentary responsibilities.

(signed) Finlay

Discussed with:

Hon. Robert L. Stanfield and Mrs. Stanfield
Senator Lowell Murray
Peter Harder
Rick Clippingdale

Appendix A

Memo from John Thompson to Brian Mulroney

List of Contents

Introduction

I have consulted with:
> Paul Weed
> Michel Cogger
> D. Matthews
> Rod Pageau
> Keith Hamilton
> Roy Perry
> Beth Moores
> 6-7 Tour people from various Ontario type campaigns
> National Party Headquarters
> Norman Atkins
> Paul Curley

Observations

- Convention campaign is out of control
- No direction or focus
- No organizational discipline
- Will cost a lot more than it should
- Currently insolvent—many overdue bills in Ottawa—Bell Telephone have frozen the phones and called National Headquarters
- Most material items have been committed for, which precludes much scope.
- Although material is not objectionable, quite good
- Most opportunities for an Ottawa based organization have been missed. I don't perceive that we have one competitive point of view.

- Most positions in the Convention Committee have been filled with Montreal based people whose only experience was the losing campaign of 1976.
- Few delegates in organization
- Too many people are being paid
- Space is fragmented in Ottawa causing lack of communication
- Our competitors and National Headquarters think we are poorly organized

Our campaign requires a focus—a game plan with fully integrated strategies for all elements. Above all the campaign requires an organization structure. *You must stop running this campaign and have some faith in your people—this lack of faith shows now and will show through to the delegates.*

The following outlines a Convention Strategy based on my analysis of:
- Our strengths and weaknesses
- What our competitors will do and
- What the delegates want

Strengths and Weaknesses

The main negative about our campaign is that:
1. Your image is fuzzy and
2. People are scared of your candidacy because
   (a) they are scared off by your organization
   (b) they don't trust you

1. Your image is fuzzy—*People perceive you to be both left and right.*
   The image must be focussed.
   I believe the book, policy sessions, speech and all the material will work.
2. It is in this latter regard that I believe our convention strategy has to focus; i.e., trust.
   - Your organization poses a threat because of the people and because it is unknown
   - They don't trust you because of the slickness, smoothness, pat answers, feeling that there is no substance, plastic image and the feeling that you are *someone's candidate*—big business or Conrad Black.

Our campaign strategy must focus on both of these weaknesses.

Strategies of Other Candidates

Our competition will run the following types of campaigns:
   Crosbie will run a campaign that will attempt to create illusions that he is going to win and that everyone should jump on board. Everything will be geared to show his support is growing. He will do all the traditional things well:

good presence at all events, constantly being surrounded by people, spontaneous demos, colourful strong advertising— much of which will be done by volunteers rather than delegates.

Clark's campaign will be similar to Crosbie's but will suffer by lack of genuine enthusiasm. It will stress his being a unifying force for the party and will be focussed in what they perceive our weakness to be; i.e., we are a threat to the existing party organization.

They will both run *presidential style* campaigns.

Everyone will be after the 4 other candidates support.

Gamble will be the most vocal anti-Clark critic and we should let him do it.

Wilson and Crombie are running on ego and futures—they will take the highroad and stress thoughtful presentations-substance.

Pocklington is running on principles and people will listen to him. We should acknowledge Peter's principles.

If we look like we are the only alternative, we should get the majority of Gamble's and Pocklington's support.

I believe we could count on not more than an even split of Wilson's and Crombie's support and that Crosbie's support is the key.

We must be behind on the first ballot by less than 200 votes and Crosbie must be at least 400 behind. Clark must be ahead.

What the Party is Looking For

Delegates want someone who can win the next election. With the high ratings in the polls there is a feeling that we are going to win. We must continue to stress that a rebuilt Liberal Party lead by John Turner is a real threat and we are the best candidate to meet that threat.

Secondly, all delegates want to be part of the process. Now—when in opposition, during an election—in the transition and in the rebuilding of the government— the salvation of Canada or whatever one's political philosophy—all want to be involved.

Neither of the other major candidates can make an appeal to the Party to be involved because they will lead presidential style campaigns.

Joe Clark ignored them, offended them after he won and then didn't make the fundamental changes most delegates wanted to see in Ottawa. While Joe talks this way he has not implemented and every delegate knows this that—next to his dreadful image with the electorate, this is his Achilles' heel—but [he] doesn't recognize it. Crosbie can't run this type of campaign because he has too far to come and it must be a presidential style bandwagon campaign.

Process is More Important than the Result

The process of selecting a candidate/leader is one of rejecting the others. All delegates want to be involved. A campaign must be organized to get as many delegates, alternatives and spouses involved as possible — because someone who is not asked to work becomes a rejected soul who looks for a home. Involvement breeds involvement.

Convention Strategy

Our convention strategy should be:
1. To run a people-oriented campaign rather than a presidential style campaign.
2. To stress involvement in the process though the maximum number of volunteers.
3. To stress *Party* and Policy.
4. To make our convention campaign an easy campaign to join.
5. To play catch-up.

In implementing these strategies:
1. We must recognize that the campaign in Quebec is over and that the battle is for the English delegates
2. We must make a smooth transition to this campaign so as not to stress problems; i.e., money

The average English delegate wants to know that you have French support, but he really doesn't want to get too buddy/buddy with the French.

Brian should start the party theme as early as Wednesday of this week stressing delegates being involved. Asking for their help and involvement, their personal commitment. He should ask for their help personally and give them a name and number to call. He should ask for their help right up to voting hour as this suggests we are behind.

Fundamental to these strategies is one that has Brian going to people than people coming to Brian — and one in which Brian asks for personal commitments by delegates on the basis that they want to be involved — Brian promises to fulfill their desires. He might say that it will start on the Monday after the convention — e.g., or that Brian will initiate a council of riding presidents to meet every other month — this would be in addition to a revised association structure. We should have *some* specific recommendations.

1. Theme WIN TOGETHER
2. Music written around theme to be played by *Hoopla*
3. Theme overlaid on existing materials
4. Use shamrock as trademark — also green colours
    lapel
    on Brian
    and on material

Appendix A

5. Go low key—frugal
6. People-oriented campaign—go to where the people are—at airports; casual
7. Stress delegate involvement—as many as possible—make up jobs with title
   Ask for their help
   Ask for their commitment
   Channel volunteers to Margaret Crook
8. Our functions will be to keep morale of our workers high—not to influence uncommitted delegates

   Early in campaign—rather than Thursday or Friday nights
   Say Thursday AM—breakfast function
9. Stress only candidate who can beat John Turner—Run Turner scare ad.
10. Stress Mulroney is his own man—writes own speeches
11. Stress energetic—Jogging in AM
12. Get out of plastic clothes
13. Must do well at Policy sessions—need advisors for each
14. Speech should be "off the cuff"
15. Demo to stress support for Brian Mulroney
16. Mila must campaign
17. Tour strategy will have spotters around them with wt (walkie talkie) so BM can move to crowds
18. Use electronic medium for on-site commercials; i.e., replay of news at hospitality suites with ad for Brian the man?
    and perhaps with his comments for previous night
    perhaps streeters stressing Brian Mulroney's strategies
19. Go after citizens of Ottawa. Visit the mayor of Ottawa and Hull when the convention starts *Tuesday / Wednesday*. They have given a lot to the party for the convention.

The style should be low key and should focus on the campaign and not on Brian. It should look inward rather than outward.

Our appeal and theirs should be:
   Together *we* can win. . .
   Let us work together—for a better Canada, Government, Party
   Travaillons Ensemble
   With Brian Mulroney
   avec Brian Mulroney
   Our theme should be *Together*

This allows us to let people vote for themselves—it humanizes Brian to being one of them which he is—a tireless party worker and it should take away the threat our campaign evokes.

TARGET DELEGATES

Our campaign should recognize that the campaign in Quebec is over and that the battle now is for English Canada. *Our Quebec support should not threaten the English delegates with a strong French presence as did Wagner's in 1976.*

THE KEYS TO COMPETITION ARE

- Testamentials [sic] by recognized people
- Good policy performances—not with repetitive answers if possible
- Obviously a good speech
- An image should be created that Brian writes his own materials and that he is his own boss

SPECIFIC

- Materials are already set—we need good exposure. We will try and work in the theme as an overlap to existing material
- We need to bring in a Irish touch to downplay the French side—perhaps shamrocks put on some material might do the trick
- Brian should go out and meet the delegates everywhere and not the converted. We will go to them wherever they are—outside competitors functions—in restaurants in teams at the airports

Brian should meet all the delegates on arrival in Ottawa—in a casual manner.

He should *jog* every morning at the convention at 6.30 AM—in non Christian Dior shorts, etc. He should start now so as not to look phoney. What he might say is that he gained weight with all the good cooking and has to take it off. Mike McSweeney obviously is not the right running mate. Perhaps he might ask delegates to come and join him. *Start now. This would show up Crosbie and Crombie's health, Clark's non-athletic body.*

Demo: I think our introduction and demo should be as follows: Brief intro by Roy McMurtry on Brian's qualifications. Then he introduces the 50 or 60 prominent people seconding the nomination on stage and then Brian comes in to theme song. *No outsiders. No bands.*

Speech: Speech strategy should be consistent with campaign strategy. It should be gutsy, emotional, and should show Brian as he will be on the campaign trail. It should touch all the bases and be his own words.

We should put together a speech advisory group.

C. McMillan	First Meeting
L. Horswell	Sunday 28
a Westerner	Second
B. Mulroney	Sunday 5
Paul Weed	Tuesday PM

Appendix A

M. Cogger
Perhaps H. Segal
J.T.

Friday afternoon, if necessary better
go to BBQ.

To be consistent with Brian approach. The speech should *not* be read, but should be a *framework to follow.*

HOSPITALITY SUITES AND FUNCTIONS

I don't think we really need them all. Perhaps just one well-publicized one with times that Brian will be there. The kids expect a bash and we should give them a good one.

I think we should go to everyone's bash—as a delegate—stressing fiscal responsibility and the fact that the party has organized a good convention.

TOUR STRATEGY

Our strategy should be move where the delegates are—Brian sells so well. Our tour organization would have spotters all over town and would call in where there are good crowds and we would move around constantly. Be everywhere— all the time. A strong friendly presence.

Perceptions of Brian Mulroney as the Candidate

PERSONAL TRAITS

In analysing perceptions I have used the following framework to highlight the weaknesses that must be focussed on:

TRUST

COMPETENCE

DYNAMISM

SOCIABILITY

Every voter is looking for these traits in political leaders. 50% is Trust, 30% competence, 10% dynamism, and 15% sociability. So will the delegates.

Deal Only with Negatives Here

Vis-à-vis Joe C. and John C., the people I spoke with would rate you as follows:

		Brian Mulroney		Joe Clark		John Crosbie	
Trust	50	4	2.0	6	3.0	8	4.0
Competence	25	6	1.5	4	1.0	6	1.5
Dynamism	10	5	0.5	4	0.4	5	0.5
Sociability	15	6	0.9	4	0.6	6	0.0
			4.9		5.0		6.9

Contenders: The Tory Quest for Power

Trust is low because—(1) image is fuzzy—(how can they trust someone they don't know)—(not certain who you are and what you stand for and I had image of impressions of political leanings from Left to Right) —(2) it is perceived that you are not your own man—that someone is pulling the strings, Conrad Black or some big business organization—that someone who is always perfect (changing shirts, Christian Dior shirts, Ken Doll image) should be suspicious [sic]. That you are opportunistic—here today gone tomorrow—(3) people around you are not acceptable—(certain party workers from Headquarters fired for being double agents), Lortie's tough…image and your own stabbing Joe in the back—your convention tactics at Winnipeg, etc. all contribute. Your campaign is a threat.

Competence: is low because you have no experience in government and while you have big business experience that does not mean anything to people in Ontario—if it where Canadian Tire, etc. it would mean something—Iron Ore means nothing to the average person. Surprisingly some people feel that running a business in Quebec is easier because the competence level on average is so low. This image flows from the former because it is perceived that your canned answers are not your own.

Dynamism: Crosbie's well-organized campaign has created dynamism for him and so did his many speeches during the 1980 campaign. Joe gets it in comparison to his colleagues, you are measured against the two and get a tie with Crosbie again because there is very little perception of anything different.

Sociability: Joe gets the lowest rating and you suffer because of the "perfect" image. While Crosbie is reserved in private he is quite socialable [sic].

John Thompson
May 22, 1983

Appendix A

Excerpts from Crosbie Memo

January 1, 1982

1981 Strategy

In June of '81 a draft campaign strategy was prepared for the campaign group which, among other considerations, developed an overall campaign strategy. One of the components of this strategy was a tour programme for the remainder of the year ('81). This June paper was a revised draft of an April proposal and contained the following points regarding tour:

Primary Objective

1. Keep a low profile in relation to the current leadership position. Allow others to speculate about a possible candidacy, but do nothing overt to cause controversy or appear to push Clark.

Secondary Objectives (re: Tour)

1. Concentrate personal appearances in B.C., Ontario and the Atlantic Provinces. Reduce number of speaking engagements after end of May '81 and put more effort into fewer speeches and targeted audiences. In June it was decided to do a maximum of one speech per week in the autumn.
2. We should aim for a majority of Party events, rather than non-Party events. (Events where we are asked to attend by M.P.'s or other Party members should be considered as Party events.) The current 1981 speech plans as of now, and using those definitions, are:

Party	50%
Non-Party	50%
Total	100%

3. It is essential to develop a constituency for the candidate. Use time to identify possible support *if* decision is made to run. Gather data into central files. Travels should be scheduled so as to maximize contact with those Party members who are or are likely to be delegates.

The tour strategy and programme was agreed upon by the campaign group with the following approved observations:
1. The tour programme was an important area of the campaign and would require sufficient funds to meet objectives. (Minutes, August 10, meeting)
2. A staffer should travel with the candidate while on tour to ensure that logistics run smoothly and, primarily, to collect names of supporters who meet the candidate. (August 10 meeting)

3. Thank-you notes should be sent out by the candidate following each tour or speaking engagements (August 10 meeting)

An analysis of the 1981 tour programme indicates that the campaign has met, and in some areas surpassed, the tour objective established in June of last year, particularly in light of the primary objective of keeping a low profile on the leadership question.

Notwithstanding the surprising statistic that touring engagements have increased by nearly 70% over 1980, the candidate's profile has met the primary objective amidst obvious turmoil and controversy within the Party of:

- a major shakeup of the caucus critics by the leader, demoting rivals and promoting loyalists;
- a revolt within the caucus with a majority supporting a leadership question;
- a declaration by two major candidates, Mulroney and Crombie, that they would seek the leadership; and
- a significant erosion amongst the grass-roots and a rekindled drive by anti-Clark forces to dump the leader.

The primary objective has worked well to the candidate's advantage. So well in fact, that in a recent interview by Crombie in the *Toronto Star*, announcing his leadership ambitions, he did not mention the candidate's name as a potential candidate for the leadership. This low profile has afforded the campaign the opportunity of meeting its internal secondary objectives in touring, communications, supporter contact, etc. While at the same time the perceived image within the party has been projected:

- that the candidate is a team player;
- that he is willing to place his personal ambitions behind the welfare of the unity of the party; and
- that he has established a clear mandate in a new policy area (external) with hard work and vigour.

1981 Tour Programme: Analysis

In 1981, a total of 65 major engagements were accepted out of some 150 formal invitations received. Countless others were declined on the telephone as not meeting the hidden objectives. The analysis by province and by category does not include the 1980 election campaign speaking engagements. The number are based on one major engagement per trip. Several party riding tours where more than one speech per constituency was made (Albert Cooper, M.P. and Fred King, M.P.) only counted as one major engagement.

The two-day fact finding trip to Washington and the three days spent at the United Nations in conjunction with the candidate's mandate as chief external affairs critic for the party are not included in the comparison.

228

Appendix A

Engagement by Province (Chart 1)

	1980	1982	Totals
Yukon	—	—	—
British Columbia	2	3	5
Alberta	2	9	11
Saskatchewan	—	2	2
Manitoba	2	—	2
Ontario	9	23	32
Toronto	12	8	20
Quebec	2	2	4
New Brunswick	—	1	1
Nova Scotia	4	6	10
Prince Edward Island	—	1	1
Newfoundland	6	9	15
Totals	39	64	103

Engagement by Category (Chart 2)

	1980	1981	Totals
Party Events	5	27	32
Service Clubs	6	9	15
Academic Forums	9	4	13
Economic/business Forums	5	5	10
Association Conferences	12	12	24
Media Speech Forums (Press Clubs, etc.)	2	3	5
Other (classified)	—	4	4
Totals	39	64	103

* * *

Tour Objective 1: *Concentrate appearances in Ontario, British Columbia and Atlantic; Fewer speeches to target audiences; Maximum one speech per week.*

Observations (Chart 1)

1. Tour engagements have increased some 70% over 1980, with 39 engagements in 1980 and 64 in 1981.
2. The regional mix has remained consistent over the two years: concentration in Ontario, followed by the east and the west. 50% of the concentration has been in "delegate rich" Ontario. In 1981, particularly in the second half, concentration moved into areas outside Metropolitan Toronto. (42% rural Ontario in 1980 to 74% in 1981).
3. In the West, while speaking engagements have increased by 10% in 1981, the overwhelming concentration has been in Alberta which represented some 60% of all western engagements in 1981. A major tour into British Columbia,

which would have lessened the Alberta concentration, was limited to the interior (Fred King, M.P.). This alteration in emphasis accommodated the primary objective of maintaining a low profile.

4. Approximately half the speaking engagements were completed in the second half of 1981 which averaged out on paper to a little over 1 per week. *However, regional concentrations at times placed strain on the candidate in terms of logistics and energy.* In the second half, an effort was placed on target audiences with fewer occasions requiring the generation of *completely* new fresh texts. As a result the fewer targeted audiences allowed for more adequate time in the limited resource of speech preparation.

	First half of '81	Second half of '81
A. Completed speaking engagements	32	32
B. Party events using a variation of a stock theme speech	8	19
C. "Other" remaining engagements (A-B)	24	13
D. Engagements (C) with selected policy topic speeches ready for press or supporter distribution (targeted)	4	7

Specific targeting, outside of party engagements, lessened "other" speech forums from 75% of all speeches in the first half to 40% or 13 in the second half. And, of those engagements the availability of "release text" speeches climbed from 16% to over 50% at 7 of 13.

* * *

Tour Objective 2: *Majority of party events;*
Party/non-Party split 50/50*
*(Party engagements are defined as fundraisers, annual meetings, special caucus speaking engagements)

Observations (Chart 2)

1. Party speaking engagements rose from 13% of all engagements in 1980 to 42% in 1981, while non-party events dropped by 30% from 87% in 1980 to 57% in 1981.
2. Of the 42% party speeches in 1981, 70% of that was reached in the second half of 1981 following the establishment of the "50% party speech objective" at the June meeting of the campaign group.
3. A provincial breakdown of the party engagements in 1981 closely mirrors the first objective of concentrating appearances in Ontario, B.C. and the Atlantic.

230

Appendix A

Ontario	14	(52%)
East	6	(22%)
West	6	(22%)
Quebec	1	(4%)

4. Category shifts between 1980 and 1981 in non-party events shows a movement away from academic forums to service clubs, with other categories remaining consistent.

* * *

Tour Objective 3: *Develop constituency for candidates;*
Maximize travel to identify support of those who will be delegates;
Maintain records.

Observations

1. Potential delegate support has been sought out on each party engagement trip. Constituency contact lists and past delegate/alternative lists have been used to reach out to party people while on tour.
2. In non-party events potential supporters are recorded for later use in a campaign structure or for fundraising (direct mail) purposes.
3. Following each tour the names and contact points are added to the communications system, with reference notes. List maintenance has been strict with regard to new executives and riding presidents following annual meetings. The personal hard-core supporters list has risen to 600 from June of 1981.
4. And, following each tour, appropriate thank-you notes are sent by the candidate to people who have helped on the tour or indicated support during a leadership convention.

1982 Strategy

By December of 1981, the tour objectives for the year had been met in terms of the overall campaign strategy. The tour concentration and mix had placed the candidate on a campaign-ready footing while maintaining the lowest profile of any potential leadership candidate. The candidate had survived the year with no scars from a war within the party that had taken its toll, not only within the party organization, but in a party leadership image perception with the general public.

The prospects for the coming year are no brighter. The leadership of the party is dug-in for another year; the faithful party grassroots is disenchanted; the party organization is one and a half to two years away from an election and in disarray; and the caucus is nowhere is addressing a policy theme and thrust for an alternative Conservative Government.

231

During the coming year, the campaign and the candidate must develop a strategy to meet these challenges. In politics, no less than war, the lessons of the last campaign are prized beyond their application to the present one. Each political campaign, like every battle, is dependent upon experience of past campaigns but itself unique. Therefore, the strategic campaign objectives for 1982, of which the tour programme is a component, are based in the past objectives of 1981 as well as the new challenges for 1982.

Strategic Goal 1: Continue to maintain a low profile in relations to current leadership position. Allows others to speculate about possible candidacy, but do nothing overt to cause controversy or appear to be pushing Clark.

Strategic Goal 2: Present a *statesman-like* image within the Party and endeavour to bring unity, loyalty and pride to a fractured national and local party organization and to protect the democratic process and principles of the party constitution. *To help prepare the organization to run a national campaign.*

Strategic Goal 3: Present a *leadership* image within the Party, and particularly amongst caucus, by endeavouring to tackle the issues (substance, theme, thrust). *To help prepare the caucus to lead a majority government.*

The second and third goals are based on the premise that despite all our desires that there be leadership convention: *Joe Clark may be there for another year and quite possibly for another election.* By the time a leadership convention arrives there may be only a few potential candidates left to pick up the pieces and lead the party. And, the candidate that maintains a low profile, a statesman-like manner, and a leadership image—*despite Joe Clark*—stands a good chance of leading the party at some future time. A sizeable percentage of the party delegates support Joe Clark simply out of loyalty for party unity and image, not because of loyalty for the man.

It is important to not play Joe Clark's game, for he is experienced at it. He experienced the 1966-67 era, won the leadership from third place, rallied fractious organization to a campaign victory and has successfully manipulated stalling tactics regarding the leadership question. He has achieved a general meeting when he wants, out-manoeuvered the national executive and caucus, and brought two potential rivals into the ring to fight a long drawn-out campaign. One of those candidates, Mulroney, he has seriously injured with the Joliette byelection and the other, Crombie, he will endeavour to injure on the issues. Only by playing an "anti-Joe Clark strategy and tactics game" can a candidate hope to get the support of the party and lead it.

In 1981 the campaign has successfully demonstrated that it can be on an election footing by not being perceived a candidate and maintaining a low profile. *We can successfully build further upon that low profile in 1982 to become even more ready, while at the same time, demonstrating the qualities needed by the party, enhancing the candidate's position, and, protecting his record in the party. (years and position)*

1982 Tour Programme Proposal

As of January 1, some twelve speaking engagements have been scheduled during the first half of 1982. This does not include two major trips as external affairs spokesman to Florida and Europe.

The tour programme should be built around the three primary campaign objectives of: low profile, statesman image, leadership image, and should establish some secondary internal objectives to guide its development.

Leadership Convention?

The proposed tour programme for 1982 has been developed under the assumption that there will be no leadership convention in 1982. Campaign planning for the year must therefore be based on a long-term strategy that secures our resources, in terms of structure and budget, and our image, in terms of profile, theme and thrust. This consistency will allow for a smooth transition into a campaign situation, should it develop, either through rapid erosion of the leader's support or strike action on his part.

Should a leadership convention develop, alteration must be made in this long-term proposal and a specific campaign tour proposal must be developed, considering the following:

Long-term Proposal

1. Party events should be honoured that have been scheduled.
2. Non-Party events should be cancelled except where benefit to the campaign strategy can be achieved.

Leadership Campaign Proposal

1. A detailed proposal must be developed consistent in style and image with our established long-term strategy.
2. A campaign tour programme must accentuate party events and consider four time periods:
   1. Pre-announcement period
   2. Post-announcement tour programme
   3. Convention days itinerary
   4. Immediate post-convention day(s)

Appendix B

Table 1: ACTUAL DISTRIBUTION OF VOTES FOR EACH CANDIDATE FOR EACH BALLOT

Candidate	Ballot 1	Ballot 2	Ballot 3	Ballot 4
Clark	1,091	1,085	1,058	1,325
Mulroney	874	1,021	1,036	1,584
Crosbie	639	781	858	—
Wilson	144	—	—	—
Crombie	116	67	—	—
Pocklington	102	—	—	—
Gamble	17	—	—	—
Fraser	5	—	—	—
Spoiled Ballots	3	1	2	19
Total Votes	2,991	2,955	2,954	2,928

Table 2: EVOLUTION OF VOTE: REPORTED AND ACTUAL

	Pre-Convention Study %	During Convention %	Actual Ballot 1 %	Post-Convention Survey %
Clark	41	39	37	38
Mulroney	24	27	29	27
Crosbie	19	18	21	21
Wilson	5	7	5	6
Crombie	3	5	4	5
Pocklington	2	2	3	3
Gamble	*	1	1	*
Fraser	0	0	0	0
(No Response)	6	2	n/a	*
[n =]	[958]	[788]	[2991]	[713]

Appendix B

Table 3: SHIFTS IN DELEGATE SUPPORT BETWEEN BALLOTS (%)

BALLOT 2

Ballot 1	Clark	Crombie	Crosbie	Mulroney	Did Not Vote	N
Clark	97	0	2	1	0	(263)
Crombie	13	52	10	10	0	(31)
Crosbie	1	1	92	5	0	(144)
Gamble	0	0	100	0	0	(3)
Mulroney	0	1	1	98	0	(188)
Pocklington	0	0	50	50	0	(20)
Wilson	12	2	35	49	2	(43)

BALLOT 3

Ballot 2	Clark	Crosbie	Mulroney	Did Not Vote	N
Clark	95	5	*	0	(267)
Crombie	30	55	15	0	(20)
Crosbie	1	94	6	0	(176)
Mulroney	1	2	97	0	(229)

BALLOT 4

Ballot 3	Clark	Mulroney	Did Not Vote	N
Clark	97	3	*	(264)
Crosbie	21	75	4	(192)
Mulroney	1	99	*	(238)

Table 4: DISTRIBUTION OF VOTES ON FOURTH BALLOT ACCORDING TO IDEOLOGICAL SELF-IDENTIFICATION

	Percentage Who Voted		
	Clark	Mulroney	Did Not Vote
Extreme Left	73	27	0
Moderate Left	67	31	2
Centre	61	38	1
Moderate Right	32	67	2
Extreme Right	13	78	9

Table 5: DISTRIBUTION OF POCKLINGTON, WILSON, CROMBIE, AND CROSBIE VOTES TO REMAINING DELEGATES UPON WITHDRAWAL FROM BALLOT

	Percentages from Previous Ballot Who Voted for				
	Mulroney	Clark	Crosbie	Crombie	Did Not Vote
Wilson Delegates on Ballot 2	49	12	35	2	2
Pocklington Delegates on Ballot 2	50	0	50	0	0
Vote Percentage on Ballot 2	33	39	25	3	*
Crombie Delegates on Ballot 3	15	30	55	—	0
Vote Percentage on Ballot 3	34	38	28	—	*
Crosbie Delegates on Ballot 4	75	21	—	—	4
Vote Percentage on Ballot 4	43	56	—	—	2

Table 6: ABC AND ABM BY REPORTED FIRST BALLOT SUPPORT (PRE-CONVENTION)

	First Ballot Support						
	Clark	Crombie	Crosbie	Gamble	Mulroney	Pock-lington	Wilson
ABC:* (N = 191)	1	5	26	2	52	5	8
ABM:** (N = 196)	79	3	9	0	0	2	5

(*) ABC: Anyone But Clark; would not vote Clark
(**) ABM: Anyone But Mulroney; would not vote Mulroney

Appendix B

Table 7: DISTRIBUTION OF FIRST BALLOT VOTES OF DELEGATES WHO IN JANUARY 1983 WORKED FOR OR AGAINST LEADERSHIP REVIEW, AND OF OTHER DELEGATES WHO SUPPORTED OR OPPOSED LEADERSHIP REVIEW*

	Attended Winnipeg		Not Attending Winnipeg but	
	Voted For Review	Voted Against Review	Supported Review	Opposed Review
Clark	2	94	12	86
Crombie	31	56	11	78
Crosbie	51	37	66	33
Mulroney	68	30	58	42
Wilson	18	77	41	59

(*) Excluded from the table are non-voters, delegates who voted for Fraser or Gamble, and those who indicated no position on leadership review.

Table 8: DISTRIBUTION OF FOURTH BALLOT VOTES BY PROVINCE

	Percentage Who Voted for		
Province	Clark	Mulroney	Did Not Vote
Newfoundland	23	63	13
Nova Scotia	60	40	0
New Brunswick	36	64	0
Prince Edward Island	63	38	0
Quebec	51	48	2
Ontario	34	65	1
Manitoba	62	35	3
Saskatchewan	53	47	0
Alberta	48	51	2
British Columbia	44	57	0
Yukon	100	0	0
Northwest Territories	40	60	0
All	43	56	(*)

(*) Excluded are those who did not vote.

Table 9: PERCENTAGE OF DELEGATES MENTIONING EACH OF A GIVEN SET OF REASONS FOR FIRST BALLOT CHOICE*

	Very Influential	Of Some Influence	Not Influence**
A belief that the candidate would be the best one to get the party back into power	74	17	7
The candidate's view on policy	65	32	3
A belief that opposing candidates would not be as able to give competent leadership to a government	58	27	15
A feeling of attraction to the personality of the candidate	51	34	14
Personal friendship for the candidate or for people working for him	43	28	28
A belief that the candidate would do the most effective job of responding to the interests of your province or region	40	34	25
A sense of obligation to the candidate or someone working for the candidate	28	18	52
Dislike for an alternative candidate or candidates or the people working for them	22	33	43
The candidate has helped the party in your community in the past	17	18	64
The hope to have a more substantial role in the party	11	22	65
A feeling of commitment to the candidate because he was a "native son" of your province or region	8	11	79
The hope for an opportunity to be able to serve in a government appointment or do work for the government	4	12	83

(*)   This data is derived from responses to the question "In making your *first ballot choice* was each of the following reasons very influential, of some influence or not influential? (Circle only *one* response for each question.)

(**)   No opinion/refused was excluded.

Appendix B

Table 10: PERCENTAGE OF THE DELEGATES APPROACHED BY THE CANDIDATES AND/OR THEIR WORKERS

1967		1983	
Diefenbaker	7%	Clark	94%
Fleming	17%	Crombie	69%
Fulton	33%	Crosbie	85%
Hamilton	16%	Fraser	15%
Hees	28%	Gamble	26%
McCutcheon	17%	Mulroney	86%
Roblin	31%	Pocklington	40%
Stanfield	30%	Wilson	76%

Note on Delegate Surveys

Three delegate surveys were conducted for the book. The first prior to the convention, the second at the convention but prior to the actual voting, and the third study after the delegates had returned home. The surveys conducted prior to and after the convention were mail surveys and the convention interviews were conducted by Queen's University students. All data processing of the responses was conducted by Decima Research Ltd. staff. The results of all three surveys may be obtained from the authors.

Notes

CHAPTER 1 "Go, Joe, Go...please!"

1. This attitude was reflected at the June 1983 leadership convention. Although they essentially came to Ottawa to throw Clark out, 74 per cent of the party's delegates agreed with the statement that "public loyalty to the leader is essential—even if it means you sometimes have to support a leader of whom you don't approve or whose policies you don't agree with."
2. See N. Nurgitz and H. Segal, *No Small Measure: The Progressive Conservatives and the Constitution*, (Ottawa: Deneau Publishers, 1983).
3. The complete text of the MacDonald memo is reproduced in Appendix A.

CHAPTER 2 "At least they don't call you 'Joe Who' anymore"

1. William Christian and Colin Campbell, *Political Parties and Ideologies in Canada*, (Toronto: McGraw-Hill Ryerson, second edition, 1983), p p. 85-93, *passim*.
2. The Mulroney organization also paid commissions for new members but, in the early days of the campaign, paid for merely the sale of a membership card. When only small percentages of the new members turned out to meetings, they began using the Clark technique of only paying when the member came to vote.
3. Results of the Broadview-Greenwood byelection held October 12, 1982: McDonald (NDP) 10,957; Worthington 9,004; Fatsis (PC) 4,999; O'Connor (L) 2,728; Others 347.
4. Crosbie had sewn up Newfoundland and PEI's system of poll workers electing representatives to delegate selection meetings precluded any invasions. In New Brunswick, Conservative Premier Hatfield simply told the candidates not to interfere with delegate selection.
5. Forty-eight per cent (48%) of those who ran as identified delegates or were opposed by identified delegates were Clark supporters.
6. A radio reporter travelling with Mulroney had recorded the sequence which verified that he did call the idea "preposterous."
7. *Le Devoir* sent questionnaires to 757 Quebec delegates and tallied its results from the 341 who returned them.

8. *Montreal Gazette*, May 28, 1983.
9. Riding delegates were restricted to the following: two youth (i.e., under 30) and four senior, at least one of whom must be female. With the advent of more and more youth delegates from post-secondary campus clubs, senior men had indeed become a minority in the delegation, though still a majority of the membership in the party. The situation was exacerbated by the fact that senior male members could vote only for senior delegates at selection meetings, whereas youth members could vote for both YPC and senior delegates. Further, female members could vote for delegates from women's caucus groups, where they existed. It was possible, therefore, for a young woman member to vote three times for delegates and, if she were a member of a campus club too, a fourth time as well. Senior male members had only one vote.
10. When asked how committed they felt to their first choice, 89% of Clark's supporters said "very." This contrasts with 85% of Mulroney's; 82% of Crombie's; 80% of Crosbie's and 69% of Wilson's.

CHAPTER 3 **"Ya dance with the lady what brung ya"**

1. Organizers had predicted a turnout of 4,000 and had unofficially suggested as many as 5,000 might arrive. The number who did attend became the subject of some contention. Mulroney organizers put out that it was "at least 3,500 to 4,000." The *National* on CBC had labelled the crowd as "over 1,000," the *Globe and Mail* described it as "perhaps 2,000" and the *Montreal Gazette* accepted the organizers' assessment of 4,000.
2. By 1980, Mulroney had given up drinking and, at the time of the Ottawa convention in June, 1983, had been an abstainer for three years.
3. Not long after, in 1978, Wagner left the PC caucus to take a Liberal seat in the Senate.
4. See Peter C. Newman, *The Establishment Man*, (Toronto: McClelland and Stewart, 1982) pp. 246-257.
5. Following the Winnipeg meeting, former party president Dalton Camp complained that Joe Clark had in part been victim of certain "offshore" interests. While some observers looked south to the Amway Corporation or certain oil interests for the culprit, others concluded he was really referring to Frank Moores, who in recent years had become involved in offshore oil and gas ventures off the coast of Newfoundland.
6. Even at the June convention, Moores' loyalty remained in question. At each plenary session he could be seen sitting in John Crosbie's reserved section but, after hours, he served Brian Mulroney as that candidate's principal conduit to the other candidates' camps. See Chapter 6 "If the numbers are right..."

7. *Canadian Business*, September 1982.

8. More of the Thompson memo appears in Appendix A.

9. This penchant for name-dropping is the subject of one of the first Brian Mulroney jokes. A friend once chided Mulroney after hearing him freely lace his conversation with the names of many of the important people he knew. "You've gotta stop all that name-dropping," his friend advised. "I know," replied Mulroney, "the Queen Mother was telling me that just the other day."

10. Long had been succeeded in 1982 by another bright young right winger, Nigel Wright, but Wright fell considerably under the influence of Long.

11. Clark was not the only target for these young zealots. At a provincial policy conference, OPPCA President Long openly attacked Premier Davis and some of his cabinet for their moderate policies. The normally circumspect premier felt forced to respond at the victory lunch for OPCYA President Zeise by warning the youth about their dangerously narrow view.

12. Randall Bocock, another Walker supported candidate of the right, and Zeise's former campaign manager, was selected.

13. Peter White continued to play an active role in solidifying the youth leaders' loyalty to Mulroney. Even after the June convention and throughout the summer of 1983 he held a number of meetings with Zeise, Long, Bocock and others in the imposing headquarters of Conrad Black's Argus Corporation at Number Ten, Toronto Street.

14. Mulroney remembered well the personal calls and private meetings with John Diefenbaker that he had so coveted as a youthful Tory at Saint F.X. and Laval, and played the game well. The Ontario leaders were not the only youth he attempted to win over. Greg Thomas of BC, the outgoing national youth president, was also courted. Thomas was a supporter of the right, but had been publicly loyal to Clark. The former leader failed, however, to call him after Winnipeg and a hurt Thomas was receptive when Mulroney phoned. The Quebecer had him flown to Montreal from Vancouver for a private meeting.

15. *Where I Stand* is explored at greater length in Chapter 8, "Right on the numbers."

16. Thanks to Claude Arpin of the *Montreal Gazette* for his account of this exchange.

17. Senior Ontario government officials first became suspicious that something was wrong when Mulroney visited the provincial caucus. He brought with him Weed, who many considered *persona non grata*, and not Meighen who most felt close to.

18. *Maclean's*, August 1, 1983, p. 56.

19. Southam News/Global Television poll published May 16th, 1983. 530 delegates sampled indicated their preference on the first ballot as:

Clark	35%	Crombie	2%
Mulroney	19%	Pocklington	1%
Crosbie	14%	Gamble	0.4%
Wilson	4%		

with 19% undecided.

As their second choice they named:

Crosbie	27%	Clark	7%
Mulroney	14%	Wilson	6%
Crombie	9%	Pocklington	2%

20. Mulroney later told interviewers on Global Television, seen in Eastern Canada, that "there has *never* been an open bar, there has never been a *bar* at any one of my meetings."

21. Ten per cent (10%) of Crosbie's support went to Mulroney in the last two weeks of the campaign.

22. They were wrong. Objective tracking shows a swing of approximately 55 to 60 votes during this time, enough to put Mulroney ahead but keep Crosbie respectable. In fact, Crosbie ended up with 639 votes on the first ballot.

23. The following day, Saturday, Thompson would be forced to spend $75 from his own pocket to pay for sandwiches for the candidate's box during the voting.

24. The Thompson memo appears in Appendix A.

CHAPTER 4 "Je suis canadien"

1. In 1978, Paul Curley replaced Laschinger as national director.

2. A regional breakdown of Crosbie's speaking engagements in 1981 shows his tour meeting "the first objective of concentrating appearances in Ontario, B.C. and the Atlantic": Ontario 52%, East 22%, West 22%, and Quebec 2%.

3. One of the major Crosbie memoranda is partially reproduced in Appendix A.

4. Crosbie argued that until entrepreneur John Shaheen put up more money and demonstrated the viability of the project, the provincial government should put up no more cash. Crosbie lost the argument to Smallwood and resigned, but was vindicated some years later when the refinery went bankrupt. Following his resignation, Crosbie entered the legislature to find that his seat had been removed from the government benches and bolted to the floor on the opposition side of the House.

5. Crosbie enjoys telling the story about his one week in French immersion in a Francophone Quebec household: After hours of silence he finally screwed up enough courage to demand of his hosts, "Avez-vous une scotch?"

6. Excerpts from the Crosbie memo appear in Appendix A.

244

7. Cambridge, Ontario, and Fort McMurray, Alberta, with large Newfound-lander communities, were notable exceptions.
8. Eighty per cent (80%) of the delegates said they supported this idea.
9. A number of newspaper columnists and editorialists in Quebec agreed in principal with Crosbie. For example Marcel Adam, in *La Presse*, noted that "other things being equal, Canadians must prefer a bilingual over a unilingual personality. But I do not believe that language must be the determining factor when a candidate is clearly superior in terms of character, ideas and leadership qualities. (*La Presse*, April 23, 1983, p. A6.)
10. Crosbie frequently let his affection for his wife show. When a street photographer presented him with a lapel button bearing a picture of Jane, he took to wearing it constantly. When delegates at the Ottawa convention noticed it, many mistook the attractive red-haired lady depicted for Britain's Conservative leader Margaret Thatcher.
11. Thanks to Charlotte Montgomery of the *Globe and Mail* for her account of this event.
12. Crosbie's advisors appear to have missed the gravity of his blunder at first. Internal memos analyzing the press coverage paid little special attention to the reports of his Longueuil remarks.
13. *Toronto Star*, June 5, 1983, p. F3.
14. *Ottawa Citizen*, June 2, 1983, p. 4.

CHAPTER 5 "...but I don't think he can win"

1. The closest thing the financial community had to one of their own in the party was Sinclair Stevens, the member for York-Peel and former president of the Treasury Board in Clark's government. But the one-time president of the now defunct Bank of Western Canada was thought to be too unpredictable by many on Bay Street. The Ontario Tories were suffering a dearth of friends, too. Most of the province's federal PC MPs were not part of the provincial team. There was no one they could count on especially in the Toronto area. Ron Atkey the MP for St. Paul's and former Minister of Employment and Immigration had been the closest thing they had to a friend but he had lost, for the second time, in 1980, and the former mayor of Toronto, David Crombie was too independent to be relied on.
2. "Red Tory" is a term that was originally used to describe a particular characteristic of Canadian conservative thought which distinguished it from American conservatism, but in the internal politics of the Conservative party it has come to be used to describe people on the extreme left of the party. Even during the period of the "progressive" leadership of Robert Stanfield, there were very few party members—only about five per cent in surveys of delegates to national meetings—who called themselves Red Tories.

3. *Maclean's*, April 11, 1983, p. 18.
4. Pocklington's name received an unexpected boost in popularity only three days after receiving Adams' report. The millionaire was kidnapped, a ransom demanded for his release, and, in the battle that climaxed the hunt for him, he was accidentally wounded by a policeman's bullet.
5. Why not release the Adams' poll if it gave such a damning account of Clark's fortunes? Ralph Lean, Pocklington's campaign manager, offered the explanation: To release the poll would have "put the knife [stabbing Clark] in Pocklington's hand" because Adams was known to be his pollster. Further, because of that relationship, people might not have believed Adams.
6. Cited in W. Christian and C. Campbell, *Political Parties and Ideologies in Canada*, (Toronto: McGraw-Hill Ryerson, second edition, 1983).
7. Less than one per cent of the delegates surveyed were prepared to make across-the-board cuts in government spending. The number who could make cuts in five out of ten representative areas was only 12 per cent. Less than two per cent would make across-the-board reductions in government regulatory activity. The number who wanted to reduce regulation in five out of nine representative areas was only 22 per cent. Only eight per cent of the delegates wanted to sell off to the private sector all of the crown corporations on a list of five representing different forms of public ownership and only 39 per cent wanted to sell off three out of the five.
8. Mary Walker Sawka received just two votes at the 1967 leadership convention.

CHAPTER 6 "If the numbers are right..."

1. Crombie's reasoning proved sound, at least on the second score. He was able to hold about 54 per cent of his vote on the second ballot, almost 30 per cent of which ended up going with Clark on the third ballot after Crombie was eliminated. He had succeeded in keeping at least 20 delegates from voting for Clark on the second ballot, enough to have shown a rise in support for Clark instead of a slight drop. There is no evidence to suggest that any of Clark's supporters deserted him for Crombie as the latter had hoped; however, Crombie did pick up a handful of delegates from both Crosbie and Wilson.
2. Pocklington was the only candidate Mulroney secretly met with.
3. Crosbie *was* uncomfortable. He'd been suffering from hemorrhoids the previous few days and they had become so painful that the following morning he was briefly hospitalized to have them removed. A less than good humoured Crosbie entered the hospital shielding his face with a

246

newspaper only to be greeted by a doctor who quipped "This is the closest I'll ever get to the seat of power."

4. Pocklington and his wife had been concerned about security ever since his kidnapping the year before. When he was robbed in Chicago during a recent visit he resolved that his whereabouts would be kept secret while in Ottawa.

5. The occasion bringing both to town was a candidate's debate also attended by Joe Clark. Clark was anxious to build bridges to David Crombie who, by that point, appeared to be foresaking his chances in order to make a more progressive pitch to the party; but when Clark called him to suggest a meeting after the debate, Crombie pleaded fatigue. In fact, the rejuvenated Red Tory was meeting with Pocklington that night over dinner to discuss how best to prevent the former leader's comeback.

6. A more complex breakdown of the vote from ballot to ballot appears in Appendix B.

7. By the fourth ballot, however, 89.5 per cent of Pocklington's original 102 delegates ended up supporting Mulroney; five or six delegates voted for Joe Clark and five or six didn't vote at all. 72.5 per cent of Wilson's original 144 votes went to Mulroney on the last ballot; 27.5 per cent returned to the former leader, Clark.

CHAPTER 7 "You can lose to us or lose to Mulroney"

1. At Bazin's request both Danis and his deputy Mario Beaulieu had met with the Mulroney representative in Montreal prior to the convention and again in Hull early in the convention week. As they had agreed, Danis met with Bazin following each ballot of the vote. Mulroney's side wanted to know what Danis would do in the event the final choice for the delegates came down to Mulroney and Crosbie. Danis made no secret of the fact that he'd personally prefer Mulroney, but insisted that, if Clark decided to support Crosbie, he would follow suit. Danis had told this to Clark, but added that even if both of them went to the Newfoundlander, he wasn't sure how many of his Quebec delegation would follow — Roch La Salle, for one had already informed them both that in such a situation he would endorse Mulroney.

2. Clark had dropped three per cent of his first ballot vote on the second ballot, a loss which was almost compensated for by gaining a handful of supporters from Crombie and Wilson and even a few from Crosbie. On the third ballot, his gains from among Crombie supporters could not make up the 5 per cent he dropped.

CHAPTER 8 "Right on the numbers"

1. This kind of response might be dismissed as reflecting a "bandwagon

effect"—an after-the-fact attempt by delegates to put themselves on the winning side—but there was no evidence of such an effect in the delegates' reporting of their real voting choices. When asked the same question pairing Crosbie and Clark, a majority of them said they would have voted for Crosbie.

2. That, too, is clear from the research. Thirty-five per cent (35%) of the delegates who said that finding a winning candidate was "very influential" voted for Mulroney on the first ballot; and, in overwhelming numbers, the rest of the delegates who cited this reason went to Mulroney as the balloting progressed. Eighty-three per cent (83%) of the delegates who said finding a candidate who could win power was a very influential reason for their first-ballot choice, and who had voted for candidates other than Clark or Mulroney on the first ballot, went with Mulroney on ballot four.

3. For a discussion of the impact of this idea (collectivism) on the Conservative party, see William Christian and Colin Campbell, *Political Parties and Ideologies in Canada*, (Toronto: McGraw-Hill Ryerson, second edition, 1983), pp. 85-99 *passim*.

4. Brian Mulroney, *Where I Stand*, (Toronto: McClelland and Stewart, 1983). Excerpts from this book have been reprinted with the permission of McClelland and Stewart.

EPILOGUE

1. The delegates wanted the country to take tough stands in dealing with the Soviet Union and to seek closer political relations with the United States.

2. In fact, in the March 1983 issue of *The Decima Quarterly Report* , it was found that 44 per cent of the Canadian population agreed with the statement... "None of the political parties in Canada really stand for the things I believe in"...Only 41 per cent disagreed.

3. John R. Williams, *The Conservative Party of Canada*, (Durham, N.C.: Duke University Press, 1956), p. 42.

4. Point six of "Notes for a speech" by M. Brian Mulroney delivered to a meeting in Montreal, May 23, 1983.

Index

Index

Index

DATE DUE

NOV 2 7 2007	

PORTRAIT OF HO CHI MINH

PORTRAIT
OF HO CHI MINH

An Illustrated Biography

Reinhold Neumann-Hoditz

Translated by John Hargreaves

HERDER AND HERDER

123456789 BPBP 798765432

FIRST EDITION

Original edition: *Ho Chi Minh in Selbstzeugnissen und Bildokumenten,*
© 1971 by Rowohlt Taschenbuch Verlag GmbH, Reinbek bei Hamburg.

Library of Congress Cataloging in Publication Data

Neumann-Hoditz, Reinhold, date
    Portrait of Ho Chi Minh.

    Translation of Ho Chi Minh in Selbstzeugnissen und Bildokumenten.
    Bibliography: p. 185
    1. Ho-chi-Minh, Pres. Democratic Republic of Vietnam, 1894?–1969.   1. Title.
DS557.A76H68613   959.704′092′4 [B]   72-2904
ISBN 0-07-073788-6

CONTENTS

THE ENVIRONMENT

NGHE An Province lies in the central part of Vietnam, which became known as Annam after the Chinese occupation and kept that name until the declaration of independence from the French. Annam means "the country in the south" (that is, to the south of China). Since the partition of Vietnam in 1954, it has, however, belonged politically to the north, as it is situated to the north of the demarcation line on the 17th parallel. It is part of the Democratic Republic of Vietnam, which is commonly referred to as North Vietnam. This province has always been of great importance in the geography and history of Vietnam—and Nghe An was also the birthplace of Ho Chi Minh.

Vietnam gradually contracts into a strip of land which is only thirty miles wide at its narrowest point in Nghe An. The province borders on the sea, but its inhabitants have little contact with the water. It is a country of peasants with few fishermen. Nghe An is a transitional area, linking Tonkin (as the northernmost part of Vietnam was known before independence), whose climate is harsh and whose inhabitants resilient, to the less stable central and southern regions. Confucianism and rigid structures have always prevailed here, but the gentler, more tolerant influence of Buddhism is also present. Here too, the mountains slope down into the plain. There is a traditional contrast between the inhabitants of highland and lowland areas in Asia. The difficulties experienced by the two groups in understanding each other are noticeable in Nghe An too, but there is no gulf between them.

Nghe An is an outward-looking province whose inhabitants are self-reliant and independent. They are never servile. It has been a catalyst in the history of Vietnam, with a dynamic influence on the south, and has brought forth many important figures: scholars and poets, rebels and revolutionaries.

In the early fifteenth century, for example, it was here that the landowner Le Loi organized resistance against the Chinese who had recently occupied the country. But the resistance was defeated, and Vietnam had to accept once again the role of a tributary power, which lasted until the beginning of the French colonial occupation.

Perhaps Ho Chi Minh was thinking of his own native province when he wrote the following lines in a Kuomintang prison:

> Suddenly a flute sounds a nostalgic note:
> Sadly the music rises, its tune is close to sobbing:
> Over a thousand miles, across mountains and rivers
> Journeys an aching grief. We seem to see a woman
> Climbing a far-off tower, to watch for someone's return.

These lines were later published in Ho's collection of poems, *Prison Diary* (Hanoi, 1967).

The poet Nguyen Du (1765–1820) also came from Nghe

An; he wrote the most famous work of Vietnamese literature, the verse novel *Kim Van Kieu*. It is an attack on the prevailing feudal system; Kieu, the young heroine, is a victim of the customs of her age.

Nghe An is not a rich province. The soil is poor and needs artificial irrigation. The country is overpopulated. The jungle of the Laos mountains spreads in from the west and reduces the already limited space available for the staple crop, rice. Nature has played a part in making the local population rebellious. But mental attitudes have been at least equally important. Because the soil was not rich enough to provide work and food for all the population, some members of the peasant community became scholars. Ho's father, for example, was a *Pho Bang* (a doctor of the second grade) who had passed the traditional competitive examinations in Chinese script and classical philology. Many champions in the learned literary competitions organized by the imperial court in Hue according to the Sino-Confucian rules came from Nghe An province. These award winners, the mandarins, were given responsible posts in the state.

It is therefore not surprising that the first resistance to the European foreigners developed here when the French (after signing the protectorate treaty) occupied the venerable imperial city of Hue (1885). Confucian scholars organized a rebellion against the French which lasted for eleven years. This rebellion has become known as the "Scholars' Revolt" (*Van Than* or *Can Vuong*) in the history of Vietnam.

Finally in 1930 and 1931 the "Nghe Tinh Soviets" were formed in the neighboring provinces of Nghe Nan and Ha Tinh; this movement was based on Marxist-Communist prin-

Near the Lam River in the province of Nghe An lies the village of

ciples and attacked both the colonial power and the local feudal structure. With the help of the Communist Party founded only a few months earlier, a kind of people's government was quickly established; it was instrumental in bringing about land reform. The only official collection of writings dealing with the life of Ho Chi Minh, *Souvenirs sur Ho Chi Minh* (Hanoi, 1962), states that 217 demonstrators from the Nghe Tinh Soviets fell on September 12, 1930 under a hail of bullets and bombs on the road leading to Uncle Ho's native village.

The only serious opposition to Communist rule also came from Nghe Tinh: this was the peasant's revolt of November 1956, directed against the brutal methods of land reform and the abuse of power by officials. The army soon quelled this revolt. But the party and President Ho Chi Minh himself found it necessary to admit to certain "errors."

The future patriot, revolutionary, and politician Ho Chi Minh grew up among people with a keen sense of history. As a child he heard tales of popular heroes from his own region: Mai Hac De who became emperor after defeating the Chinese with an army of peasants in 722 and Quang

Kim Lien, Ho Chi Minh's birthplace.

Trung (Nguyen Van Hue) who unleashed a revolt at the end of the eighteenth century which put an end to the rivalry between two dynasties, re-united the north and south after two hundred years of division and forced a Chinese army to retreat.

Hundreds of historical anecdotes are current in Vietnam, and young Nguyen Tat Than, as Ho was called when he was a boy, must have known many of them because his father is said to have been a master of the art of ceremonial story-telling. It is worth considering some of these legends and true events here because they prove the historical awareness of the simple people of Vietnam and their close ties with tradition. They show more clearly than any chronological table that this country has had to fight an almost uninterrupted series of battles for its independence. Historically speaking, the present conflict is certainly understood by the majority of the population of Vietnam as the continuation and final phase of this long struggle for national independence.

When China controlled Vietnam, its governors ruled with great cruelty. To Dinh was perhaps the worst of them all. He

11

persecuted anyone whom he disliked with unrelenting persistence. In his day two sisters of a noble family named Trung Trac and Trung Nhi lived in Vietnam.

Trung Trac was married to a man named Thi Sach. One day Thi Sach contradicted governor To Dinh on a paltry matter and the governor ordered his immediate execution without trial. His widow Trung Trac did not put on white mourning garments as other women would have done. Instead she donned her dead husband's armor and cried out to the people, "For how much longer will you tolerate this injustice? Take up your arms!" The people banded together

The Trung sisters.

under the leadership of the two sisters and drove out the
Chinese. The sisters marched victoriously on the capital and
the delighted people named Trung Trac queen; she ruled
with great wisdom and benevolence. But the Chinese emperor
did not accept defeat. He sent a great army under his best
general. Once again the Trung sisters called upon the people
to take up arms. The attack was defeated in the Vietbac
mountains (in the far north of Vietnam). But while the
Chinese received constant reinforcements the number of
Vietnamese warriors declined. The last battle was fought
by the river Cam Khe near the village of Buong Tay. When
the sisters saw that all hope was lost they threw themselves

Victory over To Dinh.

into the river to prevent the victors from taking them alive. Their bodies drifted downstream and were pulled onto the shore by peasants. Here they are said to have become stone statues which can still be seen today in a temple at the mouth of the Song Hai.

The revolt of the Trung sisters took place around 40 A.D., at a time when Vietnam had already been under Chinese rule for 150 years. And so it was to remain for nine more centuries.

Today a girls' secondary school in Hanoi bears the name "Trung Vuong" (Queen Trung), and a pagoda has been erected in honor of the sisters. When the Chinese president Chou En-lai visited the capital of communist North Vietnam for the first time, he asked to be taken to the pagoda of the Trung sisters. He bowed deeply in honor of the struggle for liberation fought against his own people and his gesture made a deep impression on the Vietnamese.

The American author Susan Sontag (*Trip to Hanoi,* New York, 1969) learned of the Trung sisters in Hanoi in the summer of 1968, when the girl who was acting as her guide in the Historical Museum pointed out that two women had led the first successful Vietnamese revolt against foreign rule more than a thousand years before Joan of Arc. The guide added: "The tradition of the sisters lives on today. Many women have distinguished themselves in our new struggle."

The "stakes of the Bach Dang river" are also exhibited in the Hanoi Historical Museum. Tran Hung Dao, a prince of the Tran dynasty who drove out the Mongols in the thirteenth century, adopted subtle methods of warfare. He ordered stakes to be driven into the bed of the coastal river Bach Dang at high tide. The Mongol fleet was decoyed into the river and trapped when the tide ebbed and the level of the river fell.

All the episodes of this kind describe the struggle of a small nation against strong invaders, to maintain the ordinary people's rights. In *Prison Diary,* Ho himself described the phenomenon in these words:

All over Asia flutter the anti-Japanese flags:
Big flags or little flags—they are not all the same.
Of course, big flags we must have, but we need the little flags too.

Many temples throughout the land are dedicated to Tran Hung Dao and Le Loi. A curious legend surrounds one of them:

When the Chinese had once again occupied the country

The Battle of Bach Dang.

the people suffered heavily under foreign rule. Resistance developed in many places. At this time a poor fisherman lived in Hanoi. His name was Le Loi (popular legend has transformed the rich peasant into a poor fisherman). While he was out fishing one day in the lake which lies in the middle of the town, the gods sent a sign to him. When Le Loi hauled in his net he found a magnificent sword in it. He understood this supernatural message and became a rebel leader. With his miraculous sword whose strength put the enemy to flight, Le Loi drove out the Chinese. After the victory he returned to Hanoi and went to the shore of the lake to thank the water spirit. But when he reached the water's edge the sword suddenly slipped out of its scabbard and changed into a jade-colored dragon that disappeared in the water. The watching

16

people acclaimed Le Loi as their king. His rule was just and benevolent and he founded the powerful Le dynasty.

The lake in Hanoi still bears the name Ho Hoan Kiem—that is to say, the "Lake of the Restored Sword." One evening in February 1930, women burnt incense sticks on its banks. That was on the eve of a revolt which the National People's Party of Vietnam intended to unleash against the colonial rulers. As Jean Chesneaux points out in his book *Vietnam* (Frankfurt am Main, 1968), the population knew of the impending revolt, but the French did not understand this sign. The Yen Bai revolt was put down with great bloodshed and its leaders fled or were executed. The National People's Party disintegrated as a result.

Subterfuge and primitive means of warfare exploiting natural advantages to the full have typified all national movements in Vietnamese history. Similar methods are still

Ho Hoan Kiem, the "Lake of the Restored Sword."

17

being used by the National Liberation Front of South Vietnam (NLF). Ho Chi Minh has often spoken of *Can Cu,* the art of improvisation and adaptation to difficulties; the term could also be translated as "skill" or "resilience" and offers a good description of the attitude of the Vietnamese people. Quang Trung, for example, had the original idea of dividing his army into groups of three. Two soldiers carried a hammock in which the third rested on the march. In this way the soldiers were able to rest alternately and the army advanced in day and night marches with unheard-of speed to take the enemy unawares and defeat him all the more easily. It is not difficult to draw a parallel with Dien Bien Phu (1954), when the logistic achievements of the Vietminh soldiers astonished the whole world (and especially the French). The Vietminh troops transported loads of up to 800 pounds on a single bicycle fitted with two supporting bars at right angles to each other. In this way heavy artillery was transported to the front in an area where roads were almost nonexistent. The French had only expected coolie loads of fifty pounds to be carried. The result was the Waterloo of the Fourth Republic. These same bicycles are still being used in Vietnam today.

Young Nguyen Tat Thanh often listened to these tales of the past. The revolutionary Nguyen Ai Quoc (later to become Ho Chi Minh) recalled historical actions when he appealed from hiding to his countrymen to rise up against the French and Japanese: ". . . The loyal and heroic spirit of our predecessors such as Phan Dinh Phung, Hoang Hoa Than, and Luong Ngoc Quyen [resistance fighters against the French between 1885 and 1917] is still alive; the heroic

18

feats of our revolutionaries in Thai Nguyen, Yen Bai, Nghe An, and Ha Tinh provinces remain forever in our memory . . . Some hundreds of years ago, when our country was endangered by the Mongolian invasion, our elders under the Tran dynasty rose up indignantly and called on their sons and daughters throughout the country to rise as one in order to kill the enemy. Finally they saved their people from danger, and their good name will be carried into posterity for all time. The elders and prominent personalities of our country should follow the example set by our forefathers in the glorious task of national salvation . . ." (*SW*, II, 152f.).*

YOUNG HO AND HIS FAMILY

Ho Chi Minh's native province was traditionally a source of nationalist ideas. The members of his own family were not people to accept the fate of their country as immutable. Some of them were actively involved in resistance to the French. There can be no doubt that the impressions Ho received in his early youth affected his whole life.

Unlike Mao Tse-tung, Ho Chi Minh never described his early life and political development to a Western observer. For details of his family history, childhood, and youth, we are dependent exclusively on second- or third-hand information published in Hanoi. Even Bernard B. Fall, the American

* For this and subsequent sources in text, see abbreviations listed in the Bibliography.

19

Vietnam expert, who obtained an interview with Ho Chi Minh in Hanoi in the summer of 1962, could not persuade the President to discuss his own life: "Ah, but you know, I am an old man, a very old man. An old man likes to have a little air of mystery about himself. I like to hold on to my little mysteries." And when Bernard Fall objected, Ho answered jokingly: "Wait until I am dead" (*BF* 2, 111f.). We have therefore been obliged to base this chapter primarily on information taken from the biographical anthology *souvenirs sur Ho Chi Minh,* but it is reasonable to assume that the contributions were approved by Ho Chi Minh.

We have no photographs of his parents. His father, Nguyen Sinh Sac,* was a village scholar and had passed the imperial examinations; he did not come from an aristocratic environment, but from a peasant family which owned a little land in the village of Kim Lien or Sen. He was the son of a concubine. (According to the old Chinese tradition, a man was entitled to have one or more concubines in addition to his wife. The children of these liaisons were recognized as legitimate). Nguyen Sinh Sac's parents died while he was still young. He then lived with his older half brother who was not well disposed towards him. He found a way out by studying. Young Nguyen Sinh Sac grew attached to the village teacher Hoang Xuan An who gave him lessons. Ho's father was not only a very attentive pupil, but also handsome; the scholar's eldest daughter, Hoang Thi Loan, fell in love with this studious young man who would sit reading his

* The first of the three names is the family name in Vietnam, Nguyen is one of the most common patronymics. The second name frequently differs according to sex; the third is the forename.

The house in which Ho spent his childhood.

book on the back of a buffalo as he drove it out to the pastures. The stepfather gave the young couple a hut on his land and a rice plot. Ho and his brothers and sisters were born in this hut.

After Nguyen Sinh Sac had passed the mandarin's examination in the capital, Hue, in 1901, he returned to his village where a great celebration was organized in his honor. It was the first time a man from this district had achieved such distinction. This was reason enough for the villagers to be proud of their comrade; they even built a new house for him on public land and surrounded it with cacti and bamboo plants. Young Ho spent his childhood in this village house in Kim Lien. It is generally referred to today as Ho Chi Minh's birthplace.

But the newly appointed *Pho Bang* was not particularly

A mandarin in the imperial court.

pleased with his changed social status. He kept on postponing his return to Hue until he was finally obliged to take up his new post as a secretary in the Ministry of Protocol. He is reported to have said: "The mandarins are slaves among slaves and their bonds weigh even heavier than those of other slaves." Because of his overindulgent attitude to the laws, the French dismissed Ho's father from his post as District Head of Binh Ke in Binh Dinh Province. Louis Arnoux, who supervised the Annamese immigrants in Paris and later set up the Indochinese Sûreté, recalled in a conversation with

The empress mother in ceremonial dress.

Jean Lacouture, Ho Chi Minh's French biographer, that nationalist leanings were the reasons for Sinh Sac's dismissal. He had refused (at this time) to learn French. Officially he was accused of minor corruption which was certainly not classified as a serious offense. On the contrary, it was welcomed in officials who proved accommodating towards the French. Arnoux, a member of the secret police and certainly no friend of the revolutionary Ho Chi Minh with whom he was in contact for almost thirty years, said: "One of his sons was called Nguyen Tat Thanh: this was the future Nguyen Ai Quoc, the future Ho Chi Minh . . . Ho's life was begun in an atmosphere of injustice, of anger and bitterness, of hatred towards France" (L, 7). Ho's father cannot have been active on the side of the resistance fighters, because the Hanoi biographers are silent on this point. After being dismissed from state service, Nguyen Sinh Sac (whose wife had died long before) traveled south where he led an unstable life. In unofficial discussions with western visitors to Hanoi, Vietnamese spokesmen have often tried to idealize the final years of Sinh Sac's life. They like to describe him as a wandering aesthete who gave medical advice and taught young people, as a man who remained vigorous in his old age. The authorized biography shows, however, that reality was different (a fact which incidentally tends to confirm the objectivity of the Communist biographers). In the mid-1920s the old doctor could usually be seen sitting in front of a Chinese shop in the Rue Lagrandière in Saigon. Like the peasants of the south he wore a simple jacket and trousers of black cotton, instead of a "black silk costume." He diagnosed his patients and wrote prescriptions for them. In return he took as much money as he needed to keep alive. According to the *Viet-Nam Courier* (October 1969), "his daily nourishment was a boiled egg, a little fish sauce and a small bowl of rice."

Nguyen Sinh Sac lived in a pagoda and helped the illiterate priests to write down their prayers. In return he was given free lodging. From time to time he felt an urge to travel. He visited the famous ruined temples of Angkor in Cambodia. He clearly had no contact with his son, Nguyen

Vietnamese healer.

Ai Quoc, who was in Canton at the time. According to the official version, Ho's father was compelled to leave Saigon by the French because Nguyen Ai Quoc's revolutionary activity was becoming increasingly well known and it was supposedly feared that the father and son might meet. There is, however, good reason to doubt that the authorities took the old doctor so seriously. In any event, Nguyen Sinh Sac now began to wander the country aimlessly. People called him the "doctor with the reed basket" because he slept, like the poor people, in woven reed mats which he always carried with him; these mats afforded protection against the mosquitoes. In 1930 he fell ill and was found unconscious by the edge of a highway. He was carried to the house of a friend, an old man, with whom he lived from time to time, but he refused all food and medicine. He was taken into the nearby pagoda and died there.

The family of Ho's mother which also lived in Nghe An province, in Chua, a village near Kim Lien, is said to have engaged in active resistance to the colonial rulers. Hoang Xuan Hanh, an uncle of Ho's mother, joined a group of rebels which held out for twenty-five years in the northern Yen The mountains. It was led by the legendary Hoang Hoa Tham (De Tham), the last of a long line of popular leaders in the monarchist-Confucian tradition. His group continued to fight a losing battle for many years until Hoang Hoa Tham was murdered in 1913. Hoang Xuan Hanh was taken prisoner by the French and temporarily deported to the infamous settlement on Poulo Condore island. Later he worked with the politician Phan Boi Chau, to whom we shall return later.

Nguyen Sinh Sac and his wife Hoang Thi Loan had four children: a daughter Thanh, born in 1884, and three sons— Khiem, born in 1888, the future Ho Chi Minh, born in 1890, and Xin, at whose birth (in 1900) the mother died. At the time of the fourth birth, the family was living in Hue. The father was in the province of Thanh Hoa, where he had been sent to conduct an examination. The mother, who had been ill for some time, was very weak when she gave birth to her sickly son. She died with her baby in her arms, and the baby took her breast until his mother's body became stiff. Later on people said that the young Xin was

26

always weak and ill because he had drunk the milk of his dead mother. He died a few years later, probably in 1905.

Ho Chi Minh used or was given more than twelve names at different times in his life. This was, however, only partly a result of his revolutionary and conspiratorial activity. In Vietnam, as in all other countries under the cultural influence of China, it is common to give young people a new name to mark a fresh stage in their lives. Ignorance of this fact has given rise to endless speculation about Ho's early names.

Nguyen Sinh Cung (Coong) was the first name given to the boy who was born on May 19, 1890 in Kim Lien village in the Nam Dan prefecture of Nghe An province. Young Cung, the future revolutionary Nguyen Ai Quoc and statesman Ho Chi Minh, had the hair shaved from the top of his head like all the other boys in the district. A lock of hair was left on either side of his head according to the local custom. He was constantly mocked by other children because of this haircut when the family later moved to Hue.

Cung grew up in the country until he was seven or eight. In the village and surrounding countryside there were many pools; it was a marvelous world for the boy. Cung's favorite occupation was to watch people fishing. Sometimes he accompanied his father on the way to the school. Like all children, he put questions with untiring curiosity. One day a thunderstorm broke. When Cung heard the thunder he gripped the hand of another older boy and asked where the noise was coming from. From the sky, was the reply. "And is there anything else in the sky? Are there men up there?" The older boy—who still remembered this episode eighty

The citadel of Hue, around 1875.

years later in an article in the *Viet-Nam Courier*—did not know what to answer.

When Cung was about eight years old, his family moved to Hue. This was a completely new experience for the boy. Early in the nineteenth century at the end of the Tay Son rebellion, Hue had become the capital of the reunited country and the seat of the emperor and his court. Here there were high fortress walls, large, solid houses, mandarins in splendid clothes, and French soldiers. The town citadel, which was severely damaged in the second Indochinese war, still played a part in young Cung's life. It was here that Bao Dai, the last emperor of the Nguyen dynasty, abdicated on August 25, 1945, a few days after Ho Chi Minh had launched the August revolution. Ho's representative received the insignia

Throne room of the imperial palace, Hue.

of the old order from the emperor's hands in the throne room of the imperial palace.

The children led a happy life in Hue. Cung went on excursions into the town and surrounding countryside with his elder brother and other comrades. They built rafts of banana branches and played on the Song Huong, the "perfumed river." After his mother's death, the family returned to their native village.

Cung was now ten years old and was given the new name of Nguyen Tat Thanh, "Nguyen who is destined to succeed." The official biographers say that after his two journeys across country (it is about 200 miles from Kim Lien to Hue), after all he had experienced in the capital and after the death of his mother to whom he was deeply attached, Tat Thanh had become more mature than his comrades of similar age in the village. He was thoughtful and read a great deal. His favorite stories included the historical tales from China called "The Three Kingdoms" and "To the West." At this time his father was constantly postponing his return to the capital and working in the village as a teacher. However, he concerned himself only sporadically with the education of his children. When he was at home he sometimes wrote aphorisms on the wall and made his children learn them by heart. At school Nguyen Tat Thanh was not particularly interested in good marks or homework. He was far keener on learning the significance of all kinds of everyday things. He rarely stayed at home, but spent his time observing life around him just as he had done in Hue. Often he walked out alone to Thanh Ca, a local shrine situated on a hill with a good view all around. The house which the villagers had built for his father when he passed the mandarin's examination and in which the family lived had five rooms. Tat Thanh shared a room with his brother Khiem. There were two wooden beds by the window. On very hot days a hammock was slung across the room. Through the window there was a view of the Ru Chung mountains in the distance. Nearby was a smithy and to the right of the house an ancient well. The villagers said that the rebels threw their swords into this old well when the enemy advanced with superior forces. But when the enemy had vanished, they fished their swords out again. There were a few old graves in the garden in the shadow of the lemon and grapefruit trees.

At this time the French administration was using forced labor to build the Cua Rao colonial highway in the upper reaches of the Lam River near the frontier between Vietnam and Laos. Its main purpose was to make the "pacification" of this area easier. (Since 1893, Laos too had belonged to the "Indochinese Union" under a French governor). The forced recruitment (*corvée*) of local men between the ages of eighteen and fifty for road building work, which Nguyen Tat Thanh had watched in his village and district, must have made a lasting impression on the growing child.

"The purpose of the *corvées* is not merely to build pathways round the houses of a few Europeans for their amusement. Always at the mercy of the resident, the local population has to do much harder work. The road construction in Tourane, Tran Ninh, and Ai Lao (Laos) has left many painful memories. The persons enrolled for forced labor had to walk sixty miles to reach the building sites. There they were lodged in miserable huts. There was no hygiene and no proper medical care. They were worked to the bone, given an inadequate ration of rice, a piece of dried fish, and forced to drink the polluted water of this mountainous region. Illnesses, exhaustion and maltreatment took their toll . . . On the way into the mountains where death awaited them, whole convoys of requisitioned workers who had to support long days without food attempted to run away or rebelled. This led to terrible reprisals by the guards and the road was littered with corpses" (*SW* II, 84f.). Tat Thanh alias Nguyen Ai Quoc wrote these sentences in French in the 1920s. They are included in his first major work, "*Le Procès de la Colonisation française*" ("French Colonization on Trial"—

31

French officers in Tonkin.

probably written in Moscow), which appeared in Paris in 1925. It is a pamphlet intended for French readers whom the author wished to inform of the crimes committed not just in Indochina, but in French colonial territories.

Doctor Nguyen Sinh Sac's family (like all relatives of mandarins) was exempt from the *corvée*. Although the Cua Rao highway was more than 130 miles away from Nan Dan prefecture, labor was raised even here. People fled from their villages into the jungle as soon as the recruiting platoons approached. Often the settlements were surrounded at night because the authorities knew that villagers who had fled returned when darkness fell. The villagers were aroused by gongs and drums, lamps and torches, wailing women and barking dogs. Nguyen Tat Thanh must have experienced this often or heard reports describing the occurrences. It was said that the doctor had sold a few rice plots and used the money to assist forced laborers from his village. In these early years of the century, most of the uprisings against the colonial power had collapsed. Even Hoang Hoa Than had provisionally concluded an agreement with the French. Resistance at this time tended to be intellectual. Educated young or middle aged men like Phan Boi Chau (1867–1941) looked beyond the frontiers of Indochina to countries where modern ideas had already gained a foothold. The new generation to which Ho's father no longer belonged wanted to "learn from the West" how to defeat colonialism. Modern education was the watchword. Even Ho's father made the concession of learning French in his old age with the help of a dictionary.

At this time Japan, having just defeated the great Russian empire (1905), was a symbol of Asian emancipation from white rule. Many Asian reformers and revolutionaries looked toward Tokyo. Suffice it to say that Sun Yat-sen (1866–1925), the "father of the Chinese Republic," settled in Tokyo—so impressed was he by this first victory in recent history of members of the "yellow race" over the whites. Here he founded his "Brotherhood of Conspirators" (*Tung Meng Hui*) in 1905 out of which the Kuomintang developed. The Vietnamese nationalism of those days was also primarily based on the Japanese example.

As mentioned earlier, Phan Boi Chau was acquainted with Ho's family on his mother's side. He met Ho's father too. He was a famous scholar and patriot who encouraged rebellions and founded the *Dong Du* ("Trip to the East") nationalist movement. Young Vietnamese were encouraged to go to the land of the rising sun and study there. He even chose a member of the imperial family, Prince Cuong De, to go with him to Tokyo; Cuong De later became a puppet of the Japanese in occupied Indochina. The two sons of doctor Nguyen Sinh Sac were also among the talented young men whom Phan Boi Chau wanted to have educated in Japan. But this proved impossible. Khiem and Tat Thanh could not make up their minds without the approval of their father and he was strongly against the proposal. Many years later, Ho's official biographers suggest that the young Thanh, who was then fifteen years old and very enterprising, declined the invitation because he already realized that a revolutionary movement could not be created with representatives of the old society such as the pretended Cuong De. But biographers have certainly idealized the young Ho Chi Minh.

When his father returned to Hue, Tat Thanh attended the secondary school in the capital (1905). Quoc Hoc Lycée in Hue was then considered the best in Vietnam. Founded by a high official of the court, it was specifically intended to train an elite of young Vietnamese who were to be initiated to Western—and particularly French—education and knowledge without identifying with the West (France). The name of the school—*Quoc Hoc,* or "studies of the fatherland"— indicates the intentions of its founders. Bernard B. Fall, the French expert on Vietnam, mentions that other leading figures attended the Quoc Hoc School or passed their final examinations there: Vo Nguyen Giap, the victor of Dien Bien Phu; Pham Van Dong, the prime minister of North Vietnam; and Ngo Dinh Diem, the president of South Vietnam and Ho Chi Minh's opponent, who was later assassinated.

The official biographers tend, however, to play down the

importance of this school. The headmaster in Tat Thanh's day is said to have been a former foreign legionary who had been given this appointment as a reward. Ho Chi Minh discovered at this school that "the only concern of the French colonialists is to train obedient servants and not men who are capable of serving the people and country in a useful manner" (*Comm.*, 35). Even when he opened the People's University in Hanoi (January 19, 1955), President Ho Chi Minh did not mention his own school days in his address, but simply made a few polemic remarks on the education of young people in the past: "During their rule lasting for many decades, the imperialists and feudalists turned our young people into slaves . . . The old society was full of poison which was injected into the young but above all they were exposed to the harmful influence of American culture" (*SW* IV, 55f.). Whether Ho felt that he too was given the education of a slave in his youth is a matter open to question.

The syllabus of the Quoc Hoc School included natural science, history, and geography. The main subject was translation from French into Vietnamese and vice versa. The language used was *Quoc Ngu*, the romanized form of Vietnamese. Tat Thanh had already learned the new script before entering the school.*

In these days, many patriotic movements were started in Vietnam but most were only short-lived. The "Trip to the

* *Quoc Ngu* became the popular written language early in the twentieth century. It replaced the complicated *Chu Nom* script which attempted to use Chinese characters for the Vietnamese language. This system had been confined to scholars because it could only be used by those with a knowledge of Chinese. Until the twentieth century, all the major literary works in Vietnam were written in Chinese.

East" movement, the *Dong Du* (1904–1909), was followed by the *Don Kinh Nghia Thuc* (Tonkin Institute), an association for free education of the people. Its aim was to propagate the national culture, as well as its own written language and revolutionary ideas. This was a movement of renewal and modernization. Just as long pigtails disappeared in Sun Yat-sen's China, men in Vietnam were urged to crop their hair and wear short jackets instead of the long traditional

Long nails: a sign of aristocracy in old Vietnam.

The marketplace.

garments; they were also instructed to use domestic rather than imported products. And once again protest demonstrations were organized against compulsory recruitment and the continual increases in taxes. Early in 1908, almost all the provinces of Central Vietnam were affected by a wave of patriotic fervor. The people converged on Hue. On the way, they cut their hair in public and trimmed their long clothing. They surrounded the citadel and house of the French resident. The population of the capital joined them. The people's uprising lasted for three days and nights until the French intervened and put it down forcibly. In the schools, Chinese script was generally replaced by *Quoc Ngu;* many scholars who had passed the mandarin's examination refused to take up their official duties and were imprisoned by the French or deported to the penal settlement on Poulo Condore island. Eighteen-year-old Nguyen Tat Thanh observed all these events closely. During the same period his own father was dismissed from the public service.

While the old doctor pursued his wanderings in South Vietnam, his two elder children, his daughter Thanh and son Khiem, were arrested in their native village because they had been in contact with the Nghe An rebels. They both served prison sentences. Ho's sister Thanh was described as particularly brave. For a time she ran a boarding house in the district capital of Vinh for low-ranking members of the local police force. She obtained weapons from her guests and passed them on to the rebels. The provincial mandarin, a Vietnamese, once said jokingly: "Other women bring forth children, you bring forth rifles." After the August revolution of 1945, the inhabitants of Kim Lien had doubts about the authenticity of the pictures of Ho Chi Minh. Was this really the Nguyen Tat Thanh who had been born in their village and grown up among them? Even his sister was not sure. She decided to see for herself. The elderly lady packed two ducks and twenty eggs in a basket as a present and set out. She met her brother again. Afterwards she returned to her village, where she died in 1954. She never married.

Ho's brother Khiem once sent a petition to the French Governor General Albert Sarraut in which he described the sufferings of men in his home district and called for reforms. He was living under poor conditions at the time. Khiem took keen interest in the teaching of Quoc Ngu at the local schools. He died—unmarried like his sister—in November 1950. Ho Chi Minh sent a telegram to the villagers (reprinted in the *Viet-Nam Courier,* November 1969):

"The onus of public affairs has not allowed me to look after him during his illness or to attend his funeral today. I humbly apologize for this failure in brotherly devotion and beg you to forgive a son who has had to put affairs of state before family feelings. Chi Minh." Khiem died at a time when Ho Chi Minh had to devote all his energies to the task of consolidating the position of the new state against the French.

After the death of the mother and the dismissal of the father, the Nguyen family finally broke up. Tat Tanh left the Quoc Hoc School after five years, evidently disappointed and without passing a final examination. He was now twenty years old. It remains a mystery why he suddenly appeared early in 1911 in Phan Thiet, a coastal town in the South where he became a teacher in a private school. The official biographers say nothing about his motives, while the *Viet-Nam Courier* of November 1969 offers a number of mysterious hints in the following quotation from a "former pupil of Schoolmaster Thanh": "There were about seventy pupils. The subjects were French, Chinese, and Vietnamese. Schoolmaster Thanh taught French and Vietnamese in the second and third classes. It was a boarding school; Thanh lived in the school. He always disappeared on Thursday and Sunday. Heaven only knows where he went. He taught at the school for eight months and then we learned one Monday morning in October 1911 that he had left without giving notice.

39

The pupils were dismayed, not only because he was a good teacher but also because they believed there were other motives for his being at the school than the need to earn a living." Did Ho Chi Minh's revolutionary activity begin in Phan Thiet, a small town about one hundred miles east of Saigon? This is unlikely. The Historical Committee of the Party and the Party Ideologist Truong Chinh simply mention that in spite of his admiration for the patriots and resistance fighters, Ho Chi Minh was already convinced that other solutions must be found. His country needed help and encouragement from outside. It was no use looking to Japan, because the assistance of that country in driving out the French would amount to "chasing the tiger out of the front door, only to let the wolf in at the back." He therefore wanted to visit France and other European countries to "watch men at work and then return to help his fellow countrymen." (*TC,* 10f.). But for the time being "schoolmaster" Nguyen Tat Thanh simply disappeared.

How could a young Vietnamese man find his way to France at this time? It was far from easy. Nguyen Tat Thanh went to Saigon and enrolled at a technical school which also trained sailors. Only three months later he had found a job which enabled him to take leave of his homeland. "He decided quickly and left the country with no possessions other than the burning faith of his twenty years" (*Comm.,* p. 35).

It would, however, certainly be mistaken to conclude from observations such as this one—which idealize the resolve of the twenty-two-year-old Ho—that he set out for the West as a young revolutionary. There is nothing to suggest that Nguyen Tat Thanh was anything more than an enterprising (if thoughtful) young man at this time who wanted first and foremost to see the world. Probably the idea was maturing in the back of his mind that his country and compatriots could only be helped from outside. He left with no fixed plan and his sympathy for his fellow countrymen had not yet turned into effective action. The young man did not know if he would find others to help him, like-minded people with whom he could join forces. Nguyen Tat Thanh had no inkling of what was happening in far-off Europe on the eve of the Great War or of the social changes brewing there. He did not set foot in Vietnam again for thirty years.

THE YEARS OF TRAVEL

LATE in 1911 or in the spring of the following year the liner *Latouche Tréville* owned by the French shipping company Chargeurs Réunis moored in Saigon harbor. One afternoon a slim young man came on board. A few Vietnamese were standing around on the deck. The young man asked them rather sheepishly if there was any work. They took him to the captain, who asked what the young man could do. The answer came: "Anything you like." "Good, then you can start tomorrow morning as mess boy." (*TDT,* 5).

The mess boy became known as Ba. This was Nguyen Tat Thanh's first pseudonym. He chose this alias so as not to dishonor his family's good name by the miserable work he did on board. This was in keeping with the Confucian scheme of order which treated the code of family honor with great respect.

Hard times now began for Ba. He started work at four in the morning. First he had to clean the kitchens and then fetch coal, stoke the kitchen boiler, and bring vegetables, meat, fish, and ice from the storeroom. Food had to be prepared for the French cooks and vegetables and potatoes peeled. Finally he had to clean the kitchen utensils. He was kept busy until nine in the evening. The work was hard, not only because Ba had no training; it was hot in the kitchen and very cold in the storeroom. Often he had to climb the gangway in rough seas with a heavy sack on his back. There were 700 to 800 passengers and crew members on board. The cooking pots in which their food was prepared were so large and heavy that he had to drag them along the floor when they needed cleaning or else stand on a chair to reach them. The sailor Mai, with whom Ba became friendly, remembers the first asparagus stems which the kitchen boy saw. He peeled them so thoroughly, including the tips, that they had to be thrown secretly overboard. While the others slept or played cards in the evening, Ba read until eleven o'clock or midnight or sat writing. He helped illiterate sailors to write letters home. At last Ba's first sea voyage was over. In Marseilles each Vietnamese crew member was paid wages of 100 to 200 francs plus tips. Ba, the kitchen boy, was given ten francs.

His first impressions of Europe with the electric streetcars and cafés of Marseilles must have been overwhelming. For the first time the young Annamese, dressed in clean clothes, was addressed as "monsieur" by a Frenchman when he went to a café on the Cannebière with his friends. Mai has noted some of the things he said: "So there are poor people in France too just as there are in Vietnam!" And when he noticed the prostitutes on board: "Why don't the French civilize their own countrymen before starting on us? Why are things like this, brother Mai?" But Ho Chi Minh was greatly struck by one thing: "The French are far better and more polite in France than they are in Indochina" (*TDT*, 7). This remark made in the early days of his stay in France certainly explains in large measure why Ho Chi Minh always had the friendliest of feelings towards simple French people.

1912 to 1917: six years of travel and apprenticeship during which Ho Chi Minh saw the world. His path to a position as a top Communist official is comparable with that of Chou En-lai. His formative years had a lasting influence. Ho Chi Minh was always an empiricist. He was never interested in dogma but was a keen observer. All that he discovered on his travels, and—above all—that he saw in the vast French colonial empire later moved him to make ironic comments: "The Gandhis and the De Valeras would have long since entered heaven had they been born in one of the French colonies. Surrounded by all the refinements of court-martial and special courts, a native militant cannot educate his oppressed and ignorant brothers without the risk of falling into the clutches of his civilizers" (May 25, 1922, in *L'Humanité* [*SW* I, 14]).

As a steward or sailor, Ba visited the ports of Spain and Portugal, the Mediterranean, and the North African coast. He traveled through West Africa down to the Congo and Madagascar. Mai recalls that Ba always went on shore in the

A postcard showing Dakar at the turn of the century.

ports, and returned with his pockets full of postcards and matchboxes.

When the ship sailed into Dakar in a heavy storm and it was impossible to use boats to reach the shore, the French port authority ordered a number of natives to swim out to the steamer. One after another the Negroes jumped into the sea and perished in the heavy waves. Although this was the normal procedure, Ba was deeply shocked. "The French are all right in France. But the French colonialists are cruel and inhuman. It is always the same. I saw something similar in Phanrang. The French burst out laughing when our country-men died on an errand for them. For the colonialists, the life of an Asian or African is not worth a centime" (*TDT*, 8).

Ba generally kept to himself on board. He avoided dis-putes and did not even take part in drinking bouts. All in all he was "a bit odd": even when he was not on duty he rose early almost every morning to watch the sunrise. In

44

his free hours he paced up and down the deck lost in thought; he would cry out in delight on seeing a picturesque landscape.

The sailor Mai probably exaggerated many of the things he reported about his colleague who later became famous. But we are left with the impression that Nguyen Tat Thanh, alias Ba, developed a healthy independence on his travels. To begin with he may have had an impression of inferiority because of his hard work and low wages, but this feeling probably soon disappeared. He must soon have realized that "natives" were not alone in being primitive and that the same backwardness could be found among white men. He learned to judge white men critically: "If one has a white skin, one is automatically a civilizer. And when one is a civilizer, one can commit the acts of a savage while remaining the most *civilized*" ("*Le procès de la Colonisation française*," *SW* II, 56).

In the summer or autumn of 1913, Ba appeared in London where he worked as a snow shoveler in a school yard, a stoker in a large apartment building, and a kitchen assistant in a hotel. He had come to London to learn English. His experience among Englishmen was evidently not unpleasant. "Snow shoveling was hard work. I was bathed in perspiration but my hands and feet were half frozen. After eight hours I was completely exhausted and hungry. I had to give up. But the director was a good man. He gave me sixpence and said in a kindly tone: 'This job is certainly too hard for you'" (*TDT*, 9). Ba is reported to have said this by a fellow countryman who worked in the famous Carlton Hotel with him. His second job, as a stoker, was not much easier. Once again Ba

The Carlton Hotel, London.

with his slim build—and despite his astonishing physical resistance—could not cope with it all. "I did not have enough warm things and I caught a cold. I had to stop for a fortnight. I used my savings to pay my rent, bread and butter, and six English lessons. I was left with six shillings and sixpence. I walked around Soho looking for work and was sent here" (*TDT*, 10).

In the Carlton Hotel things were better for him. The working hours were from 8 A.M. to midday and from 5 to 10 P.M. Ba now had time for serious study of English. He generally spent the early morning and lunch hours in Hyde Park, with a book and pencil. On his free day an Italian gave him English lessons. The Carlton was an ultra-modern hotel for the times. An electric hoist returned the dirty crockery to the kitchen where Ba and his colleagues were ready to wash up. They first had to separate the china from the silver. Ba who had learnt the meaning of hunger could not bear to let anything go to waste. He carefully gathered all the remainders—often a large piece of chicken or half a steak—and instead of throwing them away sent them back to the kitchen. This strange behavior aroused the interest of the chef. The great Escoffier asked the kitchen boy to explain himself: "Why do you not throw the leftovers away as the others do?" To which Ba replied: "It would be better to give this food to the poor instead of throwing it away." Escoffier, the head cook and probably the greatest master of his craft in his generation, seemed to like this reply: "Forget your revolutionary ideas for a moment and I shall teach you to cook so that you will earn a great deal of money. What about it?" (*TDT*, 10f). Ba was then promoted from dishwashing to the post of assistant cook in the pie bakery where he not only earned more money but became accustomed to good food. (Ho Chi Minh could have been a gourmet except that circumstances generally prevented any indulgence on his part.)

But he was still far from being a revolutionary. Ba is also described as very sentimental; he is said to have burst out in tears on seeing how the natives were treated in Dakar. And his colleague in the Carlton said that he saw Ba one day with a newspaper and tears in his eyes. "Look at this report about the mayor of Cork, a great Irish patriot. He was sent to prison by the English. He went on hunger strike and said not a word. He just lay there without even moving—for sixty-nine long days. He died for his country. How courageous! How heroic! A nation which has men like that will never give in" (*TDT,* 11). The Irish struggle for home rule affected the young Ho Chi Minh in London as much as the events in his own country of which he heard occasional reports. One major factor in his future revolutionary development was his encounter for the first time here in the British capital with men who had the same cares and concerns that he did. Ba joined an organization called *Lao Dong Hai Ngoai* ("Workers Overseas"), a group of Asians, mostly Chinese, living in London. They were opposed to colonialism and here Ho Chi Minh had his first experience of revolutionary agitation.

The sentimentality of this young man which often moved him to tears must not be confused with a weak character. His heightened sympathy may also have involved a measure of self-pity coupled with great homesickness and a feeling of abandon and anxiety in face of life. He had set out on his travels with no fixed purpose and with some misgivings. Even before leaving Indochina, he had said in Saigon: "It will be dangerous to travel alone. One may for example fall ill" (*Viet-Nam Courier,* special issue, eightieth anniversary of the birth of Ho Chi Minh, Hanoi 1970). Moreover, he would have to break all his family ties—ties that are far more important to Asians than to West Europeans. At last, however, he came to realize in London that he was not alone in his struggle against the whites. Here the twenty-three-year-old man discovered the feeling of strength that comes from belonging to an organization. As yet he had no intention of joining a political party.

At the outbreak of the First World War, Ba left for

France. He wanted to make contact with compatriots such as Phan Chu Trinh (1872–1926) and Phan Van Truong (1878–1933), both patriotic intellectuals who belonged to the reform movement. But there were obviously difficulties. Ba was also afraid of being called up for military service. In any event, he soon joined a ship again, this time on the America run.

The official biographers in the "Historical Committee of the Vietnam Workers' Party" deal with the American interlude in a few sentences, and even American sources give no further details. We are told that he studied social conditions, life, and political systems in the New World. He is said to have been shaken by the cruelty of American capitalism and the terrible lynch justice meted out by the Ku Klux Klan to the Negroes. He was also able to see how the American workers called protest strikes against the war and to demand higher wages. "On all these journeys he made one bitter observation: imperialism always looks the same: in France, England or America. By its very nature it cruelly exploits the proletariat in the mother country and the working masses in the colonial states" (*Comm.*, 37). On his journey to the U.S., Ba only visited the East Coast ports. Ten years later, Ho Chi Minh studied the American racial problem in greater depth when he attended the Eastern Workers University in the Soviet Union. He was a regular contributor at this time to the journal *La Correspondance Internationale,* and wrote two articles on lynching ("*Le lynchage*") and the Ku Klux Klan. After a detailed list and description of many appalling cases of lynch justice in the United States (Ho quotes local American press reports) he concludes in his first article on "a little known aspect of American civilization": "Among the collection of the crimes of American 'civilization,' lynching has a place of honor" (*SW* I, 105). When Nguyen Tat Thanh set foot in France again towards the end of the First World War, he saw his future mapped out before him. His immediate aim was to improve the inhuman conditions in his own country—in other words, to force the colonial regime to introduce certain reforms. As yet, however, there was no mention of a worldwide revolution by the exploited masses against imperialism. This slogan was not taken up by Ho Chi Minh until he went to Moscow.

Nguyen Tat Thanh, alias Ba, now adopted the name Nguyen Ai Quoc, "Nguyen who considers love (*Ai*) of the fatherland (*Quoc*) as the highest virtue," or "Nguyen the patriot."

THE BEGINNINGS

In Paris Nguyen Ai Quoc came into contact with international politics for the first time. Here he took up the struggle for the political rights of the Vietnamese people and became a Communist.

When the peace conference was convened in Versailles on January 18, 1919, the "modest demands of the Annamese people" were laid before the conference secretariat. They bore the signature Nguyen Ai Quoc. On behalf of a "group of Annamese patriots" he had drafted these eight points with

The Versailles conference.

Phan Chu Trinh and Phan Van Truong, who translated the document into good French. On reading the text again today, one is astonished at how modest the claims of the Vietnamese patriots in fact were. They cover the following points: 1) A general amnesty for political detainees; 2) Equal rights for the Annamese and French in Indochina; 3) Freedom of the press and freedom of opinion; 4) Freedom to meet and assemble; 5) Freedom to emigrate and travel abroad; 6) Better school and educational facilities; 7) Abolition of the principle of rule by decrees of the French president rather than by laws; 8) Appointment of permanent representatives in the French Parliament to support the interests of the Annamese.

There is no mention of independence or self-determina-

REVENDICATIONS
Peuple Annamite

TRICH DỊCH 8 ĐIỀU YÊU SÁCH
TRONG BẢN BÊN

1) Ân xá cho tất cả chính trị phạm bản xứ ;

2) Cải cách nền pháp lý ở Đông - Dương bằng cách ban bố cho người bản xứ cũng được những đảm bảo về pháp lý như người Âu châu, xóa bỏ hoàn toàn và triệt để các tòa án đặc biệt dùng làm công cụ khủng bố và áp bức đối với bộ phận trung thực nhất trong nhân dân An-Nam ;

3) Quyền tự do báo chí và ngôn luận ;

4) Quyền tự do lập hội và hội họp ;

5) Quyền tự do xuất dương và đi du lịch nước ngoài ;

6) Quyền tự do giáo dục thành lập các trường kỹ thuật chuyên nghiệp ở tất cả các tỉnh cho người bản xứ học ;

7) Thay chế độ ra các sắc lệnh bằng chế độ ra các đạo luật ;

8) Có đại biểu thường trực của người bản xứ do người bản xứ bầu ra tại nghị viện Pháp để giúp nghị viện biết được những nguyện vọng của người bản xứ .

The "eight-point demand."

tion, even though the authors had been inspired by President Wilson's Fourteen Points. But Nguyen Ai Quoc and his friends were to see their modest claims disregarded. The representatives of other nationalities—Irish, Arabs, Indians, or Koreans—were far more emphatic in their demands. They were able at least to gain a worldwide hearing. Nguyen Ai Quoc, however, had to return his hired dark suit and bowler hat without even using them. He did not gain the audience with world leaders for which he had hoped. Neither Wilson nor Lloyd George, let alone Clemenceau, received the insignificant and modest Asian. The name of Annam or Vietnam does not appear in the minutes of the Versailles conference.

Although the "demands" did not gain official recognition,

52

they did not pass unheard. The socialist newspaper *Le Populaire* was alone in publishing the opinions of the Vietnamese. With the modest funds available, leaflets were printed and distributed primarily to the Indochinese soldiers in the French army. Close to 100,000 of them—for the most part Annamese—had helped the French to win the war as combatants or workers. Nguyen also sent a few leaflets to Indochina, but only those addressed to French citizens reached their destination.

Around this time, a classified advertisement appeared from time to time in the trade union newspaper *La Vie*

Impasse Compoint, Paris XVII. Ho's room is marked with a cross.

Ouvrière: "If you would like a lifelong memento of your family, have your photos retouched at Nguyen Ai Quoc's. A lovely portrait in a lovely frame for 45 francs. 9 Impasse Compoint, Paris XVII." This was the poorest street in the poor section of the XVII. Arrondissement, an alley consisting of only four delapidated houses, three of which were rented out as storage areas. The house which was still occupied had two tenants; Nguyen Ai Quoc lived in a single room which was only three yards square. An iron bedstead and a small table were his only furniture. A French electrician, Jean Fort, lived next door. Like his neighbor, he later became a member of the French Communist Party. Between 1920 and 1922, Nguyen was permanently employed by the Lené Studio in Paris. As a photographer's assistant he was paid 160 francs a month; out of this he had to pay 40 francs for his room. Nguyen Ai Quoc, who was now thirty, attached some importance to appearances. He had visiting cards printed as he

Portrait-Agrandissements Photographiques

Nguyên Ai Quâc

9, Impasse Compoint, Paris (17)

One of Ho's visiting cards.

did later in China. But his life was far from being as bourgeois as it might have seemed.

"When he published the "eight points," Nguyen Ai Quoc met the editor of *Le Populaire,* Jean Longuet, the grandson of Karl Marx and a member of the French parliament. Nguyen was very surprised by the warmth of his reception. Longuet addressed him as "dear comrade," and encouraged the young Annamese to write articles for his newspaper so as to inform the French of the injustices perpetrated in Indochina. Nguyen was only too pleased to do so, but his French was not good enough. He asked the lawyer Phan Van Truong to polish up his style; but Phan did not like doing this and disagreed with much that Nguyen wanted to say. Thus Nguyen Ai Quoc began, with great difficulty, to write in French himself. The chief editor of *La Vie Ouvrière* also helped him by correcting in his own hand the articles written in bad French by Nguyen. Nguyen had developed a system which proved useful when he made his first steps in journalism. He always compared the copy of his own version word by word with the printed text and corrected the mistakes carefully. He slowly "learned" the art of writing with the help of his new French friends.

Nguyen Ai Quoc, sensitive as he was, suffered from his lack of formal education. He now made great efforts to improve his general knowledge by reading. He read Shakespeare and Dickens in English, Lu Hsun in Chinese, Hugo and Zola in French. His favorite authors were, however, Anatole France and Tolstoy.

Unfortunately none of Ho Chi Minh's early attempts at journalism have been preserved. The editors of his *Selected*

Works in Hanoi probably felt they were not important enough. The first of their four volumes begins with the essay (which we have already quoted) published in the Communist Party journal *L'Humanité* of May 25, 1922 under the title: "Some Notes on the Colonial Problem."

What did Nguyen Ai Quoc know at this time about intellectual movements and politics? He was aware of the conditions in his own country of which his comrades in Europe had heard very little. But he did not know the first thing about trade unions, strikes, or political parties. Nor was he interested in the difference between the Second Socialist, Second-and-a-half Pacifist, or Third Communist International (which had just been founded in Moscow). All that

Paris, 1920.

56

concerned him was whether they were doing anything to help the colonial people. "After World War I, I made my living in Paris, now as a retoucher at a photographer's, now as a painter of 'Chinese antiques' (made in France!). I would distribute leaflets denouncing the crimes committed by the French colonialists in Vietnam. At that time, I supported the October Revolution only instinctively, not yet grasping all its historic importance. I loved and admired Lenin because he was a great patriot who liberated his compatriots; until then, I had read none of his books" ("The Path which led me to Leninism," *SW* IV, 448ff.).

But under the influence of his new friends, Nguyen Ai Quoc had joined the French Socialist Party, where a heated debate raged in the immediate post-war years between the traditionalists and the left (which sympathized with the Bolshevik October Revolution). His notes continue: "The reason for my joining the French Socialist Party was that these 'ladies and gentlemen' (as I called my comrades at that time) had shown sympathy toward me, toward the struggle of the oppressed peoples. But I understood neither what was a party, a trade-union, nor what was Socialism or Communism.

"Heated discussions were then taking place in the branches of the Socialist Party, about the question of whether the Socialist Party should remain in the Second International, should a Second-and-a-half International be founded, or should the Socialist Party join Lenin's Third International? I attended the meetings regularly, two or three times a week, and attentively listened to the discussions. First, I could not understand thoroughly. Why were the discussions so heated? The revolution could be waged either with the Second, Second-and-a-half or Third International. What was the use of arguing then? As for the first International, what had become of it?"

What is striking about this passage is the frankness with which Ho Chi Minh describes his original political naiveness. Few other Communist politicians have dared to reveal their political beginnings so completely. How sure of himself and convinced of his cause Ho Chi Minh must have been when he set down this confession at the age of seventy. His epigones have not always found it in themselves to describe Uncle Ho as frankly as he himself does. Ho continues: "What I wanted most to know—and this precisely was not debated in the meeting—was: which International sides with the people of colonial countries?

"I raised this question—the most important in my opinion —in a meeting. Some comrades answered: it is the Third, not the Second, International. And a comrade gave me Lenin's "Thesis on the National and Colonial Questions" published by *L'Humanité* to read.

"There were political terms difficult to understand in this thesis. But by dint of reading it again and again, finally I could grasp the main part of it. What emotion, enthusiasm, clear-sightedness, and confidence it instilled into me! I was overjoyed to tears. Though sitting alone in my room I shouted aloud as if addressing large crowds: 'Dead martyrs, compatriots! This is what we need, this is the path to our liberation!' After then, I had entire confidence in Lenin, in the Third International. Formerly during the meetings of the Party Branch, I only listened to the discussion: I had a vague belief that all were logical and could not differentiate as to who were right and who were wrong. But from then on I also plunged into the debates and discussed with fervor. Though I was still lacking French words to express all my thoughts, I smashed the allegations attacking Lenin and the Third International with no less vigor. My only argument was: 'If you do not condemn colonialism, if you do not side with the colonial peoples, what kind of revolution are you waging?'

"Not only did I take part in the meetings of my own Party Branch, but I also went to other Party Branches to lay down my position. Now I must tell again that Comrades Marcel Cachin, Valliant-Couturier, Monmousseau, and many others helped me to broaden my knowledge. Finally, at the Tours Congress, I voted with them for our joining the Third International."

We have no reason to doubt Nguyen Ai Quoc's spirit and honest conviction as described here retrospectively by Ho Chi Minh. It seems that Nguyen was beginning at this time to think of the subject which was to become the center of his life in the next ten years or so: worldwide revolution as a means of securing freedom from injustice for his fellow countrymen.

The Eighteenth Congress of the French Socialist Party was held in Tours from December 25 to December 30, 1930. Nguyen Ai Quoc joined the left-wing group and voted for a resolution on the foundation of the French Communist Party (FCP) and its entry into the Third International (Comintern). Nguyen Ai Quoc was a founder member of the FCP. A photograph which was first published by *L'Humanité* on December 28, 1920 shows the young idealist

The Tours congress.

Nguyen looking even younger than his age in Tours beside the replete, mustachioed veterans of the Socialist Party establishment who seem to be smiling condescendingly in his direction. It is hardly surprising that Nguyen did not feel attracted to these party representatives, but turned instead to the left-wing members such as Marcel Cachin, Paul Vaillant-Couturier, and the anarchosyndicalist Gaston Monmousseau who offered him both encouragement and promises. Jean La-couture, who has retraced Ho Chi Minh's movements in France, describes a participant in the congress listening to Nguyen's short and comparatively harmless speech "with a certain apprehensiveness, as though troubled by memories of the Yellow Peril" (L, 18).

The following quotation is taken from the shorthand record of the proceedings:

Chairman: I now call on Indochina.

Representative of Indochina: Comrades, I wish I were here today to collaborate with you in the task of world revolution; but to my utmost sorrow and regret I am here today to speak out, as a Socialist, against the abominable crimes perpetrated in my country of origin [*Cries of "hear, hear!"*].

As you know, French capitalism came to Indochina half a century ago. It conquered us at bayonet-point and in the name of capitalism. Since then, in addition to being shamefully persecuted and exploited we have been hideously martyred and poisoned (I stress the word "poisoned"—by opium, alcohol, etc. . . .). It is impossible to reveal to you, within the space of a few minutes, all the atrocities which have been perpetrated in Indochina by the capitalist bandits. The prisons, more plentiful than schools, are always open and shockingly overcrowded. Any native reputed to hold socialist ideas is jailed and sometimes executed without trial. This is so-called Indochinese justice, for out there men are weighed according to two different scales. The Annamese do not enjoy the same safeguards as the Europeans or the Europeanized.

For us there is no such thing as freedom of the press and of opinion, nor freedom to hold meetings and form associations. We are not allowed to emigrate or travel abroad. We live in darkest ignorance, for we do not have freedom of education. In Indochina, every possible effort is made to intoxicate us with opium and besot us with alcohol. Several thousand Annamese have been put to death, and several thousand more slaughtered in defense of interests which are not their own.

This, comrades, is how more than twenty million Annamese, equivalent to more than half the population of France, are treated. And yet these Annamese are under the care and protection of France [*applause*]. The Socialist Party must, out of duty to itself, take effective measures on behalf of the native population [*sustained applause*] (*SW* II, 11ff.).

This brief address was certainly not a masterpiece of rhetoric; it was not even particularly logical (after all,

Nguyen himself was able to leave the country, and nobody had forced him to smoke opium or drink spirits). But all the delegates were able to sense the young man's holy anger. When conversations began in the hall and the delegates were evidently not discussing Nguyen's bitter accusations, his intellectual and colonial inferiority complex made itself felt once again. He reacted very sensitively: "I began by calling for silence! [*laughter*]"; and a little later: "Members will restrain themselves [*applause*]." And he ends with the stirring appeal: "In the name of the whole of mankind, in the name of all Socialists, right-wing and left-wing alike, we say to you: 'Comrades, rescue us!' [*applause*]."

Thus Nguyen Ai Quoc, like the majority of delegates to the conference, sided with the Communists and the Third International. When the representatives were leaving, Rose, the pretty young congress secretary, came up to the Indochinese delegate who was standing rather forlornly on one side: "Comrade, now you can see why we have discussed this problem at such length in Paris, can't you?" (Nguyen had once complained bitterly at a meeting that there were too many idle discussions while his fellow countrymen were left to suffer.) Nguyen replied: "No, not entirely." "Why then did you vote for the Third International?" "That is quite simple. I did not understand a single word of what you said about strategy, proletarian techniques, etc. But one thing I did understand. The Third International is paying considerable attention to the colonial problem. It promised to help the repressed peoples to recover their freedom and independence while the Second International did not even mention the fate of the colonies. That is why I voted for the Third International" (*TDT*, 22f.).

Here we see for the first time the *practical* aspect of Ho's communism which was to remain a dominant feature throughout his life. In this respect too he proved himself a genuine son of the people. Vietnam has never produced important theoreticians, either Confucian or Communist.

Communist dogmatists who thought they were putting Ho in a particularly favorable light wrote after his death that only his enemies branded him a nationalist whereas in reality he had become an internationalist far away from his homeland. We do not propose to examine here the complicated problems of the fluid boundary between patriotism and nationalism. However, it is clear that—particularly in Asia —all the really great revolutionaries were in the first instance fierce patriots and nationalists, characteristics which the people obviously look for in their leaders. But let Ho speak for himself:

"At first patriotism, not yet Communism, led me to have confidence in Lenin, in the Third International. Step by step, along the struggle, by studying Marxism-Leninism and participating in practical activities, I gradually came upon the fact that only Socialism and Communism can liberate the oppressed nations and the working people throughout the world from slavery.

"There is a legend, in our country as well as in China, on the miraculous Book of the Wise. When facing great difficulties, one opens it and finds a way out. Leninism is not only a miraculous book of the wise, a compass for us Vietnamese revolutionaries and people: it is also the radiant sun illuminating our path to final victory, to Socialism and Communism."

We have quoted here from Ho Chi Minh's essay "The Path Which Led Me to Leninism" because we consider it the most important testimony and confession of faith by the Vietnamese revolutionary and statesman.

Mankind was threatened not by the "yellow peril" which sent a chill down the spine of the Socialist delegate in Tours, but by white colonialism which had held back the development of the colored world. Was it surprising that Nguyen Ai Quoc and other patriots from many colonial countries welcomed the Bolshevik revolution in Russia and communism in general as the beginning of their liberation? None of the established parties in the Western democracies seemed really interested in the colonial problem. The only promise of help came from revolutionary Russia and the Communists. How could it be refused?

"The Russian revolution . . . did not confine itself to high-sounding platonic speeches and pleas for humanitarian attitudes towards the repressed peoples. Instead it taught them to fight. It gave them moral and material help, as Lenin wrote in his essays on colonialism" ("*Le Procès de la Colonisation française*," *SW* II, 130).

Let us not forget that Nguyen Ai Quoc, and thousands of idealists with him, understood communism as a doctrine of freedom and humanity.

THE REVOLUTIONARY

FROM now on Nguyen Ai Quoc was a revolutionary—a Vietnamese revolutionary and an international revolutionary, in that order. His activities in France had important personal consequences for him. He became known both to the police and to his fellow countrymen. The police watched Nguyen's movements closely. Louis Arnoux, the French secret-service agent, summoned him to frequent interviews. They generally met in a small café near the Paris opera. Arnoux remembers altogether benevolently the young man who talked to him about his country, village, and family with infectious enthusiasm. "How could I ever forgive France for perpetrating such crimes!" Nguyen said in one of these conversations (*L,* 16). The first "official" photograph of Ho Chi Minh—a photograph taken by the French police—also dates from this period, the early twenties.

Bui Lam, a Vietnamese from the Haiphong district, who had signed on like his fellow countryman to a ship of the Chargeurs Réunis line and remained in France, recalled for the *Viet-Nam Courier:* "The name Nguyen Ai Quoc had an extraordinary magnetism. We felt we were doing a good deed when we mentioned it." The articles which Nguyen Ai Quoc wrote in various newspapers, were eagerly read and discussed by the Vietnamese in France. This was particularly true of *Le Paria,* the journal of the Union Intercoloniale founded by Nguyen Ai Quoc.

The Intercolonial Union, representing the "natives" of all French colonies living in metropolitan France, had been

Photograph taken by the French police in the 1920s.

founded in 1921 in order to make the general public acquainted with the problems of the colonial people. The initial manifesto of this organization, like the "claims" addressed to the Versailles Peace Conference, made no mention of self-determination or even of independence for the colonial peoples but referred solely to human and political freedom. It concludes with a reference to Karl Marx's appeal in the Manifesto of the Communist Party: "Workers of the world, unite!"

Nguyen was the publisher and chief editor of *Le Paria*. He was responsible for financial management and distribution and wrote up to three articles himself in each edition. The journal appeared monthly between 1922 and 1926 and later at irregular intervals, especially after Nguyen had left France. It was financed by donations. Sales at newstands (25 centimes per copy) were so small that Nguyen frequently appeared at political meetings with a bundle under his arm, jumped onto the platform and handed out copies. "Comrades, *Le Paria* costs nothing. But if you feel like it, I should welcome a small contribution to cover the costs. One centime, one franc—any contribution, every centime helps" (*TDT*, 19). In the colonies the journal was forbidden but it was introduced secretly, generally by sailors.

Le Paria.

Le Paria confined its reports almost exclusively to events in the French colonies, generally in Indochina. The contributions by Nguyen Ai Quoc (Nguyen Ai Quac) usually reported in a dry style bare facts of attacks by the colonial authorities, cases of cruelty or economic exploitation. Statistics were also given. Some titles show the tenor of the articles: "The Civilizers"; "Racial Hatred"; "Murderous Civilization"; "Annamese Women and the French Overlords"; "The Martyrdom of Amdouni and Ben Belkhir"; "Just Like Home." The author wrote in great earnest; he set out his accusations and attached little importance to polish and literary style. But there was an exception in the sarcastic tone of the "Open Letter to Mr. Sarraut" (August 1, 1922), addressed to the minister for the colonies, who had just ordered more stringent measures of supervision for Annamese citizens living in France:

Your Excellency,

We know very well that your affection for the natives of the colonies in general, and the Annamese in particular, is great. Under your proconsulate the Annamese people have known true prosperity and real happiness, the happiness of seeing their country dotted all over with an increasing number of spirit and opium shops which, together with firing squads, prisons, democracy, and all the improved apparatus of modern civilization, are combining to make the Annamese the most advanced of the Asians and the happiest of mortals. These acts of benevolence save us the trouble of recalling all the others, such as enforced recruitment and loans, bloody repressions, the dethronement and exile of kings, profanation of sacred places, etc. . . . You have created in Paris itself a service with the special task . . . of keeping watch on the natives, especially the Annamese, living in France. But keeping watch alone seemed to your excellency's fatherly solicitude insufficient, and you wanted to do better. That is why you have granted each Annamese . . . private aides-de-camp . . . At a time when Parliament is trying to save money and cut down administrative personnel, when there is a large budget deficit, when agriculture and industry lack labor, when attempts are being made to levy taxes on workers' wages, and at a time when re-population demands the use of all productive energies, it would seem to us antipatriotic at such time to accept personal favors which necessarily cause loss of the powers of the citizens condemned—as aides-de-camp—to idleness and the spending of money for which the proletariat has sweated hard.

In consequence, while remaining obliged to you, we respectfully decline this distinction flattering to us but too expensive to the country.

In the summer of 1922, Bui Lam writes, he was asked by his friends who had read *Le Paria* to visit Nguyen Ai Quoc in Paris. "The articles encouraged us to act, but we did not know what to do. Then it occurred to us that we must speak to Nguyen Ai Quoc." Bui Lam—whose hagiographic description in the *Viet-Nam Courier* must be taken with a grain of salt—finally found his way to 6, rue des Gobelins, in the XIII. Arrondissement where Nguyen was living at the time. "A man of about thirty (Bui Lam himself was not yet twenty) very thin and pale, stood smiling before me . . . He wore an old suit of coarse, black cloth. And then there were his eyes—those big, shining eyes. The room was sparsely furnished. A table in one corner. A pile of newspapers, journals, and books. An iron bedstead and a small wardrobe. That was all. But it was a clean, bright, and pleasant room."

Nguyen and his young visitor soon found common ground. Bui Lam had to recount his experiences at sea, the ships on which he had sailed and the countries he had visited. He noticed that Nguyen mastered the sailors' jargon and knew almost all the places he mentioned. (However, even in those days Ho Chi Minh was not particularly communicative when it came to his own adventures.) And of course they spoke about their homeland. Bui Lam was asked to return the next morning, a Sunday.

Nguyen Ai Quoc turned out to be an art lover. When the two countrymen met again, Nguyen invited his young visitor to go to an art exhibition. They strolled down the rue Monge. Nguyen was wearing the same old black suit and heavy but comfortable boots with thick heels. The exhibition was being held in a building opposite the Panthéon. Nguyen greeted many people. Clearly he had a large circle of acquaintances. They looked at a picture painted by his friend, the Communist Party member, Vaillant-Couturier. After the exhibition Nguyen and Bui Lam went into the Panthéon and then to a Chinese restaurant in the rue Descartes.

Bui Lam also tells us how the revolutionary Nguyen Ai Quoc lived at this time in Paris. In the morning he made Chinese handicraft products for which he was paid on a piece rate. This was how he earned his living. He spent some of his earnings on the journal *Le Paria.* In the afternoon he worked at his editorial duties. He still wrote for other papers such as *L'Humanité* and *La Vie Ouvrière.* In the evening he could often be found in the Club du Faubourg where the Communist intellectuals held heated discussions of political, economic, or philosophical questions. Or else he went to the National Library. Nguyen was now gradually overcoming his complexes and counted himself as an intellectual of the young Communist Party. He now practiced to become a good orator and debater. He attended the meetings of his local party cell. Nguyen knew Paris fairly well, especially the suburbs of the "red belt" with the factories and workers' districts in which the Communist Party soon gained influence. After the first meeting with Bui Lam, Nguyen said to him as they parted: "We must join forces with the French workers. We are poor as they are, repressed and exploited" (*Viet-Nam Courier,* November, 1969). This feeling of belonging did not, however, prevent him from vigorously criticizing the French proletariat—his own comrades (proof again of his frankness).

In *L'Humanité* (May 25, 1922), he speaks of the "indifference of the protetariat in the motherland towards the colonies" and writes: " . . . the workers in the mother country must learn exactly what a colony is; they must become acquainted with the things which are happening there, with the sufferings which are the lot of their brothers, the proletariat of the colonies, and which are a thousand times worse than their own sufferings. In other words they must take an interest in this problem. Unfortunately there are many militant workers' representatives who still believe that a colony is simply a piece of land with a great deal of sand under foot and a hot sun overhead, a few green coconut palms and colored natives—nothing more. And they are not in the least interested in the colonies." Nguyen Ai Quoc then turns to the lack of education in the colonies and the prejudices which are rife: "The lack of knowledge among the two proletariats (in the colonies and mother country) about each other breeds many prejudices. The French workers look down on the natives as inferior and insignificant human beings who are incapable of taking any form of action. And the natives look upon all French people without distinction as brazen exploiters. Imperialism and capitalism take good care to exploit this mutual distrust . . ."

Nguyen Ai Quoc was then living under the same roof as the lawyer Phan Van Truong (twelve years his senior), who had given him a room in his flat in the rue des Gobelins. Phan Van Truong was not a Communist but a militant patriot. In Paris he published the weekly *Viet Nam Hon* (The Soul of Vietnam). Later Phan returned to his homeland where he founded the newspaper *An Nam,* which was the first journal in Indochina to reproduce the *Communist Manifesto* in full. Whereas in the French colonies (including the Indochinese protectorate) nationalist agitation and attacks on the colonial power were punished by heavy penalties and were therefore only possible under cover, in France itself the press was free, and the authorities could not take stern measures against agitators from the colonies because of the need to respect public opinion. Here nationalists of all kinds were able to seize their opportunity.

Nguyen Ai Quoc took advantage of this fact on his many journeys across France: he addressed discharged Vietnamese soldiers and workers who had been brought to Europe during the war and were now awaiting repatriation.

We have already mentioned that Nguyen Ai Quoc, like other revolutionaries from the colonies, soon became convinced that help in the struggle for national liberation could only be expected from the Bolsheviks and Communists of revolutionary Russia. In 1923 and at the turn of 1923/1924 the language of Nguyen's articles became more virulent and the range of subjects dealt with wider. The repression of all (colored) races now became the dominant theme, extending from Indochina and the French colonies to the workers' movement in Turkey and the English capitalist system in China. And when the Soviet delegate to the Lausanne conference, the Bolshevik V. V. Vorovsky, was assassinated on May 10, 1923, the following commentary appeared in *Le Paria:* "All working class martyrs are victims of the same assassins—international capitalism. And the souls of these martyrs will be set at rest only by belief in the liberation of their repressed brothers. After these painful lessons the repressed people in all countries should learn on which side their true brothers stand and on which side their enemies." This and other statements show the development of Nguyen Ai Quoc's revolutionary ideas; he now presented the Bolshevik Party in the young Soviet state to his own party (the French Communists) as an example to be followed in areas other than colonial policy.

He refers in particular to the twenty-one conditions which the Second World Congress of the Comintern had approved on August 6, 1920 and which the French Communists had accepted when they joined the Third International. These were Lenin's famous guidelines for all parties wishing to join the Third International. However, Nguyen Ai Quoc must have been particularly impressed by Lenin's theories on the national and colonial problem which the leader of the Soviet Union had drafted for the Second World Congress. For Nguyen Ai Quoc, the Comintern and Lenin presonally had become symbols of the liberation of the colonial peoples.

In 1923 Nguyen must have decided to leave France and

continue his revolutionary activity in the Soviet Union. None of his articles indicates clearly why he reached this decision and he has not explained his motives elsewhere. It cannot have been easy for him to move into a completely strange environment in spite of his enthusiasm for the new revolutionary Russia and in spite of the opportunities which the new social order seemed to offer him. He had found many staunch friends among the French comrades. And it was France (and French culture) with which his own homeland was still associated because of the facts of history. He himself often drew a clear distinction between the true France and the French colonialists.

But the indifference of the French proletariat which he had already criticized earlier must have come as a hard and disappointing blow to him. His comrades in the party were far too concerned with their own problems and the revolution in Europe whose failure was now becoming evident, to help this overenthusiastic young man from the colonies solve the special problems confronting him. Nguyen Ai Quoc sought salvation in the East. He turned his back on Paris in a manner befitting a revolutionary: without saying where he was going and without leaving any trace.

One Saturday afternoon his Senegalese, Moroccan, Algerian, and Madagascan colleagues on *Le Paria* turned up as usual to discuss the next week's edition. But the offices were closed. Was Nguyen ill, had he left, or had he been arrested? They went to see a lawyer from the French West Indies with whose family Nguyen was acquainted. A letter written by Nguyen was lying on his desk:

Dear Friends,

We have worked together for a long time. We are men of different races, from different countries and we believe in different religions. Nevertheless we feel an attachment to one another like brothers in a single family. We share the same fate: the cruelty of colonialism. We are fighting for a common ideal: for the liberation of our peoples and the independence of our countries.

We are not alone in our struggle. We have the support of our entire people and of the French democrats, the true French who stand shoulder to shoulder with us. Our common work on *l'Union Intercoloniale* and *le Paria* has borne fruit. Because of it France, the true France, is fully acquainted with what is going on in the colonies. France now realizes that the 'colonialist sharks' are misusing the name and honor of France to perpetrate unimaginable crimes. Our work has aroused our own people. At the same time they also realize that there exists a free and brotherly France. But now we must achieve still more. What are we to do?

The answer to this question must be given deep thought. The answer is dependent on the special situation in each country. As far as I am concerned the answer is clear: we must return to our homeland and work with the masses, educating, organizing, uniting, and training them in order to assist them in their struggle for freedom and independence. Perhaps some of you could and should do the same. Others should continue our present work, strengthening *l'Union Intercoloniale* and developing *le Paria*.

Dear Friends,

I must now say farewell to you; I shall be far away but my heart will always be with you. I am sorry that I could not take my leave personally. You know that all my movements have been closely watched. When this letter reaches you, your friend Nguyen will have left France at least twenty-four hours ago. My compatriot Dai will give you the keys to our office together with the papers and documents of our Union and journal as well as its funds. I have paid the rent of the offices until the end of the year. The printing costs have also been settled. We owe money to no one. The library list is in the drawer on the right. All the books which were on loan have been returned except for those borrowed by persons who are on holiday. In short, I have put everything in order before leaving. I shall write to you, but I can make no promises because it is difficult to maintain a correspondence when one is working underground. Even if I do not write to you, you may rest assured that my sympathy is always with you. Please shake hands with our French friends on my behalf.

And now a few words to my niece and nephew.* You love me very much and I too am very fond of you. That is true, isn't it, children? I shall tell our young friends in Vietnam that you are good children. I shall shake hands with them for you. Perhaps you will not see Uncle Nguyen again for a long time; you cannot climb onto my knees or back now as you have done so often and a long time will elapse before I see my Alice and Paul again. When we meet again I shall probably be old already and you will have grown up like your mother and father. But that is not important. I shall always be thinking of you. You will always remain my dear little Alice and Paul.

Be good children. Study hard at school. Obey your mother and father. Do not hit your little dog Marius. When you grow up you will fight for your country, like your parents, like Uncle Nguyen and all your other uncles. My little niece and nephew, I kiss you both tenderly. Give your mother a kiss from me.

Uncle Nguyen (*TDT*, 25ff.)

This was probably in the early summer of 1923. We do not know the date of the farewell letter but the Historical Committee of the Vietnam Workers' notes in its official biography that Nguyen Ai Quoc left Paris in June 1923. He went to Moscow to attend the Congress of the Peasants'

* Reference to the lawyer's children.

Red Square, May 1, 1923.

International in October. On October 16, 1923, Nguyen was elected to the Executive of the Krestintern (*Krestjanskij international* = peasants' international); it had been founded in the same year as the central organization of the revolutionary peasants' unions. As a representative of the colonial peoples, he now belonged to the executive committee of this branch organization of the Comintern. The official sources do not say who sent him as a delegate to the Soviet capital, though it was probably the French Communist Party. In any event, from now on Nguyen Ai Quoc was known as an expert on colonial problems in the world Communist movement.

In Moscow he translated the manifesto of this first congress of the Peasants' International into Vietnamese. However, he was still only calling upon the peasant masses in the colonial territories to unite and not to bring about a violent revolution. In *"Le Procès de la Colonisation française,"* his best known work of the 1920s, Nguyen Ai Quoc quotes a later appeal of the International which was directed specifically to the "working peasants of the colonies." He talks here of capitalist exploitation of the "modern slaves" and of the "pariahs of the colonies," but the appeal simply ends with a call for "common emancipation" and "salvation" of the natives in the colonies. The colonial revolution had not yet gotten underway, but Nguyen Ai Quoc was one of the leaders who prepared the ground for it. With the backing of his wide experience he was finally able to lead Vietnam to independence under Communist rule—the only Western colony in which this happened.

For the next twenty years, however, Nguyen's movements remain shrouded in obscurity.

We still do not know whether (as Ruth Fischer, the former German Communist leader, has claimed) Nguyen Ai Quoc in fact went to Moscow a year earlier to attend the Fourth World Congress of the Comintern (November to December, 1922). Since no sources in either the East or the West confirm this statement, Ruth Fischer was probably mistaken; she may in fact have meant the Fifth Comintern Congress in the summer of 1924 (which Nguyen did attend). However, Ruth Fischer's observations on "this young revolutionary nationalist . . . in whose ascetic face two soft, intelligent eyes shine brightly" are so interesting that they are quoted here: "I met Ho Chi Minh . . . fairly often in Moscow early in the 1920's. With his friendly, almost shy nature he soon became popular in Comintern circles. We

European Communists who were used to a rather monotonous, abstract form of internationalism were already deeply impressed by Ho's passionate nationalism." Ruth Fischer goes on to report certain currents of opposition in the Comintern to exclusive control of the national groups by the Moscow central body and continues: "Ho observed this opposition from the wings and often sympathized with it without taking part in these arguments between groups. His main interest was then—as it still is today—the struggle for the independence of his own country" (*RE*, 178). In his letter of farewell, Nguyen had indicated his desire to return to his own country in order to continue the struggle for liberation. The official biographers also stress this intention which Nguyen may actually have had at the time. The stay in Moscow in the autumn of 1923 and in the first half of 1924 must then have led to a different decision after discussion with Comintern officials. The time to establish a local Indochinese Branch of the Comintern was not yet ripe. Instead of returning to educate and work with the masses in his homeland, the thirty-four-year-old revolutionary now embarked upon a course of intensive development of his own talents in the bastion of world communism.

First of all, however, an event occurred which shook the world Communist movement and the Soviet states: the death of Lenin on January 21, 1924.

Like millions of Soviet citizens and Communists throughout the world, Nguyen Ai Quoc was afflicted with deep sorrow. He had now become such an important figure in the Moscow central organization, that *Pravda* allowed him space for his opinions on January 27, 1924:

Lenin shortly before his death.

Lenin and the colonial peoples. "Lenin is dead! The news has gone out like a bolt from the blue. It has spread across the fertile plains of Africa and the green fields of Asia . . . After liberating his own people, this great leader wanted to liberate others . . . At first they did not believe that there could be such a man and such a program anywhere on this earth. But later on they heard rumors of Communist parties and of the organization known as the Communist International which is fighting for the exploited peoples; and they

80

Lenin's burial.

learned that Lenin was the leader of this organization. We for
our part are deeply shaken by this irreparable loss and share
with our brothers and sisters the general sadness of all the
peoples. But we are convinced that the Communist International and its branches which exist even in the colonial
countries will succeed in respecting the experience and implementing the doctrines which our leader has handed down
to us. Surely the best way of proving our love for him is to
complete the task with which he has entrusted us? In his
lifetime he was our father, teacher, comrade and advisor.
Now he is our guiding star pointing the way to social revolution. Lenin lives on in our actions. He is immortal."

An episode which had occurred shortly before is characteristic of the young revolutionary's enthusiasm. After attending
the first congress of the Krestintern, Nguyen returned briefly

to France. The Japanese author Kyu Komatsu, who was then living in Paris, reported that in November 1923 Nguyen asked him to go with him to Moscow. When the Japanese writer said he would rather devote himself to art and literature in Paris, he received the characteristic reply: "What kind of art is possible in a putrid society like this? We shall carry out the revolution and then you'll be able to write for the free members of a classless society" (L, 32).

And so Nguyen returned to Moscow alone, accompanied only by his hopes. He was not to set foot in France again officially until 1946 when he came as president of an independent Democratic Republic of Vietnam.

The sea voyage was the normal route taken by revolutionaries in those days to reach the promised land of the Soviets from Western Europe. Two days after Lenin's death, Nguyen Ai Quoc reached Leningrad on board a Soviet ship and went on immediately to Moscow. He arrived in a city in which Communist leaders from all over the world had assembled for the funeral ceremony. The official reason for his journey was the impending Fifth Congress of the Comintern to which he had been sent as a representative of the colonies by the Central Committee of the French Communist Party. The congress was postponed by a few months because of Lenin's death. Soviet sources stress, however, that Nguyen had been hoping to meet Lenin face to face.

The Fifth World Congress of the Communist International was held in the Soviet capital from June 17 to July 8, 1924. One recurring theme of the congress was the struggle against Trotskyism which had now broken out in the Soviet party after Lenin's death. Trotsky himself, however, did not attend the congress. Stalin had already forced him into isolation in the party and in the International too. But, as Ruth Fischer has noted, Nguyen Ai Quoc was not concerned with internal disputes. With rare and fanatic stubbornness he pursued his own strictly personal aim, apparently failing to notice that a struggle for power was developing in the central body of world communism and was bound to influence his own plans.

Moscow, 1924: Nguyen Ai Quoc (first row, seated at left) with delegates of the Fifth Comintern Congress.

His report on national and colonial problems has been set down in the shorthand record of the congress. Nguyen Ai Quoc had prepared his subject thoroughly and appeared before the assembled officials from the whole world with astonishing self-confidence. The dispute surrounding Stalin's policy line had already begun but Stalin had not yet stifled free criticism; the delegates' speeches were still free from servile obedience to their own party or to the will of an individual.

83

After a short statistical introduction to the subject of colonial possessions and the colonial powers, Nguyen launched an attack on his comrades in Indochina. Referring to Lenin and Stalin, he said: ". . . so long as the French and British Communist parties have not brought out a really progressive policy with regard to the colonies, have not come into contact with the colonial peoples, their program as a whole is and will be ineffective because it goes counter to Leninism . . . As for our Communist parties in Great Britain, Holland, Belgium, and other countries—what have they done to cope with the colonial invasions perpetrated by the bourgeois class of their countries? What our parties have done in this domain is almost worthless. As for me, I was born in a French colony and am a member of the French Communist Party, and I am very sorry to say that our Communist Party has done hardly anything for the colonies" (*SW* I, 143ff.). Here there is no longer any trace of the shy young man who, only three and a half years earlier, had to call for silence from his amused socialist comrades in the party establishment in Tours in order to finish his speech. And his colonial inferiority complex seems to have disappeared under the protective shadow of the Kremlin.

Nguyen bitterly criticized *L'Humanité* (the central organ of his party) for devoting even less space than the bourgeois press to conditions in the colonies. He quoted a dozen examples in support of his theory. What was one to think, he asked, when *L'Humanité* repeatedly praised the victories of the Senegalese boxer Siki but did not mention the reprisals to which Siki's brothers, the dock laborers in Dakar, had been subjected. And he described how the central organ of the

Party contained daily reports of d'Oisy's record-breaking flight from Paris to Saigon but did not mention the punitive expeditions by the colonial authorities against the Vietnamese peasants, while French slave traders in Indochina still sold the inhabitants of North Vietnam to planters on the Pacific islands. The newspaper had not even found it necessary to publish the appeal (referred to earlier) by the peasants' International to the population of the colonies. "This attitude is completely unacceptable. We can only assume that our party wishes to disregard everything concerning the colonies" (*SW* I, 146). The French Communist Party, he stated, had committed mistake after mistake in its handling of the colonial problem (which is inseparable from the national problem). Nguyen refers to the lesson of the Ruhr where German troops were called into action against starving German workers and unreliable French regiments. Even the use of colored soldiers as strikebreakers in France has not forced the party to take a firm stand on the colonial problem.

In a second statement, the virulence of Nguyen Ai Quoc's attack on the exploitation of the peasants and on the particular role played by the Catholic Church is also striking. "The Catholic mission alone occupied one quarter of the areas under cultivation in Cochin China [the southern part of Vietnam] . . . The mission exploited believers no less ruthlessly than the planters" (*SW* I, 150). (The disfavor in which Ho Chi Minh later held his Catholic countrymen may thus have had much earlier origins). Finally, Nguyen claims that the economic measures taken by the French authorities have caused a threat of starvation in the colonial territories. "In all the French colonies, famine is on the increase and so

85

is the people's anger. The native peasants are ripe for insurrection. They have risen often in many colonies, but their uprisings have been drowned in blood. If the peasants still have a passive attitude, it is only because they still lack organization and leaders. The Communist International must help them to revolution and liberation" (*SW* I, 156).

The slogan of revolution in the colonies had now been proclaimed in the highest body of the organization whose aim was a world Communist revolution. What is more, Nguyen Ai Quoc had spoken of a peasants' revolution, while in the standard Communist version the industrial proletariat in the cities was the standard-bearer of all revolutionary activity. Observers in the West have highlighted this point and expressed the opinion that Ho Chi Minh postulated the theory of revolution of the peasant masses long before Mao Tse-tung. In doing so, however, they misrepresent the Vietnamese revolutionary and practical leader as a theoretician—a role he never played. The passage concerning the peasants who are ripe for rebellion must rather be viewed in the context of Ho's report. Here a man who came from peasant stock was speaking in anger of the fate of his own compatriots in the narrower sense. He made a point of mentioning that ninety-five per cent of the population of all French colonial territories were in fact peasants. He did not need to consider the role of an urban proletariat: there was no such group, just as there was no local party organization to lead it.

Like Mao Tse-tung in China, Nguyen started out pragmatically from the special conditions in his own country—an agricultural land.

It is equally misleading to suggest that Nguyen Ai Quoc revealed himself in his true colors at this Comintern congress as a follower of the Stalin line. In his report he referred (rather offhandedly) to Stalin as the comrade who attached true importance to the colonial problem, and also quoted him in the same breath as Lenin. But he certainly did not pay homage to the future strong man of the Soviet party. We shall consider Ho Chi Minh's attitude to Stalin and Stalinism later on. Nguyen Ai Quoc equated the masses of the colonial peasant population with the proletariat for whose unification the Communists appealed. This is reflected in the title page of his newspaper *Le Paria* for which Nguyen continued to write articles while he was in Moscow. Up to 1924, the subtitle of the newspaper was "Tribune of the Population of the Colonies"; after this point it became "Tribune of the Proletariat of the Colonies."

During his first months in Moscow between the autumn of 1923 and the summer of 1924, Nguyen Ai Quoc's intentions and views evolved in a distinctly radical direction. What is more, he was far in advance of the overwhelming majority of his revolutionary colleagues from the colonies. At the Fifth Comintern Congress, Nguyen Ai Quoc was appointed a permanent member of the Eastern branch of this organization. In this capacity he was responsible for the southern region—so, at least, the official biography published in Hanoi tells us.

Only a few years previously, he had confessed to having no idea of what was meant by a party or communism or what the difference was between the Internationals. His career since then had been rapid. Side by side with personalities such as the Indian M. N. Roy, a fellow traveler in Moscow and China, he now belonged to the elite of Comintern officials from the colonial territories.

We have already pointed out that the disputes between factions in the Soviet party were bound to influence the Comintern's work. Stalin began to develop his concept of "socialism in one country" and was later able to use this argument against his opponents—from Trotsky to Zinoviev. It was the reply to Trotsky's "permanent revolution," born out of the failure of the revolution in Western Europe, especially in Germany, and intended to consolidate Stalin's own position of power in the Soviet party machine. One consequence was the shift in Comintern activities, and Asia, more precisely the Far East, provided new ground for experiments. Moscow anticipated a threat to its security from the imperialist powers and there had already been a revolution against semi-colonial dependence in China. Perhaps Communist revolutionary successes seemed most probable here.

For the Vietnamese nationalist, Nguyen Ai Quoc, the omens were favorable. His shift from France to the Soviet Union had already loosened his formal organizational dependence on the French Communist Party, and his emotional ties with the central party in Moscow grew correspondingly stronger. He spent the year 1924 on (hitherto neglected) theoretical studies at the Moscow University for Oriental Workers which Nguyen had particularly recommended in his report to the Comintern congress as a training center for Communists from the colonies. Although throughout his life Nguyen considered theory less important than revolutionary practice, he must have felt in his element at this school of revolution attached to the Comintern center. He describes it in a detail in several articles.

"At present this university has 1,022 students, including 151 girls. Eight hundred and ninety-five of the students are communists. They represent the following social groups: 547 peasants, 265 workers and 210 proletarian intellectuals" (*SW* I, 81ff.).

Nguyen explained the high proportion of students of peasant origin by pointing out that the Asian countries have an almost exclusively agricultural economy. As a particularly interesting detail, he noted that the students included seventy-six pupils between ten and sixteen years of age. "One hundred and fifty teachers give instruction in social sciences, mathematics, historical materialism, history of the workers' movement, natural sciences, history of revolutions, economic policy, etc. Young persons of sixty-two different nationalities are fraternally united in the classrooms." (Unfortunately he does not list the nationalities.) "Food, clothing, and lodging for the students are free, and each student is given six gold rubles a month as pocket money. The university for Oriental Workers teaches the avant-garde fighters of the future the principles of the class war, principles about which they have become confused because of racial conflicts on the one hand and patriarchal customs on the other" (*SW* I, 84).

Nguyen Ai Quoc was the first of a series of Vietnamese revolutionaries to attend this Moscow University. Others included Tran Phu (1904–1931), the first secretary general of the Indochinese Communist Party, who died in prison; the French had detained him because of his political beliefs.

In December 1924, Nguyen's first visit to Russia came to

Canton harbor, about 1920.

an end; his stay in Europe was drawing to a close. A new field of activity awaited him in China, much nearer to his homeland.

Canton, the South Chinese port some 400 miles from the northeast corner of Tonkin, was a hotbed of agitation and a center of Vietnamese nationalist activities. In June 1924, the year in which Nguyen Ai Quoc arrived in China, the revolutionary Pham Hong Thai had made a bomb attack on the French governor general of Indochina, Monsieur Merlin. The attack failed, but it gave a strong impetus to the Vietnamese living in exile in Yunnan and Canton.

The party ideologist, Truong Chinh, later described Nguyen's attitude to this attack as follows: "He came to the conclusion that the colonial regime could not be overthrown merely by assassinating a governor. In order to lead the revolution to ultimate victory, a strong political party was needed to organize the masses and provide them with the necessary leadership" (*TC*, 15). But some time was to elapse before this party was founded.

Michail M. Borodin.

Once the decision was taken in Moscow to shift the center of world revolutionary activities to East Asia, it was not long before revolutionary experts set out from the central organization. (China had already been a playground for Comintern agents of different colors and nationalities for several years.) Official Communist sources today all fail to mention that Nguyen Ai Quoc was attached to the mission which advised Sun Yat-sen's Kuomintang government under the Soviet ambassador Michail Borodin and General Galen (later to become Marshal Blücher).

Nguyen's status in the mission which resided in Canton has never been clarified. Officially he was described at the time as Borodin's interpreter, although it soon turned out that he was devoting most of his time to Indochinese affairs and very little to what was going on in China. Pham Hong Thai belonged to a revolutionary organization of Vietnamese known as the *Tam Tam Xa* ("league of persons with united ideas," or "league of hearts"). It had been founded in Canton in 1923. The bourgeois politician and patriot Phan Boi Chau, who had known Nguyen's father, was also in China. At the time when Nguyen was active in Canton, Phan Boi Chau was arrested by the French authorities in Shanghai and taken to Hanoi for trial (1925). His arrest sparked a wave of protests throughout Indochina.

While south China was a melting pot for Vietnamese nationalists of all shades of opinion and splinter groups, Nguyen Ai Quoc saw it as his duty to bring his revolutionary compatriots together in a unified organization. In June 1925, he founded the League of Vietnamese Revolutionary Youth in Canton (*Viet Nam Thanh Nien Cach Mang Dong Chi Hoi*—abbreviated to *Thanh Nien* Youth). This was the germ cell of a Vietnamese Communist Party.

Nguyen believed that as a nationalist and a Communist he had to also make efforts to establish international links on the Asiatic stage which he had just entered. In the same year

Seat of the Tanh Nien in Canton.

he helped to form a League of the Repressed Peoples of Asia
with the Intercolonial Union in Paris as its model. It was,
however, only moderately successful and its function was
gradually taken over by national Communist parties in the
individual Asian countries. A certain dualism was apparent
in the statements made by Nguyen at this time. On the one
hand there was the guerilla Pham Hong Thai, who drowned
in the Pearl River during an escape, and who had become
a modern national hero and martyr of the Vietnamese people.
On the other hand Nguyen also spoke of Lenin over and

over again in a tone of native faith. "Lenin was the first to realize that there can be no socialist revolution without participation by the colonial peoples" (*SW* I, 140).

At this point it seems relevant to consider briefly the home of the revolutionaries who fought for liberation from colonial rule in neighboring China by so many different methods. Admittedly the direct effects of the World War had been less noticeable in Indochina than in India or China, but the colonial authorities found themselves obliged to implement certain reforms. This was particularly true in the sphere of education and the legal system, where certain excesses such as forced labor (the *corvée*) were abolished. The resistance to colonial rule had in the meantime shifted from what were generally secret societies before 1914 to new, semi-legal organizations which were joined by increasingly large numbers of officials and intellectuals. Their leaders were, however, not ready to cooperate with the organizations in exile, such as the Thanh Nien movement with its Communist leanings.

As Phan Boi Chau's example shows, the French made persistent efforts to put their hands on the revolutionaries who agitated against them. Because of this Nguyen Ai Quoc decided to adopt a new pseudonym for his stay in China, and chose the name of Wuong. In view of the fact that Nguyen Ai Quoc belonged to the Comintern apparatus, "Comrade Wuong" now adopted highly unconventional methods to persuade his politically active compatriots to fall in with the cause of communism. The documents published in Hanoi on Ho Chi Minh's life surprised us with their frankness—a characteristic not often found among Communists of any nationality.

The biographers even mention specifically that Comrade Wuong did not organize a single training course on dialectical materialism, because he realized that purely theoretical arguments (which in any case did not appeal to him) would tend to dismay the young Vietnamese who had entered the country illegally from Indochina (*Viet-Nam Courier,* February 1970). The agenda of the first political seminar held by Wuong in Canton in August 1926 included subjects such as: What is revolution? Why and how we should make the revolution; a comparison of communism and other doctrines; the different revolutions—national liberation, bourgeois, democratic, and socialist; political regimes (including in particular the system of "councils" in the Soviet Union); the different international organizations—the First, Second, and Third International; revolutionary activity—reconnoitres, contact, propaganda, organization, and training; and finally: agitation among workers, peasants, soldiers, youth, and women. No doubt these questions were far more interesting than abstract debates to the young people who had crossed the frontier at great risk (many of them had already been under arrest).

Wuong directed the courses personally. Each course lasted two months with about twenty participants. Wuong had a Vietnamese assistant and "Soviet and Chinese comrades sometimes came as guest lecturers." Borodin and his people therefore kept an eye on Wuong and his activities and approved of them. The last of the themes mentioned above, agitation, was dealt with by the Chinese comrades, according to the recollections of a course participant. At this time the Chinese, of course, had more practical experience than comrade

Wuong. (The Chinese Communist Party had been founded in Shanghai in July 1921; in 1923, Canton was the scene of the Third Congress of the Chinese Communist Party and the First Congress of the Kuomintang, which was Sun Yat-sen's party.)

Kuomintang functionaries with family members and advisors. Far left: Borodin; third from left, Mrs. Borodin; behind the chair, General Galen; to his right, General Chiang Kai-shek.

As the *Viet-Nam Courier* reports, the lectures given by the future Ho Chi Minh were not a dry affair. Sometimes he stopped in midstream to ask, "Can you hear me? Do you understand what I am saying?" He would often intervene in discussions with simple statements and arguments. After a lesson on the personality and work of Lenin, the question arose as to whether a hero creates his time or the time its heroes. Wuong listened attentively to the lively discussion of this subject and then went to the blackboard, took a piece of chalk and drew a circle, saying as he did so, "Time, hero =

hero, time," and when the circle was finished he added, "And now can someone tell me which came first?"

He constantly hammered into his audience the Comintern principle that revolution in a particular country such as Indochina is closely linked with world revolution—and vice versa. (By contrast with the situation in Western Europe, the prospects for a chain of revolutionary events in Asia seemed very promising.) A collection of lectures by Comrade Wuong were published in Canton in 1929 by the League of Repressed Peoples of Asia. It bears the title *The Path to Revolution* and is Ho Chi Minh's confession of faith corresponding to his idealistic attitude of the time, one which was still untroubled by setbacks:

"There are two kinds of revolution: a) the Vietnamese drive out the French, the Indians the British, the Koreans the Japanese, the Filipinos the Americans, and the Chinese all the different imperialists . . . That is national revolution; b) all the peasants and workers in every country throughout the world join forces like brothers in the same family to overthrow capitalists everywhere, so that all the countries and peoples can live in happiness and mankind move forward in universal equality. That is world revolution."

In addition to the peasants, Wuong specifically mentions the exploited workers of the Hong Gay coal mines and refers to the workers and peasants together as the source of the class revolution. As a pragmatist he had no objection to manipulating historical truth for domestic consumption, by forecasting that the workers and peasants would eventually unite in Indochina as they had done in Russia and sweep away the capitalists. This, he said, was the class revolution.

97

The world revolution would ultimately be led by the proletariat which according to Wuong's definition consisted, in contrast with the orthodox Marxist-Bolshevik doctrine, of peasants and workers (sometimes in that order, sometimes in the opposite order).

Nguyen Ai Quoc, alias Wuong, alias Ho Chi Minh, does not deserve any laurels as a pre-Maoist theoretician for reaching this conclusion. If he aimed at a revolution led by the peasant masses, he was merely seeing things in their true perspective from his own homeland. But the industrial proletariat was included in his plans. In 1928 there were 3,300 industrial workers in Vietnam, especially in the coal mines of the North, and a few thousand workers in the cotton mills and weaving factories; these figures were to rise constantly with the influx of French capital. However, at the time of independence in 1945, the industrial proletariat only accounted for two to three per cent of the population of Vietnam as a whole and this proletariat was "demographically concentrated" in Tonkin in the North.

Another fact which has remained of great importance for Vietnam as a whole up to the present time is openly reported by Wuong: "The people are normally split into groups and factions. In Vietnam, for example, our compatriots in the South do not trust those in the center, while the latter look down on the inhabitants of the North. Accordingly their strength is diminished, just as chopsticks are useless if their ends are held wide apart. The revolutionary forces must therefore be united, and for this purpose we need a revolutionary party." For the time being, however, there was no true revolutionary party and the professional revolutionary

Wuong could not count on the support of "class revolutionaries." His best pupils in Canton came (like Wuong himself) for the most part from families of village scholars who did not suffer from colonial repression or capitalist exploitation. They included Nguyen Luong Bang, then twenty-two years old, who has been vice president of North Vietnam since Ho Chi Minh's death. He joined the Thanh Nien in Canton and was sent back to Vietnam by Wuong on a special mission. And Pham Van Dong, the prime minister in Hanoi since 1955, was even a young mandarin whose father had held a senior position at the imperial court in Hue.

It was not only the contrasts between the different areas of this long country (the distance from the north of Tonkin to Cape Ca Mau is just over 1,000 miles) that complicated Wuong's plans for unification. In spite of the frankness which characterizes the Vietnamese Communists in comparison with their comrades in other countries, the party historians fail to mention the fact that there was resistance among the ranks of the patriots to Nguyen Ai Quoc, alias Wuong, the man from far-off Moscow, and to his words. An effective solution was found for those students who refused to follow the orders of the Communist leaders after training in China. The French secret service in Indochina "learned" their names and acted quickly when they returned to their homeland. On completing their course in Canton, the most promising young revolutionaries were sent by the Comintern mission at the recommendation of Comrade Wuong either to the Kuomintang military academy in Whampoa, which had been founded and was led by General Chiang Kai-shek with the assistance of the Soviet officer general Galen, or to

Moscow for further training. In a period of only two years (mid-1925 to mid-1927), more than two hundred reliable "cadres" were trained in this way and sent back to Indochina as instructors.

Possibly Wuong himself may have been at the military academy for a short time; one of the Vietnamese who went

Mao Tse-tung in the 1920s.

to Moscow believes he saw him there, but the official sources do not confirm this information. It is also uncertain whether Wuong met Chinese leaders during his stay in China, such as Chiang Kai-shek, Chou En-lai, or Mao Tse-tung (who was in South China in late 1925 and early 1926). Perhaps he met Chou En-lai in Whampoa; the latter recalled absentmindedly in a conversation with André Malraux, "We have not forgotten that you were persecuted at the same time as Nguyen Ai Quoc." Chou En-lai also suggested that this persecution occurred in China.

Comrade Wuong's Chinese mission was at an end when Chiang Kai-shek launched his first attack against the Communists in the spring of 1927. Michail Borodin has reported his parting words: "The revolution must now go underground." Nguyen Ai Quoc now left China again to seek refuge with the Comintern in Moscow. "Borodin did not understand the peasants," Mao Tse-tung said almost forty years later. But the Russian's Vietnamese aide did. He was to move along other devious roads, however, before reaching his objective.

WITH THE COMINTERN

IN 1923, Nguyen Ai Quoc had already been paid a special honor in Moscow. The famous author, Ossip Mandelstam, who was later murdered during Stalin's reign of terror, visited the revolutionary from Vietnam. He wrote an essay on

101

Нюэн Ай-Как.

В гостях у коминтерпщика.

Очерк О. Мандельштама.

Ossip Mandelstam's article in *Ogonjok*.

the "international fighter for Communism" and his people, which was published in the popular journal *Ogonjok* on December 23, 1923. "A guest of a Cominternchik" was the title of this article and "Cominternchik" was in fact an honorary designation for a member of the Comintern—a man who devotes his whole life to service of the Communist International.

Nguyen Ai Quoc was such a man. He remained a member of the International when his mission to China came to an abrupt end. He had gained so much experience in the difficult area of Asian revolution, reports Ruth Fischer, that after his return to the metropolis of world communism he became a "privileged advisor of the Comintern leaders."

What was the man Ho Chi Minh really like in those years? He refused to talk to strangers about himself and his personal feelings, and the official Communist biography obviously paints an idealized portrait of him. Ruth Fischer is the only responsible Western witness with anything to say on this subject. She wrote as follows about the early days of the Cominternchik in Moscow: "When he first arrived, he seemed very inconsequential. He had neither the dash nor the presence of that other Asian revolutionary, the Indian leader Roy. But he immediately won the respect and even affection of us all. Amid these seasoned revolutionaries and exacting intellectuals, he struck a delightful note of goodness and simplicity. He seemed to stand for common decency—though he was cleverer than he let on—and it was his well-earned good name which saved him from getting caught up in internal conflicts. Also his temperament inclined him far more strongly towards action and putting ideas into effect than towards doctrinal debates. He was always an empiricist within the movement. But none of this detracted from his colleagues' regard for him, and his prestige was considerable. He played a very big part in things, bigger than some of the better-known Asian leaders of the time: Mao did not come to the fore till later" (L, 32).

Ruth Fischer repeatedly stresses that Nguyen did not become involved in "party conflicts"—meaning the debate surrounding Stalinism. But this certainly did not make Nguyen Ai Quoc a Stalinist, a supporter of the methods of the secretary general of the Soviet party. It must, of course, be remembered that at this time (in the late twenties) discussion still centered on the "correct" line of the Russian Communist Party, the line of the secretary general. The reign of terror against its opponents had not yet begun.

103

Joseph W. Stalin.

And when the terror did begin in the 1930s—when the Comintern officials Zinoviev, Radek, Bucharin, and countless others to whom Nguyen Ai Quoc had been a "privileged advisor" were liquidated or disappeared without a trace— Nguyen kept his silence and nothing happened to him. We have never learned whether he regretted the disappearance of his earlier comrades such as Borodin or Marshal Blücher. His attitude may be criticized as opportunism. But he certainly did not change his tactics for personal gain. The Asian Cominternchik was not concerned with internal Soviet problems. He had problems of his own. Mao Tse-tung also remained indifferent to Stalin's reign of terror. Ho Chi Minh has repeatedly been referred to—particularly in this connection—as an empiricist and pragmatist; yet pragmatism seems to be a common quality among people within his cultural sphere, and among the Chinese in general.

There is another important factor. The shift in the emphasis of Communist activities towards Asia, which must have suited Nguyen Ai Quoc's purposes admirably, was due in no small measure—whatever the motives—to Stalin's policies. Indeed, Stalin was often referred to as a semi-Asian. The stress he placed on the colonial problem was already apparent at the Fifth Comintern Congress in 1924. It became even clearer at the Sixth meeting of the International July 17 to September 1, 1928) when the green light was given for the anticolonial revolution. In this respect, and in this respect alone, is it possible to say that Ho Chi Minh followed the Stalinist line. But in all other policy areas, Nguyen, the expert on revolution in the colonial territories, fell back on his personal oasis of Leninism, and when he was beset by doubts (as he must have been) he repeatedly thought of his master Lenin, to whom he referred in his testament—only a few months before his death—as the "man who must be honored." In all probability Nguyen Ai Quoc did not attend the Sixth Comintern Congress. His movements in 1927 and 1928 are unknown. The Cominternchik had indeed gone underground, and we do not know what instructions the central organization gave him. He appeared in Western Europe to attend a peace congress in Brussels and then visited France again. But he had to exercise caution at this point; the French secret service was apparently aware of the fact that Nguyen and Wuong were one and the same person. He went to Switzerland, Italy, and Germany, but the exact dates of his moves have never been established.

Several East German newspapers have referred to Nguyen's stay in Berlin without giving any details. The authors of these articles base their reports on several conversations with President Ho Chi Minh, who mentioned with obvious pleasure his stay in the Berlin district of Neukölln. Perhaps he spent his time among the treasures of the Berlin libraries as his great mentor Lenin had done thirty years before. But we have no precise information. The President liked to keep his "little secrets" to himself.

Traveling was no problem for Nguyen. Other Vietnamese who knew Ho Chi Minh well have mentioned his liking for "tourism" which he indulged in from time to time, during his first years in France, as a kind of hobby. His knowledge of languages must have stood him in good stead during his new political "tourism." He mastered the main Chinese dialects, spoke French fluently, knew some Russian and English, and a little German as well.

In the autumn of 1928, Nguyen Ai Quoc made another major move. He boarded a ship—probably in Italy—for Southeast Asia. The sea voyage from western Europe was the usual route by which the representatives of the Comintern, couriers and agents of all kinds, traveled to Asia. After the about-face of Chiang Kai-shek, who was now hunting the Communists, it was too dangerous to journey through China.

Nguyen's destination was Siam, now known as Thailand; the Cominternchik was keenly interested in the few million Vietnamese who live there. In those days they lived in the northeast of the country, roughly speaking between the Menam and Mekong rivers, and were peasants and small tradesmen. They included fugitives from neighboring Indo-

Buddhist monks in northern Thailand.

china; some had actively opposed the French and fought under Phan Dinh Phung or Hoang Hoa Tham. Nguyen Ai
Quoc's role was to win these Vietnamese over to the cause
of the revolution and to spread the message of communism
among the nationalists.

Buddhism was a vital force in Siam in those days, as it is
today—a religion shared by the whole population. Service as
a monk was one of the duties of a faithful Buddhist and
"the students of perfection" traveled the land, as they still do
today, supplied with all the necessities of life by the local
population. Nguyen Ai Quoc profited from these ideal conditions. He and his comrades cropped their hair short and
donned the orange robes of Buddhist monks. They wandered
through the villages, making contacts and spreading the word
of revolution as well as the leaflet entitled *"Than Ai"* (friend-

107

ship" or "blood-brotherhood") which was printed especially in Siam for the Vietnamese and also smuggled across the nearby border into Indochina.

Anyone who has studied the history and influence of Buddhism, particularly in recent times, will not be surprised that the revolutionary disguised himself in monk's clothing. Throughout Southeast Asia, Buddhism is an eminently political force. As early as the nineteenth century, the *Sangha* (organized monks) in Ceylon and Burma embodied the will to eliminate the British colonial power; the Buddhist monks were at one and the same time revolutionaries and nationalists. This still holds good in South Vietnam today where messages from the North are not uncommonly echoed in the pagodas and bonzes burn themselves to death in political protest. Nguyen Ai Quoc grew up in an area where Confucianism was the dominant faith. But the doctrines of Buddhism were by no means alien to him. Did he come into conflict with them as a Communist? Buddhism and communism are not necessarily conflicting beliefs. The pragmatist Nguyen could seek out those elements which best suited him. But Thau Chin—the venerable Uncle Chin, as the man from Moscow called himself in Siam—carefully avoided mention of the word "Buddhism" when he attacked the capitalists and imperialists who used religion and culture to hold the people in a state of uncertainty.

Little is known about the practical achievements of Nguyen's stay in Siam which lasted for less than a year. It cannot have been particularly fruitful. With his cooperation, a "Vietnamese mutual aid association" was founded, but the long arm of the *sûreté* reached out beyond the Mekong frontier and Nguyen often had to seek refuge in a pagoda. More important than cooperation between the Siamese authorities and the French was the fact that the majority of Vietnamese in Siam were completely passive at this time. Today, of course, the situation in northeast Thailand has changed substantially. The two Indochinese wars brought new fugitives into the country. And with the escalation of the conflict, sympathy grew among the Vietnamese in Thailand for Ho Chi Minh, who had once adopted the robes of a monk to teach brotherly love and revolution.

In general, the prospects for communism were bleak in East Asia at this time. The disastrous defeat of the Canton commune in 1927 had paralyzed the work of the Comintern, and the Thanh Nien was going through a serious crisis. The colonial police in the French and British colonies repeatedly took measures against the Comintern agents and Communists. Their position was desperate in China, and not much better even in countries such as Siam. The most radical followers of the Thanh Nien called for the movement's conversion into a genuine Communist Party. But they remained a minority. The result was the formation of three splinter groups. The regionalism which Nguyen Ai Quoc condemned in his "Path to Revolution" now gained favor even among the revolutionaries. The League of Revolutionary Youth of Vietnam founded by Nguyen in Canton in 1925 disintegrated in June 1929. As early as March 1929 the Thanh Nien representatives of the north had founded the first Indochinese Communist cell in Hanoi. After the failure of their attempt to found a Communist Party at the Thanh Nien Congress in Macao in May, they acted independently and the

Communist Party of Indochina (*Dong Duong Cong San Dang*) was founded on June 17, 1929. Its sphere of influence extended to Tonkin and north Annam. The Annam Communist Party (*Annam Cong San Dang*) was founded in October, followed by the League of Indochinese Communists.

In view of the confusion and uncertainty which prevailed among the Communists of East Asia it is astonishing how quickly and confidently the Comintern center in Moscow reacted to end the rivalry in Indochina. When the news arrived from Macao, Comrade Tran Phu (who was studying at the University of Oriental Workers) was immediately dispatched to Asia. He was instructed to travel home via Paris and establish contact with Nguyen Ai Quoc in Siam. He carried with him an appeal from the International to the Communist groups in Vietnam to unite as quickly as possible.

There was a real need for urgent action. The French police were profiting from the disputes and the fact that some comrades did not hesitate to denounce their rivals. Strikes broke out in the cities of Haiphong and Namdinh in the North and in Saigon and the rubber plantations in the South. But the revolutionary section of the population was leaderless. The governor, General Alexandre Varenne, who had affinities with the socialists and in whom the Vietnamese patriots had placed some hope, was recalled in 1929. His reforms were partially set aside. Nguyen Ai Quoc did not appear again until January 1930, this time in Hong Kong. Had he come directly from Bangkok, or had he been on the Chinese mainland in the intervening period? Even his closest comrades did not know the answer. At all events, he brought clear directives from the International. The lack of a united

110

Communist Party was presented as a major threat to the future of the revolution in Indochina. "The most important and urgent task for all Communists in Indochina at present is to found a revolutionary party of the proletariat, in other words a Communist Party of the masses. It must be a united party and the only Communist Party in Indochina" (*Comm.*, 61).

The Vietnamese comrades obeyed their central organization. A congress for the unification of all three Communist organizations was held on February 3, 1930, in Kowloon in the British crown colony of Hong Kong. It was presided over by Nguyen Ai Quoc, as the Communist sources stressed. However, the secretary general of the new party was Tran Phu, who had brought the message from Moscow. Until 1930, it was known as the Communist Party of Vietnam (*Viet Nam Cong San Dang*) and from then on as the Communist Party of Indochina (*Don Duong Cong San Dang*) which more accurately described the area for which the party was responsible.

The Vietnamese revolutionaries met to work out the preliminaries for their important measures under picturesque conditions: on the cheap upper stands of a football stadium where they could discuss their problems freely and pass unnoticed among the human masses of Kowloon. Nguyen Ai Quoc summarized the results and published them on February 18, 1930 in the form of a call for the foundation of a Communist Party in his country. It begins with an appeal: "Workers, peasants, soldiers, youth and students! Oppressed and exploited fellow compatriots! Sisters and brothers! Comrades!" It is an appeal to the feelings of the simple people

111

and contains neither theoretical phraseology nor party jargon, but simple, readily understandable sentences such as the following: "Imperialist contradictions were the cause of the World War of 1914–18. After this horrible slaughter, the world was divided into two camps . . . World War II will break out. When it breaks, the French imperialists will certainly drive our people to a more horrible slaughter . . . The Communist party of Indochina has been established. It is the party of the working class. It will help the proletarian class to lead the revolution in order to struggle for all the oppressed and exploited people . . ."

The appeal ends with ten practical demands. Seven of the ten points directly concern the ordinary man and woman: "To confiscate the banks and other enterprises belonging to the imperialists . . . To confiscate the whole of the plantations . . . and distribute them to poor peasants . . . To implement the eight-hour working day . . . To abolish public loans and poll tax. To waive unjust taxes on the poor people . . . To carry out universal education . . . To implement equality between man and woman" (*SW* II, 145ff.).

Nguyen, the patriot and Cominternchik has come a long way: this official document represents his first demand for complete independence for Indochina.

CONSPIRACY

On June 5, 1931 the man of whom *Pravda* wrote that he was a "master of the art of conspiracy for the sake of the party" (May 19, 1970) was arrested for the first time. Fortunately, Nguyen fell into the hands of liberal colonial authorities in the British crown colony of Hong Kong, and was not handed over to the French. By now events had taken place which had made the French authorities extremely nervous.

For the first time since 1916, bloody uprisings had occurred on a large scale against the colonial rulers in Vietnam. On February 9, 1930, army units mutinied in the Yen Bai garrison northeast of Hanoi in Tonkin. This rebellion had nothing to do with the Communists who were building up their party organization in Hong Kong at the same time. It was instigated by the radical-bourgeois National People's Party of Vietnam (*Viet Nam Quoc Dan Dang,* abbreviated to *VNQDD*) which had been founded a few years earlier and was in sympathy with the Kuomintang. This mutiny, though it claimed the lives of a few French officers, did not give the signal for a general uprising as its instigators had hoped. The VNQDD was popular among the people; but the rebellion was poorly prepared and carried out too quickly. No doubt the Communists learned their lesson from it. They were able to observe the rapid and brutal reaction of the French military forces. The leaders of the rebellion were executed unless they managed to escape across the Chinese border.

An event of the same year which the Communists now attribute to their own influence had a far more lasting effect than the shots of Yen Bai: the foundation of the first Soviet in Indochina—the famous *Xo Viet Nghe Tinh.* Was it merely the anger of the exploited peasants that finally erupted in the summer of 1930 in the provinces of Ha Tinh

113

and Nghe An (in which Ho Chi Minh was born), or had the Communists been directly responsible for this development? The most probable version is that the party intervened after the first disorders, seizing the opportunity to organize the peasants' uprising.

In any event, the first mass revolutionary uprising in Vietnam was brought about by the peasants, just as Nguyen Ai Quoc had so often demanded on the basis of the situation in his own homeland. The columns of peasants set out and marched through the rice fields to the provincial capital of Vinh where they were mown down on September 12, 1930 by the French army and police. But their movement still continued into 1931. Peasant Committees and people's courts were set up. Units were formed for self-defense and land reform was demanded in a flurry of red flags and violence. Landowners and usurers were killed. A series of bad harvests, high taxes, and falling prices for their crops, had driven the peasants to despair.

The *Xo Viet Nghe Tinh* which was bound to arouse national feelings brought prestige to the young Communist Party as well as the revolutionary experience it needed. However, the party also suffered substantial losses. A French pro-Communist source speaks of some 700 executions without trial in 1930 (including reprisals after other revolutionary actions) and a total of ten thousand political prisoners in 1932 (*JC*, 239). The best-known victim in the Communist Party was its secretary general, the teacher Tran Phu. He died on September 6, 1931, after torture in a French prison. Other Communist leaders were also sentenced to imprisonment. Pham Van Dong, the future prime minister of North Vietnam, and Ton Duc Thang (who later took over as state president after Ho Chi Minh's death) were sent to the infamous penal island of Poulo Condore in the South China Sea. (This penal settlement again attracted attention in 1970 under the regime of the generals in Saigon as Con Son—"the island of tiger cages").

During these events, Nguyen Ai Quoc remained outside Vietnam. He played no active part in the revolutionary movement which could have led to the fulfillment of his dreams. The explanation must surely be that the Comintern had other tasks for him. This would also explain why Tran Phu took over the leadership of the party although (according to the official version) Nguyen Ai Quoc himself had completed the process of unification. On the other hand, Tran Phu is mentioned only rarely as a martyr of the movement; it therefore seems likely that there was some conflict between these two leading figures of the Indochinese party. Be that as it may, Nguyen's role was well-known to the French secret service and a court in Vinh sentenced him to death in his absence in 1931; he had now adopted the new alias of Tong Van So.

Where was Nguyen Ai Quoc (alias Tong Van So) during the months between the foundation of the party and his arrest by the English? Truong Chinh speaks in his biography of "revolutionary activities in China" (*TC,* 19), and specifically mentions that Nguyen did not lead the revolutionary work in Vietnam. Apparently he paid another short visit to Thailand. As a representative and right-hand man of the Comintern, Nguyen probably had the task of supervising the young party and restraining its revolutionary zeal by prevent-

115

Hong Kong.

ing a sharp movement to the left and a defeat. On April 20, 1931, he wrote to the Central Committee attacking the "errors and mistakes" of his inexperienced comrades. He speaks of a formalistic working style, lack of realism, insufficient attention to the concrete local situation, narrow-mindedness in the mass organizations, and underestimation of the anti-imperialist front. He also issued a directive containing the draft of a detailed program of action for each district and province. Unfortunately, the official biographers in Hanoi do not tell us the actual significance of his criticism. We must therefore fall back on suppositions which suggest that the peasants of Nghe An and Ha Tinh and the Communist officials working there relied too much on their own strength and rejected all aid from bourgeois circles. Truong Chinh even mention the reproach of sectarianism which Nguyen is said to have made. The errors must have been serious: even the Far Eastern bureau of the Comintern with its offices in Shanghai (to which Nguyen Ai Quoc was responsible as leader of the southern section) warned a little later (May 1933) against "left-wing and sectarian" trends which "do not accord with the principles of communism" (F I, 118).

The dispute which broke out here and must have been linked with the failure of the Nghe Tinh movement was interrupted by an event with serious implications. On June 1, 1931, the British police in Singapore arrested the French Comintern agent, Josef Ducroux. This lead pointed to Nguyen Ai Quoc in Hong Kong, to the Swiss citizen Hilaire Noulens alias Paul Ruegg in Shanghai, and to the discovery of the entire Far Eastern apparatus of the Third International. The French and British secret police, the colonial authorities throughout East Asia, the agents of the Kuomintang, and the international police in Shanghai cooperated brilliantly. But the international Red Aid (MOPR) Organization also functioned smoothly; it included left-wing personalities from many countries and prepared a campaign to liberate the detainees.

It also provided a lawyer for Nguyen Ai Quoc: the British citizen Frank Loseby, who defended the Vietnamese case with vigor, skill, and perseverance. He is reported to have said on meeting the prisoner: "Dr. Sun Yat-sen was saved by an Englishman.* I shall do everything to secure your release. Just tell me what I must know to defend you successfully. Say no more than is necessary, for all revolutionaries have their secrets" (*TDT*, 34). Nguyen Ai Quoc certainly did have his secrets. The English authorities took their prisoner so seriously that his case was judged by the Supreme Court, the second highest legal authority in the colony. The charges were attempted violent revolution in the crown colony and activity as an agent for a foreign power (the Soviet Union).

But Nguyen's lawyer—who entered into heated arguments with the prosecutor during the public hearing—obtained his client's release. The indictment was rejected. Nguyen, who still nominally had French nationality, was sentenced to be deported and taken away from the colony on a French ship. Loseby intervened again, realizing what it would mean if his client were deported to the French colonial territory, where he was threatened with execution. The story went as far as London, where the lawyer Stafford Cripps, then an extreme left-wing Labor member of Parliament, took up the case. The British legal system may well have saved Nguyen's life. It was argued that the mere fact of being a nationalist or Communist would not be interpreted as an

---

* In 1896 Dr. Cantlie, an Englishman, had launched a storm of protest in London after the revolutionary Sun Yat-sen had been enticed into the imperial Chinese embassy.

Nguyen Ai Quoc in Hong Kong before his arrest (1930).

infringement of British law. Nguyen was rather to be treated as a political refugee, and released.

Nguyen Ai Quoc was detained by the British for almost a full year. He spent part of this time in the prison hospital after contracting tuberculosis. Even after his release in Hong Kong, Nguyen was in danger, for the Kuomintang authorities and the agents of the *sûreté* were waiting to lay hands on their dangerous opponent. An attempt to reach England was thwarted when he was taken off ship in Singapore and re-

Nguyen Ai Donc after his release from prison.

turned to Hong Kong. Once again, it was Loseby who took in the fugitive. Disguised as a wealthy Chinese merchant, Nguyen left the colony and disappeared on the mainland farther north. Friends of the Losebys offered him refuge in Amoy, in the quiet coastal province of Fukien. After more than six months of rest, walks in the forest, and regular physical exercise, their guest finally recovered from the trials of imprisonment and disease, only to embark upon a new period of conspirative activity. He disappeared once again and rumors circulated that Nguyen had died of "advanced tuberculosis" in British custody in 1931. The news was published by *L'Humanité* and the Soviet press.* Vietnamese students in Moscow organized a mourning ceremony for Nguyen and Tran Phu in Moscow at which a speech was made by a representative of the Comintern. (Years later, the fact that Nguyen Ai Quoc had been able to leave the British colony in spite of the attention of French and Chinese secret agents led to the theory that he had helped the British secret service and had been hidden by the English. However, there is no serious evidence to support this claim.)

What was the revolutionary like now almost ten years after his first Moscow years? Josef Ducroux, who contacted his colleague in Hong Kong in January 1931 before his own arrest, described his fellow conspirator many years later as follows: "He looked astonishingly thin and lithe. He was clean-shaven at the time, apart from a few hairs on his upper lip. His face was sharp and seemed almost charred . . . I've seldom met a human being who lived so frugally and was so disdainful of every comfort. The energy he showed! He was taut and quivering . . . He had only one thought in his head —and it has, I think, obsessed him all his life long. His country. Vietnam. I won't say he wasn't a sincere internationalist, a true revolutionary, but to him Vietnam has always come first . . . He devoted little time to doctrinal wranglings. He was first and foremost a militant, an organizer . . ." (*L,* 48).

* According to the Historical Commission of the party in Hanoi, the French published the message of his death to discourage the revolutionary movement in Indochina. This version lacks credibility because even official French sources believed Nguyen to be dead. Perhaps the Comintern itself spread the news.

This "quivering" activity prevented the convalescent from staying for long in his haven of refuge in Amoy where he led the "idle life of a rich man on holiday" (*TDT*, 37). Early in 1933 he was in Shanghai, where he attempted to establish contact with the Chinese Communists who were desperately fighting the Kuomintang troops and had already left their central committee in Shanghai. In November, Nguyen Ai Quoc met an old friend from his Paris days in the international branch, Paul Vaillant-Couturier, who had just reached East Asia with a secret mission from the French Communist Party. Nguyen left Shanghai a little later. He sailed on a Soviet ship to Vladivostok and then took the Trans Siberian Railway to Moscow.

THE PEOPLE'S FRONT

IN July 1935, representatives of the Communist International met for the seventh time in Moscow. It was to be the final congress of this worldwide secret organization and the long interval which had elapsed since the last conference (seven years) in itself showed that the directives determining the Comintern's work were certainly not drawn up in free discussion between the delegates of different nationalities. Nguyen Ai Quoc attended the final congress of the Comintern.

In the Soviet Union, foreign and domestic policy had now been consolidated over a period of several years. Revolutionary pathos had given way to Soviet patriotism. Recognition by the U.S. (1933) had been followed by Soviet membership of the League of Nations (September 1934). World revolutionary agitation no longer fitted in with the tactical turn which Stalin had taken in face of the threat from Nazi Germany. The policy of collective security in league with the Western democracies was bound to influence the work of the Comintern which was increasingly harmonized with the policy of Moscow. Following the line of Stalin and Georgi Dimitrov, the Seventh Comintern Congress developed the people's front policy as a guideline for the Communist Parties. Nguyen the patriot certainly found this shift to more flexible methods easier than many of his comrades. He had already warned against the risk of underestimating the value of cooperation with "noncommunist forces" (by which he understood the association of all anticolonialist groups). But Stalin's new policy also led to an alliance with the mortal enemy, the French colonialists, represented by the bourgeois camp. How could he explain the new tactic to his radical friends at home? In March 1935, in Nguyen's absence, the First Congress of the Communist Party of Indochina in Macao had found the revolutionary situation extremely favorable (most of the official party publications fail to mention this fact today).

Nguyen realized that the balance of power in Vietnam excluded any possibility of independent action at this time. Far away from the scene of action, in the Moscow central organization, it was easier for him to analyze coolly the implications of the failure of the Nghe Tinh movement and the changes in world politics. He wrote: "1. For the time being, the Party cannot put forth too high a demand (national independence, parliament, etc.) ... It should only claim democratic rights ... a general amnesty for all political detainees, and struggle for the legalization of the party. 2. To reach this goal, the Party must strive to organize a broad Democratic National Front. 3. The Party must adopt a wise, flexible attitude towards the bourgeoisie, strive to draw it into the front, win over the elements that can be won over and neutralize those which can be neutralized ... 4. There cannot be any alliance with or any concession to the Trotskyite group ... 5. ... The Indochinese Democratic Front must keep close contact with the French Popular Front because the latter also struggles for freedom, democracy, and can give us great help. 6. The Party cannot demand that the Front recognize its leadership ... It is only through daily struggle and work that the masses of the people acknowledge the correct policies and leading capacity of the Party and that it can win the leading position. 7. To be able to carry out this task, the Party must uncompromisingly fight sectarianism and narrow-mindedness" (*SW* II, 149ff.).

These extracts from a report to the Comintern of July 1939—"The Party's Line in the Period of the Democratic Front (1936–39)"—show the reversal of Nguyen's attitudes and his return to the policy of International (Stalinism).

We have already tried to explain the indifference with which Nguyen Ai Quoc viewed internal Soviet conflicts. The great purge had now begun with the public trials. He may well have been equally indifferent to the reasons for which Stalin changed his foreign policy tactics towards the

Western democracies. For him the decisive factor was that the political situation had also changed completely in East Asia. The increasing number of Japanese attacks—Manchuria had already been separated from China—had led to a "people's front" policy in China as well. Here, however, Mao Tse-tung took the initiative without directives from the Kremlin. In his explanation of the need for a united front, Nguyen Ai Quoc looking back on this stage in his career mentioned the plans of the Japanese Fascists, without, however, examining them in any detail.

It took the Indochinese Communist Party one whole year to correct its policy and become an anti-imperialistic people's front in July 1936 in accordance with a decision of the Central Committee. The "anti-fascist-colonialist" formula enabled it to establish contacts with the representatives of the Paris People's Front Government without losing face. The victory of the People's Front in the French elections therefore had implications for the Indochinese colonial territory too. Prominent political detainees such as Pham Van Dong were freed and the Communist Party of Indochina was even able to operate legally in an Indochinese congress. The 'Trotskyites' in the nationalist movement whom Nguyen described in his report as political tools of the Fascists who "must be destroyed politically" (*SW* II, 150) therefore had the ground cut from under their feet.

It must not, however, be assumed that these opponents of the new Comintern policy and their representative Nguyen Ai Quoc now had close contacts with Trotsky (who had been deported abroad). It has always been an easy way out to describe all the opponents of the party line as "trotskyites."

Nguyen Ai Quoc suffered the same fate. But the conflict appeared to be largely confined to the south, to Cochin-China, where Trotskyites under Ta Thu Thau sometimes cooperated with the orthodox Communists and did not break with them until 1937/38. Ta Thu Thau was murdered in 1946 by Communist opponents when the hostile groups entered into open conflict in the general confusion. But officially approved excesses against "Trotskyite" deviationists never occurred in Ho Chi Minh's Communist state.

Externally the years between 1934 and 1938 were the quietest Nguyen Ai Quoc had ever known. He had enrolled at the International Lenin School in Moscow, the training ground for officials who had already proved their merit. At the same time, he worked at the Institute for National and Colonial Problems, an establishment of the Comintern. He is said to have gone to Sotchi on the Caucasian Black Sea coast for treatment of the after-effects of his tuberculosis.

Finally the time for new action came in the autumn of 1938. Once again the political landscape had changed radically. The end of the People's Front Government in France meant a return to illegality for the Indochinese Communist Party. But in China the Kuomintang and Communists continued their alliance after the outbreak of the war with Japan in 1937. Almost all the leading Vietnamese Communists took refuge in China.

Once again Nguyen's tracks become blurred; we do not know when he left Moscow to return to China. We come across him again in North China in Chensi Province where Mao Tse-tung had set up his capital after the Long March. How did Nguyen reach Yenan—directly from the Soviet

126

Union, or by a more devious route? Was there any contact between the remote headquarters of the Chinese party in the hillside caves and far-off Moscow? Was Nguyen supposed to establish contact in order to bring the independent Chinese comrades under the control of the Kremlin?

"He did not stay long in Yenan," we are told, "and he lived there in an apple orchard" (*S,* 75). Did he meet Mao? And what was the purpose of his stay far up in the north of China, if he was supposed "simply to establish contact with the movement in Vietnam" (*Comm.,* 64)? He is now described as a member of the Eighth (Communist) Field Army, and when Chiang Kai-shek called for advisors on guerilla warfare from among his new Communist allies, Nguyen Ai Quoc was a member of this group of experts. The years previously, Comrade Wuong had been obliged to leave China when Chiang Kai-shek defeated the Canton commune; as Nguyen Ai Quoc, he now trained Chiang's soldiers to become partisans. He was promoted from leader of political training courses for the Vietnamese to "political commissar" of a Chinese army unit.

By February 1940, Nguyen Ai Quoc had traveled throughout China, from north to south. He now reached the provinces of Yunnan and Kwangsi bordering on Indochina, where he met his comrades who had taken refuge from the French. Among them was Vo Nguyen Giap, the small man with the delicate features who, with Mao Tse-tung, was to become one of the greatest guerilla strategists of all time. Here in the Yunnan mountains the plans were prepared for national revolution as the first stage toward liberation.

Vo Nguyen Giap has described his first meeting with the

now legendary older comrade who was referred to respect-fully as "*bac*" ("uncle") by his fellow soldiers: "A man of mature years stepped toward us, wearing European clothes and a soft felt hat . . . He had let his beard grow. This was the first time I had set eyes on him, yet already we were conscious of deep bonds of friendship . . . He spoke with the accent of central Vietnam. I would never have believed it possible for him to retain the local accent after spending so many years abroad" (*L*, 56).

And the "uncle" joked: "Our Dong (Pham Van Dong) hasn't aged much." Then turning to Giap: "He's still as fresh-looking as a girl of twenty" (*S*, 75). In Vietnamese there is an expression, *thoi co*, which means the "favorable moment." This concept has played a constant role in Viet-namese revolutionary history and is still important today in the Indochinese war. For Ho Chi Minh and his friends there were many "favorable moments," opportunities to be seized quickly after a long period of waiting.

One such moment came in the winter of 1940/41. The Japanese who had entered Indochina in the summer set out to occupy Vietnam. France had been defeated by Hitler's Germany and offered no resistance in Indochina. The colo-nial power was floored; some of the colonial authorities collaborated with the Japanese occupying forces. There were spontaneous uprisings against the Japanese and French.

Then Nguyen Ai Quoc decided to return to his homeland. After thirty years' absence he set foot on Vietnamese soil again in December 1940. The clod of earth he kissed after crossing the frontier is preserved today in the Hanoi Revolu-tionary Museum. Close to the Chinese frontier in Cao Bang

The clod of earth that Nguyen Ai Quoc kissed on his return home after thirty years.

province, the small group of revolutionaries discovered a limestone cave with strange rock formations and a profusion of stalagmites and stalactites. This made an ideal hiding place. The cave in Coc Bo became the Yenan of the Vietnamese revolution.

Here the future Ho Chi Minh instructed his comrades—who naturally saw things only from the narrow angle of their local situation—and gave them the benefit of his worldwide experience. He realized that a long partisan war was inevitable if the double foreign domination was to be shaken off. He therefore translated Sun Tsu's *Art of Warfare* and wrote the pamphlet entitled "Guerilla Warfare: Experiences of the Chinese Guerillas." Mao Tse-Tung had also carefully

The cave in Coc Bo, the Yenan of the Vietnamese revolution.

studied the theories of Sun Tsu, who may well have been the world's first philosopher of war, and borrowed his aphorism "Know your opponent and know yourself; you will then be invincible" for inclusion in his writings on military theory. Nguyen Ai Quoc's short stay in Yenan had born fruit. But he did not forget his Moscow teachers. In the cave at Coc Bo he also translated the *History of the Russian Communist Party* (*B*), the standard work of Soviet party history in the Stalin era.

Close by the jungle hideout at Pac Bo, the Central Committee of the Communist Party of Indochina held its eighth congress in May 1941 under the chairmanship of Nguyen Ai Quoc. Nguyen is reported to have led the meeting as a "representative of the Communist International" (*TC*, 24) while Truong Chinh was elected secretary general of the party. The Moscow-trained revolutionary apparently still had other important tasks outside the country. But first of all important decisions were taken affecting work at home. Because the moment was favorable—Truong Chinh later spoke of an opportunity which "occurs once in a thousand years"— it was decided to found an organization which thirty years later still remains one of the most widely discussed political movements in the world. On May 19, 1941 in the jungle of Tonkin near the Chinese frontier, the Vietnam League for Independence was founded—the *Viet Nam Doc Lap Dong Minh,* abbreviated to *Vietminh.* This famous name has two significant features. First of all, the ancient national concept of Viet Nam (Viet = nation and Nam = south, the country's geographical position seen from China) was once again brought to the fore. (As we have seen, it had been replaced by Indochina in the name of the Party). Secondly, mention was again made of independence—only six years after Nguyen had gone back on this concept in line with the Comintern policy.

This is another classical example of a rapid change in tactics when local conditions were found to be suitable. It must be counted to Ho Chi Minh's credit in the Communist movement that he recognized the true situation for Vietnam, his homeland.

At the same time work began on the establishment of support points for guerilla campaigns to be led from this northern frontier area. And on June 6, 1941, Nguyen Ai Quoc published his famous letter from abroad in which he struck a distinctly patriotic tone and praised the heroic deeds of the past:

In the cave: thoughts about the war.

("Elders! Prominent personalities! Intellectuals, peasants, workers, traders, and soldiers! Dear Compatriots!" (His words leave no doubt that this call for national insurrection comes from a true patriot.) "Now the opportunity has come for our liberation. France itself is unable to dominate our country. As to the Japanese, on the one hand they are bogged down in China, on the other they are hamstrung by the

British and American forces, and they certainly cannot use all their forces to contend with us. If our entire people are united and singleminded, we are certainly able to smash the picked French and Japanese armies. Compatriots throughout the country! Rise up quickly! Let us follow the heroic example of the Chinese people! Rise up quickly to organize the association for national salvation to fight the French and the Japanese . . . National salvation is the common cause to the whole of our people. Every Vietnamese must take part in it. He who has money will contribute his money, he who has strength will contribute his strength, he who has talent will contribute his talent. I pledge to use all my modest abilities to follow you, and am ready for the last sacrifice . . ." The final paragraph appeals to the "revolutionary fighters" who are called upon "to guide the people throughout the country." The appeal ends with the words, "Victory to Viet-

Guerillas in South Vietnam.

133

nam's revolution! Victory to world revolution!" (*SW* II, 151ff.). At the end of this patriotic appeal—an appeal which takes into account national traditions and the role of the eldest members of the population, and which praises the victory over the Mongols in the thirteenth century as an exemplary achievement—we encounter once again Ho Chi Minh's typical mixture of nationalism and internationalism. Patriotism seemed to be his major concern in this decisive hour. Not only the choice of words (but specifically the fact that there is no reference to communism) indicates this. The Central Committee concerned itself with organizational problems. It considered the name which the new state should be given after its liberation, and chose the designation "Democratic Republic of Vietnam" and a revolutionary symbol consisting of a red background with a five-pointed golden star in its center. As the flag of the Vietminh and the symbol of a revolutionary fight for liberation, this emblem has now taken over, in many parts of the world, the position once enjoyed by the Soviet hammer and sickle.

Although concrete results of the June appeal were not immediately apparent—the Vietminh had few guns and had to confine their activities to agitation—the events of the early summer of 1941 were the most important in Vietnamese revolutionary history. For Nguyen Ai Quoc, who had celebrated his fifty-first birthday on the date of foundation of the Vietminh, they meant the end of thirty years of conspiracy beyond the frontier. He had finally returned to help his compatriots on the spot. From now on he took over the leadership in his own country. His leadership was interrupted by his year's imprisonment in China; but it was never called into question.

PRISON

WHEN Nguyen Ai Quoc crossed the Chinese frontier again in the summer of 1942, he had chosen a new alias: Ho Chi Minh, which is officially translated as "Ho with the clear will."* This time he was to keep his new name.

The newly founded League for the Independence of Vietnam needed help. It had neither weapons nor money. If the Vietminh were to overcome their isolation in the jungle of Cao Bang, they had to establish links with the outside world. The obvious answer seemed to be to seek aid in neighboring China since both the Kuomintang and the Chinese Communists were fighting against the Japanese. Of all the comrades, Ho was best acquainted with the conditions in China, and was most proficient in spoken Chinese. And so he set off once again. He wanted to reach Chungking on which Chiang Kai-shek's government had fallen back after the Japanese attack. In Chungking, however, there were also Americans who had set up an air lift to China after the Japanese occupation of Burma. Ho Chi Minh probably also wanted to make contact with them.

* The following other translations of the name Ho Chi Minh are current in the West: "Ho, the bringer of light"; "Ho, the bright light"; "Ho, the enlightener"; "Ho, who has become wise."

135

However, his aims were thwarted. After marching for several days he was arrested one evening in August in a town in the frontier province of Kwangsi. The circumstances and immediate reasons for his arrest remain unknown. Ho Chi Minh has failed to give any explanation. The Vietnamese publisher of the *Prison Diary* suggests that the Chinese police had doubts about the true identity of their prisoner although the revolutionary Nguyen Ai Quoc was believed to be dead. The fact that he was making for Chungking has also been suggested as a reason for his detention. This assumption is probably correct. The Kuomintang generals in the provinces set great store by their independence. It is not improbable that the authorities in Kwangsi wanted to prove their independence from Chungking and then simply forgot the prisoner. But Ho certainly made himself look suspicious. He was found with a visiting card which suggested that he was a Chinese journalist, living in Vietnam (we already saw Ho's liking for visiting cards when he was in Paris); on the other hand, he claimed to be a representative of the Vietnamese patriots. But the latter, if they come from Vietnam itself, were anything but favorites of General Chiang Fa-kwei, the war lord of the province. He preferred the Vietnamese who had already been living in China for many years and wanted nothing to do with the new Vietminh whose representatives spoke of revolution and liberation in a manner reminiscent of the Communists in China. A difficult time—certainly the most difficult of his whole life—now began for Ho Chi Minh. With his hands and feet shackled, chained together with bandits, he was dragged from prison to prison for fourteen months. Ho has described his period of detention in the more than one hundred four-line verses and poems of *Prison Diary,* written in the classical Chinese and Vietnamese style (*Tuc Tuyet*). He wrote them in Mandarin Chinese in order not to arouse the distrust of his guards, working during the endless nights when he could not sleep:

At "Abundance and Glory" street, shame was thrust on me
So as to delay my journey:
I am an honest man with a clear conscience,
But I was accused without ground of being a spy.

Ho Chi Minh seems initially to have been surprised at the fate which befell him.

I.

With hungry mouth like a wicked monster,
Each night the irons devour the legs of people:
The jaws grip the right leg of every prisoner:
Only the left is free to bend and stretch.

II.

Yet there is one thing stranger in the world:
People rush in to place their legs in irons.
Once they are shackled they can sleep in peace.
Otherwise they would have no place to lay their heads.

Often the prisoners covered more than thirty miles on foot in a single day before they reached a new prison. Sometimes they were loaded onto junks.

Carried along by the current, the boat glides towards Nanning.
Our legs are tied to the roof, as though we were on the gallows.

Along both banks of the river are lively prosperous villages.
The boats of the fishermen glide swiftly in mid-stream.

In spite of this harsh treatment, Ho attempted to bear his
fate with dignity.

The supple rope has now been replaced with iron fetters.
At every step they jingle as though I wore jade rings.
In spite of being a prisoner, accused of being a spy,
I move with all the dignity of an ancient government official.

But he was depressed and cursed the fate which condemned him to inaction.

The whole world is ablaze with flames of war,
And men compete as to who will be the first at the front.
In jail inaction weighs heavily on the prisoner.
My noble ambitions are valued at less than a cent.

In a newspaper the prisoner read reports of "Alarm in
Vietnam."

Better death than slavery! Everywhere in my country
The red flags are fluttering again,
Oh, what it is to be a prisoner at such a time!
When shall I be set free, to take my part in the battle?

Ho was evidently well informed about political develop-
ments. The Americans and British were negotiating in
Chungking. He too was a friend of China, arrested on the
road to Chungking. Why, then, were different standards applied to him?

The Americans have come, and now the British arrive.
Their delegation is welcomed everywhere.
I am also a delegate on a friendly visit to China,
But the warm welcome given me is of another kind!

But Ho was not only concerned for himself and his country. He commented sarcastically in verse on the fate of some of his fellow prisoners and conditions in general in China.

The Wife of the Deserter

One day you went away, not to come back again,
Leaving me alone in our room, with sadness for companion.
The authorities having pity on my loneliness,
Invited me to live temporarily in the prison.

The Child in Pin Yang Prison

Oh, oh! oh! My father's run away,
My father is afraid to be a soldier.
So I'm in prison, though I'm only six months old.
I had to come with my mother.

After a year's detention, Ho Chi Minh set down this poem:

Autumn Night

My heart travels a thousand li towards my native land.
My dream intertwines with sadness like a skein of a
  thousand threads.
Innocent, I have now endured a whole year in prison.
Using my tears for ink, I turn my thoughts into verses.

One may be tempted to compare his lines with the poems of another great Asian leader, Mao Tse-tung, who also set down his thoughts in verse at different periods of his life. Unlike Mao, Ho did not write for pleasure or out of passionate poetic inspiration. His poems were born of suffering and sympathy. He was not kept in solitary confinement, but surrounded by other men in his cell—gamblers, opium addicts, syphilitics. In *Prison Diary,* Ho describes how, in all this filth, surrounded by sick men and vermin, "we lived as a single family, preparing tea on our own cooking stove and eating with pleasure (when there was anything to eat) after first hunting for lice." Ho observed the people around him and their misery. Were they not typical of China at this time? In the evening he took out his dog-eared notebook and brush and wrote the impressions of the day in the language of his guards. Generally they were immediate impressions rather than the sweeping lyrical associations found in Mao's poetry. Ho does not like abstractions. He reports concrete events: everyday life in the prison, the cell and its occupants, the guards, the roof, and even—not without humor:

Goodbye to a Tooth

You are hard and proud, my friend,
Not soft and long like the tongue:
Together we have shared all kinds of bitterness and sweetness,
But now you must go west while I go east.

My Cane, Stolen by the Warder

All your life with me, you have been upright and strong.
Together we have passed through seasons of snow and mist.
Cursed be the thief who has separated us!
And will it ever be over, the sorrow he caused us both?

Since we have no other personal records, the *Prison Diary* in verse is the only text to give us any insight into Ho Chi Minh the man, whom we shall consider later on. The prisoner proved unsentimental but highly sensitive. His verses are short but full of the tenderness we encountered for the first time in his parting words to the children in Paris. In later years Ho Chi Minh wrote other poems, generally devoted to current events.

After only four months in prison, his health had been seriously undermined. He wrote that he had grown more than ten years older while his hair had turned gray.

> . . . And lean and black as a demon gnawed by hunger.
> I am covered with scabies. Fortunately,

Fishing.

Being stubborn and patient, never yielding an inch,
Though physically I suffer, my spirit is unshaken.

Ho suffered increasingly from an eye disease and recovered only very slowly after his release. In the military prison of Liuchow (Kwangsi Province) he was finally given the status of a political prisoner. He now had enough to eat and the bonds were taken away from him. Here he learned for the first time why he had been held so long in a total of thirty prisons.

The Chinese saw him as a threat to the parallel organization to the Vietminh which they had set up in the meantime. This was the Patriotic and Revolutionary League of Vietnam (*Viet Nam Cach Mang Dong Minh Hoi*)—sometimes confused with the Vietminh by Western authors. This league was developed by the Kuomintang government with the ultimate idea of using it to gain influence in Indochina after the victory over the Japanese. Discussions had already been held to this effect between the Americans and the authorities in Chungking long before the Allies approved the occupation of North Vietnam by Chiang Kai-shek's troops at the end of the war. It was obvious that Ho Chi Minh stood in the way of these Chinese intentions. At this point Ho Chi Minh proved himself as a Moscow-trained tactician who did not mind compromising as a means of achieving his ends. He quickly abandoned the idea of contacting the important figure he was to meet in Chungking and came to an agreement instead with General Chiang Fa-kwei, the man at whose command he had been held captive. The compromise consisted in Ho's release and return to Vietnam with a number of members chosen by himself from the Revolutionary League. In October 1943 a conference for unification of the two revolutionary organizations was held in Liuchow. The groundwork was now laid for the first coalition government of an independent Vietnamese state in which the Communists were, however, to call the time from the outset. We are reminded of the first poem which Ho Chi Minh wrote down in his tattered diary:

> The body is in prison,
> The mind escapes outside:
> To bring about great things
> The mind must be large and well-tempered.

INDEPENDENCE

IN the winter of 1944/45 Ho Chi Minh established his first contacts with the power which was to present a deadly threat to his country twenty years later. The Americans seemed to him (as they then did to many Asians, including the Communists) to be the only effective allies in the war against the military power of the Japanese and colonial rule. Unlike the French, English, and Dutch, the U.S. had no colonies and it had taken on the main burden of crushing the Japanese military machine.

Ho Chi Minh had another special reason for seeking to establish these links. His mistrust of the Chinese intentions in Vietnam was justified. He had to dissuade the Americans

143

from backing Chiang Kai-shek's plans. But he could only do this if he and his movement put forward a valid alternative to convince the American secret-service officers operating in South China.

We have already seen how the imprisoned Ho was disillusioned by the dual standards applied to the different allies in the struggle against the Japanese. As soon as he was released his first task was to gain prestige as an ally of the Allies. Were the Americans bothered by the fact that Nguyen Ai Quoc was a Communist and had grown up with the Communist International? The Comintern had in fact been officially disbanded for similar reasons by Stalin (May 1943). And Ho Chi Minh's name did not figure on any list of Communist agents. He carefully drew attention to this fact when the opportunity arose.

The members of the American foreign information service in China known as the OSS (Office of Strategic Services) had no qualms about accepting Ho and his Vietminh as allies. (Anyone who wanted to help fight the Japanese was welcome.) OSS officers parachuted into Vietminh territory in Tonkin and arranged the delivery of some light American weapons (twenty years later this led to the ironic observation from North Vietnamese commentators that they had previous experience with American visitors from the air).

At this time Ho Chi Minh's contact with Americans was certainly not unpleasant. In spite of their later anti-Communist polemics, at this time they were only interested in defeating the Japanese, and Ho himself has repeatedly praised the U.S. on that score.

This was a period in which the slogans of patriotism and

nationalism completely replaced communism (there was a parallel development in the Soviet Union during the "Great War for the Fatherland"). Ho Chi Minh gave instructions that Vietminh activity should concentrate on the dissemination of propaganda among the population until the general revolt could be fomented. In this way a Vietnamese Propaganda and Liberation Army (*Viet Nam Tuyen Truyen Giai Phong Quan*) was founded at the end of December 1944. It was the precursor of the modern North Vietnamese people's army and its commander was (and still is) Vo Nguyen Giap, the victor of Dien Bien Phu. Ho Chi Minh remained a close friend of Vo (who respectfully referred to Ho Chi Minh as the "father of the Vietnamese revolutionary army"), and described several years later how his teacher dissuaded him from hasty action in the summer of 1944: "The phase of

Vo Nguyen Giap (left), with a unit from his army, in the jungle of Cao Bang, December, 1944.

peaceful revolution is over, but the hour for the general uprising has not yet struck . . . For the time being, political action must take priority over military measures." And he then gave a few words of advice: "Remember that secrecy is vital. The enemy must think you are in the west when in fact you are in the east. Attack by surprise and withdraw before the counterattack" (S, 202f.).

Like Mao Tse-tung, Ho Chi Minh subscribed to Sun Tsu's theory that the resistance of the enemy should be broken by agitation. He repeatedly stressed this in his instructions to the propaganda army. "Your very name implies that political action is of paramount importance. This is a propaganda unit . . . As far as tactics are concerned, we shall pursue guerilla action. We shall move secretly, quickly, and actively in the east and west alike. We shall strike when we are least expected and depart again unnoticed" (SW, II, 155f.).

The French, split into Vichy supporters and Gaullists, did not remain inactive. The former were in Hanoi while the latter had their headquarters in Chinese Kunming, the capital of the other neighboring province of Indochina, Yunnan. Both groups wanted to shake off the Japanese rule, but both also wanted to restore colonial control of Indochina. Ho Chi Minh was bitterly disappointed by de Gaulle's declaration on this subject.

When the Japanese military authorities took over full power on March 9, 1945, the French plans to destroy the weak guerilla units in a rapid campaign were thwarted. While the French local and military administration had remained intact up to then, the Japanese now disarmed all the forces of the Vichy authorities. The Japanese therefore remained the sole opponents of the Vietminh. This Japanese move was well thought out. At a time when the sun of Japan was already setting, Tokyo tried to win over the Vietnamese (and the inhabitants of other colonial territories) by granting them independence. Bao Dai, the last ruler of the Nguyen dynasty (who had already been used as a front by the French), cooperated and proclaimed the end of the protectorate.

But the Japanese met with hostility wherever they went, for Vietnam had experienced the worst famine in its history under the Japanese occupation. Even under French rule the peasants had not been plundered as they were in the war years when Indochina was used as a source of supplies for Japan's great campaigns in East Asia. According to official figures confirmed by Western estimates, two million Vietnamese died of starvation between 1943 and 1945.

It is therefore not surprising that more and more people joined the guerilla movement in which Ho Chi Minh's Vietnam League for Independence now played a vital part. Early in June 1945, two and a half months before the Japanese capitulation, all six provinces to the north of the Red River belonged almost completely to the "free zone." Ho Chi Minh's guerillas had reached the suburbs of Hanoi. The new *Thoi Co* was drawing near. Referring to this period, Vo Nguyen Giap reports—in a tone of idolization—how Uncle Ho lay seriously ill with a fever in a jungle hut. In a lucid moment, he said: "Now the circumstances are favorable. Independence at any price. Every sacrifice is justified even if

147

the whole Truong Son mountains are set ablaze" (*S*, 211).*

Such was the position in mid-August. After Hiroshima, Japan soon capitulated. On August 16, a national congress was convened at the initiative of the Vietminh and was attended by representatives of all political parties in favor of an independent state of Vietnam. It set up a national liberation committee to take over the duties of a provisional government. The position of the Vietminh in the independence movement had become so strong that Ho Chi Minh naturally spoke on behalf of the government and made his famous appeal for a general uprising. This was the last time he used the name Nguyen Ai Quoc by which the people knew him.

Emperor Bao Dai.

* Truong Son is the mountain range that crosses Vietnam from north to south.

His language had become more concise and specific since the Letter from Abroad (to which he made specific reference). Obviously Ho no longer entertained any doubts about his victory. "This is a great advantage in the history of the struggle waged for nearly a century by our people for their liberation . . . Our struggle will be a long and hard one . . . Because the Japanese are defeated, we shall not be liberated overnight . . . The Viet Minh Front is at present the basis of the struggle and solidarity of our people. Join the Viet Minh Front, support it, make it greater and stronger! . . . The decisive hour in the destiny of our people has struck. Let us rise up with all our strength and free ourselves!" *SW*, II, 157ff.).

Here the only emotion is one of patriotism. Now that he had drawn noticeably closer to his goal—liberation of his homeland—the Communist and internationalist sides of Ho Chi Minh's character seemed to have receded almost completely into the background. It is certainly no accident that the word "revolutionary" appears only once in the appeal and that no mention is made of "world revolution" (or even of communism). If the French had been willing to make concessions at this stage, perhaps a Communist state would never have been formed in North Vietnam.

While de Gaulle's representative in Kunming, Major Jean Sainteny, was preparing to fly to Hanoi to present the French claims, a general revolt broke out on August 19, 1945. This has gone down in Vietnamese history as the "August Revolution." Ho Chi Minh, who only arrived in Hanoi a few days later, did not yet appear in public. But side by side with the words *Doc Lap* ("independence") and *Tu Do* ("freedom") which decorated the towns and villages, streets and squares as far down as Cochin-China, red flags with the five-pointed gold star began to appear. They clearly indicated who the instigator of this was.

The triumph when Emperor Bao Dai received the representatives of the Vietminh in the old imperial city of Hue on August 25, 1945 and signified his abdication in favor of a Democratic Republic of Vietnam was no less impressive. Nobody had forced him to make this move. The revolution of Ho Chi Minh—who had carefully avoided using the normal Communist vocabulary in these decisive weeks—had not only won the day with the support of a majority of the population, but had even been legalized afterwards by the monarch.

The rest was little more than a formality. On August 29

Ho Chi Minh with the first government of an independent Vietnam. Hanoi, 1945.

the provisional government was officially installed under Ho Chi Minh as president. On September 2, 1945, the solemn proclamation of Vietnamese independence was made in Hanoi. The provisional government spoke specifically on behalf of the whole Vietnamese population. The declaration of independence was drafted by Ho Chi Minh himself. As a tribute to the United States (in whom the new republic saw an ally against the French), it began with the words: " 'All men are created equal; they are endowed by their Creator with certain inalienable rights: among these are Life, Liberty and the pursuit of Happiness.'

"This immortal statement was made in the Declaration of Independence of the United States of America in 1776. In a broader sense this means: all the peoples on the earth are equal from birth, all the peoples have a right to live, to be happy and free." And the Declaration ends with the words: "For these reasons, we, members of the Provisional Government of the Democratic Republic of Vietnam, solemnly declare to the world that Vietnam has the right to be a free and independent country—and in fact it is so already." (SW, III, 17f.).

After September 2, 1945, Ho Chi Minh underwent a transformation. Up to then he had been a revolutionary, conspirator, and agitator; now he became first and foremost a statesman. The time had come to set up and defend the independent state of which he had dreamed for such a long time. With the proclamation which he read from the platform in Da Binh Square in Hanoi, Ho Chi Minh had moved far ahead of events. For all the others involved in these difficult hours, Vietnam was anything but free and independent.

151

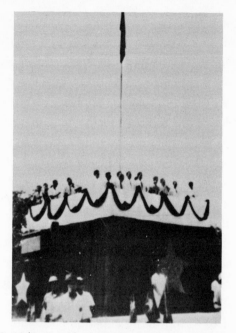

September 2, 1945: President Ho Chi Minh proclaims independence.

Ho Chi Minh had intentionally confronted the allies with a *fait accompli.* He felt himself one of them; but he already knew or suspected that they had quite different plans. The Americans were well-intentioned toward him but they had to make allowances for their Chinese allies. Only folly and ignorance of historical facts and resentments could have allowed them to send Chinese troops to replace the Japanese. Ho Chi Minh was "amazed," as Jean Sainteny put it later.

And the former colonial power, initially represented by General de Gaulle, had resolved to return to Indochina at any price. The "greatness" of France demanded this, de Gaulle said. While Great Britain was preparing to grant independence to India, the symbol of its colonial power, General Leclerc was putting together his expeditionary force.

In view of this situation, Ho Chi Minh realized that he would have to negotiate with the French. This brought him a third opponent and one in his own camp: the militant non-Communist nationalists.

Contrary to all the clichés which have been spread in the West (and above all in the U.S.) about Ho Chi Minh, he proved to be a man of moderation in the difficult negotiations which ensued. Almost all his French negotiating partners recognized his honesty and genuine desire to reach an agreement.

A speech in Hanoi, 1946.

On the whole the August Revolution had been bloodless and power was taken over in Hanoi under disciplined conditions. Apart from individual acts of revenge there was no general outburst of hatred against the French. Even Sainteny confirmed this fact (*L,* 56). The majority of the population favored a peaceful settlement with the French and Ho Chi Minh also expected a peaceful outcome. Were not his own political friends, the Communists, represented in the new Paris coalition government, and had he not maintained a strong emotional attachment all these years to the other France—the French people in metropolitan France? When the new president received the first French journalists in October 1945, he said: "France and Vietnam became wedded a long time ago. The marriage has not always been a happy one but we have nothing to gain from breaking it up. France is a strange country. It is a breeding ground of admirable ideas, but when it goes traveling, it does not export them." And a few months later: "A race such as yours, which has endowed the world with the literature of freedom, will always find friends in us, whatever it may do. If only you knew, monsieur, how passionately I returned to Victor Hugo and Michelet year after year! There is no mistaking the tone of their writings . . . Ah monsieur, colonialism must certainly be evil if it has the power to transform men to such a degree" (*L,* 97f.).

Ho Chi Minh took one more important step forward. The turn from communism to nationalism seemed complete when the Communist Party of Indochina gave news of its own dissolution in November 1945. But this step, in which the French comrades (let alone the Chinese or Soviet) had not been consulted because of the break in the links between them, must be interpreted as a tactical maneuver for power in the internal Vietnamese tug of war. The first elections in the history of Vietnam were not far off. How could a Communist Party program be made acceptable to a population which was living through the turmoil of revolution but had no experience of politics? It was much safer simply to abandon the Communist label. This was a bleak period in Ho Chi Minh's life as a Communist. His decision meant that for tactical reasons he turned his back temporarily on his own party. Significantly enough, the decision is not mentioned in any of the official party accounts of the revolution. Once again Ho Chi Minh proved himself capable of cool calculation when political power was at stake. And what about the people and electors? They had already decided in favor of the Vietminh; they supported the revolution and the League of Independence. The elections of January 6, 1946 which resulted in a substantial majority for the Vietminh were not a vote for communism. The vote did not concern communism at all (as yet no election had been held on party political lines either in North or South Vietnam). It was a vote for independence and for Ho Chi Minh, the only man who could guarantee its maintenance.

The "History of a Lost Peace," as Jean Sainteny has called it, had already begun when Ho flew to France early in June 1946 as a guest of the French state. Paris had decided to grant only minimal concessions to this troublesome Asian. The "freedom" of Vietnam was only acceptable to the French within the Indochinese Federation (a revival of a notion dating back to colonial days) and the French Union. They had worked out special arrangements for the South, for Cochin-China or Nam Bo as it is known in Vietnamese. Meanwhile Leclerc's troops had landed in the South. France promised to recognize the results of a popular decision in the South. But even today no real general elections have been held there. Finally, the most important point was that French troops were to move into the North and replace the Chinese. To avoid bloodshed, Ho Chi Minh had reluctantly agreed to all these conditions. After the signature of the agreements on March 6, 1945 in Hanoi, Ho Chi Minh said to his satisfied French partner: "I'm not so pleased, for really it is you who have benefited; you know perfectly well I wanted more than this . . . Still, I realize one cannot have everything overnight." And he added: "Friendship is my one consolation" (*L,* 107).

Ho Chi Minh did not find it easy to restrain opposition to these agreements in his own camp. His position became so precarious that he found it necessary to address the people directly. He said in a message in Hanoi: "It testifies to our intelligence that we should negotiate rather than fight . . . I, Ho Chi Minh, have always led you along the path to freedom, I have spent my whole life fighting for our country's independence, you know I would sooner die than betray the nation. I swear I have not betrayed you . . . !" (*L,* 109).

By proclaiming an independent Democratic Republic of Vietnam, Ho had created a *fait accompli.* With the establishment of an autonomous republic of Cochin-China the French now made a decisive move before the final negotiations in Paris had even begun. Ho Chi Minh must have felt himself cheated, and the timing of the French move was even more offensive. The declaration was made on June 1, 1946, two days after Ho's departure; the news reached him in his aircraft. The official visit of Ho Chi Minh and his delegation to France which lasted until mid-September took place in an atmosphere of hypocritical expressions of satisfaction on both sides while Uncle Ho indulged in a public relations campaign. He embraced his left-wing socialist friends demonstratively while behaving in a more reserved manner towards the Communists in the government; he handed flowers to ladies present at receptions and made witty replies at press conferences.

The official French mood is best reflected in a report which the head of protocol, Monsieur Dumaine, later made on the traditional July 14 parade which Ho Chi Minh attended as a guest of honor: "We were obliged to supervise the official visit of Ho Chi Minh. Age and calm have lent polish to his cannily goodhearted manner, and he conducts

The unwelcome "guest of honor": Ho Chi Minh at the parade in Paris on July 14, 1946.

157

himself with natural ease and a certain dignity . . . He caused me an additional headache on Bastille Day when he had to decide where he should be seated for the review. M. Bidault did not want him at his side. Uncle Ho insisted on being next to the Premier. The positioning of his chair in the official stand was a detail which I had to calculate to the last inch . . ." And referring to an official meal with Uncle Ho: "One can only admire the mastery with which this self-taught man controls his language, conveys his thoughts and endows his designs with the semblance of moderation and the stamp of courtesy. Those about him are highly-strong, fanatical and unmindful of their behavior. He, on the other hand, gives the impression of being wise and perspicacious. If he can obtain a little more than the possible, perhaps he will not ask for the impossible? Would that not be the lesser of two evils? (L, 120).

The guest of honor obviously felt ill at ease in a society which did not accept him. Did he suspect that the self-assured General de Lattre de Tassigny sitting near him would do all he could a few years later to starve out the population of the Vietminh zone?

Considering the gulf between the initial positions of the two negotiating partners, it is astonishing that the Fontainebleau coexistence formula was ever arrived at. The Vietnamese worked on the assumption of independence and equality within an alliance, whereas the French stuck to their supposed rights as they already had done in March; they were only prepared to allow a "free" Vietnam with its own government under the mandate of the French Union. Ho Chi Minh banked on the assumption that the French

Ho Chi Minh with Foreign Minister Georges Bidault.

would keep their promise to organize popular elections in the South. On the first anniversary of independence he cabled Hanoi: "The festivities must be devoid of any anti-French connotation," and in an interview he said: "Our differences are of the kind which are to be found in every family." He almost begged the Minister for the Overseas Territories: "Don't let me go back empty-handed!" (*L*, 123f.).

The Fontainebleau agreements of September 14, 1946 eventually merely confirmed the military (and political) presence of France in North Vietnam. This led to the first Indochinese war with the French, a war which Ho Chi Minh had not wanted.

And since it was not even possible to solve the problem of the South because the people were never consulted and the ambitions of politicians and military men on both sides came into play while terrorism and counterterrorism stirred up passions, the conflict in which Ho Chi Minh's successors are still invoked today can be traced back to this year in which reconciliation was no more than superficial.

THE MAN AND HIS WORK

WE have tried to throw light on the character of a unique man, the greatest revolutionary figure of our times, whose life is cloaked in extreme secrecy. This is a convenient point

On the front in 1950.

Dien Bien Phu: a conference at the office of the Lao Dong party.
Left to right: Pham Van Dong, Ho Chi Minh, Truong Chinh,
Vo Nguyen Giap.

to pause because the aim of his life—independence for his
country—had been achieved in spite of Fontainebleau and
the separation of the South. The task now was to defend that
independence.

The events between the bloodbath of Haiphong on
November 23, 1946 (with which the French practically
began the first Indochinese war) and the victory of the
Vietminh in Dien Bien Phu in May 1954 (which marked the
defeat of the French) were shaped primarily by the military
leaders. But Ho Chi Minh still remained the driving force
behind the resistance. As a politician who wanted to put
things straight with the French, he eventually resigned himself to reality. In a reply to a representative from Paris he

161

answered the arrogance of the French officers and officials in the same tone: "There is no place for cowards in the French Union. I would be a coward if I accepted these conditions." (*JC*, 300). But he appeared so convinced of victory that he was able to say to a French friend even before the war broke out: "You would kill ten of my men for every one I killed of yours. But even at that rate you would be unable to hold out and victory would go to me." (*L*, 138).

Let me now briefly consider the human personality of Ho Chi Minh, leaving aside the legend which has grown up around him.

Uncle Ho had returned to the highland jungle after the failure of the attempt by the Vietminh associations to gain control in Hanoi (December 19, 1946). After his death many of his fellow combatants remembered those years; their stories have all the elements of hero worship, and there is no doubt that Bac Ho really was a kind of father figure for his people. The legend included the simple uniform he wore right through the war and the army coat he placed over the shoulders of a wounded soldier in battle. He was always on the move with his brown jacket and sailcloth pouch containing the bare essentials of life—precooked rice or a few ears of corn. Sometimes he wore a handkerchief round his neck and head against the heat.

And then there were the famous sandals made out of an automobile tire. Uncle Ho wore them during the first Indochinese war on the jungle trails at Pac Bo and Dien Bien Phu. According to the *Viet-Nam Courier* (October 1969) his nephews and nieces "use the same sandals when they climb

Ho in his brown jacket and sailcloth pouch.

the Truong Son mountains and go down to the Mekong Delta: Ho Chi Minh sandals on the Ho Chi Minh trail."

There was the bamboo house in the jungle with its roughly hewn table and portable typewriter on which the president recorded his commands or thoughts, and a camp bed on the floor.

Uncle Ho led a spartan existence. His private life is one of the secrets about which we have learned nothing, even after his death. One of his constant wishes has therefore been respected.

The president's jungle residence.

We know that Ho never married and that he had no children. But he liked to have his say in the family matters which play so important a role in Communist Asia. With a mixture of humor and pathos he said to a party meeting when the subject of a new marriage and family law was raised: "There are people who believe that I as a bachelor understand nothing of all this. I have no family of my own, but a much wider family to care for—the working class of the world and

Issuing orders from the jungle.

the Vietnamese people. My experience of this great family enables me to judge personal families too" (*SW*, IV, 370).

He himself had a strong family feeling, as we recall from the telegram on the death of his brother in which he regretted that his family feelings had been sacrificed to affairs of state. After thirty years abroad Ho returned to his own country; after fifty years he set foot in his native village again. When he was invited to tea in the guesthouse of Kim Lien village he replied: "The guesthouse is for guests; I have returned home." And the *Viet-Nam Courier* notes that the president stopped for a while before the altar of his ancestors

Uncle Ho with a group of "nieces and nephews."

in the house where he had spent his childhood and visited the family shrine in the garden.

Ho did not marry, but he was certainly not a misogynist. On the contrary, he proved a gallant charmer of women on many occasions. Bernard B. Fall remembered the following incident: "I brought him one of my books and mentioned that it contained a portrait of him drawn by my wife. 'Where is it,' he asked, 'let me see! I hope she has got my beard right. I hope my beard looks good.' He was satisfied with the portrait. He looked around him for a moment. Then he took a small bunch of flowers from a vase on the table and handed it to me. 'Tell her that the drawing is very good. Give her

Ho's visit to his home village after fifty years.

the flowers and kiss her on both cheeks from me'" (F, I, 112).

Clearly Uncle Ho with all his modesty was not without a touch of vanity. It was never possible to be sure when his modesty was genuine and when it was merely assumed. Bac Ho was, however, (to our knowledge) the only Communist politician to refuse the Order of Lenin, the highest Soviet distinction, when it was offered to him on the fifteenth anniversary of the October Revolution. On November 6, 1967 he wrote to the Central Committee in Moscow: ". . . At present the American aggressors are stepping up the war against our homeland of Vietnam. They are brutally murdering thousands of my compatriots in the South and North alike . . . I should have no peace of mind if I were to accept this high honor. I therefore convey my warmest gratitude to you and would ask you to postpone conferring the high distinction on me until the day when our people has driven out the aggressive American imperialists. When the whole of Vietnam is free, I shall accept the order which bears the name of the great Lenin, fully conscious of the

Vietnamese newspaper clipping: Ho refuses the Order of Lenin.

honor which has been shown to me and with great pleasure on behalf of all my compatriots." The same thing happened when Ho was offered the order of the Golden Star (*Sao Vang*). "Only when the country is reunited," he said, "shall I be worthy of this honor." And so this Vietnamese distinction has not yet been awarded to any leader.

A man becomes wise at sixty—such is the rule of the Confucian order under which Ho Chi Minh began his life. Ho therefore became wise when the war against the French was at its height. But he was also wise enough to avoid any cult of his own personality even after the victory when his position in North Vietnam was practically unchallenged. In Ho's lifetime there was no personality cult of the kind which has surrounded Mao Tse-tung. His picture was rarely displayed on public buildings. And the theoretical party journal *Hoc Tap* was able to note on one of the president's birthdays that Uncle Ho was loved and respected but not revered as a god.

Ho's title of "*Bac*" must also be understood in the context of Chinese culture in which the eldest members of society (Ho himself refers to them repeatedly in his appeals) enjoy especial veneration. *Bac* means "big uncle"; it is the term used to denote the elder brother of a father or mother while the younger brother is referred to as *Chu*, "little uncle." It was only natural that people began to speak of Bac Ho because his closest colleagues already belonged to a younger generation. *Bac* is therefore a familiar term and the Communists in North Vietnam like to point out that every family considered Bac Ho an honored member. In addition, *Bac* is synonymous with democratic conduct; the father can com-

The president planting rice: dedication of a new machine
constructed in North Vietnam.

mand, but the uncle only advises. The relations were unique
between this leader of a Communist Party and state and his
people from whom he demanded the most severe depriva-
tions.

Perhaps Ho Chi Minh would in fact have become a Vietnamese Gandhi, as some observers suggest, after the revolution was completed, if the French and then the Americans
had not robbed him of the fruits of his victory. After gaining
independence, he sought understanding and not violence. If
the revolutionary youth of the West today identify Ho Chi
Minh with violence, they are doing him a bitter injustice.
And it was the misfortune of the politician Ho Chi Minh to
be at one and the same time a nationalist and Communist.
The Americans therefore viewed him as their enemy once the
cold war began.

Working the soil. Ho is wearing the traditional black pyjama.

This was the origin of the bitter enmity between Communist Vietnam, represented by Ho Chi Minh, and the United States of America, to which the Vietnamese revolutionaries had originally looked with high hopes and expectation. Here again there is a strange paradox. Two American presidents, Lyndon B. Johnson and Richard Nixon, wrote polite letters to the President of Communist North Vietnam in the middle of the war. Ho's reply to Nixon, written on August 25, 1969—one week before his death—includes the sentence: "But I am also deeply moved by the growing number of young Americans who are dying senselessly in Vietnam for the policy of the governing circles of the U.S." However hard this judgment may be, Ho Chi Minh's last official statement (printed in the *Viet-Nam Courier*, Novem-

171

Ho with an antiaircraft unit.

ber 1969) still sounds rather conciliatory: "With good will on both sides we can seek together a fair solution to the Vietnam problem."

In spite of his strong words, the conflict with a world power must often have depressed him. But the letter to Nixon is not a document of cheap triumph. Did Ho Chi Minh ever have doubts about himself or his mission? There is no evidence that he did. But he suffered internal political setbacks. Even before the outbreak of the war with France, resistance was growing—as it had in the days of the People's Front— within his own party, which in spite of the official dissolution continued to exist as a Marxist cadre organization. On the one hand, there were the militant Trotskyite elements and on the other the Vietnamese anti-Communists. These included in particular the active Catholic minority in the North which voted after 1954 in favor of the state in the South under the Catholic president Ngo Dinh Diem. Reprisals were taken against people who held different ideas on the grounds that they had betrayed the patriotic cause. Ho Chi Minh never exposed himself personally in this respect. Unlike his master Lenin he did not call for a reign of political terror against the opposition in any specific phase of the revolution. The seemingly fragile man who destroyed his opponents with an iron fist—that man is merely a legend created by the other side.

We come closest to the truth by recognizing both Ho Chi Minh's iron will and his absence of hatred for his opponents. He was able to push his personal feelings to one side when it came to the building of an independent state. When the peasants of Nghe Tinh and other counterrevolutionaries revolted in 1956 against the excesses of land reform and also against Communist rule, the rebellion was put down by force of arms. But even today the agricultural policy of those years and the stern action by overzealous officials are officially described as "errors." Significantly, Communist Vietnam chose cooperatives rather than an extreme form of collectivization. Stalin was not the example to be followed. Ho Chi Minh himself intervened to depose the militant secretary general of the newly founded Lao Dong Party (Party of Vietnamese Workers), Truong Chinh, and took over his post. With the rapid "correction" of errors and astonishingly frank language in the party press, Ho Chi Minh followed the softer line of the post-Stalin era sooner and more unreservedly than all other leading Communist officials.

We have already discussed Ho Chi Minh's relations with Stalin. It would be idle to try to answer the question as to which successor of the Soviet dictator at the head of the world Communist movement—Khrushchev or Mao Tsetung—was closer to Uncle Ho in personality and ideas. We do not know, but he seems to have preferred Khrushchev the pragmatist, who was so close to the people. Ho Chi Minh was not a man of letters like Mao Tse-tung, but a practical man, and the idolization of Mao must also have been foreign to him.

China was the neighbor; all the intellectual influences—and also foreign conquerors—had come from China in the two-thousand-year history of Vietnam. He retained close links with the Chinese culture and traditions throughout his life. (In his will he quoted Tu Fu, the poet of the Tang dynasty). But his political beginnings can be traced back to Moscow and the political influences in the main phases of his life came from the Soviet Union. He never took sides in the ideological war between Moscow and Peking. It would have been easy for him to play the two Communist giants off against each other for the benefit of his own country. But he tried to act as an intermediary between them. And when he wrote *Loi Di Chuc,* his last will and testament, on May 10, 1969, he not only called for unity within his party but also for the world Communist movement to close its ranks: "Being a man who has devoted his whole life to the revolution, the prouder I am of the growth of the international com-

Ho's will.

munist and workers' movement, the more pained I am by the current discord among the fraternal Parties. I hope that our Party will do its best to contribute effectively to the restoration of unity among the fraternal Parties on the basis of

Marxism-Leninism and proletarian internationalism, in a way which conforms to both reason and sentiment. I am firmly confident that the fraternal Parties and countries will have to unite again."

In reality his death did not reconcile the two Communist camps, but at least it brought them to the same table. During the funeral ceremonies, the Russians and Chinese established contacts which afterwards led to Mr. Kosygin's visit to Peking. And this journey in turn resulted in negotiations which led to the resumption of governmental relations. Even the last will of the old revolutionary helped the cause he stood for.

Ho Chi Minh could be justly proud of his life's work. His state, the first independent Communist country in Asia, had been created entirely through his own strength. No Russian troops were there to help him (as in Mongolia and North Korea). And no help came from neighboring China; the Democratic Republic of Vietnam already existed when Mao's troops reached the Vietnam frontier after their victorious advance. Ho Chi Minh and his fellow fighters needed no foreign advisors or assistants like Borodin or Che Guevara. The cooperation with American forces shortly before the Japanese defeat was an insignificant episode. It had no influence on the course of events: there was no Fitzroy McLean among the Vietnamese guerillas to give Western aid against the common enemy.

Ho Chi Minh was occasionally described as an Asian Tito. But this comparison is only true if it is applied to him as the president and head of a socialist state which remained independent from the two Communist giants. Ideologically, Ho

Ho Chi Minh greeting the President of the Provisional Revolutionary
Government of South Vietnam, Huynh Tan Phat, in Hanoi,
only a few weeks before his death.

was not a Tito, because Titoism arose under the special conditions of Stalinism to whose direct and threatening pressure
Yugoslavia was exposed. Marshal Tito is a special European
case.

After achieving independence, Ho was able to face the
Chinese in particular as an equal with justified pride. In his
report to the party conference in 1951 at the height of the
"war of resistance" against the French we find these significant words: "Comrade Mao Tse-tung has skilfully Sinicized
the ideology of Marx, Engels, Lenin, and Stalin, correctly
applied it to the practical situation in China, and led the
Chinese revolution to complete victory. Owing to geo-

graphical, historical, economic and cultural conditions, the Chinese revolution exerted a great influence on the Vietnamese revolution which had to learn and indeed has learned many experiences from it" (*SW,* III, 238).

He could not have expressed himself more coolly. And at the height of Stalin's glorification, Ho simply included the leader of world communism in a short sentence as the teacher of the world revolution with Marx, Engels, and Lenin. Stalin and Mao were clear-sighted and highly meritorious "elder brothers." But nothing more.

In spite of everything, Ho Chi Minh's work remained incomplete. He had created and defended an independent Vietnamese state. But it has not managed to represent the whole of Vietnam. Since the end of the Second World War probably no other politician has felt himself so cheated of the fruits of his victory and personally betrayed by the great powers. When Ho Chi Minh died, Vietnam was divided and civil war raged in the South. American troops were still in the country and the bomb attacks on his own people were liable to begin again any day.

It had been precisely this kind of disappointed hope which had brought the Communist variant of Ho Chi Minh's personality back to the fore beside his nationalist facet. Ho Chi Minh had been the driving force behind the resistance against the French. All those who later fought the Saigon regime and the Americans in the South—and who are referred to simply as "Vietcong," Vietnamese Communists—put their faith in Ho Chi Minh. Uncle Ho's will begins with the following sentence: "Even though our people's struggle against U.S. aggression, for national salvation, may have to go through more hardships and sacrifices, we are bound to win total victory." And it ends: "My ultimate wish is that our entire Party and people, closely joining their efforts, will build a peaceful, reunified, independent, democratic and prosperous Vietnam, and make a worthy contribution to the world revolution."

The meteorological office in Hanoi issued one of its terse hurricane warnings for September 2, 1969. The weather soon became stiflingly hot and the humidity rose. When the heat becomes as sultry as this, people in Vietnam say that the "sky is turning"; and when the sky turns, they add, old people become ill.

On the evening of September 1, Uncle Ho did not make

Mourning.

179

his customary appearance to give an address marking the national day. The news ran through the town that the president was unwell. Groups of people formed at once, waiting in silence for news. And they went on waiting for two more days. Then early on September 4, the Voice of Vietnam radio station broadcast the sad news. On September 3, 1969, Ho Chi Minh died of a heart attack at 9:47 A.M. He was seventy-nine years old.

On September 9, a vast crowd assembled on the Ba Dinh, the square on which Ho Chi Minh had proclaimed the independence of Vietnam, twenty-four years earlier almost to the day. Le Duan, the first secretary of the Central Committee,

Le Duan reads the will.

180

now read out the will of the party chairman and president. And in his funeral oration, Le Duan quoted from Ho's will: "I have only one wish, one burning wish: to achieve complete independence for our homeland and freedom for our people so that our compatriots can all be properly fed, clothed and educated."

Ho conducting.

Then the crowd took up the song "*Ket Doan*"—"Unity is our strength." Ho Chi Minh had often beaten time to the same music.

"When I am gone, a grand funeral should be avoided

Vietnam takes leave of Ho Chi Minh.

in order not to waste the people's time and money." Perhaps a mausoleum will one day be built for uncle Ho in spite of his expressed wish, because (as one commentator in Hanoi said) Ho has an assured place in the people's memory beside

the two Trung sisters or Quang Trung, the people's hero of Vietnamese unification. Veneration of noble ancestors has persisted even under communism. As Ho himself said, he was leaving his will "in anticipation of the day when I shall go and join Karl Marx, Lenin and revolutionary elders." And he appended his signature.

The achievements of Ho Chi Minh's life may not have been very great in themselves. A revolutionary created a radical party and fought for the independence of a small nation. But this seemingly insignificant Asian also defied a world of power, and as a Communist he stood squarely for independence. He demanded suffering and deprivation of his people but he stood by them. As a man and politician, Ho

Ho Chi Minh, eight months before his death, receiving a group of visitors from the Air Force.

Chi Minh enjoyed the respect even of the opponents. As a revolutionary, he was not an advocate of violence even though many see him as such. A man who treats his enemies in this way will always set an example for others to follow.

一更…二更…又三更，輾轉徘徊睡不成。

四五更時才合眼，夢魂環繞五尖星。

睡不著

昔君送承至江濱，問我歸期指谷新。

現在新田已種好，他鄉汆作織中人，

替誰友們寫報告

同舟共濟義難辭，替友編修報告書，

「奉此，等因」今始學，多多博得感恩詞。

Ho Chi Minh's autograph

184

BIBLIOGRAPHY

1. *Works by Ho Chi Minh*

Against U.S. Aggression, For National Salvation, San Francisco, 1967.
Ho Chi Minh on Revolution: Selected Writings, 1920–1966. New York, 1967.
President Ho Chi Minh's Testament. San Francisco, 1967.
Prison Diary of Ho Chi Minh. New York, 1971.
Selected Works (SW). Hanoi, 1960–1962.

2. *Biography*

Chesnaux, Jean. *Vietnam. Geschichte und Ideologie des Widerstandes (JC).* Frankfurt, 1968.
Fall, Bernard B. *The Two Viet-Nams (BF1).* New York, 1963.
———. *Viet-Nam Witness, 1953–1966 (BF2).* New York, 1966.
Fischer, Ruth. *Von Lenin zu Mao (RF).* Düsseldorf/Cologne, 1956.
Lacouture, Jean. *Ho Chi Minh (L).* London, 1968.
Le President Ho Chi Minh: Par la Commission d'Histoire du Parti des Travailleurs du Viet Nam. (Comm.) Introduction by Prime Minister Pham Van Dong. Hanoi, 1961.
Souvenirs sur Ho Chi Minh (S). Hanoi, 1962.
Tran Dan Tien. *Glimpses of the Life of Ho Chi Minh (TDT).* Hanoi, 1958.
Truong Chinh. *President Ho Chi Minh (TC).* Hanoi, 1966.

CHRONOLOGY

1890   May 19: Ho Chi Minh born in the village of Kim Lien.

1905   Attends secondary school in Hue.

1911   Mess boy on the *Admiral Latouch Tréville*. Extensive travel at sea, either as steward or as sailor.

1913   Works as snow shoveler and stoker in London. Kitchen assistant at the Carlton Hotel.

1915. In America.

1917   In Paris.

1919   Presentation of the "eight-point demand" at Versailles.

1920   Founding member of the French Communist Party. Photographer's assistant and journalist.

1923   Member of executive committee of the Krestintern, Moscow.

1924   Delegate to the Fifth World Congress of the Comintern.

1925   Revolutionary activities in China.

1928   Works for Comintern in Western Europe and Thailand.

1930   In Hong Kong. Foundation of the Communist Party of Indochina.

1931   Arrest in Hong Kong.

1934   Return to Moscow.

1935   Participates in the Seventh World Congress of the Comintern.

1939   Contact with Chinese Communists in Yenan.

1940   December: Ho returns to Vietnam for the first time in thirty years.

1941   Foundation of the Vietnam League for (Vietminh) Independence.

1942   Arrest in South China.

1945   September 2: Ho Chi Minh reads the proclamation of Vietnamese independence.

1946   Negotiations in France.

1947   Back in Vietnam.

1954   Dien Bien Phu. Return to Hanoi.

1957   Travel through East European Communist countries. Participates in celebration of the fortieth anniversary of the October Revolution, held in Moscow.

1960   Second World Conference of Communist Parties, Moscow. Ho Chi Minh attempts to arbitrate between Moscow and Peking.

1966   Ho calls for total war to be waged against American troops.

1967   Correspondence between Ho Chi Minh and President Johnson.

1969   Ho announces he will continue war until the complete withdrawal of American troops and the end of the Saigon regime.

        Correspondence with President Nixon.

        September 3: Ho Chi Minh dies at the age of seventy-nine.